THE EAST AFRICA FINANCIAL SYSTEM:
TOWARDS AN OPTIMAL REGIONAL INTEGRATION

MUGERWA PAUL
MBA-Investment Management
CFA-1 (CFA, Institute); IISI & Islamic Finance (CISI, UK)
Plus other Short Technical Courses & Consultancies

Lecturer: Financial Economics & Risk Management;
Scholar: Investments, Financial Systems
(Conventional & Islamic Finance)
School of Business and Computing
Bugema University, Uganda

CEO, Asante Capital Hub Ltd
Financial services, Tax & Business Consultancy
Kampala, Uganda
E-mail: tatagracia2007@gmail.com / asantecap@gmail.com
invest@asantecapitalhub.com

+256 782 640448

Glimpses into the Global Financial Systems & Integration.

THE EAST AFRICA FINANCIAL SYSTEM:
Towards an Optimal Regional Integration

ISBN:

9 789970 532018

Investment Editor: Obatsa Barrack, CFA,
Production Editor: Kerosi Josephat Bosire, PhD- Finance
Managing Editor: Munyambonera Ezra, PhD Economics
Sole Contributor: Mugerwa Paul, P.O Box 36750 Kampala;
+256 782640448

Text Designer: Wakabi Joe

Printer: Corporate Impressions Agency (Ssenono Emmanuel)

Marketing Manager: Nakisozi Rebecca

Cover Designer: Wakabi Joe

Publisher: Mabira International Publishing & Media Company.

Content Fields: Financial economics & Systems; Investments;
Islamic Finance; Regional Economic Integration; Financial Markets;
Monetary Studies; Financial Management.

ABOUT THE AUTHOR

Mugerwa Paul was born on 27th September 1983 to Mr. Paul Mukisa Ssali & Mrs. Ritah Namiiro Ssali at Bunamwaya – Wakiso District, Uganda (East Africa). He completed his B.A (Economics & French Language) at Kyambogo University in 2008; MBA-Investment Management in 2013; partly pursued a CFA-1 (Chartered Financial Analyst) at CFA Institute, USA. Currently, he is progressing with Investment & Securities certifications at the Chartered Institute of Securities and Investments (CISI, UK); besides, he has done courses in Islamic Finance, including Bsc Islamic Economics, Banking & Finance that he is pursuing at the Islamic Online University (India). This, is coupled to a diversity of short courses and seminars attended in: Financial markets & Investments; Resource mobilization, Strategy, Risk Management, and Research analysis.

He has been a lecturer of financial economics and Insurance at Bugema University and other Tertiary institutions from 2011. He is currently the CEO of Asante Capital Hub Ltd (a consultancy firm in financial services that has done consultancy up to the East African Community level). He has done consultancies; published reviewed books and journal articles (including the popular, "The Ugandan Financial System"; presented papers in International Conferences; an active investor in East African financial markets; and he has a passion in financial systems. He speaks at least six (6) languages including English, French and Spanish but also EAC regional popular languages. He is an Associate researcher at Economic Policy Research Center; a resource person in the Ugandan financial sector (Ministry of Finance, financial regulators and institutes, financial sector players associations, etc); and a research and policy expert at the Islamic Chamber of Commerce & Industry Uganda). He has interacted with most top CEOs, Directors and finance gurus of the financial and educational sectors in the East African Community

He is happily married to Rebecca Nakisozi Mugerwa, with two gorgeous children (Gracia Ritah Namuli & Gentil Reuben Katumba). During his leisure time, he is an athlete (plays basketball, table tennis & badminton); besides, he does vocal music with his family as a passion; and he enjoys travelling in quest for information and knowledge.

SUMMARY OF CONTENT

DETAILED TABLE OF CONTENTS

ACKNOWLEDGEMENTS

In an effort to present a complete, accurate and harmonized panorama, as humanly possible, of the rapidly evolving and nitty-gritty of the East Africa financial system environment (both existent and prospective), the Scholar reached out to a diversity of finance gurus. This was in a bid to respond to William Safire's proposition to scholars like me, "Write what you see, because what history needs more is first-person testimony". These more than 65 respondent firms were from the global and Supranational financial institutions, the EAC Secretariat and institutions, the Public sector, the Private sector, the Academia as well as domestically and internationally-based financial system and regional integration experts. The study benefited from high levels of engagement among many of these contacts and I'm grateful for their insights regarding comparisons of the development of the Six financial systems but above all the proposed model of an Optimal Regional Integration in the financial subsystem of the EAC regional bloc. Heartfelt appreciation go out to my resourceful respondents from the 20 EAC and Supranational Institutions; 25 Ugandan financial and education institutions; 9 Rwandan financial and academic institutions; 7 institutions for Kenya and Tanzania each; 3 institutions for Burundi and South Sudan each for their suggestions, counsels, and encouragement. These have been highlighted at the end of the Book, after the Bibliography section. Nonetheless, the following financial system authorities were exceedingly incremental to the whole research initiative:

Prof. Mwape Bonard   (Director General - East & Southern Africa Management Institute)
Prof. Alexandre Lyambabaje (Executive Secretary - Inter-university Council for East Africa)
Prof. Dr. Ashraf Hashim   (CEO – International Shariah Research Academy for Islamic Finance)
Dr. Ssewanyana Sarah (Executive Director, Economic Policy Research Center)
Dr. Josephat Bosire Kerosi   (Professor & Consultant in Finance – Rwanda)

Dr. Ezra Munyambonera (Senior Research Fellow – Economic Policy Research Center)

Dr. Kihangire David & Anne Mpendo (East African Community Secretariat)

Dr. Martin Brownbridge (Advisor to the Governor – Bank of Uganda)

Dr. Kaberuka Donald (formerly President, Africa Development Bank; now, Harvard Univ.)

Dr. Enos Bukuku (Deputy Secretary General (P&J) of the EAC Secretariat)

Bekabye Moses (Macroeconomic Advisor to the Government)

Stephen Kaboyo (MD – Alpha Capital Partners)

Mulema Stephen, CFA (Director, Financial Markets Dep't): Bank of Uganda

Keith Kalyegira (CEO – Capital Markets Authority)

Barack Obatsa, CFA (Chief Investment Officer - African Alliance Investments East Africa)

Byarugaba Richard (Managing Director, NSSF-Uganda)

Rwabukumba Celestin (CEO – Rwanda Stock Exchange; & Chairman – EASEA)

Mkama Nichodemus (Director – Capital Market & Securities Authority-Tanzania)

Paul Mathaura (CEO - Capital Market Authority-Kenya)

Nyakundi David Bonyi (CEO - Uganda Retirement Benefits Regulatory Authority)

Mutimba Patrick, CFA, FAIA, MBA (Director, MEFMI of Eastern & Southern Africa)

Mutahakana Franklin (Office of the Country Director, World Bank Group)

Kassami Jasi (Office of the Director General, East Africa Development Bank)

Dieudonne Nyunguka (Monetary & Financial Markets, Bank of Republic of Burundi)

Girish Raipuria (Founder Director : Shrikaam Fincom Consulting Ltd)

Kasolo Ronald, CFA (GenAfric Investments)

Lutwama Joseph (Capital Markets Authority Uganda)

DEDICATION

This publication is dedicated to:

My gorgeous wife – Rebecca Nakisozi Mugerwa

My charming children – Gracia Namuli Ritah and Gentil Katumba Reuben

My beloved parents – Mr. Paul Ssali Mukisa and Mrs. Ritah Namiiro Ssali

BOOK REVIEWS

Mugerwa's Book is technically profound, analytically rich, regionally inspirational, and provides benchmarks that inform policy to the current initiatives on EAC integration in the financial system. The Book is meant for use by different stakeholders including policy makers, central banks, other financial services industry, and investors, practicing managers, and academia for research and teaching purposes. It provides background analysis and understanding of the current East African Community's financial systems and proposes an efficient and integrated model that is applicable to the sub-region.

MUNYAMBONERA EZRA (PhD)

Senior Research Fellow & Financial economist, Economic Policy Research Center (EPRC)

Paul Mugerwa's new book " The East African Financial System" is probably among the first books published, exploring the East African Financial System in greater depth. The book takes us back to history tracing the origins of modern monetary and financial systems. The author explores not only conventional finance and banking but also introduces one area that is usually not captured in most writings and books in this areas i.e. Islamic Finance. While Islamic Finance is slowly becoming a maintsream area of finance, there has been limited research , works and writing in this area. The author brings to our attention this area of finance. A good reference to practioners. Following from his previous book, the Author explores in-depth the key regulatory instituitions in East Africa and different markets operating and currently under development like the derivative and commodity markets. The writer further explores in an eloquent way the

Public Private Patnerships, The scholar dwells on the mechanics of investing various investment instruments including their risks. For those students who want to understand how thier monetary, regulatory and financial systems work in East Africa this is the book, for those already practising finance, banking or investments, the book is an inavaluable tool to have.

BARACK OBATSA, CFA

(East Africa Portfolio Manager, African Alliance Investment Bank; and arguably the 1st CFA holder in EAC)

In the current economic juncture, globalisation is a phenomenon that cannot be avoided. This book focuses on the East African market where, we are experiencing profound changes in the structure and functioning of the economy that has generated outstanding performances in the technical and technological production, trade, services and information system.

The book is an intellectually stimulating read. I couldn't stop reading page after page, while relating with the simplicity and intellectual insightfulness that Mugerwa provides as he weaves the otherwise complex terminologies. A Very pragmatic and easy to understand as it not only informs but also clarifies as well as provides comparison.

His emphasis is that nowadays, in the context of globalization, the world economy recorded significant changes in the structure and function of its main subsystems, especially in the financial subsystem. Under globalization conditions, this subsystem, which includes capital flows (loans and bonds) and investment (foreign direct investment, shares and money), has recorded a high rate of increase of the volume business. The spread of capital circuits, plus a strong institutionalized infrastructure, have created a global financial market the developments of which are felt very quickly on our east African markets. I call upon the economic Policy architectures, scholars and financial and economic enthusiasts to make it a must read book.

Dr KEROSI J BOSIRE, (PhD)

(CEO, THRUWAY ATOZ – Management firm; and formerly, DVC-Academics, University of Kigali)

Towards an optimal regional integration, is an excellent resource for students, academicians and financial markets practitioners. The organization of the book meshes well with its lay out and lends itself successfully to the pillars that put together a well-functioning financial system. The author supplies an in-depth analysis of the various aspects of the financial structures, the current status, the desired, the critical elements necessary for regional integration. The author's enthusiasm for this topic is obvious throughout the book. I can't recommend this book enough. It's a must have.

KABOYO M. STEPHEN
(MD, Alpha Capital Partners; formerly, Director, Bank of Uganda)

I have been given an opportunity to read the part related to Islamic finance and I found it very interesting and informative. The development of Islamic finance has been elaborated and most importantly the issues and challenges have been highlighted. All these are vital to be tackled by various stakeholders to ensure the positive development of Islamic finance. This is a must-have book for those who are interested to learn more about EAC financial system and its development but also the Islamic Financial system.

Prof. Dr. ASHRAF Md. HASHIM
(Sharia Advisory Council, Central Bank of Malaysia; & CEO, International Shariah Research Academy for Islamic Finance –ISRA Consultancy)

FOREWORD

In this century, regional integration is taking a new shape in Africa. Africa has now several blocks with the aim of creating a continental block. Indeed there are both benefits and challenges that arise out of such a development. Therefore, understanding key financial related issues to that regional integration will equip Africa to make sound policies to foster effective integration and to prepare for any risks.

This book is one of its kind on integration and therefore an eye opener on what really it entails to create economic integrations. It tries to explain a number of key financial issues that must or will go on in the East African countries to have sustainable integration. From that point of view, this book is the first of its kind on integration, and the author discusses and pulls on a variety of financial issues that have not been discussed on integration.

For the Academic, it is a source of inspiration in building theory on and about regional financial integration; for the policy maker, the book presents issues in a simple and easy to use manner. It uses simple language and simplifies complex financial terms that make easy reading and understanding. I highly recommend this book for anybody or those involved and interested in integration as it brings in a dimension, financial bases for integration, often forgotten in the discussion on integration.

Prof. BONARD MWAPE

Director General, ESAMI

(East & Southern Africa Management Institute)

Globally, financial economists have accentuated how imperative financial system soundness is to regional integrations, domestic macroeconomics, and global competitiveness but also to rational corporate and personal financial decision-making. Financial systems make possible the creation of productive capital so as to meet the demands of the economy; this is done through mobilizing and allocating domestic savings and foreign investments by operating as an efficient conduit between savers and investors.

This Book is technically profound, analytically rich, regionally inspirational, and provides a benchmarks that informs policy to the current initiatives on EAC integration in the financial system. The Book is meant for use by different stakeholders including policy makers, central banks, other financial services industry, and investors, practicing managers, and academia for research and teaching purposes. It provides background analysis and understanding of the current East African Community's financial systems and proposes an efficient and integrated model that is applicable to the sub-region.

With Mugerwa's publication focusing on "The East Africa Financial System: Towards an Optimal Regional Integration", we now have a comprehensive text that links theory and practice on finance/investment, economic integration aspects of the financial systems. The assessment begins from the evolution of monetary economies to the various types of financial systems as determined by economic ideologies, but more specifically puts a strong case for embracing the "Islamic Financial System". In details, the writer provides a deeper analysis of the: EAC Financial Institutions; the Commodity & Financial Markets the EAC Financial assets; a break-down of EAC Financial Infrastructure, Risks & Intermediation; an exploration of EAC financial system players. Finally, the writer proposes an efficient and Integrated Financial System model that would work for the EAC economies to achieve regional and global competitiveness.

This Book is a must-have by all stakeholders in the EAC financial systems but also prospective investors from the global financial world.

SSEWANYANA SARAH (PhD) & Dr. EZRA MUNYAMBONERA
Executive Director, Economic Policy Research Center (EPRC)

PREFACE

Why Study "The East Africa Financial System: Towards an Optimal Regional Integration"?

Most of us (stakeholders) wonder whether our crucial institutions that have served us for close more than a Century can continually function well, and work for the poor communities that are greatly characterized of the EAC region. These institutions of the financial system include: a wide array of the banking system, non-bank financial intermediaries, pooled investment vehicles, Central banks, and other financial services providers; this, coupled to, a diversity of financial markets players that render the financial system complete and efficient in allocation and distribution of funds. This EAC regional financial system may look solid and secure, but in the face of global financial crises, most of these regional financial systems have been adversely affected and are significantly vulnerable. There is, therefore, need to align and/or benchmark the integrated financial system constituents with international best practices such as BCP for banking, IAIS for insurance, IOPS for pension, among other international finance bodies.

The banking system enjoying the lion's share with more than 70% of assets in the combined EAC financial system but largely serving a small percentage of the EAC population. Unfortunately, some few largest players in the banking sector in some EAC countries collude (in form of a cartel market structure) in the primary bond markets to set high interest rates (yield) on government debt securities during auctions, given most EAC governments' high appetite for borrowing and fiscal indiscipline. This has seen a comparatively high interest rate environment in the EAC vis-à-vis her other African regional peers. On the other hand, mobile money and other pro-poor financial infrastructure have significantly contributed to improvement in financial inclusion and financial system development.

For regional integration basically in the financial sector, much as the small, fragmented and globally invisible financial markets in EAC regional bloc are a huge disincentive to the achievement of sustainable development for both individual economies and the regional bloc at large, the business sense (value proposition) should guide all initiatives – the business community and the household sectors should be incentivized by the business/ value element and rational financial decisions so as to transact with each other within the EAC region but NOT laws and policies taking precedence over the business sense. Besides, policy makers at both national and EAC regional levels ought to facilitate the harmonization and synchronization of policies, guidelines, systems, and laws so as to boost the business sense (as a driver or regional integration, at the same time financial inclusion and financial system development). These will significantly contribute to making financial services work for the poor in the EAC region, stimulate healthy competitions, and procure efficiency in resource allocation across the EAC regional bloc but also serve to contribute to achieving the EAC Vision 2050.

This publication discusses all of the major constituents/ players in the financial system in a flexible order that accommodates the needs of different stakeholders: financial sector players and regulators at all levels, regional integration policy makers, training and academic institutions, financial systems scholars, investing community, and other readers who often approach the financial system from unique perspectives. This book is quite comprehensive though analytical in approach, but among other themes it majorly focuses on: Financial inclusion, Financial system development, and Regional integration.

TOPICS COVERED IN THE BOOK

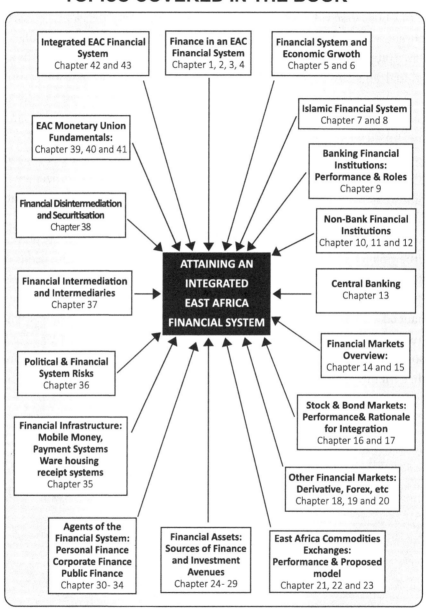

Integrated EAC Financial System
Chapter 42 and 43

Finance in an EAC Financial System
Chapter 1, 2, 3, 4

Financial System and Economic Grwoth
Chapter 5 and 6

Islamic Financial System
Chapter 7 and 8

EAC Monetary Union Fundamentals:
Chapter 39, 40 and 41

Banking Financial Institutions:
Performance & Roles
Chapter 9

Financial Disintermediation and Securitisation
Chapter 38

Non-Bank Financial Institutions
Chapter 10, 11 and 12

ATTAINING AN INTEGRATED EAST AFRICA FINANCIAL SYSTEM

Financial Intermediation and Intermediaries
Chapter 37

Central Banking
Chapter 13

Political & Financial System Risks
Chapter 36

Financial Markets Overview:
Chapter 14 and 15

Financial Infrastructure:
Mobile Money, Payment Systems
Ware housing receipt systems
Chapter 35

Stock & Bond Markets:
Performance& Rationale for Integration
Chapter 16 and 17

Other Financial Markets:
Derivative, Forex, etc
Chapter 18, 19 and 20

Agents of the Financial System:
Personal Finance
Corporate Finance
Public Finance
Chapter 30- 34

Financial Assets:
Sources of Finance and Investment Avenues
Chapter 24- 29

East Africa Commodities Exchanges:
Performance & Proposed model
Chapter 21, 22 and 23

PART 1:

INTRODUCTION/ FINANCE IN A FINANCIAL SYSTEM

"Greater access to finance can help households escape poverty & tap the talents of the less privileged"

Chapter 1

EVOLUTION OF MONETARY ECONOMIES

To better appreciate the imperativeness of money in a financial system, it is logical to imagine a society without any financial services. How on earth would folks go about their daily business in the absence of either money or financial intermediaries, and this can be exhibited in a two sector model in a given society: the household and the business sectors. The business sector produces goods & services, through the exploitation of resources such as labour, land among others resources which are owned by the household sector. Then the household sector is in turn given goods & services produced by the business sector in exchange of their resources. In this barter system of economy (simple economy), there is neither government nor foreign trade sectors, not even money as a medium of exchange. Therefore, the household sector is left with two options upon receipt of the goods & services:

> *a) Consumption; commodities provided from the place of work can either be consumed/ enjoyed directly now or be exchanged with other households so as to widen the variety of consumption*

> *b) Investment; a portion of current consumption can be fore gone so as to create resources for asset-building, hence producing higher levels of consumption in the future when the household also enters the business sector and produces more resources.*

The obvious challenge with this system that was faced by our ancestors was spending a lot of time and resources in search for other households interested in exchanging their commodities.

This definitely necessitated a mechanism that would facilitate transactions and render them more efficient by converting commodities into something small, portable, standardized, and generally acceptable.

MONETARY ECONOMY

The introduction of money in the financial system facilitated the transaction and exchange of, for example labour and dodge the inconvenience of carrying tins of beans or pieces of meat to the market to exchange them for medical or teaching services. Before the money facility, many items have been used as means of exchange, in quest for simplification of transactions, ranging from commodity money to the contemporary electronic money. The production of cash crops and some food crops in the current EAC economies is largely responsible for the initial monetization of the region's economies, which were all influenced by the goals of the British and the Belgians (colonial masters) basically for production of raw materials for export to home industries.

It has been recognized that the evolution of money has so far gone through seven important stages depending on the progress of human civilization at different times and places. These include:

i) Commodity money:

where various types of commodities have been used as money depending on the level of civilization and means of livelihood of a given society such as pastoral, agricultural, hunting, fishing, among other societies. Stones, axes, shells, grains, tobacco, animal skins (both domestic & wild), spears, bows & arrows, but due their defects as a medium of exchange, societies went ahead to look for better alternatives as money.

ii) Metallic money:

with the discovery of precious metals and their being valuable due to improvement in civilization and trading activities amongst communities, metallic money was introduced. Silver, copper, gold, tin were initially used as money in its raw form, but later coins of predetermined weight were used as a medium of exchange. On the contrary, due to their shortcomings as a form of money such as unreliable supply, lack of portability and other merchants would actually melt it to earn more money selling it; these forced societies to look for other convenient alternatives of money.

iii) Paper money:

this development came as a result of goldsmiths who kept strong safes to store their gold since they were believed to be honest merchants, where people would keep their gold for safe custody. In return, goldsmiths would give them a receipt promising to avail the gold on demand. These receipts from the goldsmiths were given to sellers of commodities by buyers since they represent value that was in store/ custody of the goldsmiths. Later, this system was used by central banks, whereby they would issue paper money that is backed by gold reserves which would regulate the supply of paper money. However, this type of money was affected by changes in supply and prices of such metals as gold and silver, and such as system would not be responsive to changes in level of economic activities in a given society.

iv) Credit Money:

this evolution of money in modern financial world was characterized by the use of cheques as money; since it performs the same function as bank notes in the transfer of money and obligations from one entity to another. Of course, a cheque is not real money but a written order since it expires with a single transaction, and it has a specified sum. On the contrary, due to safety and convenience in the contemporary financial system, large transactions are made through cheques nowadays, leaving bank notes to small transactions.

v) Near Money:

this stage has been characterized as the use of close substitutes for money that are highly liquid assets; at this stage, money has become intangible. Financial assets such as insurance policies, unit trust funds' certificates, bills of exchange, saving certificates, debentures, treasury bills and notes, bonds, share certificates, etc; where ownership is now transferable merely by book entry.

vi) Electronic Money (e-money):

this is one of the most recent stages in the evolution of money whereby money as actually become not only intangible but invisible through payment and transaction systems such as mobile money, Electronic Funds Transfer (EFT), Real Time Gross Settlement (RTGS), plastic money (credit cards), etc. This has enabled the monetary authority to streamline and monitor funds/money transfer within the financial system. It has brought a lot of safety, convenience but also the integration of many households who were initially in the informal financial systems closer to the formal financial system.

vii) Crypto Currencies:

these are also called virtual currencies, and Bit-coin is apparently the newest form of such currency with a uniquely designed and decentralized platform. These currencies provide a way to transfer digital property from one internet user to another; which transfer of assets has potential to be used in buying and selling financial assets like stocks and bonds. In the future, this could prompt investors to consider investing in assets denominated in a virtual currency as part of their overall investment strategy. This is evidenced by the fact that of all the bit-coins minted in 2009 – 2010, more than 60% remain unspent and some took more than a year to be spent: implying that some investors may already be using bit-coins as an alternative investment. The bit-coin system has potential to interrupt the existing payment systems though its development has addressed outstanding issues that were characterized with other stages of money such as: market risk, counterparty risk, transaction risk, operational risk, privacy risk, and regulatory risk. Since its inauguration in 2009, it has facilitated more than 60 million transactions between 109 million accounts; and currently, there are 14 million minted bit-coins worth USD 3.5 Billion. Many financial institutions, corporations and now even central banks are currently contemplating using these digital currencies like bitcoins or some analysts refer to them as "distributed ledger" due to the fact that they, among other advantages, make it easier to comply with anti-money-laundering and other regulations since they provide a record of all past transactions. They operate through a database which is maintained by a single actor like a bank but collaboratively by a number of participants whose computers regularly agree on how to update the database using a consensus mechanism. Financial institutions are getting excited with this kind of currency because, instead of having to keep track of their assets in separate databases as they do now, they can share just one, and trades can be settled almost instantly without need of lots of intermediaries. This has resulted into: less capital tied up during transactions, reduced transactional risks

On the other hand, many central banks are equally excited with this newly introduced technology (currency), and this has seen Russia' central bank set up a working group to this effect; the People's Bank of China is showing interest. World central banks plan to interest individuals and firms open digital currency accounts at the central bank since this would save on printing costs if people held more bits (digital currency) and fewer banknotes but also it would be quite hard to forge the currency

Monetization of the financial system has ushered in investments, which has trained households to put aside some resources currently so as to produce a return in the future. This has seen many people, basically in modern economies, significantly reducing on their current consumption in a bid to put resources into capital formation (asset-building) such as building industries, purchase of machines, buying financial assets (like stocks, bonds, insurance policies, pension funds, etc). And this is done by majorly the household sector but also the business sector. Economies need people who are ready to sacrifice current consumption in anticipation for fruits that come with investments; they should be willing to defer present consumption and put their resources at risk within the productive business sector upon a promise for attractive returns, with the use of risk management systems. In contemporary sophisticated financial systems, households (real owners of assets) invest their aggregate resources in the business sector which acts as stewards for resources of the household sector for more value/net-worth creation on the part of the households. This state-of-affairs has ushered in the philosophy of economies of collective strategies, whereby households now pool their resources through a variety of investment vehicles (shall be discussed later) for better risk management and value creation. This has consequently led to the development of the financial markets to assist the flow of funds from the households to the business sector; and thus create more value to the household, the business and the government sectors through, among others the multiplier effects. It is actually this reason that the author decided to make an analysis of the East Africa financial system (and provide a model for an Optimal Regional Integration), but also glimpses of financial systems of the Sub-Saharan Africa since there are lots of commonalities amongst them: financial institutions, financial markets, financial assets, financial agents, and financial intermediation.

Chapter 2

FORMAL AND INFORMAL FINANCIAL SYSTEMS

FINANCIAL SYSTEM

This is a system of rules and practices which coordinates & regulates the monetary & economic affairs of a country. It is an interaction of policy makers, a monetary system, financial institutions, financial markets, financial agents & intermediation so as to accelerate the flow of financial capital from savings to investment. It also entails the legal, political and institutional frameworks that govern them.

A financial system refers to a system which enables the transfer of money between investors and borrowers. It could be defined at an international, regional or organization level. The term "system" in "Financial System" indicates a group of complex and closely linked institutions, agents, procedures, markets, transactions, claims and liabilities within an economy.

Financial system consists of institutions that help to match one party's savings with another's investment. It moves the economy's scarce resources from savers to borrowers: whereby savers save for various reasons such as child's education, retirement, owning a house, taking advantage of future opportunities, etc; yet borrowers borrow for also various objectives like buying a house, starting a business, etc. Savers supply their money to the financial system expecting to get it back with interest (cost of capital) at a later date, and borrowers do so knowing that they will have to pay back with interest at a later date.

Uganda's financial system has grown tremendously in terms of size with total assets equivalent to 35.53% of GDP in December

2014. In terms of structure, commercial banks dominate the financial system in Uganda accounting for over 77% of financial assets and with total assets equivalent to 27.43% of GDP. Other financial intermediaries are limited in number and relatively small in size.

Tanzania's financial system was as follows: banking sector accounted for 70.8%; Pension assets were at 26.7%; Insurance at 1.9%; and Collective Investment Schemes at 0.6%.

SOUTH SUDAN FINANCIAL SYSTEM

By 2011, the economy performed relatively well thanks to favorable oil prices, higher levels of donor support, and considerable increase in FDIs basically from East Africa and China. The economy had 10 commercial banks and 42 branches; with only one locally owned bank called the Agriculture Bank of Sudan. There were 6 microfinance institutions with 76 branches, and only 5% potential clients in the Capital Juba, and less than 1% of potential clientele in the whole region.

By 2013, the financial sector was still small and limited/ underdeveloped, whereby the government would majorly manage its finances through using officials to hold and disburse funds. Only 1% of the population had bank accounts, and the economy was characterized by very poor banking infrastructure. But 2014 saw a significant improvement in the financial system, with 27 banks, 79 forex bureaus, 12 multilateral financial institutions, and 10 insurance companies. All of these with over 80% foreign ownership; and Central bank's oversight of commercial banks was very weak; the banking system's adherence to the Basel core principles was limited. All this implied that the health of financial system could not ascertained with confidence.

Currently, she still largely relies on Uganda and Kenya for external financial transactions eg money transfers; and minimal geographical coverage, weak regulatory framework, limited management and expertise. The financial system is characterized by very few banks, and majorly by Uganda and Kenya; besides, bank services rendered are limited to forex transactions for remittance and bank transfers; limited provision of loan, finance and savings transactions; and very high transaction costs.

i)   Formal Capitalistic Financial System

The East Africa financial system can be broadly classified into the formal financial system and the informal financial system. The formal financial system is one that is well regulated and domiciled under the Ministries of Finance; EAC Central banks; the Capital Markets Authorities (CMA); Retirement Benefits Authorities (Pension regulators); Insurance Regulatory Authorities; money, capital and foreign exchange markets; insurance companies; brokerage firms; deposit money banks; development finance institutions; fund managers; and other regulatory & self-regulatory bodies in the East African Community (EAC).

ii)   Informal Financial System

On the other hand, the informal financial system is one that is not regulated and there is a weak relationship/ integration with the formal financial system. This includes the following:

- *Individual money lenders such as neighbours, relatives, traders, landlords, and store owners*
- *Groups of persons operating as funds or associations, and functioning under a system of their own rules, and brand themselves as fixed funds, associations, saving/ investment club, SACCOs, financial cooperatives, microfinance institutions, Rotational Savings & Credit Associations (ROSCAs), Community-Based Organisations (CBOs).*
- *Partnership firms consisting of local brokers and non-bank financial intermediaries such as finance companies.*

This financial information on the EAC financial systems clearly indicate deliberate steps taken by the government to achieve both the domestic and global targets in line with financial inclusion and deepening compared to many Sub-Saharan African economies that are faring very poorly in many dimensions. However, there is still a long way for the regional bloc to attain a position of developed financial system given the appalling statistics as will be presented in subsequent chapters just to compare with her counterparts in Southern and North Africa.

Chapter 3

ALTERNATIVE FINANCIAL SYSTEMS: COMMUNITY CURRENCY

Community currencies have been used world over to facilitate financial transactions in many a rural communities, to strengthen community spirit and foster self-sustenance in socio-economic life of informal settlements in Africa, Asia, and South America. In East Africa, originally called "Eco-Pesa" but later rebranded to "Bangla-Pesa" or generally community currency are various names of a particular community currency used in Kenya that serves to reduce poverty and support environmental conservation in various communities in Kenya and but also existent in South Africa, and soon to be initiated in Uganda. Introduced by William Ruddick in 2010 to three informal settlements in Mombasa County but later developed into the Bangla-Pesa model in 2013 based on the results of Eco-Pesa whereby residents could obtain Eco-Pesa through being part of a business network or participating in community events. Once registered, local businesses become part of an Business Network where businesses are allowed to exchange their Eco-Pesa vouchers for the national currency (Kenya Shillings) backed by donors funds. Such businesses include among others general shops, poultry sellers, transportation providers, water sellers, etc. Eco-Pesa vouchers were security features such as: security designed backgrounds, watermarked paper, and serial numbering.

On the other hand, Bangla-Pesa uses a mutual credit model where there is no longer need for national currency or donor funds to keep it running. Unlike vouchers that are used for a particular good or service, Bangla-Pesa coupons are accepted for many transactions and therefore represent a complementary currency acting as a means of exchange in informal settlements (it operates alongside the official government legal tender currency). The Bangla-Pesa program aims at cushioning residents against falling below the poverty line during periods when business slow and poor. It also aims at stimulating the local economy and increase overall efficiency in the market. Besides, it seeks to create an avenue for the poor to enhance their participation in a market economy, and it should provide a means for the poor to purchase goods and services from the market even without normal currency. This program is only used within the membership network and serves as a mutual-credit clearing; it is described as credit since traders receive goods and services without paying any cash but only presenting coupons. Such complementary currencies have had positive impact on communities in the following ways:

- *It serves to strengthen community spirit*
- *It increases community participation in socio-economic activities.*
- *It reduces imports into the community and leads to quality life*
- *It helps to stabilize the community in the face of monetary volatility by allowing network members to trade with each other without using the national currency.*

On the contrary, complementary currencies which are a growing phenomenon in developing economies have broader implications such as their use weakening linkages with other communities and the larger economy that could have macroeconomic problems. Besides, what might be the impact on the economy if many other informal settlements in various communities adopt their own complementary currencies? Or could this turn out to be "bad money" driving out "good money"?

Chapter 4

HISTORY / EVOLUTION OF FINANCE AS A DISCIPLINE

Before the invention of money, temples were the first places for safekeeping of valuables, which consisted of items such as grain, cattle and agricultural implements, later followed by precious metals such as gold. The reasons to store valuables in temples included:

- *Continuous stream of visitors: this made it difficult for any thief to go about his business unnoticed.*
- *Building strength: temples tended to be well-built, and gaining unauthorized entry was difficult.*
- *Places of worship: sacred places were deemed to provide additional protection against potential thieves.*

The lending of money is not a recent practice - there is evidence of priests in Babylon lending money to merchants as early as the 18th century BC. The Code of Hammurabi, written around 1760 BC, includes laws governing banking operations in ancient Mesopotamia. The laws regulate, among others, risk and reward sharing between lender and borrower, compensation for loss of articles in safekeeping, and the amount of rent to be paid for having the use of land and different species of livestock was clearly defined.

In the wake of the 20th century, finance, though closely linked with economics, emerged as a separate field from economics; in financial economics, we actually define finance as the applied economics due to its usage of economic tools of analysis. The major focus of this study reflected the developments of finance, such as, the building of giant Industrial Corporation by Rockfeller,

Carnegie, Du Pont, among others. These ushered in the usage of financial instruments that were so key in major investment decisions like mergers and acquisitions.

With the development and implementation of antitrust laws, corporate consolidations became less prominent, and alternative patterns of growth were emphasized. Attention shifted to financial assets like stocks and bonds and other securities used for raising capital; and the role of the wholesale banks or intermediaries in security offerings also received much interest. No doubt, the great bull market of the 1920s in the Western economies contributed to the emphasis in raising capital using modern avenues.

On the contrary, the shock of depression in 1930s ushered in an era of conservatism, and attention shifted to such topics as preservation of capital, maintenance of liquidity, re-organization of financially distressed corporations, and the bankruptcy process. Governments of many frontier-market economies assumed a much larger role in regulating business through the establishment of Securities and Financial services Acts which would later serve to monitor the corporate performance of companies but also to protect the investors' interests.

The 1940s and 1950s offered new knowledge in the study and practice of corporate finance. However, in the mid-50s a major shift in finance took place: from a descriptive approach to a more analytical and decision-oriented approach. Up to that time, the study procedures of finance had been descriptive or definitional in nature; and the orientation had been from the viewpoint of a third party or an outsider.

The first area of study to generate the newfound enthusiasm for decision-related analysis was capital budgeting; where the financial manager was presented with analytical techniques (capital rationing techniques) for allocating resources among the various assets of the firm. The enthusiasm spread to other decision making areas of the firm such as cash and inventory management, capital structure formulation, and dividend policy. The emphasis shifted from that of the outside looking into that of the financial manager forced to make tough routine decisions affecting the performance of the firm.

Finance originated from economics and accounting: economists use a supply-and –demand framework to explain how prices and quantities of commodities are determined in a free enterprise economy. On the contrary, accountants provide the record-keeping mechanism for showing ownership of financial instruments used in the flow of financial resources between savers and borrowers; and they also record revenues, expenses, and profitability of firms that produce and exchange commodities.

i)   Finance as a Discipline

The field of finance is quite broad in perspective; and simply defined, finance is a body of facts, principles and theories dealing with the raising and managing of money by individuals, businesses and governments. It covers essential areas of financial planning and financial institutions as well as managerial finances by the above three financial agents of the financial system. Melicher & Norton (2003) define finance as the study of how individuals, institutions, governments, and businesses acquire, spend, and manage financial resources. Besides, finance is also defined as a field that studies how people make decisions regarding the allocation of resources over time and the management of risks.

It is technically separated into three sub-categories: personal finance, corporate finance and public finance. All these categories are concerned with activities such as pursuing sound investments, obtaining low-cost credit, attracting funds for liabilities, and for banking. Yet each has its own specific considerations: for example, individuals need to plan for retirement expenses, which mean investing enough money during their working years and ensuring that their asset allocation fits their long-term plans. On the other hand, a large firm may have to decide whether to raise additional funds through a bond issue or stock offering or sale of its assets. Merchant banks may advise the firm on such considerations and help them market the securities. On the contrary, public finance, in addition to managing funds for its day-to-day operations, a government body has larger social responsibilities whose goals include attaining an equitable distribution of income for its citizens and enacting policies that foster macroeconomic stability.

Figure 1.1:
CAREER AT A GLANCE

Finance Job/Position	Job/ Career Description
Cash management analyst	This involves monitoring and managing the firm's daily cash flows.
Tax analyst/ expert	This is about preparing financial statements for tax purposes.
Insurance broker	This entails selling insurance to individuals and businesses, but also participating in the process of claims.
Mortgage analyst	This comprises analyzing real estate loan applications and assisting in arranging of mortgage financing.
Financial analyst	This involves evaluating financial performance and preparing financial plans
Stock broker	This entails assisting clients in purchasing financial securities and building investment wealth.
Capital expenditure analyst	This comprises estimating cash flows and evaluating asset investment opportunities (capital budgeting).

Cost analyst	This involves the comparison of actual operations against budgeted operations.
Research analyst	This entails analyzing the investment potential of real property and securities for institutional investors.
Loan analyst	It involves evaluating consumer and commercial loans applications.
Bank teller	This involves assisting customers with their daily checking and banking transactions.
Security analyst	This engrosses analysing and making recommendations on the investment potential of specific securities
Financial planner	This entails analyzing individual client insurance needs and investment plans to meet one's financial goals.
Investment research analyst	This engrosses conducting research on investment opportunities for a corporate treasury.
Investment banking analyst	It entails conducting financial analysis and valuation of new securities that are being issued. He is also in charge of creating securities
Portfolio Manager	It entails a process of combining securities in a portfolio tailored to the investor's preferences and needs, monitoring that portfolio, and evaluating its performance.
Risk / insurance Manager	

Source: Researcher's Data

Chapter 5

OVERVIEW OF THE FINANCIAL SYSTEM

Figure 1.2:

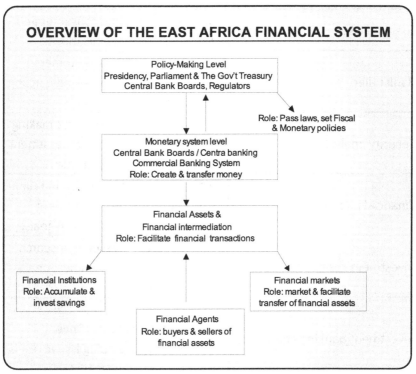

OVERVIEW OF THE EAST AFRICA FINANCIAL SYSTEM

Source: Researcher's Data

i)   **Relationships amongst constituents of a financial system**

To better understand the operations of the financial system; and the interconnectivity amongst all its constituents, allow me use this hypothetical illustration:

Gentil Company wants to establish an efficient inexpensive factory (production unit) that produces beverages from fruits and vegetables that are produced by rural small-holders hence linking small income earners (retail farmers) basically from the particular rural areas in the East African Community (EAC) with the commodities markets but also availing them technical advisory in their lines of production in real time. But the company does not have funds to actualise this brilliant and ground-breaking invention. On the other hand, Ritah has some good savings she amassed through both inheritance and also her work life, which is lying under-utilised some in her ceiling and others on her bank account. If only Gentil Company and Ritah could be linked so that Ritah could avail the finances required for the establishment of this production unit that will create a lot of value for Gentil Company, Ritah, rural dwellers, corporate bodies, and the economy at large; all financial agents will be better off. This could be actualised through the working of the financial system: Gentil Company (manufacturer with deficit financing) would be advised (financial intermediation) by Asante Capital Hub (financial institution) a financial services firm on how it can access funds through issuing shares, bonds and other instruments (financial assets) so that Ritah (household/ net saver/ financial agent) with surplus funds on her bank account (financial institution), can transfer some of her money (via financial system infrastructure) through either buying equity or debt instruments from Gentil Company via the securities exchange (financial markets) which are regulated by the State (government) so as to protect the investors' interests..

Likewise, when a local government needs to construct a bridge, a road, a school, an airport, etc; it will definitely require more funds than the collections from local property taxes and other financial hand-outs. Therefore, a good financial system is crucial to the economic health (individually and socially). That is why it is critically important to scrutinise the whole structure and operation of our financial system so as to appreciate its contribution to the economy.

Simply put, a financial system should make possible the creation of productive capital so as to meet the demands of the economy. And productive capital formation takes place whenever resources are used to produces commodities, buildings, machinery or other capital goods that are essential in the production of both consumer goods.

NB: Globally, the above constituents of the financial system are efficiently connected and work to facilitate the flow of financial resources from points of surplus to points of deficit yet with productive uses of such resources, basically in developed economies. Contrarily, EAC's situation is one of constituents that either deliberately dis-intermediate the financial flows or due to high financial illiteracy that many financial agents are largely not informed of opportunities within the financial system so they choose to keep their funds in pillows, ceilings, pots and some in bank accounts (household) yet for the corporates, they keep excess funds in highly illiquid and less profitable real assets.

ii) Functions of a financial system

A major role of the financial system is to mobilise and allocate domestic savings: by operating as an efficient conduit (link) for the allocation of resources from net savers (people with surplus incomes) to net investors (individuals, institutions, and organisations with deficit financing).

- *It serves to monitor the corporate performance of investments in financial markets and institutions: by exerting corporate controls on underperforming firms in an economy.*

- *It provides efficient payment and settlement systems across geographical regions and industries: this ensures quick and safe movement of funds so as to create value for households, businesses, and governments.*

- *It serves to optimise the allocation of risk-bearing and reduction: by limiting, pooling, and trading risks involved in saving &*

allocating credit. This aims at containing risks within acceptable limits.

- The financial system helps to disseminate price-related information which is critically valuable in both economic and financial decision-making among financial agents.

- It offers portfolio adjustment facilities done by financial markets and intermediaries like banks and unit trust funds including: services of providing a quick, cheap and reliable way of buying and selling a wide variety of financial assets.

- The financial system serves to lower transaction costs that are incurred in the trading of financial assets: research has established that frontier market economies are characterised by high intermittent transaction costs which adversely affect the development of financial markets and financial system depth.

- It promotes the process of financial deepening and broadening such as: increasing of financial assets as a percentage of GDP (equity, bond, insurance assets).

- It serves to determine the return that equates aggregate savings and borrowing which renders the whole economy a good investment environment.

iii) Characteristics of a good financial system

A good financial system allows entities to achieve their purposes; in particular facilitates financial markets to be complete and efficient, where:

- Investors can save for the future at fair rates of return determined by the Market.

- Creditworthy borrowers can obtain finance.

- Hedgers can manage their risks.

- Traders can obtain the currencies, commodities, and other assets they need for their operations.

If markets can perform these functions at low transaction costs, then they are said to be operationally efficient. If asset prices reflect all the information associated with fundamental value in a timely fashion, then the financial system is informationally efficient, with prices reflecting fundamental values. Besides, in informationally efficient markets, capital is allocated to its most productive use, due to allocation efficiency.

Informational efficiency is brought about by traders who bid prices up and down in response to new information that changes estimates of securities' fundamental values. If markets are operationally efficient, asset prices will have more informational efficiency since low transaction costs encourage trading based on new information.

Below are the Critical areas necessary for designing (and/or features of) a good financial system:
A well-functioning financial system should:

- *It should have a strong legal and regulatory environment that protects the rights and interests of investors so as to attract and facilitate more investments.*
- *It should have a stable currency (money): large fluctuations and depreciations in value of money leads to financial crises and hinders the growth of the economy.*
- *A good financial system ought to have established sound public finances and public debt management such as: setting and controlling public expenditure priorities; and raising adequate revenues to fund the national budget.*
- *It should have an efficient central banking institution that supervises and regulates the operations of the banking system in the country.*
- *It should maintain a sound banking system with both domestic and international banking operations: since these are the core financial intermediaries in all economies.*
- *This financial system should have efficient information systems with proper disclosure practices and networking of information systems.*

- *It should have well-functioning securities markets which promote economic growth by mobilising and deploying funds into productive uses; lowering cost of capital for firms; enhancing liquidity; and attracting foreign investments.*

A country's financial system includes its banks, securities markets, pension and mutual funds, insurers, market infrastructures, payments and settlement infrastructures, central bank, as well as regulatory and supervisory authorities. These institutions, structures and markets provide a framework for carrying out economic transactions and monetary policy, and help to efficiently channel savings into investments, thereby supporting economic growth. Problems in financial systems not only disrupt financial intermediation, but they can also undermine the effectiveness of monetary policy, exacerbate economic downturns, trigger capital flight and exchange rate pressures (a case for 2015 volatilities in the global financial system), and create large fiscal costs related to rescuing troubled financial institutions. Furthermore, with increasing connectivity among financial institutions and tighter financial and trade linkages between countries, financial shocks in one jurisdiction can rapidly spill over across financial sectors and national borders as the case was for the 2008/09 Global financial crisis, and the 2015 global currencies' volatilities as a result of the economic rebound in the U.S economy (along with the USD). Therefore, resilient financial systems that are well-regulated and well-supervised are essential for both domestic and global economic and financial stability.

Chapter 6

FINANCIAL SYSTEM & ECONOMIC GROWTH

"A well-functioning financial system requires a supporting infrastructure"

i)   Introduction

Financial systems tend to evolve around a banking sector seeking to achieve economies of scale in order to offset the costs of collecting and processing information designed to reduce uncertainty thereby facilitating a more efficient allocation of financial resources. Efficient financial systems help countries to grow, partly by widening access to external finance and channeling resources to the sectors that need those most. A well-developed financial system also can help an economy cope better with exogenous shocks such as terms of trade volatility and move them away from natural resource based development. In a well functioning economy, banks tend to act as quality controllers for capital seeking successful projects, ensuring higher returns and accelerating output growth. However, a competitive banking system is required to ensure that banks are effective forces for financial intermediation channeling savings into investment fostering higher economic growth.

Mugume (2008) argues, in reference to the performance of Uganda's banking industry that a financial system's contribution to the economy depends upon the quantity and quality of its services and the efficiency with which it provides them.

ii)   Role of Financial System in Economic Development

The economic development of any country is dependent on its financial system: its banks, stock markets, insurance sector, pension funds and a central bank with authority or at least influence over currency and interest rates. In developed countries, these two sides of the economic coin work together to promote growth and foster macroeconomic stability. Therefore, a country like Uganda which is still in a developing stage and characterized by the lack of a strong & sound financial system normally works against the national economy which would otherwise contribute to economic development. For this reason, we need to explore the relationship between financial system and economic development. And below are some of the roles of the financial system in economic development of a country:

The Country's banking system: Banks are the cornerstone of a national financial system and their key services are to provide a safe haven for the earnings of individuals and finance to companies in need of capital for a variety of investment objectives. Without this source of available capital, businesses would be hard-pressed to continue growing and returning a profit to their stakeholders. By channeling savings into the business sector through loans and also offering loans to individuals for asset-building in form of cars and homes, banks boost overall economic growth and development.

The Economy's financial markets: Stock markets provide an opportunity for households to invest in companies; and by issuing shares, public companies pay off debt or raise capital for their operations. The bond market provides another means to raise money: when a household or an investment company buys a bond, it receives a steady stream of interest payments over a set period. The bond market is accessible to companies as well as governments, which also need a reliable stream of funds to operate. Without the bond market, a government could only raise money by levying taxes, an action that tends to dampen business activity and investment within the economy. Besides, the money markets;

foreign exchange markets; mortgage markets; derivative markets all work together to provide liquidity within the financial system, manage investment risks, facilitate global transactions, and avail finance for huge capital investment to all financial agents which significantly contributes to economic development.

Management of financial crisis: Globally, confidence and trust in an economy's banking system are central to macroeconomic health: if banks cannot redeem savings accounts and savers begin to fear a loss of their money, a bank crisis results. This quickly drains cash from the bank and can eventually lead to a systemic failure (where a couple of banking institutions fail simultaneously). Bond and stock markets rise and fall with the demand for securities; when individuals fear risk or lose their trust in those capital markets, they sell their securities and cause the value of companies to fall. This, in turn, complicates businesses' capacity to raise money, either from banks or capital markets. Therefore, the regulators' capacity to foster financial system soundness (through prudent management of financial institutions and markets to shield the economy against financial crises) significantly correlates with the achievement of economic development.

Management of monetary policy instruments: Issuing currency and setting interest rates policy is the function of central banks, such as B.O.U, which are responsible for monetary policy. The central bank through their credit control measures loan out new money to the banks; by controlling this flow, B.O.U also keeps currency exchange rates steady, which is vital for foreign trade and new investment. A restrictive monetary policy (setting a higher interest rate) tends to support currency value, while lowering the rate encourages lending and investment but at the risk of currency devaluation and inflation. Reliable and consistent monetary policy fosters economic stability and growth. Hence, the prudent management of the monetary policy instruments through the interest rate and foreign currency rate regimes (which are a function of a well-functioning financial system) would facilitate the economy's development.

iii)   EAC GDP Growth Rates & Investment Implications

GDP = Current Account + Capital Account. Current account (exports Vs imports) yet Capital account (FDI, government bond, etc)

Current account should be kept strong because when it is in deficit, it means that the economy is using lots of foreign currency for imports which will negatively affect the local currency; the case of UGX in 2015 depreciation.

Figure 1.3 GDP Growth Rates Across EAC Region

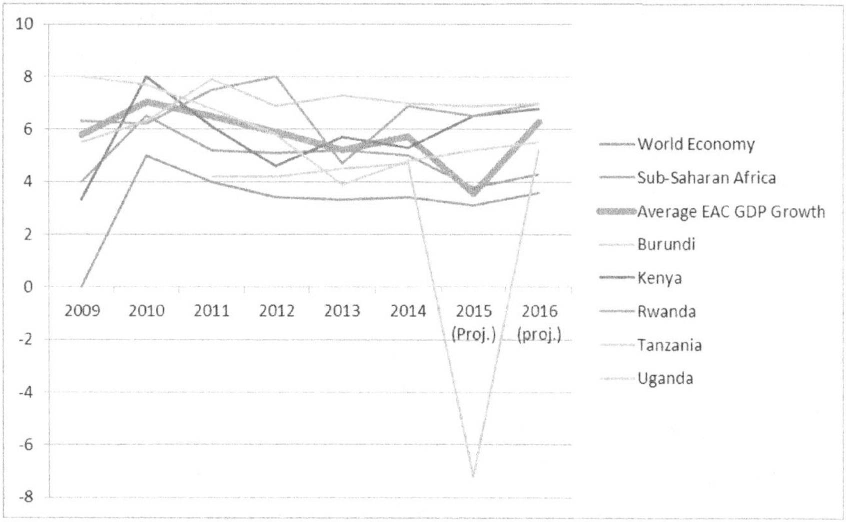

Source: IMF; WBG; EAC Central Banks (2015)

The Sub Saharan average has been on a downward trend, but projections for 2016 indicate a likely improvement in the state-of-affairs.

The EAC average enjoyed an economic peak in 2010 (due to the fact that these are Frontier market economies which are not really integrated into the global financial system, and so somewhat insulated). This was a period when many emerging markets and developed economies were struggling with the global financial crisis, but a couple of economic fundamentals were good for the EAC economies. This was followed by a significant deceleration from 2011 to 2013 when a spike in GDP growth was witnessed, but it didn't last long enough since the region went into a near recession in 2015 majorly caused by the performance of Burundi and South Sudan whose output contracted), but also partly Uganda owing to significant volatilities in exchange rate and other fundamentals. Generally, the GDP Growth rates for East Africa are higher than the average GDP growth for the world economy and that of the Sub-Saharan Africa which definitely positions the EAC to be a better investment destination for those investors who are looking for exposure high growth areas and with moderate risk profiles.

The growth in real GDP for Uganda has been on a downward trend since 2009, briefly recovering in 2013. It is currently experiencing minimal growth. Despite the massive economic potential for this economy; an uncertain global outlook, low commodity prices and relatively high cost of borrowing could potentially adversely affect her growth in 2016 and beyond. But on a positive note, given the recent rebound in commodity price in the first quarter of 2016, this is likely to offer some relief to commodity exporting countries (including the whole EAC region) although the subsequent recovery in exports may be offset by ambitious investment in infrastructure thus fueling strong import demand.

Kenya rebased its GDP in September 2014 thereby raising its GDP per capita from USD 930 to USD 1,246; and this saw her move to lower middle income economy status (the only one with such status in the EAC region).

Burundi has consistently had the lowest economic growth rates in the East African region. In 2015, the GDP growth rates reflect the political instability, with negative growth projected for 2015, projected to improve in 2016. Economic expansion in this economy has been undermined by the year-long political crisis; continued fiscal challenges and donor withdrawals will continue to adversely affect public investments as well as private investors' confidence.

Kenya has been having higher growth in the region, and is expected to flatten out in 2016. By and large, this middle income economy remains a silver lining in the whole of the EAC and possibly the Sub-Saharan Africa; and its expansion is underpinned by sustained growth in agriculture, financial services, trade, and services in general as well as construction. This is well cushioned by a healthy domestic demand in the form of resilient household consumption and continued infrastructure investments.

Tanzania has recorded consistently high economic growth rates. This usually reflects an economy that is shielded from adverse external shocks. The ambitious infrastructure investments will sustain growth at 7.0% in 2016; and such key projects include: the construction of USD 6.8 Billion Standard Gauge Railway (SGR), and the Uganda-Tanzania oil pipeline. Though may later boom-rang in the way of fiscal deficit getting out of hand.

The Rwandan economy experienced a temporary shock 2013, but picked up again and is projected to stabilize in 2015 due to sustained growth in service, industry and agriculture sectors. On the other hand, the economy growth is expected to slow down in 2016 due to adverse impact of a turbulent global commodity markets which will further weaken the current account position of the economy.

South Sudan's GDP grew by 30.7% in 2014 but 2015 was projected to have significant negative growth (-7.5%) as the prevailing civil conflict and compounded by declines in national oil production (but also momentous global oil prices) devastated the young economy. The outlook for economic growth largely depends on a recovery in global oil prices and a comprehensive conflict resolution rather than the simplistic pressures for cessation of hostilities. Improving political certainty since April 2016 should help renew both investors and donor confidence in this economically distressed country. Nonetheless, the leadership faces an uphill task of turning around the economy which is largely dependent on oil, whose prices remain subdued. There are indicators of the local currency (South Sudanese Pounds) turning around as fundamentals still suggest scarcity of US Dollars; a weak SSP has led to hyperinflation of 165% as of April 2016.

Figure 1.4
AFRICAN REGIONAL GDP GROWTH RATE PROJECTIONS

Region	2015 (Projection)	2016 (Projection)
African Continent	4.5	5.0
East Africa	5.6	6.7
North Africa	4.5	4.4
Southern Africa	3.1	3.5
West Africa	5.0	6.1
Central Africa	5.5	5.8

Source: AfDB; IMF (2015)

According to the African Development Bank, Africa's GDP growth is expected to strengthen in 2016 after subdued expansion in the last three consecutive years (2013 to 2015) and this position the continent as a preferable investment destination. Fortunately, even amid general growth prospects in the continent at large, the East African Community still has an edge over all the other regions include the compounded African continent. This is evidenced by the 2016 GDP growth rate projection that puts EAC way above all other continental peers with a towering 6.7% growth projection; which implies that the region will have an upper hand in attracting both FDIs and also domestic investments so as to take advantage of her growth story. This is because every investor would wish to identify with and/or partner with high growth potential regions, and this is partly due to natural endowments in the EAC which have not been exploited but also the improving business environment and relative political stability in most EAC regional economies.

iv) EAC Growth & US Dollar Strengthening

Despite the positive outlook for EAC economies, key risks to the region include continued decline in commodity prices (which is likely to lead to lower economic growth for four straight years according to the IMF's 2016 Regional Economic Outlook); and further strengthening of the US Dollar. The continued economic growth slowdown in emerging market trading partners particularly China may further hamper demand for EAC commodity exports, widening Balance of Payments (BOP) deficits. With possibilities of more US Federal Reserve Quantitative easing programs, the USD may strengthen further causing more exchange pressures on EAC currencies. EAC economies with significant short-term portfolio investments are at risk of more capital reversals, which would further exert additional pressure on exchange rates. Fortunately, the depreciation in EAC currencies against the US Dollar in 2015 didn't fully translate into higher inflationary tendencies, thanks to efficient Central banks in EAC which adopted tight monetary policies, through among other tools, hiking the Central bank rates; however the full effects are not yet suppressed but could materialize later on.

Figure 1.5
US Dollar Index

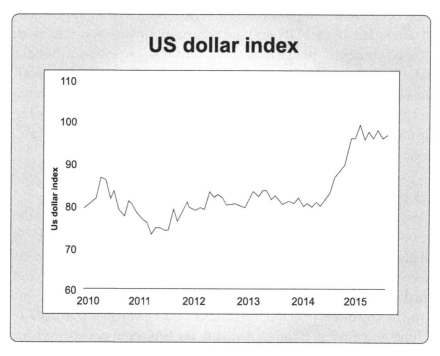

Source: EADB; IMF (2015)

v) EAC Currencies Depreciation Causes (Exchange Volatilities)

The following are the factors that significantly affected the volatilities of EAC regional currencies majorly in the year 2015:

Domestic woes like Balance of Payment deficit (sizeable current account deficits that are worsening by the day)

Regional issues like geo-political factors such as political instability in Burundi, South Sudan, and D.R Congo; which are key regional trading partners.

U.S economy & USD strengthening effect like the surge of the USD and the rebound in the U.S economy occasioned by the Federal Reserve System macroeconomic policy stance. The U.S Federal Reserve increased its policy interest rate from zero bound in 2015; although the hike was only 25 basis points, and the policy rate remains low, floating between 0.25 and 0.5, the consequent interest rate rise in 2015 was monumental because it succeeds almost ten years of no change and represents the first advanced economy to embark upon monetary policy tightening.

Global economic factors like slower growth in Europe and declining industrial growth in China & Japan (China is the region's largest trading partner, and she is a key commodity export destination & source of FDIs).

Reduction in global commodities exports: though EAC economies are not significant commodity exporters, they are also suffering from reduced global risk appetite, and government bond yields were evidently increasing up to the beginning of 2016 due to U.S/UK monetary policy normalization. This was further exerting pressure on the depreciating exchange rates.

This was further compounded by weak domestic demand, a key element in currency depreciation.

Besides, an elevated fiscal expenditure was equally further compounding the currency depreciation trends. But a stronger USD means debt repayments are more expensive in real terms.

vi) Global Economy & EAC Financial System

The global economy significantly affects both EAC as a bloc and also each individual financial system despite the fact that EAC economies are not so interlinked to the global financial system. This, in a way, insulates the EAC financial system from direct and adverse shocks, leaving it with largely spill-overs and secondary effects that still destabilize the financial structures. Otherwise, if the EAC was fully integrated into the global financial system, then the effects would be so catastrophic since these economies are characterized as Frontier market economies that are so weak and vulnerable. These spillovers were affected by a country's economic fundamentals, whereby those economies, world over, which had stronger fundamentals experienced smaller spillovers. This entail, among others, real GDP growth, stronger current account positions, lower inflation, and smaller shares of local debt held by foreigners; such financial systems expressively dulled spillover effects even during the period of unconventional monetary policy by the U.S Federal Reserve System. Frontier market economies like the EAC region ought to learn that adverse effects of spillovers from either U.S, UK or any other globally strong economy's monetary policy are related to the macroeconomics of the recipient economy like Tanzania. In other words, economies with better fundamentals and more liquid markets help to weather external shocks arising from monetary policies of strong world economies. Besides, other macro-prudential interventions like foreign exchange interventions just like most EAC central banks resorted to, capital flow management measures can equally be used to arrest the excess volatility and disorderly market conditions, along with prudent economic policies.

IMF periodically publishes an analysis of the global economic performance, and so, in its October 2015 World economic Outlook, it revised downwards its earlier global growth projections. This was largely due to sharper slowdown in emerging markets and developing economies that are forecasted to grow between 4.0 – 4.5 for the year 2015/16; and this marks the 5th consecutive year that emerging markets and developing economies have experienced a growth slowdown. This has basically been occasioned by the weakening of macroeconomic fundamentals such as: commodity prices, capital flows, exchange rates, and tightening of financial markets conditions.

For EAC, the growth outlook is even more pessimistic since, for instance, in July 2015 the average growth between the five countries (before the inclusion of South Sudan) was forecast to be considerably above the Sub-Saharan Africa average of 6.3%, but it had fallen to 3.6% by October 2015. This was due to the political situation in Burundi; and IMF forecasts for Burundi had fallen from 4.8% in July 2015 to -7.2% in October the same year. On the contrary, the other East African economies were expected to grow at a higher pace in 2016 and beyond which would serve to paint a positive picture for prospective investors (local and international) that exposure to EAC bloc would be a rational investment decision for growth objectives and the fact that the region is largely producing in excess capacity of its endowed potential.

On the issue of global oil prices, there is need to examine the new developments in the oil and gas industry since most East African economies are soon becoming oil economies due to wide discoveries and later plans to produce oil in a bid to boost their financial systems. Although oil prices had slightly picked up from September 2015 since February 2009, global oil prices are still at their lowest with an annual fall of more than 50%, and more forecasts indicate a further fall in oil prices. Besides, reports present a significant elasticity between high oil prices and increased oil & gas investments. This implies that the forecasted fall in global oil prices will reduce investments in the oil & gas production over the coming years below the previous 10 year average. This poses huge adverse effects on the East African Community financial system since most FDIs (of recent) have been directed to oil & gas industry; which is currently at stake and likely to affect other financial system constituents like the financial markets, financial institutions, and the futuristic financial assets such as derivative instruments in commodities like oil & gas. Furthermore, the massive collapse in global commodities markets like oil, minerals and agricultural products; coupled to both the strengthening of the USD and the downward trajectory of the Chinese economy have depleted foreign exchange reserves of East African countries to the point that they need to devise ways for survival. This is because empirical research has confirmed that crude oil prices are likely to rise slowly and reach USD 60 per barrel by 2020 yet, for instance, Uganda needs USD 75 per barrel to pay for costs alone associated with oil production; implying that Uganda's oil will not be profitable by then.

Although the Chinese economic slowdown had been pre-determined and was significant to the economy's long-term sustainability, it has provoked a global spill-over effect through reduced global trade, subdued global commodities prices, increased global market nervousness, and relatedly increased global financial market volatilities that will likely characterize this decade.

vii) Financial Systems & Sustainable Real GDP Growth in EAC

In developed economies, the labor force generally grows at approx. 1% per year but in Africa (particularly EAC) with young population, economies enjoy a demographic boost as more and more people enter the labor force, as long as there is productive employment. That is why for some economies like Rwanda (which are largely devoid of natural resources and are inclined at establishing knowledge-based economies), long-term productivity growth should be focused on such factors as education, training, and utilization of labor-saving new technologies. Productivity gains are more difficult to extract in post-industrialized economies than in ones with manufacturing and knowledge-based environment in frontier markets. This is further evidenced by economic statistics whereby the EAC GDP growth rate projections averaged 6.3% for 2016 (of course some member states were faring way higher); compared to the economic growth rate of the US that averaged nearly 3%.

Most East African economies forecast real GDP growth and other economic fundamentals but they don't have real indicators for sustaining such growth ie the growth is not premised on real competitive and comparative advantage sectors. This renders most regional economies risky to invest in, and it also compromises their long-term sustainability of such nominal economic growth. And below are the current realities but also proposals for each economy to beef up and sustain her GDP growth rates so as to progressive attract investments based on their respective competitive advantage and also revealed comparative advantage on an EAC regional basis:

Kenya's growth is premised and also covered by a vibrant manufacturing sector (basing on the East African scale and comparator); coupled to its developed horticulture industry that make it one of the best exporters in the whole world. By early 2015, agriculture accounted for: 65% of Kenya's total exports; 26% of GDP; 60% of employment; and 80% of rural livelihood. Besides, floriculture (flower industry) accounted for 1.3% of the total GDP growth yet the world market of flowers is projected to grow at 5% year-on-year. On the other hand, horticulture (fruits and vegetables) contributed approx. 36% of Kenya's agricultural GDP, yet Kenya is a major global market for value-added mixed vegetable packs sold in Europe. With the manufacturing industry, Kenya enjoys the whole regional market and its neighborhood; and all these are enhanced by her access to the sea. The economy ought to further build on those advantages but also progressively strategize to leverage on its developed financial services industry.

Tanzania ought to use her advanced preparation levels in oil & gas production, since much as most East African economies have discovered oil, the process for production (with the exception of South Sudan that is already producing) has been sluggish elsewhere apart from Tanzania which is very soon beginning commercial production. This will be a buffer to its outstanding GDP growth, hence an incentive to many more FDIs; this, coupled to her huge potential in agriculture but also access to the sea, will boost further GDP growth and the financial system.

Uganda, as Winston Churchill branded it "The Pearl of Africa", is uniquely endowed with favorable climate, fertile soils, and enterprising & dynamic workforce that all should be used as bulwarks for her GDP growth. She ought to capitalize on agriculture so as to boost its real GDP growth rates that are comparatively the lowest among its regional peers (of course with the exception of Burundi and South Sudan); this will further enhance her financial system. World record has it that Uganda produces some agricultural products that are the world's best and in particular the tastiest in the world export market like pineapples, bananas, coffee. This, coupled to vast chunks of fertile yet redundant land in Uganda without any activity; the advantage of a huge but unemployed and/or under employed workforce can truly position Uganda so well. Despite all the excess capacities, she has been and still can be the regional food basket and actually a global food basket at large since food will always be in high demand, given also the dramatic population growth rates world over. There is need for Ugandans to make good use of producers' cooperatives to enjoy economies of collective strategies, standardize their products and position themselves for bigger markets. This would equally boost the commodities exchange activities which would in return stimulate the financial system at large. Currently, there exists EU-EAC (European Union – East African Community) negotiations for Economic Partnership Agreement (EPA) which includes issues like EAC economies being included among the Most Favored Nations (MFNs) clause, export taxes, domestic and export support; all of which will significantly boost the EAC bloc.

Rwanda, with her vision of becoming the I.T hub for Africa and a net producer of I.T products and solutions to the region, should bank on the knowledge-based economy to be a net producer of key/unique skills due to her comparative disadvantage in real tangible and resource-based economies (sectors). Rwanda should develop its niche in knowledge creation so as to produce knowledge intensive goods and services for the East African region and the Sub-Saharan Africa. This is because Rwanda's real GDP growth rates can't be sustained and also cannot be able to further attract more investors if she doesn't have a sector that can shoulder and sustain such impressive GDP growth projections since currently she doesn't have one to really be proud of. This proposition was further supported and re-emphasized by Dr. Kaberuka Donald (former President of the African Development Bank) during the World Economic Forum 2016 hosted in Kigali- Rwanda, stressed on the establishment of knowledge-based economies as EAC bloc through education and technical training. This can serve to build a competitive advantage in Africa that would make the EAC bloc to be competitive, productive and a significant player in the global financial system but also commodities market.

Burundi and South Sudan need to work on their political systems since it is currently it is their highest risk that is hindering their growth, sustainability, and possibly competitive advantage. Besides, South Sudan which largely depends on oil & gas contributing close to 90% of their GDP; needs to develop its skills set and also agriculture (Gum Arabic and Shea nuts – these can create lots of jobs and government revenues) because oil production world over doesn't have a long future due to many global forces against the future of the oil & gas economy. These include: a shift from combustion engines (energy) to renewable energy solutions; global political conflicts between US and Iran on oil production; advocacy for a green economy; etc.

NB: The revealed comparative advantage is an index used in international economics for calculating the relative advantage or disadvantage of a certain country in a certain class of goods and services as evidenced by trade flows (country's total exports divided by total world exports in that good/service. A comparative advantage is "revealed" if this ratio is larger than 1; but if it is less, then it is a comparative disadvantage. Most EAC economies don't have any revealed comparative advantage in any good or service but once integrated as a Single financial system or economic bloc, then both the EAC regional bloc and also individual economies will be rather competitive and highly visible. Besides, the usage of revealed comparative advantage is on the EAC regional basis analysis (in my study) but not global basis; hence, various EAC economies can position themselves and also take advantage of revealed comparative advantages in various goods and services.

viii)   Fundamentals of a strong Economy

A fundamentally strong economy that would be good to invest in, should have the following:

- *A good banking system*
- *Inflation-controlled environment.*
- *Low levels of unemployment.*
- *GDP growing.*
- *High exports so as to earn forex.*
- *A strong currency.*

DEDUCTION OF PART 1:

After understanding the background to the EAC monetary and financial systems, and the fact that the financial system is largely informal, there is need to stimulate and incentivize financial flows from the informal to the formal financial system in a bid to develop the EAC economies (given the advantages of large formal and integrated financial system for the EAC Bloc). The relationship between the financial system and economic development (contribution, and forward-backward linkages) cannot be overemphasized world over. In comparison to other regions, both in Africa and the world economy, the EAC Bloc's GDP growth and outlook is, by far, competitive which can potentially position the EAC (once integrated) to attract both regional and foreign investments thanks to its resource endowment and other fundamentals. Nonetheless, the EAC ought to beef up its macroeconomic fundamentals and financial system resilience against volatilities in domestic variables and also external shocks from the global financial system like volatilities in forex markets, commodities prices, among others. But above all, each EAC economy ought to work on sustaining her Real GDP growth through identifying and harnessing certain sectors where each economy has a competitive advantage, and possibly a regional real comparative advantage. Policymakers should strive to achieve higher levels of efficiency in public investment management arena since this is so key in attaining real returns across the value-chain of investments.

PART 2

ISLAMIC FINANCIAL SYSTEM IN EAC

The British Prime Minister (David Cameron) during the 2013 World Islamic Economic Forum announced that he wanted London to become "one of the greatest centers of Islamic finance anywhere in the world". This has since then seen the UK develop more than 20 banks offering Islamic products, issuance of USD 38 Billion in Sukuk market in London; besides the growing operation of this financial system in other developed western economies like France, Denmark, Luxembourg, Switzerland, among others.

This alternative financial system, if deliberately embraced, it has all favorable factors to drastically take off within the East Africa financial system given the primary backing of the significant population of Muslim in the EAC region. On the other, it is so imperative to appreciate that Islamic finance is NOT for Muslims but for every agent/player in the financial system. In fact, in even economies like Malaysia and others were this financial system has been strategically embraced, most of the financial agents (governments, corporations, and households) who have taken advantage of its financial opportunities are not Muslims; so, it is not a religious issue but a financial asset/ avenue available for diversification purposes.

Figure 2.1
Table Showing Muslim Population in the EAC Region

East African Country	Total Population (Millions)	% of Muslim Population	Number of Muslims (Thousands)
Burundi	10.82	4.5%	486.9
Kenya	44.86	10%	4,486
Rwanda	11.34	4.6%	521.6
South Sudan	11.91	6.2%	738.4
Tanzania	51.82	35%	18,137
Uganda	37.78	13.7%	5,175.8
Total	168.5	----	29,545.8

Source: EAC Statistics Bodies (2016)

With such a huge population of close to 30 Million Muslims across the EAC region, this can provide a good start and a prospective uptake of a wide variety of Islamic financial products once well sensitized, but coupled to the remaining close to 140 Million non-Muslims but rational financial agents; the Islamic financial system is poised to become the next big thing in personal financing, corporate and public financing.

Chapter 7

INTRODUCTION

Islamic financial system is an alternative and fast growing financial system (with a whole product suite) that is based on Shariah; the value-based legal framework of Islam (though not only for Muslims but very compatible to non-Muslim financial agents). These values are shared by all the Abrahamic Faiths (Christianity, Muslims, Judaism, etc) but also by other religions. This ideology is drawn from scriptures such as: Exodus 22:25 and Leviticus 25:34-36 for Christian & Judaism; but also Surah Al-Baqara verse 274 in the Qur'an karim for Muslims. This is because their adoption and implementation contributes towards the formation of a sustainable society based on honesty, equitable, wealth distribution and social justice. Islamic financial transactions are either asset-backed or asset-based; and investors have a claim on the underlying assets which is better designed to support productive economic activities but also endogenously beefed up to weather global financial crises and financial market burbles.

This financial system is premised on the principles of the Quran and Islam that have a sense of cooperation- helping one another and aiming at eliminating exploitation so as to establish a just society through the elimination of "Riba" or interest in all its forms in the financial system. Islamic finance may be viewed as a form of ethical investing/ lending in an interest-free banking environment. Besides, other ethical restrictions include prohibition on alcohol, gambling, and the consumption of pork: such funds would never knowingly invest in companies involved in such business. On the other hand, the following are allowed in Islamic financial transactions: profit from trading activities, profit sharing from joint ventures, rental from leasing activities, and fees from services.

This financial system offers a balance between extreme capitalism and communism by helping households the freedom to produce and create wealth under an environment guided by Divine principles of goodness and piety, and human trusteeship of resources. In capitalistic systems, competition for resources and markets breeds wastage and consequently uncontrolled greed but in Islamic financial system, the idea of man representing God on earth gives business people a feeling of co-operation with other for the good of society as a whole leading to prudent and conservative management of God given resources. This system forbids the use of its finances for misleading, dishonorable, immoral and other purposes harmful to society. It is grounded on the philosophy that money is not a commodity in its own right and as such it can't be traded without an underlying asset; this helps the system to keep a close linkage between the financial sector and the real sectors of the economy.

GENESIS OF ISLAMIC FINANCIAL TRANSACTIONS

During medieval times, Middle Eastern tradesmen would engage in financial transactions on the basis of Sharia'a, guided by the principles of fairness in exchange and the prohibition of riba, which were similar to the principles that were applied by their European counterparts at the time. Riba is considered to be one of the seven evil sins (Al-Saba – al- Mubiqat), together with murder, magic, unlawfully taking orphans money, fleeing the battlefield, adultery, and belief in Gods other than Allah.

Finance and trade were undertaken without interest and were either based on profits from trades or shared profits and losses. The instruments that were introduced to cater for the financing of trade and other enterprises were effective before, during and after the era known as the Islamic civilisation which lasted from the late 6th to the early 11th century AD. Middle Eastern and Asian regions became important trading partners for European companies and European banks started to establish branches in these countries which typically were interest-based. On a small scale, credit union and co-operative societies continued to exist, but their activities very much focused on small geographical areas.

DEVELOPMENT OF RECENT ISLAMIC FINANCIAL INFRASTRUCTURE

Contemporary Islamic financial system is generally accepted to have started with the Mit Ghamr savings project set up in 1963 in the Egyptian town of Mit Ghamr. The project was based on co-operative principles and was established to allow the local population access to financial services; and anybody who deposited funds also had a right to take out small loans for productive purposes. Unfortunately the growth of this financial system was partly suffocated by the already established conventional financial system, not until it resurfaced later in the early 1970s.

During the same period, financial services based on Sharia'a were set up in Malaysia to cater for the generally under-banked Muslim population, starting with savings plans for the pilgrimage (hajj) to Mecca. In 1975, the Islamic Development Bank (IDB) was established in Jeddah as a multilateral development bank assisting in mobilizing funds for investment in projects in the member states. In the same year the first Islamic commercial bank, Dubai Islamic Bank was founded in the United Arab Emirates. Economies like Saudi Arabia, Iran and Malaysia have the largest sharia'a-compliant assets. Islamic business laws of transaction (Fiqh al mua'amalat) strictly prohibit such elements as: Riba (interest/ usury); and Gharar (excessive uncertainty); others.

FUNDAMENTALS OF ISLAMIC FINANCE

- *It is premised on the principle of trusteeship keeping in mind that all earthly resources belong to God who has made humans trustees for them. Humans are therefore accountable to God for* the use of these resources; this is in direct contrast to extreme capitalism and communism.

- It is based on caring for others contrary to self-interest that is engrained in human nature; implying that individual happiness and collective interests go hand in hand. It maintains that the wealth and integrity of a society can only increase when the haves give part of their wealth to the have-nots basically to please God

- Productive efforts as a means of serving God: productive enterprise is looked upon as a means of serving God, and wealth should be spent in the cause of God.

- It strongly advocates for the protection of consumers against the exploitations of the traders and manufacturers.

- It advocates for treating wealth as a means and not an end: this is because economic welfare is viewed as a means to peace, freedom from hunger and fear of others.

- It strongly supports the proper functioning of the market since it prohibits dishonesty, fraud, deception, coercive practices, hoarding, speculations and collusion among producers and traders against consumers' interests as is common with monopoly and oligopoly in capitalistic economies.

THE EMERGING MARKETS OF ISLAMIC FINANCIAL SYSTEM

Over the past decades, the Islamic financial system has evolved into a comprehensive financial system of its own right: ranging from capital markets, banking, to Takaful sectors (insurance), Islamic Pooled investment vehicles, asset management, among others. Currently, the total global assets of the Islamic financial industry are estimated to be above USD 2 Trillion and estimated to surpass USD 3 Trillion by 2018. However, this expansion has been skewed towards the Gulf Cooperation Council (GCC) economies such as Saudi Arabia, United Arab Emirates (UAE), Kuwait, Qatar, and the South East Asian regional economies like

Malaysia, Indonesia and Pakistan. Absolutely, given the value proposition of Islamic finance, new markets are now emerging, and these include among others: East Asia, Africa (including my East Africa), North and South America, Caribbean, Europe.

THE AFRICAN EXPERIENCE

Currently, the contribution of Islamic finance in the African region remains relatively low; nonetheless it is touted to be a key development region for the Islamic finance product markets especially after the GCC-based Islamic banks viewed the region as a key target market. With reference to the Sukuk market (bond), the sector has become an area of interest in a diversity of African economies like Senegal, South Africa, Nigeria, Ivory Coast, and Niger; whereby at least Senegal and South Africa have made their inaugural sovereign Sukuk offerings in 2014 at USD 500 Million and USD 168 Million issuances respectively; but also Ivory Coast has recently issued 150 Billion CFA Sukuk priced at a profit rate of 5.75% in November 2015. On the other hand, Niger and Nigeria are planning for debut deals soon, Kenya is deliberating on establishing Islamic capital markets including Sukuks and equity offerings. Uganda has approved a dualistic financial system (including Islamic financial system) and it can position herself as the EAC regional center for Islamic financial system given its sole member State subscription to the Islamic Development Bank Group in the whole EAC bloc. Kenya's population of approx. 44 million has approx. 10% Muslims; and Uganda's population that is 35 Million has a Muslim population of 4.6 Million (13.7%) as of 2014, which has seen an increase from 12.7% in 2002 population Census

Given the success of the inaugural sovereign Sukuk by Senegal, the country is now looking to issue a second Sukuk through funding assistance from the Saudi-based Islamic Development Bank whereby the Sukuk issued is hoped to fund strategic infrastructure projects like the regional train facility. In South Africa, as part of facilitating the Sukuk issuances, the country's treasury has proposed extending the tax reforms to allow for the issuance of Sukuk by listed companies with effect from 2016. Besides, just at the EAC neighborhood Sudan's Islamic financial institution, Bank of Khartoum is trying to establish its first overseas branch in the Kingdom of Bahrain.

On the whole, along with a diversity of opportunities discussed regarding the relatively new entrant in the global financial arena, the Islamic financial system has the potential to grow but also to boost the EAC regional financial system and bridge the gap between the formal and informal financial systems particularly from the Muslim community but also from the huge non-Muslim financial agents. Scholars believe that this alternative financial system has enough hedging mechanisms to protect banks' exposure against interest rate since many Shariah contracts have been used in the derivatives products like Waad, Urbun, Salam and also the commodity Murabahah. Besides, the Islamic financial system represents relatively rapid growth in many economies due to large pool of savings in oil-exporting economies looking for Shariah-compliant investment opportunities like the EAC region.

Chapter 8

IFS OPERATIONS
GOVERNING PRINCIPLES

Islamic financial system is based on Shariah laws, and the governing principles that ensure that financial relationships in this financial system remain participatory and fair to all parties; and these include:

> Avoidance and prohibition of Riba (interest);
> Avoidance of Gharar (excessive uncertainty);
> Prohibition of Maisyir (speculation and gambling);
> Avoidance of Zulm (Oppression);
> Promotion of socio-economic justice via Islamic tax (Zakat);
> Promotion of Waqaf (mutual trust);
> Provision of Qard Hasan (benevolent loans);
> Prohibition of Zulum (oppression and exploitation);
> Prohibition of Haram (engagement in economic activities / transactions contrary to Shariah law like alcohol and others);
> Promotion of 'Adalah & Musawamah (justice and fairness in distribution of resources);
> Upholding Maslahah (principles of universal social interests, moral and ethical values).

COMPONENTS OF THE SYSTEM

Similar to the global conventional financial system, the Islamic financial system has the following components:

> *a) Islamic Banking, which is function of:*
>
> *Deposits; Financing; and Payment systems*
>
> *b) Islamic Capital Markets, which comprise of:*
>
> *Sukuk markets (Islamic bonds – sovereign and corporate bonds), Structured products, and investment funds.*

c) *Islamic Money Markets, which are composed of a variety of liquidity facilities.*

d) *Islamic Asset Management, which includes:*

   Unit Trusts, Mutual funds, and Islamic REITs

e) *Islamic Insurance, which consists of:*

   General Takaful, Family Takaful, Agricultural Takaful, and Re-Takaful products.

f) *Islamic Social Finance, which constitutes:*

   Zakah, Sadaqah, Mutual cooperation, and Islamic Microfinance.

g) *Other Sectors, which include:*

   Islamic Endowment (Waqf), and Islamic Treasury (Baitul Mal)

h) *Regulators of these Islamic financial sub-sectors.*

OPERATING MODELS FOR THE SYSTEM

In addition to fully fledged Sharia'a-compliant financial institutions, Islamic financial services are also offered by large conventional banks. Once conventional financial institution want to offer Islamic financial services they need to ensure that their accounts and operations are segregated lest they defile the system. Either one of the following models is typically used:

Islamic windows: whereby the services are offered to clients using the same distribution channels of the conventional financial institution; which means, for example, that retail clients can obtain both types of financial services via their local branch. In a branch, the services are offered to clients using physically separate distribution channels.

Subsidiary: this model operates in such a way that the services are offered to clients via a separate legal entity which operates independently under the overall strategy of the parent company.

ISLAMIC PARTNERSHIP CONTRACTS

This financial system operates mainly under two basic partnership contracts: A mudaraba transaction which also recognizes two distinct types of role for the partners: the provider of capital (rab-al-mal), and the provider of skill and expertise (mudarib). On the other hand, in a musharaka arrangement, each of the parties (musharik) provides both capital and expertise, albeit not necessarily in the same quantities. Islamic financial contracts can generally be divided into two distinct categories:

- *Profit and Loss sharing partnerships: These transactions are based on the principles that profit is for those who bear risk, and losses are proportionately distributed on the basis of the share of capital provided. Although preferred by the majority of Islamic scholars, such contracts are generally not preferred by financial regulators and management.*
- *Predictable Return transactions: These transactions are based on trade, project finance, or lease and provide a return that can be predicted for the life of the contract.*

Besides, a variety of other contracts exist in this unique financial system, such as **foreign exchange**, **agency contracts and contracts of security.**

In a nutshell, the main Islamic finance contracts can be broadly categorized and broken down into the following:

1) Transaction Contracts, these include:

- *Murabahah (cost plus sale contracts).*
- *Ijarah (leasing contracts).*
- *Istisna (manufacture-sale contracts).*
- *Bai Salaam (payment for future delivery)*
- *Kafalah/Darman (fee-based contracting and guarantee)*

2) Equity Contracts, which comprise of:

- *Mudaraba (Participation or Trust finance).*
- *Musharaka (Equity financing).*
- *Musaqaa (Aggregation).*
- *Muzara (Cultivation).*

3) Hybrid Contracts

- *Musharaka-Mutanaqisah –MMP (diminishing partnerships like Musharaka plus sale contracts).*
- *Islamic Derivatives (Islamic forex).*
- *Arbun (Pre-purchase of right to acquire)*

4) Debt Contracts

- *Sukuk (Islamic Bonds issue)*
- *Qard Hassan (Interest-free loan)*

ISLAMIC FINANCIAL PRODUCT SUITE

The global market for Sharia-compliant financial products was estimated at above USD 2 Trillion by 2015, and this indicates a significant growth in importance and uptake of products in this alternative financial system that would be worth embracing by the EAC region. The rationale for the development and also trading of Sharia-compliant financial products should be viewed as a strategy through which to attract investments from the large Islamic finance sectors in the Middle East and South East Asia.

ISLAMIC DEVELOPMENT BANK GROUP (IDBG)

It envisions, "fostering the economic development and social progress of member countries and Muslim communities individually and collectively in accordance with the principles of Sharia. This is a multilateral financial institution for Islamic financial system (just like the World Bank is for the conventional financial system), and it has fifty six (56) member States, with more than USD 150 Billion in capital, and rated AAA. All these member States have a dualistic financial system (including Malaysia which has the most developed Islamic financial infrastructure) because all central banking (monetary policy) world over is still undertaken in the conventional financial system but plans are underway to establish a central banking infrastructure for Islamic finance. The IDBG has its Head Quarters in Jeddah, Saudi Arabia but also well-furnished with regional supervisors, and Dakar (Senegal) will be supervising the East African Community activities. In the whole EAC region, it is only Uganda that is a member State with the IDBG; which avails her a lot of opportunities and offers. This can further boost Uganda to become the financial center for this alternative but fast growing financial system. The IDBG is prominent in the following interventions: project finance, development assistance, poverty alleviation, technical assistance, trade cooperation, SME financing, Resource mobilization, Research and training in Islamic finance, Scholarship, emergency relief, public and private sector advisory, among other initiatives.

ISLAMIC CHAMBER OF COMMERCE AND INDUSTRY (ICCI)

The Islamic Chamber of Commerce and Industry, an affiliate of the Organization of Islamic Cooperation (OIC), consists of fifty-seven Arab countries. The idea of setting up an Islamic Chamber of Commerce, Industry & Agriculture (ICCIA) was mooted in the Seventh Islamic Conference of Foreign Ministers held in May 1976 in Istanbul-Turkey, which was approved by the First Conference of the Chambers of Commerce and Industry held in October 1977 in Istanbul. Its constitution was adopted by the Second Conference of Chambers of Commerce and Industry held in December, 1978 in Karachi – Pakistan.

Uganda is among the very few non-Arab member countries and the only economy in the East and Southern Africa regional Blocs; and Uganda attained this prestigious status during the OIC meeting in Uganda in 2008. This means that she is entitled to all the benefits, including the package of the ratified OIC-TPS (Trade Preferential System for the promotion of Intra-Islamic Trade) that was declared in the 16th Private Sector meeting for OIC Member Countries in Sharjah, United Arab Emirates in March 2014. The Islamic Chamber of Commerce and Industry Uganda seeks to position Uganda as the financial center for Islamic finance and trade within the Tripartite environment of the 3 Regional Economic Cooperation that includes the East African Community (EAC), the Southern Africa Development Community (SADC),and the Common Market for East and Southern Africa (COMESA).

Its main objective is to encourage international trade among member countries (private Waqf Funds and funding portfolios of international trade). This global Chamber also seeks to strengthen the ethical principles in international affairs and promote the principles of Islamic finance. The headquarters of the Islamic Chamber of Commerce and Industry are in Pakistan. It further aims at strengthening closer collaboration in the field of trade, commerce, information technology, insurance/reinsurance, shipping, banking, promotion of investment opportunities and joint ventures in the Member countries. Its membership is comprised of the National Chambers / Unions / Federations of Chambers of Commerce and Industry of the member countries.

Member States

The member countries of the Islamic Chamber of Commerce and Industry (Organization of Islamic Cooperation) include: Afghanistan, Algeria, Chad, the Arab Republic of Egypt, Guinea, Indonesia, Iran, Jordan, Kuwait, Lebanon, Libya, Malaysia, Mali, Mauritania, Morocco, Niger, Pakistan, Palestine, Saudi Arabia, Senegal, Sudan, Somalia, Tunisia, Turkey, Yemen, Bahrain, Oman, Qatar, Syria, the United Arab Emirates, Sierra Leone, Bangladesh, Gabon, the Gambia, Guinea-Bissau, Uganda, Burkina Faso, Cameroon, the Comoros, Iraq, Maldives, Djibouti, Benin, Brunei Darussalam, Nigeria, Azerbaijan, Albania, the Kyrgyz Republic, Tajikistan, Turkmenistan, Mozambique, Kazakhstan, Uzbekistan, Suriname, Togo, Guyana, Ivory Coast

Core Activities

The General Secretariat of ICCIA has been undertaking activities in line with its objective by holding the following activities:-

- *Organization of business forums: Private Sector Meetings and Businesswomen Forums.*

- *Workshops, Training programs on capacity building, poverty alleviation, upgrading marketing and managing skills, value-addition, gender development, economic empowerment of women, promotion & development of Small & Medium Enterprises, utilization of microfinance, developing Entrepreneurship, particularly in women and the youth.*

- *Playing a role for increasing the level of Intra Islamic Trade to 20% by 2015.*

- *Promoting the concept of Zakat, as a means to economic development.*

- *Clarifying the concepts of Halal.*

- *Creating awareness about the various OIC agreements for enhancing economic cooperation, particularly the Trade Preferential System among the Member States of the Organization of Islamic Cooperation (TPS-OIC).*

- *Implementing the relevant aspects of the OIC Program of Action.*

- *Cooperating with OIC & other related International Organizations for the development of SMEs.*

ISLAMIC INSURANCE

Takaful insurance products have a variety of covers such as: motor Takaful scheme for truck owners; fire Takaful scheme. These have proved to be more consumer-friendly; the profit-sharing agreements as well as the adoption of a financial policy of not charging the operator's overhead & management expenses to the participants' contribution demonstrates the principle of putting the interest of consumers first.

The Takaful agricultural insurance product line includes: Takaful (Sharia-compliant) livestock insurance that is key in improving food security majorly in pastoralist communities; the Takaful index-based crop insurance which monitors weather and feed supply conditions to determine losses suffered by crop farmers.

In Kenya, Takaful Insurance of Africa (TIA) was the first Sharia-compliant underwriter that launched its services in 2011. In Nigeria, Noor Takaful has been granted license to operate a wide range of Takaful products in 2016.

ISLAMIC BANKING PRODUCTS

Commercial banks in Uganda, Kenya and other EAC economies can now offer Islamic banking products: this banking model is different from the conventional model of banking. Whereas charging of interest is at the heart of conventional banking, in Islamic banking model that is not permissible. Instead the financial institution shares the profits or losses that accrue, if any, with the clients. Islamic banking model has gained prominence internationally due to its exponential growth and resilience to financial crises, a case in point is the 2008 global financial crisis. This is in addition to the nature of Shari'ah-compliant finance models that focus on the principles of investment in real assets and risk-sharing. In this model, each contract is backed by an underlying asset or investment activity which creates a direct link between financial markets and economic activity (this is absolutely different from the capitalistic financial market which hardly have any direct linkages with the real sectors of the economy). The Islamic finance model has thus contributed to the spread of real-asset-based finance principles in many jurisdictions and is regarded as an ideal option for the financing of infrastructure projects. This implies that the EAC bloc's exposure to this alternative financial system will significantly contribute to growth of real linkages between the financial system and the real sectors of the economy that affect the livelihood of most East African; besides, it will stimulate the growth of real-asset-based financing that betters the welfare of all the financial agents across the value-chain of both financial investments (assets) and the real investments (assets) such as infrastructure, agriculture, extractive industries, among others.

Musharakah agreements where a bank and borrower establishes a joint business and all contribute capital as well as labor and management. They share profits in agreed proportions while loss will have to be shared in strict proportion of capital contributions; the liability of all partners is unlimited.

Islamic Mortgage (Islamic home financing). In this model, the financial institution and client jointly purchase the house where ownership is split between the bank and the customer. It is agreed that the customer will purchase the share of the bank in the house gradually, thus increasing his own share until all the share of the bank is purchased by the customer, rendering him the sole owner of the asset. But during the purchase period, the bank's share is leased to the customer who pays rent for using the bank's share.

By 2015, there were at least two fully fledged Islamic banks in Kenya: the Gulf African Bank, and the First Community Bank. However, other conventional banks by this time had begun moving to introduce Islamic banking products such as Standard Chartered Bank that opened an Islamic window in 2014; and Kenya Commercial Bank had been given all approvals to provide an Islamic window. On the other hand, in Uganda, the Financial Institutions Act 2015 was amended so as to accommodate the Islamic financial system in the Ugandan financial system, and currently various regulators are working on guidelines that will be followed by financial services players in those particular fields during their transactions in Islamic financing.

ISLAMIC FINANCIAL MARKETS

This financial system has a wide offering in the capital markets such as the bond market, equity markets, forex markets, money markets and derivatives markets that are well regulated and quite competitive globally. In the emerging markets like Africa, there has been some activity in the recent past majorly in the government bonds market (Sukuks) but also other financial products; Senegal has issued a Sukuk but also Gabon, Cameroun, South Africa, and Mozambique are planning to issue Sukuks for infrastructure development. This would be a virgin financing avenue for EAC governments to cheaply fund their infrastructural deficits.

In the Sukuk market, investors provide funds used to purchase assets that are then sold or leased to borrowers with payments made gradually over time. The principal amount is typically not guaranteed (like in the conventional bond market), and the return is linked to the underlying purchase price of the asset and the profits it earns which are then used to compensate the investors. Sukuks are well suited for infrastructure financing thereby supporting economic development since economies like Malaysia Jordan, Saudi Arabia, among others have used them for airports, marine ports, roads, etc due to their operation as Islamic-financed public-private partnerships (PPPs)

NB: The global financial crisis showed how the toxins of Riba (interest) can cause the whole global financial system to collapse. The Riba-based financial system is championed by the US, and that is why the collapse and crisis begun from and/or is linked to Riba/interest. Incidentally, the Islamic banks and financial institutions withstood/weathered the global financial crisis largely because Islamic contracts are widely stable and are pre-determined upfront unlike conventional financial systems that are so volatile depending on changing interest rate regime.

ISLAMIC FINANCIAL PRODUCTS

There is need to develop a harmonized and comprehensive regulatory framework for Islamic finance by relevant regulators: Central banks; Capital Markets Authorities; Insurance Regulators; Retirement Benefits Regulators; etc. Kenya's population of approx. 44 million has approx. 10% Muslims; and Uganda's population that is 35 Million has a Muslim population of 4.6 Million (13.7%) as of 2014, which is has seen an increase from 12.7% in 2002 population Census. Currently, there is need to establish Sharia'a Boards since this is a crucial prerequisite for the smooth rolling out of Islamic banking and finance, but also a great deal of sensitization is required for the public.

Malaysia and the Gulf Cooperation Council funds are seeking for new markets to invest in their Sharia-compliant finance; besides, other Arab-related institutional investors. There is need to benchmark from economies with established and efficient Islamic financial systems like Malaysia, Oman, Bahrain; these economies have Sharia boards at national level, accounting & audit systems that are compliant to Islamic finance.

SHARIAH GOVERNANCE IN ISLAMIC FINANCE

Islamic finance was approved in laws of some EAC countries like Uganda in December 2015 when the President assented to the then bill (Financial Institutions Act 2015). Islamic Financial Institutions need to operate on sound governance frameworks so as to apply best business practices and good governance; there is need to establish an **Islamic Financial Services Act** with the following:

Licensing authorities and requirements

Establishment of Shariah committees charged with various duties across the Islamic finance value-chain.

Establishment of compliance standards.

Functional Shariah Boards.

Clear civil Actions for the offenders of the system.

Clear Criminal Actions for the lawbreakers.

Besides, firms ought to have Shariah risk management committees to manage Shariah risks such as compliance risks, reputational risks, etc.

SHARIAH GOVERNING ORGANS

These should have the following organs or structures:

Board of Directors

Islamic Financial Institutions management

Shariah Board

Other Organs such as research, risk management, audit, etc.

SHARIAH GOVERNANCE FRAMEWORKS

There are a diversity of types of Shariah governance frameworks, but among others these are:

Regulated Centralized Framework (National Shariah Advisory Council). This model oversees the system at the macroeconomic level, and it is the model in use in economies like Malaysia, Oman, Maldives, Nigeria, UAE; but it is also the one that Uganda is currently pursuing for her dualistic financial system but also Kenya has opted for this model.

Regulated Decentralized framework.

Unregulated framework

ISLAMIC FINANCIAL SYSTEM & FINANCIAL STABILITY

In the search for a new financial architecture, there is a general consensus on the need to return finance to its basic function – to provide financial services that add value to the real economy since it is the real economy that practically creates and/or distributes value to various financial agents across the value-chain of production. This, in fact, represents the very essence of Islamic finance: the very elements found in the Shari'ah principles that form the foundation of the Islamic financial system

It is these inherent elements that contribute towards the overall stability and resilience of the Islamic financial system. This foundation is further reinforced by the values that are extolled in Islamic finance that are similar to those found in ethical finance and socially responsible investment (SRI). The key strength of the Shari'ah injunctions is its emphasis on a strong linkage to productive economic activity, its inbuilt checks and balances and its high level of transparency and disclosure that is widely absent in most corporate transactions in the conventional financial system.

The Islamic financial services industry has thus been in a relatively stronger position to weather the global financial crisis, demonstrating its robustness as a stable form of financial intermediation. The inherent features of Islamic finance have the potential to serve as a basis to address several of the issues and challenges that have surfaced in the conventional financial system during the current crisis that saw the global financial system almost collapse.

As the role and relevance of Islamic finance in the global financial system gains significance, it has potential to contribute to greater global financial stability and towards strengthening global growth particularly in the real sectors like agriculture, manufacturing, extractive industries, among others that redistribute wealth (value) along the value-chain.

The Islamic Finance Key Pillars – Strengthen the financial system as well as economy. Islamic Finance provides underlying productive economic activity that will generate legitimate income and wealth. This underlying productivity establishes a close link between the financial transactions and real productive flows. This link further reduces the Islamic financial system from over exposure to risks associated with excessive leverage and imprudent risk taking. Thus, in the Islamic finance business model, financing or equity participation can only be extended to activities in the real sector that have economic values.

As a result, Islamic financial assets are expected to grow in tandem with the growth of underlying economic activities. This fosters a better financial stability both domestically and globally.

CHALLENGES OF ISLAMIC FINANCIAL SYSTEM

Lack of trustworthiness amongst East Africans unlike in the Arab world where trustworthiness is an integral part of their culture. This calls for a model that will address such a systemic shortfall in the EAC region.

Ethical considerations. This financial system doesn't believe in some economic activities like piggery, betting, among other unethical enterprises according to Sharia law; which poses a challenge of being selective in financing. This may find hardships in working in the EAC, hence need to separate between religion and financing.

Small global market share. Islamic financial assets are just slightly above 1% of the global financial assets; making the conventional financial assets almost 99%. This has rendered it practically incapable for Islamic financial system to influence global financial regulation and policies; this is because there is no central banking activities particularly monetary policy that is in line with Islamic financing up to now. This is why central banking activities are still undertaken in the conventional window even in economies with well-established Islamic financial system.

The various Shariah interpretations in the Islamic world and also harmonizing them with financing the commercial viability of businesses are also a challenge with this system.

The open mismatch between governing laws of the Islamic financial system and the national laws (EAC economies) where it is going to be implemented present a huge hurdle.

Conflicts with the already established global financial system modus operandi such as the double taxation agreements amongst States, and other nonmonetary controls that have existed for long. This would require a comprehensive revision of policies, agreements, and regulations.

There is an evidently relative scarcity of Shariah scholars (in Uganda, close to 10 professionals), and coupled to the low consumer literacy levels compound the problem of absorbing Islamic financial products.

Inadequacy in supervision and prudential regulatory frameworks due to limited expertise in many emerging economies in the Islamic financial system context.

The potential advantages of the Islamic financial system have not been fully tested and may be at least partly offset by Islamic banks' balance sheets' heavy investment in sectors relatively vulnerable to cyclical booms like real estates and housing. This can be addressed by improved capacity in monitoring the buildup of systemic risk but also development of regulatory and other macro-prudential instruments to manage this failure.

Tax policy implication in Islamic finance: conventional tax systems typically favor debt over equity-based financing. Thus, there is need to ensure a level playing field for the tax treatment of Islamic financial transactions lest it becomes a competitive disadvantage for this system in the face of conventional financial system.

Prevalence of shallow financial markets and high levels of illiquidity in financing imply that insolvency frameworks need to be strengthened further to avert a possible systemic risk. In response to deepening the Sukuk markets, there is need to develop legal and regulatory frameworks, to strengthen the infrastructure, to step up sovereign issuance with diversified maturity to manage public debt under a strong public financial management framework, and secondary market development.

The limited options in the Shariah-compliant money market instruments and markets which have potential to undermine Islamic finance's scope for effective liquidity management, forcing institutions to hold greater cash balances than necessary and constraining their ability to invest their deposits in the best interest of depositors and their country's financial system.

This system poses hardships in the area of consumer and investor protection due to lack of Shariah-compliant deposit insurance and lender-of-last-resort facilities as opposed to its conventional/capitalistic financial system counterpart.

DEDUCTION OF PART 2:

With the Islamic financial system astronomically growing in all spheres such as global assets, geographical coverage, product engineering and uptake; this should attract a special interest of policymakers and business community in the EAC Bloc. With Kenya, Uganda, Tanzania and others embracing the system at different fronts, ranging from: financial institutions and products, markets (Sukuks), Islamic Chamber of Commerce and Industry; coupled to the region's rich history in Islam and Arab trading; plus a significant portion of EAC population being Muslims. This alternative financial system, once embraced due to its socio-economic advantages, can leverage on all the above merits to become a game changer in the regional financial system due to its balance between extreme capitalism and socialism, guidance by Divine principles but above all being an asset-based/backed kind of financing (linking the financial sector to real sectors of the economy). Despite all its would-be merits and also good Sharia governance systems, the financial system has a diversity of loopholes and challenges that need experts and scholars to address before fully rolling it out as an independent financial system just like its counterpart, the conventional financial system.

PART 3

FINANCIAL INSTITUTIONS

"A sound banking system will increase opportunities for access to credit for development."

These are institutions which serve the purpose of channeling funds from lenders to borrowers; this is done through a complex system of hold money balance or borrowing from individuals, risk reduction through allowing specialist institutions to evaluate borrowers' credit worthiness so as to lend out at an established interest rate to those borrowers.

Over the last Century, the financial services industry has significantly evolved. Initially, the banking industry operated as a full-service industry with all financial services: commercial banking, investment banking, stock brokerage, insurance providers, etc. In the early 1930s, the economic and industrial collapse resulted in the separation of some of these activities. In the 1970s & 1980s, new relatively unregulated financial services industries sprung up such as: unit trust funds, brokerage funds, securitizers, etc; that separated financial services functions even further. In the wake of the 21st Century; regulatory barriers, technology, and financial innovation changes were such that a full set of financial services could again be offered by a single financial services holding company.

These institutions have been classified according to their nature of operation and the legal mandate, and these are: banking financial institutions; non-banking financial institutions; collective investment vehicles; the Central Bank; and other regulatory bodies of the financial system.

Chapter 9

BANKING FINANCIAL INSTITUTIONS

"Banking is the most fragile part of a financial system"

"A sound banking system will increase opportunities for access to credit for development."

The banking financial institutions comprise all the banks that operate within the financial system, and these include: commercial banks, credit banks, merchant banks, development banks, and others like MDIs that are allowed to mobilize deposits and loan out to the public. On the other hand, banking has also been categorized depending on the nature of the clientele and category of predominant transactions, such as: retail banking; wholesale banking; and international banking.

i)   **Historical Background of the Banking sector in EAC Region** (A case for Uganda)

Uganda's banking sector has evolved from the first commercial bank established in 1906 – the National Bank of India (this later became the Grindlays Bank; and is the current Stanbic Bank) to the current 25 commercial banks, three credit institutions and four Microfinance Deposit-taking Institutions (MDIs). Despite the rapid growth in the semi-formal and informal financial system in the country, the formal financial system has also undergone several policy, structural, legal and regulatory reforms with various degrees of results.

This evolution, basically in the banking sector, has been characterized by bank closures, mergers and acquisitions for more than a century of banking experience in Uganda. Before independence in 1962, the banking sector was dominated mainly by foreign-owned commercial banks. In addition to the National

---

Bank of India, the following banks began operation: Standard Bank in 1912; Bank of the Netherlands in 1954, which later merged with Grindlays Bank.

Later, the Uganda Credit and Savings Bank which became Uganda Commercial Bank (UCB) in 1969 following an Act of Parliament in 1965; and this was the first local commercial bank established in the country to cater for banking needs of indigenous Ugandans. Bank of Baroda had been established first in 1953, but regularized as a commercial bank in 1969 with the enactment of the Banking Act of 1969 (the first legal framework for regulation of the banking sector following the country's independence).

On the other hand, the country's central bank (Bank of Uganda) was established in 1966 under the Bank of Uganda Act 1966; and this was followed by the institution of the Uganda Development Bank under the UDB Decree of 1972. These two banks revolutionized banking in Uganda since the government-owned banks dominated the banking industry: UDB received all foreign loans and channelled them to the local companies for development; and UCB, with the biggest number of branches around 67 in number, handled the majority of the domestic customers. Then, the East African Development Bank which was established in 1967 would handle the East African Community (EAC) business and regional customers.

By 1970, Uganda had more than 290 commercial bank branches but this number reduced to 84 in the period between 1970s & 1980s following volatilities in political and economic atmosphere during that period; of which UCB owned a total of 50 branches. Privatization and divestiture of the public sector that was championed by IMF & World Bank significantly changed the banking landscape in Uganda as the dominance of state-owned banks between the 1960s and 1980s visibly decreased as several privately-owned banks were established in the 1990s.

Bank of Uganda licensed over 10 private banks (mostly locally owned) between 1988 and 1999 to operate in the country. A significant number of these banks were private local banks; and these included the Nile Bank Ltd, the Greenland Bank Ltd, the Cooperative Bank Ltd, the Gold Trust Bank Ltd, the Teefee Bank Ltd and Sembule Investment Bank, Equator Building Society, International Credit Bank, the TransAfrica Bank Ltd, Kigezi Bank of Commerce. Almost all of these banks and non-bank financial institutions have closed through merger, acquisition or outright closure. The implications of the bank closure or restructuring have been a reduction in branch network and limited access to financial services; though it has also occasioned a stronger and sound financial system that has resulted in improved confidence in the domestic economy.

ii)   The Four Tiers in the Banking Sector

A tier is a French word which means to rank; it is a row or a layer in a series of similarly arranged objects. Tier is the core measure of a bank's financial strength from a regulator's point of view. It is composed of core capital, which consists primarily of common stock and disclosed reserves (or retained earnings), but may also include non-redeemable non-cumulative preferred stock. The Banking sector in Uganda is categorized into four Tiers as follows:

Tier 1-comprising of commercial banks E.g. Centenary Bank, Exim Bank, CfC Bank, BPR Bank.

Tier 2-comprising of credit and finance companies E.g. Opportunity bank Uganda.

Tier 3-comprising of Microfinance Deposit-taking Institutions (MDIs).

Tier 4-all other financial intermediaries including SACCO's, Women groups, NGOs e.t.c

Tier I – Commercial Banks

This class includes commercial banks which are authorized to hold checking, savings and time deposit accounts for individuals and institutions in local as well as International currencies. Commercial banks are also authorized to buy and sell foreign exchange, issue letters of credit and make loans to depositors and non-depositors. Commercial Banks are regulated under the Financial Institutions Act of various EAC countries. They are supervised by the central banks of respective economies and are subject to prudential regulation by EAC Ministries of Finance. These banking regulators have set minimum paid in capital requirements for commercial banks as per the Financial Institutions Acts of each Member State though currently the EAC committee on Central banking activities is establishing harmonized policies and regulations for EAC regional banks in preparation for the EAC Monetary Union

Figure 3.1   EAC BANKING SYSTEM PERFORMANCE

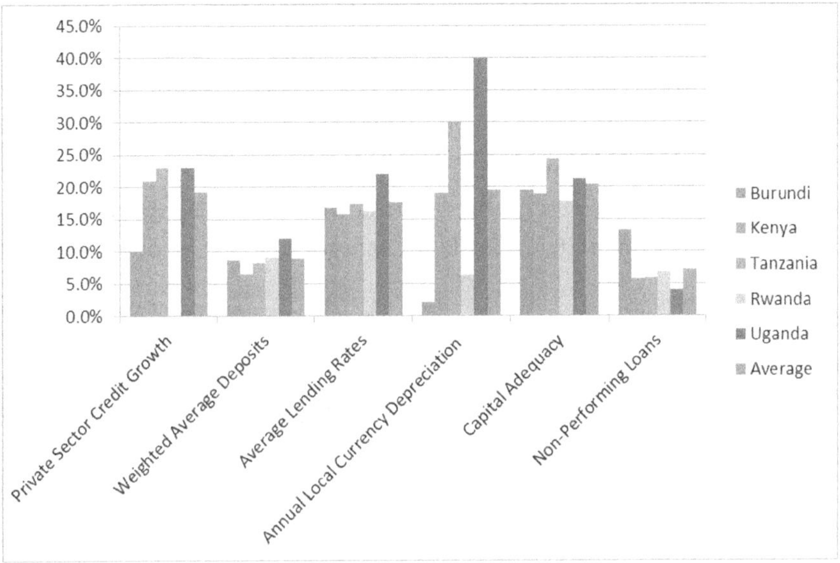

Source: EADB; EAC Central Banks (2015)

a)   Non-Performing Loans

Ugandan banks hold the lowest NPLs at 4%, followed by Kenya at 5.7% and Burundi banks have the highest NPLs ratio at 13.3%. This is indicative of a relative good regional performance in this indicator and the fact that the banking system is striving to achieve operational and allocative efficiency in its banking and financing initiatives. Non-Performing Loans among East African banks stood at an average of 7.1%. Burundi, possibly due to the volatile political environment, had the highest percentage of non-performing loans at 13.3%, while Uganda had the lowest at 4.0%.

b)   Private Sector Credit

These are major indicators for financial depth: private sector credit to GDP, & intermediation of deposits to lending. Private Sector Credit Growth is an indicator of how much additional funding is being made available to the private sector in a given year. From the above graph, the additional funding availed to the private sector in 2015 in Tanzania and Uganda was the highest in the region, at 23% each. Burundi received the least additional credit availed to the private sector, at 10%. The average for the whole region stood at 19.3% which is relatively good for frontier economies that are largely characterized by being intermediation constrained rather than savings constrained. This further indicates an improvement in banking financial intermediation (regionally and especially for Uganda and Tanzania) that as much resources that are mobilized through deposits, a considerable portion is extended to the private sector for absorption in the real economy. This ought to inform more creation of investment funds through the financial markets industry and also tapping into more foreign institutional investors including Islamic financing that can be so instrumental as an alternative financial system.

Why EAC has High Interest Margins?

Lack of financial infrastructure (credit rating agencies)

Low competition in domestic banking due to curtail-like market structure in the banking system whereby four (4) large banks (foreign-owned) control/own a huge portion of the banking assets, market size & influence the market significantly.

Riskiness of lending, combined with weak property rights that are occasioned by poor land tenure system especially in Uganda.

c)   Commercial Banks Weighted Average Deposits & Lending rates

Commercial Banks Weighted Average Deposits were highest in Uganda at 12%, and lowest in Kenya at 6.5%. The EAC average was 8.9%.

Commercial Banks Average Lending Rates reflect the cost that commercial banks charge for lending to the public in the region. From the graph, the highest lending rates were in Uganda at 22% while the lowest rates were in Kenya at 15.7%. On this measure, the average lending rates in Uganda are far above those of the fellow East African states, thereby making it more expensive to invest in Uganda using domestic debt.

d)   EAC Currencies Depreciation

Annual Local Currency Depreciation in 2015 measures the percentage by which a local currency has depreciated. The Uganda shilling depreciated the highest in 2015, far higher than the other states in the region. The lowest local currency depreciation was experienced in Burundi. This implies that many EAC economies are quite exposed to external shocks that easily lead to currency depreciation

U.S Economy Rebound in 2015

The US economy (oil sector) affected the global financial system due to a rush in production of oil so as to exhaust their oil reserves before the phasing out of combustion engine vehicles in favor of electric & other non-fuel vehicles globally. This saw huge investments in the US – that called for huge capital investment requirements (with higher returns on capital). Many global investors had to withdraw their investments/ savings from other economies which drastically increased demand for USD globally leading the USD to appreciate in value & the economic rebound (astronomic growth) at the hand of other major currencies that had to depreciate in return. Economies with fewer transactions in USD were not as severely affected as those that let the USD freely transact in their financial systems as if it were a second national currency. Some EAC economies like Uganda, Kenya & Tanzania have allowed the USD to transact freely even in basic financial activities like paying rent on property in major cities; salaries for highly skilled nationals & foreign workers; paying school/ college tuition fees. Such economies had to feel the real effect, and this saw EAC major currencies like UGX, KSH and TZS depreciate significantly to record lows during the 2015 forex volatilities, much more than other economies like Rwanda, Burundi, South Africa which have promoted the primary use of their domestic currencies for macroeconomic reasons & external-economy vulnerability management. In some EAC economies, people hoard USD like nothing yet in some it could take someone a lot of time to even see USD on the street.

On the same note, the Secretary to the Treasury of Uganda warned that awarding of contracts in foreign currencies was piling pressure on the Uganda Shilling; he argues that this practice has significantly contributed to the increased pressure on the Uganda Shilling resulting into its depreciation and budget shortfalls which culminate into supplementary expenditure. The entire budgeting process is done in Uganda Shillings, yet expenditure is done in dollars when contracts are being awarded.

Considering that the Uganda Shilling depreciated by more than 30% against the dollar between 2014 and 2015, that means government expenditure on dollar-denominated contracts had gone up. The additional expenses arise out of requiring more Uganda Shillings to pay for dollar-denominated contracts. He therefore maintains that in order to streamline the budget implementation and minimize shortfall and supplementary requests, all government contracts shall only be issued in Uganda Shillings going forward. This practice has seen many EAC governments and their agencies spend a lot of money on contracts to supply materials, build office facilities, consultants, repair contracts and infrastructure projects (especially during the forex volatilities)

Figure 3.2

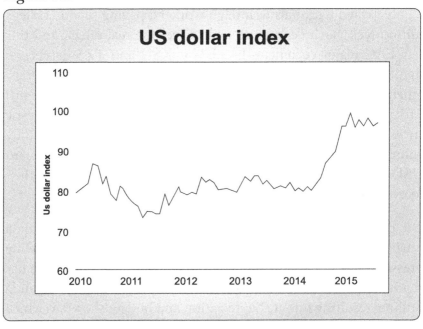

EXCHANGE DEPRECIATION EFFECTS ON THE BANKING SYSTEM

Banks in the region recorded a low 3rd quarter earnings growth and their stock fell to record lows in difficult operating environment triggered by depreciation of local currencies, rising interest rates, and collapse of some banks. This was further compounded by tight monetary policies adopted by regional Central banks to shore up local currencies in the wake of the USD strengthening against all currencies.

However, despite the significant losses in currency value; import cover in these countries remained strong averaging at least 4 months; there was growth in banks revenue boosted by high interest rates charged on loans and advances. On the other hand, many EAC banks also recorded slow growth leading to many issuing profit warning by November 2015. This, coupled with the closure of mid to lower Tier banks eg Dubai Bank (Tier 3 bank) and Imperial Bank (Tier 2 bank) which further compromised the crisis of confidence in the banking system and doubting the Central banks' ability to effectively supervise banks. Besides, putting Chase Bank under receivership by the Central Bank of Kenya (CBK) in April 2016 to operate under Kenya Commercial Bank (KCB) partly due to poor corporate governance on the part of the management whereby they awarded themselves 15 years loans without interest under the guise of Islamic Finance further complicated the public's trust in the Kenyan banking system. The high interest rate environment has adversely impacted banks' capacity to lend which has ultimately increased the level of Non-performing loans, thus further affecting their profitability, and stock prices (for those listed on stock exchanges).

These events in the banking system could undermine the effective transmission of the policy actions restraining CBK's action; but also they have distorted liquidity distribution with remarkable deposit flight from the lower tier banks. This weak confidence in the aforementioned banks may prolong liquidity constraints in the whole sector limiting optimal credit flow in the coming years; besides, concerns about corporate governance in the banking system have somehow undermined credit supply as banks' risk evaluation is becoming more stringent.

## e)	Capital Adequacy Ratio

Capital Adequacy Ratio (CAR) among East African Banks stood at an average of 20.3%. This ratio measures the adequacy of the bank's capital to shoulder the risks it is exposed to. Tanzanian banks have the highest Capital Adequacy Ratio in East Africa, at 24.3%, while Rwanda has the lowest at 17.7%.

This indicator remains highly capitalized & liquid; and by FY 2014/15, the Capital Adequacy Ratio remained above the Basel minimum standard of 8% in all EAC countries. Kenyan banks solvency status is so important to the regional financial stability and these have opened branches in the region. Besides, the liquidity ratio in the region averaged around 47.0% (liquid assets to total deposits) which is way above the 20% prudential limit. This renders EAC banking system relatively stable and an engine that would attract more FDIs to further deepen the financial system and provide the requisite financial resources to all section of the EAC public. On the other hand, there is need to scrutinize and heavily supervise the banking system of some regional economies like Kenya (the giant economy) because issue that are arising suggest a strong need to comprehensive revision of the regulatory and/or supervisory framework given the three banking institutions that have been closed and/or put under receivership by the Central Bank of Kenya.

ADVANTAGES OF COMMERCIAL BANKS.

- *More locations: the most noticeable advantage of commercial banks is their retail store setup. Most are large, global companies, and they have hundreds of retail locations in major cities. This gives a household the ability to access his/her money and account from virtually any location.*

- *Discounts: commercial banks can provide low prices. They are like wholesale companies buying in bulk and selling at a discount. Most commercial banks will not charge fees to open or maintain checking and savings accounts, and their real estate loans are usually offered at low interest rates.*

- *Personal Services offered: commercial banks are setup to close thousands of deals every day. Because of this, personal service is sacrificed. One can talk to manager at a local bank, but commercial banks have centralized call centres to handle problems and disputes.*

- *More product offerings: commercial banks can offer more products and services to their customers. A commercial bank will offer everything a small local bank does, plus CDs, investment accounts, Commercial real estate loans and credit and debit cards.*

- *They are regulated institutions fulfilling the conditions of ownership, financial disclosure and capital adequacy that help ensure prudent management.*

- *Many have physical infrastructure including a large network of branches, from which to expand and reach out to a substantial number of microfinance clients.*

- *They have well established internal controls and administrative and accounting systems to keep track of a large number of transactions.*

- *Their ownership structures of private capital tend to encourage sound governance structures, cost-effectiveness and profitability, all of which lead to sustainability.*

- *Because they have their own sources of funds (deposits and equity capital) they do not have to depend on scarce and volatile donor resources.*
- *They offer loans, deposits and other financial products that are in principle, attractive to a microfinance client.*

TIER II - FINANCIAL INSTITUTIONS

This class includes Credit and Finance companies. They are not authorized to establish checking accounts or trade in foreign currency. They are authorized to take in customer deposits and to establish savings accounts. They are also authorized to make collateralized and non-collateralized loans to savings and non-saving clientele. These Credit institutions are also regulated by the Financial Institutions Acts of various EAC economies. The banking regulators have set minimum paid in capital requirements for these financial institutions as per the Financial Institutions Acts of each Member State though currently the EAC committee on Central banking activities is establishing harmonized policies and regulations for EAC regional banks in preparation for the EAC Monetary Union

Advantages of Credit Institutions

- *Customers are owners: members of credit institutions have voting rights, thus, apart from receiving better services, members have a say in the operation of the credit institution.*
- *Credit institutions are non- profit: non- profit status means that more of the profits are shared with the owners/customers e.g owners/customers of credit institutions receive dividend payments.*
- *There are fewer fees and higher saving rates: credit institutions typically offer free accounts with no minimum balance requirements and fees are absent.*
- *Interest rates on savings, certificate of deposits and some checking accounts often exceed those offered by financial banks.*

- *Interest charged for loans and Credits are often lower: some credit institutions are regulated such that the interest rate on loans and credit cards must not exceed a certain limit.*

TIER III - FINANCIAL INSTITUTIONS

This class includes microfinance institutions which are allowed to take in deposits from customers in the form of savings accounts. Members of this class of institutions are also known as Microfinance Deposit-taking Institutions or MDIs. MDIs are not authorized to offer checking accounts; and operate under various Financial Institutions Act of various EAC Member States.

Advantages of MDIs.

- *MDIs provide financial services that allow poor people to save in times of prosperity and borrow or collect insurance when necessary allowing them to maintain a consistent level of consumption without selling off income producing assets.*
- *MDIs also provide an opportunity for expanding or pursuing new business opportunities that allow poor people to increase or diversify their sources of income.*
- *MDIs promote the development of traditional financial sector. By alleviating poverty, MDIs can deepen the market for poor traditional financial services.*
- *MDIs can also generate important non-economic benefits e.g access to financial services by women through MDIs enhance women's power and influence in the household, that is, their ability to make decisions over certain purchases.*

TIER IV - INSTITUTIONS

These institutions are largely not regulated by central banks. They are not authorized to take deposits from the public. However, they may offer collateralized or non-collateralized loans to the public. There is no minimum paid up capital since central banks do not regulate these institutions. These include:

- All other Financial intermediaries such as: SACCOs, Women groups, NGOs, CBOs, ROSCAs, etc. These are regulated by three sets of institutional legislations. These are regulated by various Acts of Parliament, stipulating their activities such as Companies Act 2012 (Uganda and Kenya).

Advantages of SACCOs and MFIs in East Africa.

- *Close to customers/members: SACCOs operate hand in hand with the members since the members are also responsible to its governance apart from being members.*

- *Easy access to internal funds: members of SACCOs and MFIs can easily access their financial accounts and records. Members can also access internal funds through borrowings.*

- *Low operating costs: interest rates on savings, certificates of deposits and some checking accounts often exceed those offered by banks.*

- *Member-based ownership: SACCOs operate in member based ownership, thus, members of a SACCO are the owners of that particular SACCO.*

- *Democratic & Participatory: every member of a SACCO has voting rights, thus, they influence its operation through democratic decision making using their rights.*

Figure 3.3
East African Community Financial systems Data:

	Uganda	Kenya	Rwanda	Tanzania	Burundi	Total EAC
Contribution of NSSF to GDP	6%	50%	1%	20%	0.24%	
	Not liberalised	Liberalized	Not liberalized	Liberalized	Not liberalized	
% of Public Debt to GDP	35.4%	49.8%	29.4%	39.9%	14.2%	
Tax to GDP	11.7%	19.3%	13.6%	12.6%	14.1%	
Stock Market Capitalisation to GDP	30.7%	29.4%	N/A	4.7%	No Stock exchange.	

Data: World Bank estimates; Mix Market; Trading Economics.

Source: World Bank estimates; Mix Market; Trading Economics (2015).

iii) Retail Banking

Commercial banking: entails the acceptance of deposits that can be withdrawn by cheques, and they perform a wide range of services that are quite unique from other financial institutions as discussed among the functions of banks (later in "vi").

Agricultural Banking: these are established mainly to provide the requisite finance for agricultural development projects and agribusiness initiatives such as: poultry, farming, fisheries, animal husbandry, forestry and timber production, but also for storage and marketing in this sector.

Industrial banking: these aim at encouraging the establishment and growth of medium and large-scale industries through the provision of medium and long-term finance for the private and public sector; provision of financial, technical and managerial assistance to indigenous enterprises.

Cooperative banking: these are responsible for promoting and giving assistance (financial, technical and managerial) to cooperative societies, companies and government agencies such as advice and preparation of feasibility studies.

Agency banking: this is a retail or postal outlet contracted by financial institution or mobile network operator to process clients' transactions; rather than a branch teller, it is the owner/employee who conducts the transaction and lets clients deposits, withdraw, and transfer funds, pay their bills, inquire about account balance, or receive Government benefits or a direct deposit from their employer. Banking agents can be post offices, supermarkets, convenience stores, pharmacies, lottery outlets, etc; and this is an emerging concept in the EAC region that has potential to significantly contribute to financial inclusion basically in the rural areas. Currently, most EAC Governments like Kenya, Uganda, and Tanzania have passed these regulations and what is required is standardizing and applying the guidelines at both national and EAC regional level but also facilitate for EAC Act on agency banking.

## iv)	Wholesale Banking (investment/ merchant)

These banks were previously known as "merchant banks" because more than a century ago, they were bankers to merchants. Trade in the 19th Century was carried out using bills of exchange; so, these financial intermediaries would serve to facilitate the acceptance of trade bills of companies due their knowledge of the merchants since they were able to assess their credit risks and then facilitate trade transactions. In the early 1800s, most American securities were traded in Europe; and so most securities firms developed from merchants who operated a securities business as a sideline to their primary business. For example, the Morgans built their initial fortune with the railroads: in a bid to raise the money to finance railroad expansion, J. P. Morgan's father resided in London and sold Morgan railroad securities to European investors. Over time, the profitability of the securities businesses became evident and the securities industry expanded.

Due to modern development and sophistication of trade, the use of bills of exchange declined significantly, and so merchant banks found a lot more new things to do which later changed even their identity to "investment banks". In the EAC region, there are a variety of such institutions include: African Alliance Ltd, Baroda Capital Markets Ltd, Orbit Securities, Baraka Capital, Crested Stocks & Services Ltd, Dyer & Blair Ltd, Equity Stock Brokers Ltd, UAP Financial Services Ltd, SBG Securities Ltd, ICEA financial services Ltd; which now specialize in giving financial advisory to companies and in fund management. As financial advisers to companies, they: give advice on takeover and merger strategies and defenses; give advice on investment projects; advisory on the best way to raise capital; act as issuing houses; arrange underwriting of new issues; issue Eurobonds.

Investment banking became so popular due to lots of competition so they realized that when so many units join hands and pool their resources, it can make economic sense for them other than small units competing against each other. Such huge funds can't be put into banks due to risks of possible failure of banks, so they decided to invest it with fund managers who could invest in a diversified portfolio of government bonds, stocks & off-shore investments.

But also in the line of fund management, they: provide management for unit trusts and investment trust companies; manage pension funds and large private portfolios; organize the Eurobond market.

In money market operations, they: accept/guarantee bills of exchange; hold treasury bills and local authority bills; issue certificate of deposits; provide finance to companies; act as trustees especially in debenture issuing.

Since these firms are always in the market advising and doing analyses for various companies, they provide more than expertise to security issuers. They are bound to suffer with investors if it turns out that the securities they have underwritten were either faulty or exaggerated prices. Among the international wholesale/investment banks are: Merrill Lynch, Goldman Sachs, etc.

v)   International Banking (Eurocurrency/ Offshore banking)

This is a kind of foreign banking transactions that deals in Eurocurrency/Euro-deposits banking for transactions in a currency other than the domestic currency such as Rwanda Francs (RwF) with both residents and non-residents of Rwanda. A Euro-deposit is any currency deposited outside its country of origin such as RwF held in a Zambian bank. There is a huge market in our financial systems for Eurocurrencies like Eurodollars, Euro-yen, etc; and the major part of international banking in the contemporary financial world is borrowing and lending in foreign currency. There are many foreign banks operating in East Africa whose main function is to provide services to nationals from other jurisdictions/ countries, for instance, for export and import transactions but also speculation in the foreign exchange markets.

Incidentally, the genesis of Eurocurrency banking was due to political factors way back in the 1950s during the Cold War between the U.S.A and the U.S.S.R; whereby USSR acquired dollars basically through the sale of its gold and other raw materials to the USA in a bid to purchase goods eg grains from Europe. The Soviets feared that the US might confiscate its dollars that were deposited in American banks if the Cold War heated up; so, Soviet dollars were placed in European banks which were outside of America's jurisdiction. Thus, it is believed that international banking and Euro-banks originated as the telex code of a Soviet-controlled Paris bank. Later, the Eurodollar system mushroomed in the 1960s as a result of new U.S restrictions on capital outflows and subsequent banking regulations. By and large, Eurocurrency banking grew as a percent of banks total stock of liabilities world over due to the following reasons:

- *The growth of global trade: a drastic increase in international trade, coupled with the increasingly multinational nature of business activities basically financial services have sparked off such a growth in that sector.*
- *Government financial regulations and taxation: stringent financial regulations have for ages been the major stimulant to financial innovation and creation of alternatives, which saw many banks opt for the Eurocurrency market that has been loosely regulated yet highly profitable.*
- *Political factors: such as the USA – USSR relations significantly paved way for creation of such facilities in a bid to make business operations sustainable even in the face of political differences and hostility.*

Eurocurrency banking has been criticized on the following grounds:

Stimulant to global inflation: this unregulated business process has led to a production of vast pools of international liquidity that has potential to spark off global inflation because such volumes of money supply are not included in any measure of money supply eg M1, M2, etc. These Eurocurrency deposits are near-money instruments which may go unnoticed by many a Central banks and later influence an economy's price levels leading to macroeconomic disequilibrium (inflation).

Eurocurrency system complicates the financial system's capacity to monitor and control money supplies by the monetary authorities, hence destabilizing the operation of the money multiplier in an economy.

vi)   Development banking:

These institutions are set up to provide banking services that will help in the development of a particular sector or aspect of the economy. They are usually government-owned institutions that serve basically to enhance economic development rather than for profit motives; they bridge the gap in the provision of long-term finance for their clients. Each EAC Member State has at least a local development bank (apart from South Sudan), and all these collaborate so well with the East African Development Bank (an EAC regional institution).

EAST AFRICAN DEVELOPMENT BANK

EADB was founded in 1967 as one of the key institutions of the East African Community, and it has built a reputation as a provider of long term finance for enterprises in East Africa. In a region where demand for long term finance is growing, the Bank has cultivated a diverse client base.

From its founding in 1967, as a key institution of the East African Community, the EADB has built a proud track record supporting capital projects in both the public and private sectors. It was founded by the original three members of the EAC – Kenya, Uganda and Tanzania – with a mandate to stimulate economic growth and social progress in the region. Its shareholding was subsequently expanded with the joining of multilateral development financiers and commercial banks, including the African Development Bank (AfDB); the Netherlands Development Company (FMO); German

Investment and Development Company (DEG); SBIC Africa Holdings, Commercial Bank of Africa, Standard Chartered Bank and Barclays Bank Plc as Class B (Institutional) shareholders. In 2008, Rwanda joined as the fourth Class A (Member State) shareholder; and Burundi has been accepted to join towards the end of 2016. In April 2015, the governing council resolved to admit the Republic of Burundi as member Country of the EADB at an increased authorized share capital of USD 2.16 Billion; entailing the issuance of 80,000 new shares at par value of USD 13,500 each. The 100% increase in shareholder capital is aimed at catering for Burundi's admission, but also to increase "Class B" authorized shareholding.

The bank has recorded significant benefits to the East Africa Community as at early 2015:

- *Awarded African Banker of the Year 2014*
- *Improved Bank's capital position with USD 932 Million as at end 2014 out of its USD 1.08 Billion Authorized capital base.*
- *Growing income base with 219.39 Million in Total Shareholders' Equity; and USD 17.87 Million as Total Comprehensive income in 2014 compared to USD 8.47 Million in 2013.*
- *Sharp decline of non-performing loans from 32% of Gross loans in 2010 to a mere 1.4% as at early 2015.*
- *Significant decrease in Bank's operational costs*
- *Total usable equity more than fully covered the investment portfolio, representing 192% of the sum of Gross loans outstanding and equity operations.*
- *Rated best performing financial institution in Africa by AADFI in 2015*
- *It is the highest rated Multilateral Development Bank in Moody's rating (June 2015) for the region at Baa3 with Stable Outlook.*

EADB recognizes the importance of having vibrant and diversified regional capital markets as a critical force for regional integration; and so, it has championed the strengthening and deepening of the region's capital markets through its local currency resource mobilization programs (issuance of bonds). The Bank pioneered the issuance of corporate bonds in East Africa and continues to raise local currency resources by issuing bonds in the region's capital markets. Since its first issue of 1996 on the Nairobi Stock Exchange, the EADB has had a successful bond issuing and servicing experience in the sub-region, mobilizing about USD 90 million from 6 issues, with the proceeds being invested in the productive sectors of the East Member States.

Besides, being the only regional DFI for East Africa, EADB has played a leading role in strengthening financial institutions in EAC with a view to promoting financial inclusion. This has been done through funding of micro finance institutions and strengthening the capital base of institutions that serve SMEs through direct equity participation.

In another development, the EADB signed an agreement with the Arab Bank for Economic Development in Africa (BADEA) in January which pledged USD 12 Million for private sector development in the East African Community. This new line of credit is in line with one of EADB's key areas of priority from 2016 to 2020 since private sector development is so critical for sustainable economic growth through generating employment and economic diversification. This comes at a time when the EAC is characterized by enormous youth employment, weak public revenues and the dominance of the informal sector.

WORLD BANK GROUP

This global development bank is one of the world's largest sources of funding and knowledge for developing economies like the EAC, comprising of five institutions with a common commitment to reducing poverty, increasing shared prosperity, and promoting sustainable development. This multilateral financial institution disbursed more than USD 44,582 Million in the year 2015. These five institutions include the following:

International Development Association (IDA): which provides interest-free loans or credits and grants to governments of the poorest economies. This institution disbursed more than USD 12,905 Million in the year 2015

International Financial Corporation (IFC): which provides loans, equity, and advisory services to stimulate private sector investments in developing economies, and this saw an investment value of USD 9,264 Million in the year 2015.

International Bank for Reconstruction and Development (IBRD): which lends to governments of middle-income and creditworthy low-income countries. This institution disbursed more than USD 19,012 Million in 2015 up from USD 18,761 Million in 2014.

Multilateral Investment Guarantee Agency (MIGA): which provides political risk insurance and credit enhancement to investors and lenders to facilitate foreign direct investments in emerging economies. This saw the institutions issue USD 3,155 Million in 2014 and USD 2,828 Million in 2015.

International Centre for Settlement of Investment Disputes (ICSID): which offers international facilities for conciliation and arbitration of investment disputes.

The World Bank Group has always served as a trusted partners for countries that seek to develop dynamic and resilient economies, expand market opportunities, and enable private initiative. Through its institutions, the World Bank offers comprehensive solutions to the pursuit of sustainable growth. These initiatives have facilitated governments and the private sector world over that are seeking more effective ways of enhancing their investment climate, improving competitiveness, boosting the volume and value of trade, and fostering innovation and entrepreneurship (indicators of successful growth strategies).

Impact on the EAC Region

The multilateral institution has supported projects to strengthen the business environment in the EAC region worth USD 9.5 Million in the East Africa Community Investment Climate Program, which facilitates regional trade and investment by improving legal and regulatory frameworks for doing business and strengthening capacity to implement the East African Community Market Protocol. This is in addition to huge investments annually in a program aimed at rendering the EAC private sector competitive by giving matching grants to eligible organisations specific production lines like agriculture, information technology, among others.

Exposure in Sub-Saharan Africa

The Bank approved USD 11.6 Billion for the region for 103 projects for the fiscal year 2015/2016 for lending in the sectors like Public administration, Law and Justice, Health and Social services, and Transportation. Besides, its activities in the region includes supporting regional integration, increasing access to power, supporting small farmers and boosting agricultural productivity in frontier market economies.

The World Bank believes that regional integration in Africa remains a critical piece of its work to improve connectivity, leverage economies of scale, and enhance productivity. The Sub-Saharan Africa's regional integration-related lending was close to USD 2.3 Billion in the fiscal year 2014/2015.

vii)   Role of Banking System in Economic development/ Financial deepening of EAC Region

Increasingly, scholars acknowledge that supportive policy for financial sector development is a key component of national development policy, and comparative analysis of the growth rates of different countries has produced convincing evidence that having a deeper financial system contributes to growth (Honohan and Beck, 2007). Countries with deep financial systems also seem to have a lower incidence of poverty than others at the same level of national income. At the firm level, growth also responds to access to credit and to the conditions that favor such access.

Financial systems tend to evolve around a banking sector seeking to achieve economies of scale in order to offset the costs of collecting and processing information designed to reduce uncertainty thereby facilitating a more efficient allocation of financial resources. The importance of a strong banking sector to a country's economic growth and development can't be over-emphasized. Efficient financial systems help countries to grow, partly by widening access to external finance and channeling resources to the sectors that need those most. A well-developed financial system also can help an economy cope better with exogenous shocks such as terms of trade volatility and move them away from natural resource based development. In this, banks tend to act as quality controllers for capital seeking successful projects, ensuring higher returns and accelerating output growth. However, a competitive banking system is required to ensure that banks are effective forces for financial intermediation channeling savings into investment fostering higher economic growth.

Banks are the predominant financial institutions in most developing countries and in the EAC region, they comprise over 70 percent of the financial system's assets and loans. Banks are the primary mechanisms for the transmission of monetary policy and they play an important role in determining the supply of money in the economy. They also form the backbone of the payments system. Therefore, changes in the structure and performance of banks can have far-reaching implications for the whole economy but above all facilitating financial deepening in our under-developed financial system. The following are the functions/ roles of the banking sector in economic development and financial deepening:

- *Banks offer a wide array of loans to financial agents in form of: personal, business, mortgage and agricultural loans. These may be short, medium and long-term loans for both consumption and investment expenditure.*
- *They avail finance through discounting bills of exchange and also giving loans against the bill which serves as security for the loan facility.*
- *They offer trustee facilities such as: acting in trust for money or property whose owners are either dead, incapacitated or minors.*
- *They provide tax planning and management facilities to the business community.*
- *Banks offer various accounts to their clients which serve as safe custody for depositors' savings, such as: savings, current, investment, fixed deposit, among other accounts.*
- *They facilitate payment and settlement systems which minimize risks of funds transfer, such as: cheques, standing orders, credit transfers, electronic transfer of money.*
- *They provide foreign exchange to business community that engages in foreign trade by intermediating between Central bank and the business community.*
- *Banks provide investment advice to business community in the way of risk management and investment appraising (new ventures).*
- *They offer a wide array of financial services such as: investment banking; lease financing; hire-purchase financing; guarantee services for their customers to acquire any kind of finance.*
- *Banks offer safe custody for valuable that are kept in banking strong-rooms, such as: gold, title deeds, bond certificates, wills, academic documents, among other valuables for their customers.*

viii) Factors responsible for the growth of the Banking Sector

- *Most EAC countries have witnessed a relatively stable political environment from at least the mid-1990s; this has been rather conducive to the development of the financial system. This can be evidenced by: the growth in GDP; development in financial institutions, markets and services; growth in foreign direct investments (FDI); among other economic variables and metrics.*

- *The growth in financial literacy among East Africans; and the subsequent (though still slow) transition from short-termism to long-term perspective towards investment and business has served to boost the growth of banking sector in the region. Households and business sectors now view banking sector as safe for the custody of their funds and also as a means for asset-building through loans, among other financing facilities.*

- *Macroeconomic stability: Besides political stability, the country is also enjoying high levels of macroeconomic stability in the way of: reasonable inflation; relatively good interest rate and foreign exchange regimes; improved levels of employment; GDP growth rates; among other factors. These have led to higher confidence levels among foreign investors; and boosted the country's credit rating among foreign creditors.*

- *The strategic positioning of the EAC region in the heart of Africa and bordering the Indian Ocean; coupled by its Member States' status as powerhouse in the field of regional peace-keeping that have facilitated trading relations within the region. This has served to attract financial institutions from the Anglophone, Francophone, Arab, among other worlds so as to connect to both East and Central African economies.*

- *Reduction in the levels of poverty: There has been significant and visible reduction in percentage of both rural and urban poor in Uganda, this has been due to: steady flow of income from agriculture; growth of both the service and tourism sectors that have employed many East Africans.*

- *Favourable government policies that have stimulated small-scale industries; attracted foreign investments through tax incentives; and the establishment of the Microfinance Support Centre that has both streamlined micro-financing but also provided start-up financial resources to those in need.*

ix) Financial Innovations & Inclusion

"Financial innovation promotes financial inclusion and financial stability."

Globally, close to 2.5 billion people (half the world's adult population) lack one of the most basic amenities of modern life: a bank account. These folks are among the world's poorest, and are struggling to obtain the money they need to feed their families or start a business and create jobs, but their exclusion from the modern financial system represents a significant obstacle to the global effort to end extreme poverty and boost shared prosperity. Modern financial facilities like e-money accounts, debit and prepaid cards, mobile money conveniences and low-cost accounts are so instrumental in increasing financial access (deepening), reducing poverty, and empowering the poor in our struggling economies. This reality actually prompted the World Bank Group president Jim Yong Kim to call for universal access to finance by 2020 by all financial agents such as governments, the private sector, and other players to that effect.

By and large, the level of access to formal financial services across the six EAC economies remains quite dismal. By 2012, an average of 60% of the population in Kenya, Uganda and Tanzania were either with no access to formal financial services or served by the in formal financial system. On the other hand, for Rwanda and Burundi, formal financial services remained a huge challenge since the biggest population had no access to any form of finance. Improving access to financial services by the underserved communities and businesses cannot be overemphasized in the development of an equitable financial system since this directly contributes to increasing incomes and reducing vulnerability for the poor. Simply put, bringing more people and also more money into the formal financial system can lead to overall economic development but also increased financial stability.

Financial inclusion implies building a financial system that serves as many people as possible in an economy. Access to and use of financial services provide opportunities for facilitating individual prosperity and economic development. By early 2015, below is how the EAC regional economies were faring in financial inclusion (which is a significant improvement from the 2012 situation):

Kenya made significant strides in advancing financial inclusion, whereby 75% of adults held an account with a formal financial institution or mobile money provider or both. Central Bank of Kenya has been so key in facilitating this financial inclusion and digital services.

Rwanda had 38% adults holding an account with a formal financial institution; and 26% saved at financial institutions; and 18% of the adults used mobile money accounts.

Tanzania made momentous progress in bettering its financial inclusion commitments through various key stakeholders like National Council for Financial Inclusion. More than 40% of adults had an account with a formal financial institution and/ or mobile money provider; digital financial services like mobile money are quite valuable in Tanzania given her highly dispersed population.

In Uganda, mobile money services have bettered access to finance since studies indicated that by 2015, 33% of adults held a mobile money account and 28% had an account at a formal financial institution; unlike by July 2014, whereby 62% of adults were totally excluded from the formal financial system.

Chapter 10
NON-BANK FINANCIAL INSTITUTIONS

"Sufficient capital & liquidity levels in the financial system provide a buffer for financial institutions to absorb the adverse impacts of shocks."

i)   Types of NBFI

BUILDING SOCIETIES

These institutions channel private individuals' excess short-term money to households to borrow for the purchase of a house. Among their investments are: grant houses, mortgage purchases, and some personal loans; then surplus money is invested in treasury securities and local authority bonds, other banks using certificates of deposits.

The building industry in East Africa has drastically improved in the past decade due to good government policy that has favored the provision of adequate and decent shelter for all across the EAC (a range of policies such as political, economic and social). This industry has for years been championed by, Akright company, among other players in this sub-sector which have made projects such as Lubowa Housing estates.

These societies are rather crucial in the economy because: they avail mortgage loans to qualifying citizens to purchase houses and repay later; they sell housing and infrastructural bonds that individuals and organizations can invest their surplus funds; they also offer savings facilities which act as a custody for depositors' money.

INSURANCE COMPANIES

These institutions protect financial agents against a variety of risk exposures that arise within the financial system by spreading losses of the unfortunate few over many policyholders through the collection of premiums. They perform financial intermediation since they mobilize /pool funds from the public which they use to compensate losses from their clients but the residue is invested in a wide variety of both real and financial assets of companies. They are so critical in: facilitating risk transfer; provision of long-term investment resources; development of financial markets; stimulate a savings culture; securities underwriting; among other functions they play.

Most activity in the global insurance industry is concentrated amongst three economies: US, Japan, and UK, accounting for close to 50% of worldwide premium income.

INSURANCE INDUSTRY IN THE EAC

Insurance density measures the premium amount per capita in a given economy; while insurance penetration measures the gross premium as a percentage of GDP. Basing on these indicators, the EAC insurance industry is operating under excess capacity (below their potentiality) since, for instance, African insurance penetration average is at 3.5% but all the EAC economies including Kenya are below this average. This implies that there are lots of opportunities for prospective investors in the insurance industry since a huge number of East African have not taken up any insurance policy yet nationals are increasing becoming concerned about personal risk management, coupled to the progressive increment in income levels and general standards of living. But the industry has a bright future, as highlighted below:

The introduction of Banc-assurance in economies like Uganda (already existent in Kenya); this will foster partnerships between insurance underwriters and financial institutions.

Proposal to EAC governments to offer tax rebates (refunds) of up to 20% on most life, health and education insurance products.

Venturing into project insurance as the EAC region prepares to roll out a host of mega infrastructural projects in power supply, infrastructure like Standard Gauge Railway, and commercial oil production; which will benefit both insurers and reinsurers.

The Oil economy risks; this will present more insurable property risks, transportation risks, refinery and storage risks which will significantly contribute to insurance industry.

The introduction of Micro-insurance in economies like Uganda that will tap into the large informal sector.

The expected National Health Insurance Scheme in Uganda so as to match with other EAC economies which already implemented it.

The long awaited liberalization of the Pension sector in Uganda, and its subsequent advantages.

The growth and activity of the Islamic insurance (Takaful) that will attract Sharia-compliant funds and products from within the EAC and globally.

Figure 3.4
Performance of Insurance and Pension Sectors in the EAC region

EAC Country	Total Population (Millions)	No. of Insurance Firms	Total Premium (USD Billion)	Share of Region's Gross Written Premium	Insurance Density (USD)	Insurance Penetration (% of GDP)	Target Market (25 years +)	Domestic Saving (% of GDP)
Burundi	10.82	6	0.016	1%	2	0.50%	35%	2%
Kenya	44.86	53	1.572	74%	30	2.93%	40%	3.9%
Rwanda	11.34	14	0.110	5%	4	0.60%	39%	10.9%
South Sudan	11.91	10	N/A	N/A	N/A	N/A	N/A	N/A
Tanzania	51.82	31	0.226	11%	6	0.90%	36%	20.6%
Uganda	37.7	30	0.193	9%	5	0.85%	31%	22.1%
Total	168.5	144	2.116		47	5.78%		

Source: EAC Central Banks; EAC IRAs (2015)

By end 2014, Kenya pension schemes had over USD 7 Billion funds under managements; and Tanzania schemes had USD 3 Billion. Rwanda had 64 SACCOs, 416 Umurenge SACCOs, 1 public pension fund, and 54 private funds by June 2015.

On the other hand, Uganda's performance was as follows: NSSF-Uganda had approximately UGX 6.2 Trillion as of February 2016; the registered occupational schemes (provident funds) totaled to 63 with assets under management of UGX 1.144 Trillion (approx. USD 227 Million) by June 2015. Besides, there were close to 8,000 investment clubs and approximately 20,000 SACCOs with an unknown value but at least DFCU Bank had 6,000 accounts for investment clubs worth UGX 6 Billion (USD 1.6 Million)

By and large, once the EAC financial system is integrated, there will all reasons to rely on the domestic schemes (saving capacity) for corporate resource mobilization since these volumes of funds can be so practical in boosting the whole financial system. This is because the EAC Gross Domestic Savings average as a percentage of GDP was close to 13% of the estimated EAC GDP of USD 110 Billion as at end 2014 (approx. USD 14.3 Billion). All this could be available for local financing and investing, coupled to more than double that value which is unknown but exchanging hands within the extremely large informal financial system that can be tapped into using financial inclusion drives like mobile money facilities.

EAC region may not need to issue Eurobonds because we can raise such finances within EAC markets from locals if well sensitized & all informal funds linked to the formal financial system through incentives and rendering the process simple and convenient to all would-be investors (savers).

SAVINGS AND CREDIT COOPERATIVES (SACCOS)

These are most popular non-bank financial institutions, and they have significantly contributed to the development of the economy. Originally created to facilitate mortgage loans to their own members, they have now increasingly established their savings institutions, catering for small investors but also local and central governments in some cases. Many SACCOs actually pay good interest that is higher than what commercial banks and other investment avenues give to their savers' deposits. Some are actually allowed to issue large denominations of certificates of deposits that have boosted their resource mobilization capacities.

DISCOUNT HOUSES

These financial intermediaries originated in Britain (UK), and had never existed in other countries. They were so popular in the 19th Century when bills of exchange were frequently used, and their role was to discount bills of exchange, and act as a buffer (shock absorber) between the Bank of England and the clearing banks. They also acted as money market intermediaries by channeling banks' excess short-term funds to institutional borrowers such as: Central government, local authorities, companies, and banks.

PRIVATE EQUITY INVESTMENT

Unlike stocks and bonds that are sold to the public and are subject to oversight by the CMA, and whose dealings are managed by brokers and dealers in these publicly held securities; private equity investments are an alternative to public equity investing. With private equity investing, instead of raising capital by selling securities to the public, a limited partnership is formed that raises money from a small number of high net-worth investors; and within the wide universe of private equity sectors, such as: the venture capital funds and capital buyouts. In the real financial world, firms actively operate in both the above areas, and among the prominent players in the private equity industry are: Fanisi capital Ltd; Mara launch-pad Ltd; Assent Capital Ltd; and Genesis Kenya Ltd, etc

Venture capital firms provide the funds a start-up company needs to get established despite the absence of concrete financial soundness data and requisite cash flows that conventional sources of finance like commercial banks would require so as to fund and develop an innovator's brilliant business idea. This is normally called money supplied to young and start-up firms that can't sell stock to the public through investment bankers because the firms and their products are so new and have not yet proven that they can be successful. It is worth to noting that equity interests in these firms are very illiquid and the investment horizons are long-term, at least five years to a decade, which requires investors with a long-term perspective towards investing

Originally, true venture capitalism begun in the USA in the 1940s by the American Research and Development (ARD); though most venture capital funding during the 1950s and 1960s was for the development of real estate and oil fields. The late 1960s, witnessed a shift toward financing technology start-ups; and still high technology remains the dominant area for venture capitalism despite the fact that the source of venture capital funding has shifted from wealthy individuals to pension funds and corporations. Many a firms consequently have benefitted from venture capitalism, such as: Apple Computer, Starbucks, Netscape, Cisco Systems, Genentech, Staples, Microsoft, and Sun Microsystems.

Africa generally has not seen lots of activity in private equity investments like the U.S & UK. Africa's largest communities of private equity are: South Africa, Egypt, Nigeria, and Kenya; and it is due to fear/ riskiness of investors' ability to exit an investment deal when time comes. Despite this fear, Uganda has had one critical success story of a smooth exit: Umeme Ltd, the main electricity distribution firm in Uganda that was privatized in 2004 by the Government of Uganda, and changed its ownership to Actis Capital (London-based emerging markets private equity investor and a subsidiary of the UK government's CDC Group). In November 2012, Actis sold 38% stake on the USE and later cross-listed on the NSE; this IPO exit proved that private equity firms can use this as a credible alternative for exit. As a matter of fact, private equity is drastically growing in EAC as investors seek opportunities and exposure in high-growth markets due to the effects of the 2007/08 Global Financial Crisis, and the Quantitative Easing programs in the West that have shifted hot money flows to Africa rising in inbounds activities in Frontier markets, EAC inclusive.

The venture capital industry is still young in many EAC economies, except Kenya that even funded the first ever mobile money technology in the whole world under the M-pesa product; this has been so successful that many economies and telecommunication firms are replicating this product with their brands.

Private equity firms are normally medium to long-term finance provided by firms in return for an equity stake in potentially high-growth firms through venture capitalism and/or buy-outs. These firms are focused on growth investment strategies and it has seen many turn to the African continent so as to take advantage of the continent's growth story. Some provide both long-term funds and also active skills required for corporate management. After an investing period, the private equity can exit the deal through one of the following (exit) strategies:

- *Selling its shares back to the management of the investee firm similar to Islamic financing.*
- *Selling the share to another investor, especially another private equity firm.*
- *A stock market listing so as to divest its holdings through the stock exchange infrastructure like Actis.*

NSSF-Uganda, the largest pension fund in East and Central Africa by assets, anticipates to establish a private equity fund so as to diversify its large asset and income base into this trendy asset class with huge return potential basically in the EAC region given its mandatory investment horizon to the region. Besides, there are also other private equity firms that are enjoying this virgin market of EAC like Vanguard................

SOVEREIGN WEALTH FUNDS

This is a state-owned investment fund that holds financial assets eg equities, bonds, real estate, or other financial instruments. These normally hold funds in order to preserve revenues from commodity exports for the benefit of future generations. African sovereign wealth funds currently manage approx. USD 160 Billion; these are increasingly becoming crucial in the global financial system due to their size, investment strategies but also political objectives since their activities could hamper the international flow of capital.

ASSET/FUND MANAGERS

These are intermediaries that are authorized/ mandated to manage pension resources of savers; and they are licensed by both the capital market regulators and/or the pension sector regulators given the nature of operations and the products they have. By the end of 2013, there were 9 (nine) licensed fund management companies in Uganda: NSSF-Uganda, Insurance Company of East Africa (ICEA), UAP Financial Services, Jubilee Insurance, Genesis Kenya Investments, African Alliance Uganda Ltd, Stanlib Uganda Ltd, Pine Bridge Investments, Pearl Capital Partners (PCP). By early 2015, Kenya's fund management sector had total assets under management at KSH 501.5 Billion, of which majorly four large fund managers accounted for more than 90% of industry's assets: PineBridge had KSH 161.8 Billion; NSSF with KSH 147.7 Billion; Genesis Kenya had KSH 114.3 Billion; and ICEA-Lion with KSH 53.9 Billion.

Chapter 11
SOCIAL SECURITY SYSTEMS IN EAC

Globally, social security systems are a crucial element in not only social/individual welfare but also in boosting the overall financial system thanks to their large and long-term funds that are available to both corporations and governments. In fact, Article 22 of the Universal Declaration of Human Rights accentuates that, "everyone has the right to social security and is entitled to realization through national efforts and international cooperation, and in accordance with the organization and resources of the State, of the economic, social and cultural rights indispensable for his dignity and the free development of his personality".

National Social Security Funds (for Uganda, Kenya and Tanzania);

Rwanda Social Security Board; Securité Sociale du Burundi are government agencies responsible for the collection, safekeeping, responsible investment, and distribution of retirement funds for the employees in both formal and informal sectors across the East African Community. Most of these operate both as pension funds and provident funds in their respective countries, but South Sudan currently does not have one.

NSSF institutions were established in various years in East Africa by various Acts of respective EAC Parliaments; their basic function is the provision of a more comprehensive and reliable social security system for EAC private sector employees since they were not covered in the public sector pension system. NSSF-Uganda has customer centric, innovation, integrity, teamwork, and efficiency as its corporate values; and it has strived to prove to its investors that its strategic thinking coupled to its values are turned into realities for the betterment of each saver. These institutions mobilize funds through a statutory and compulsory contribution to the fund by the private sector employers and employee, which funds are used to provide pension benefits to contributors. They invests these funds using their authority and capacity in investment management in a diversity of real and financial assets such as: real property, real estate, corporate and government debt instruments, listed equities and a few private equities basically within East African Community given their mandate regarding the permissible investment universe. Besides, almost all sectors of the EAC economies are permissible: real estate development, energy, water, education, health, mortgage finance and SME development.

Figure 3.5
Table Showing Social Security Fundamentals across EAC Region

Social Security Fund	Year of Establishment (Act)	Pension Contribution (% of Income)	Assets Under Management	Nature (Mandatory Horizon)	Regulators
S.S du Burundi	N/A	14.4%	N/A	Not liberalized	Central Bank
NSSF-Kenya	1965 but amended in 2013	27%	KSH 147.7 Billion	Liberalized	Retirement Benefits Authority
RSSB-Rwanda	N/A	6%	N/A	Not liberalized	Central Bank
South Sudan	N/A	N/A	N/A	N/A	N/A
Tanzania	1997	20%	TZS 2.93 Trillion	Liberalized	Retirement Benefits Authority
Uganda	1967 but amended in 1985	15%	UGX 6.2 Trillion	Not liberalized	Retirement Benefits Authority (URBRA)

Source: RBA-Kenya (2014); NSSF-Tanzania (2016); NSSF-Uganda (2016);

EAC Central Banks (2016)

FEATURE: NSSF-UGANDA PERFORMANCE DURING ITS 30 YEARS OF EXISTENCE

a)   Operating Income

In Uganda, Social Security Fund (SSF) was first established in 1967, under section 17 of the Public Finance Act of 1967 which instituted a compulsory savings scheme for the private sector employees. Later, it was amended to NSSF Act that was assented in 1985 to render NSSF-Uganda a fully-fledged autonomous body (financial institution). And below is its performance over the 30 years of existence basing on selected financial metrics:

The operating income of NSSF refers to revenue from interest earned, rental income, dividend income and all other incomes to the institution. It is a measure of how well the income generating activities that the institution is involved in are performing. A growth gross operating income indicates that the income generating portfolio choice of the institution is yielding the desired results. Over the past 30 years, NSSF has realized positive operating income, save for 2009 when negative operating income recorded.

Figure 3.6
NSSF Growth in Operating Income from 1986 to 2015.

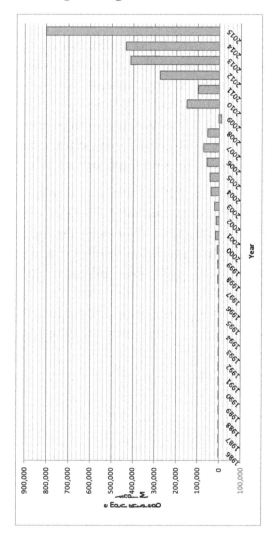

Between 1986 and 2000, there was relatively slow growth in operating income. There was a slight improvement in the 2000s. Between 2010 and 2015, there has been phenomenal growth in operating income. NSSF has been able to grow operating income to over UGX 800 bn as at June 2015.

b)   Total Assets

Total Assets refers to valuable property owned by NSSF that is available to meet commitments, debts, legacies and any other attendant liabilities that may arise. It is composed of Cash and bank balances, deposits with banks, securities, receivables, investment properties, intangible assets, among others. Over the past 30 years, NSSF has been able to grow its total assets to a tune of over UGX. 5.5 Trillion by the year 2015.

Figure 3.7
NSSF Growth in Total Assets between 1986 and 2015.

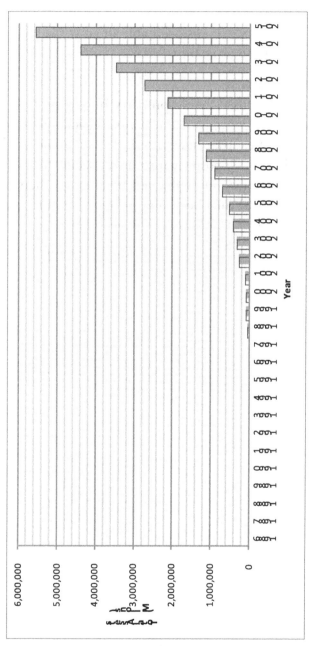

The first ten years of the fund (1986 to 1995) saw an aggressive buildup of total assets, with growth rates averaging 207%. The next ten years (1996 – 2005) saw the growth rate reduce, with average growth in total assets of 50%. The latest ten year period (2006 to 2015) has seen growth rates at an average of 26%, building on the earlier asset base.

The trend in growth of total assets is reflective of the trend in the growth of accumulated members' funds. Increase in members' funds over time has made more funding available to NSSF, thereby enabling more assets to be acquired.

c)   **Accumulated Members' Funds**
Over the past 30 years, NSSF members have continued to make contributions. These contributions accumulate and also include interest credited to members' funds as and when declared. The amount reflected in the books of NSSF as accumulated members' funds refers to the net of accumulated members' funds received to date less total benefits payments made. The performance has been as shown in the table below:

Figure 3.8
NSSF Accumulated Member Funds

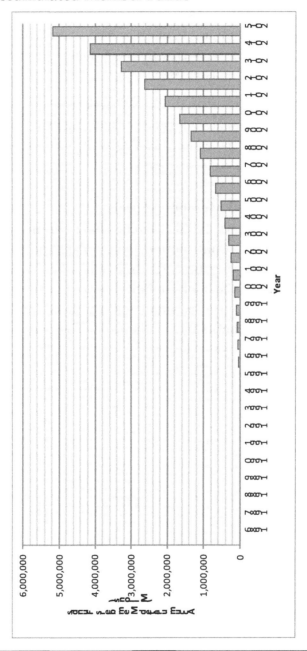

In the first 10 years of the fund (1986 to 1995), there was an aggressive growth in members' funds, as more organizations sent employees' social security contributions to NSSF. The average growth rate for the first 10 years stood at 114%. The next ten years (1996 to 2005) saw reduced growth, with average growth of 38%. The latest ten years (2006 to 2015) has seen growth stabilize at 26%, reflecting the fact that many of the organizations are registered and compliant with remittances of social security contributions for their staff. NSSF currently holds members' funds worth over UGX 5 trillion.

It is worth noting that whereas total assets held by NSSF are UGX 5.5 trillion, accumulated members' funds stand at UGX 5 trillion, indicating that NSSF has enough assets to settle member's obligations as and when they fall due.

d)   Contributions collected during each year

On a monthly basis, members make contributions to NSSF. Analysis of contributions collected each year is a good measure of the efficiency with which NSSF is inducing compliance from employer organizations in remitting their employees' contributions.

Figure 3.9
NSSF Annual Contributions Growth 1986 to 2015

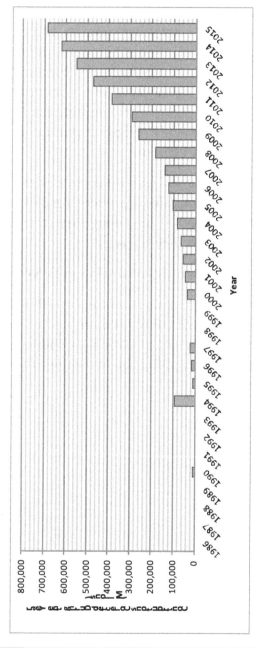

In the first 10 years of the fund (1986 to 1995), many organizations were joining the fund for the first time. This led to high contributions collections growth rates of 343%. The next 10 years saw the number of contributors stabilizing, leading to a decrease in growth to 7%, which was reflective of the general economic growth rates at the time. The past 10 years (2006 to 2015) has seen average growth of 4%, which is a reflection of the general performance of the economy, since economic performance in terms of employment is a major determinant of social security collections. In 2015, NSSF collected close to UGX 700 Billion.

e) Interest Rate Declared on Savings

NSSF utilizes members' savings to acquire assets, which assets generate operating income. In accordance with section 35 (2) of the National Social Security Fund Act, (Cap 222), the Minister of Finance, Planning and Economic Development may declare Interest payment to members. The interest so declared is then allocated to members, thereby increasing the Accumulated Members' Funds.

Figure 3.10
NSSF Trends in Interest Rates declared over 30 years

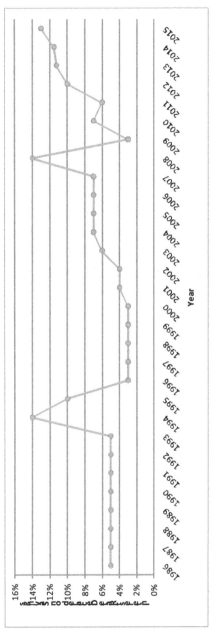

The lowest interest rates received by members were between 1996 and 1999, when members received 3% as interest. The highest over the past 30 years has been 14%, declared for members' savings of 1994 and again in 2008. Subsequently, there has been a steady growth in interest rates declared, rising to 13% declared for 2015.

It has become the largest pension fund in East Africa, and a benchmark for the industry within and outside East African region.

Besides, the fund has grown by over 150% over the last 5 years, becoming the largest financial institution in Uganda, and it had invested in a wide portfolio of asset classes: fixed income UGX 3.4 Trillion (81% of total portfolio); Equities UGX 432 Billion (10%); yet the fund is highly liquid. NSSF holds 40% of all government treasury bonds; 15% of all deposits in commercial banks; 80% of all equities listed on USE; yet 25% of its portfolio is invested in East African region due to domestic absorption incapacity and diversification strategy. Among its real estate include: Workers' House, Lubowa land, Pension Towers, and Temangalo land. Pension resources are often the only form of savings that many households have for their retirement; and they part of the employment income available to employees which are deferred until an employee has completed his/her work life. Besides, they contribute volumes of reliable investable resources to the financial sector before they are cashed out, which significantly boost long-term financing in our financial system.

By February 2016, NSSF-Uganda had the following monthly statistics/ financials that are critical to the EAC financial system:
- *UGX 160 Billion available for Investments.*
- *UGX 70 Billion in Collection from members.*
- *UGX 40 Billion in Earnings from its assets.*

- *UGX 70 Billion Maturities.*
- *UGX 14 Billion in Benefits payments.*
- *UGX 6 Billion in expenses*

ROLE OF NSSF IN BOOSTING THE FINANCIAL SYSTEM

Provision of patient capital to firms and SMEs such as private equity with a view to exiting via the stock exchange.

Provision of long term finance to Government for infrastructure projects.

Supply the market with liquidity when no one has it at an acceptable premium depending on the risk.

Market making on listed securities. Examples include: Bonds, REITS, shares.

Offering housing solutions to address the housing deficit in Uganda. For example: mortgages, affordable housing…etc.
Underwriting listings on both stock markets and bond markets.

Chapter 12
POOLED INVESTMENT VEHICLES (P.I.V)
"Collective savings media help strengthen & upgrade the financial system"

These are financial intermediaries that pool funds from individual investors (households) and invest them in a wide portfolio of securities/assets. Each investor has a claim to the portfolio established by the P.I.V in proportion to the amount invested; it is a mechanism for small holders to team up so as to enjoy economies of collective strategies, simply put, benefits of large scale investing. These are achieved through the following roles that P.I.Vs play: fund administration which is diversification of funds by investing in different assets; professional management thanks to their full time staff of security analysts and portfolio managers; and lower transaction costs due to large blocks of securities.

These investment vehicles are organized in such a way that investors either buy units or shares of ownership into these vehicles; and the value of each share/unit is called "Net Asset Value" (NAV).

i) Open-ended Funds

Kenya should become the main regional center for creation of investment funds that can later be distributed to investors across the EAC region due to its competitive advantage in having many operational funds and her long experience in both financial markets and institutional investing compared to other regional peers. The legal structure of such funds must be of a company domiciled like in Kenya's capital (Nairobi) with some key administrative aspects conducted there but the investment management can be undertaken in each major Capital city of the EAC member states.

ii)   Closed-ended Funds

These are also called investment companies, and they normally invest in more illiquid securities. Some don't actively trade their investment portfolios (buy relatively fixed portfolios of securities), and are preferable for illiquid markets like Africa (whose securities exchanges are very illiquid). This is because such funds don't alter their fund sizes since their investors buy and sell the shares to each other in the secondary market, unlike the open-ended funds that may have to sell/buy shares when many more investors buy/sell their units. This would be very practical for the EAC since they give their investors an opportunity to invest in a diversified portfolio of assets and exposure to good investments in the EAC region, Africa and the global financial markets. The pricing of such funds is determined by the price mechanism (forces of demand and supply) on the stock market but not the net asset value (NAV) as the case for open-ended funds.

iii)   Exchange-Traded Funds (ETFs)

In South Africa, there used to be a lot of liquidity amongst the public, and investors were not interested in the equities markets; so the financial system devised a means of tapping into this liquidity by creating an asset class called ETFs. Since then, South Africans are more interested in money markets. These serve to bring more clients on board since they trade on index not equities per se, which brings a decent return since this is passive investment management. ETFs are so critical in boosting liquidity levels in the financial markets; and they are designed to attract investors to invest since they track indexes in various industries eg manufacturing, banking, telecom, real estates, etc and they deal with such industry indexes. South Africa deliberately used the ETFs to attract investors across Africa and then channel them to equities markets which were not operating well, and majorly with an objective of creating the JSE as the power house of African capital markets.

The EAC ETFs ought to be created so as to give exposure to all markets in the region to foreigners in a bid to boost activity in the highly illiquidity regional stock markets. But also, there should be regional ETFs that provide East Africans exposure to other markets like South Africa, Egypt, Middle East, Europe and US to diversify their portfolios.

NB: The more people invest in an economy/ stock market, the more risks are reduced and liquidity problems are solved.

iv)   Real Estate Investment Trusts (REITs)

These are increasingly becoming popular in African markets eg Botswana, Ghana, Kenya, Lesotho, Namibia, and South Africa. Globally, this market is worth more than USD 400 Billion. These pool investors' funds to invest in commercial and residential property. These provide access to property returns without the inconvenience of double taxation (since of old, the tax system would levy both corporation tax and also tax on dividends/ any growth on investors who held property company shares). This investment also removes a further risks of holding direct property eg liquidity risk. These are closed-ended funds which are listed on stock exchanges (shares are traded in the same way as investment trusts), and in the EAC, the just recent listing was of Stanlib Fahari REITs in 2015 on the Nairobi Stock Exchange though Uganda Securities Exchange, and Rwanda Stock Exchange are very optimistic that towards the end of 2016 they will also list REITs.

These are similar to a closed-end fund; and they invest in real estate or loans secured by real estate. Besides issuing shares, they raise capital by borrowing from banks and issuing bonds or mortgages. Most of them are highly leveraged, with a typical debt ratio of 70%.

There are two principal kinds of REITs: Equity trusts which invest in real estate directly, whereas mortgage trusts invest primarily in mortgage and construction loans. REITs generally are established by banks, insurance companies, or mortgage companies, which then serve as investment managers to earn a fee.

EAC PROPERTY BILL

The East African Legislative Assembly (EALA) is currently discussing the East African Property Bill, aimed at:

Advocating for a harmonization of property/land ownership and tenure system; this comes at a time when almost all East African economies have different land tenure systems that would significantly affect not only regional integration but even productive capacities since land (majorly its ownership) is very key in the production process.

Designing and facilitating for collective strategies of investing in commercial and residential property by all East Africans. This would be done through collective investment vehicles like REITs that could give nationals an opportunity to buy/own units of property across the region without any hindrance whatsoever. This would render property investments (that are so lucrative in the region) access to and affordable to all residents so as to benefit from this asset class regionally.

v)   Depository Receipts

This instrument helps to attract funds from global investors into the domestic financial markets. American Depositary Receipt (ADR) is an investment vehicle where the U.S stock brokers can mobilize funds globally to buy U.S securities, hence giving global investors exposure to U.S markets and also mobilize funds elsewhere so as to channel them into U.S financial markets.

These instruments are pick up in popularity in African markets basically for listed equities, for instance, JSE currently trades South African Depository Receipts (SADRs) representing ownership in securities listed for trading on other exchanges like the Nigerian Stock Exchange. These trade, settle and pay dividends in local currency (South African rands) just like other equities on Johannesburg Stock Exchange (JSE).

The EAC financial markets can utilize this asset class by creating an EAC Depositary Receipt or local ones like UDR (Uganda Depositary Receipts). Brokers hold the DRs for their clients, then invest on their behalf for a return: these are created by brokerage firms and they help their clients to escape exchange rate risk and domestic taxes in some financial systems. These DRs are now demutualized (no longer physical certificates but computer-based system that indicates ownership). DRs can either be single security DRs or multiple-securities DRs: for multiple DRs, they hold a couple of securities and give investors exposure to foreign markets through a portfolio of securities. These investment vehicles are majorly in the 1st world economies due to cross-border hot money but are becoming popular in emerging and frontier markets. The depository bank owns the shares in the issuer's local market. Depository receipts and notes for equity and debt issues denominated in major international currencies like USD, Euro and GBP can be listed on foreign exchanges to make the more accessible to international investors. This could serve to improve knowledge of EAC financial products and liquidity in such products developed overseas would later be channeled to the EAC markets.

vi)   Hedge Funds

These are high-risk funds for majorly the wealthy investors and institutions that can afford to heavily invest in illiquid frontier markets like the EAC but with huge objective of absolute return regardless of the general movements of the markets.

Like unit trust funds, hedge funds are vehicles that allow private investors to pool assets to be invested by a fund manager. Unlike unit trust funds, conversely, hedge funds are commonly structured as private partnerships and thus subject to only minimal regulations in economies where they operate (but not yet popular in the EAC region). They typically are open only to wealthy or institutional investors. Many require investors to agree to initial lock-ups, that is, periods as long as several years in which investments cannot be withdrawn. These periods allow hedge funds to invest in illiquid assets without worrying about meeting demands for redemption of funds. Moreover, because hedge funds are only lightly regulated, their managers can pursue investment strategies involving, for example, heavy use of derivatives, short sales, and leverage; such strategies typically are not open to mutual fund managers.

Hedge funds by design are empowered to invest in a wide range of investments, with various funds focusing on derivatives, distressed firms, currency speculation, convertible bonds, emerging markets, merger arbitrage, and so on. Other funds may jump from one asset class to another as perceived investment opportunities shift.

There is need to create a hedge fund for the "Kwagalana Group" in Uganda (an association of wealthy traders in Kampala) because this group would perfectly fit in the requirements of investors in such fund. This entails: high net-worth individuals with minimum of at least USD 40,000; structured in an unregulated collective investment scheme for financially sophisticated investors; with high levels of investment flexibility into any asset they wish; with an investment style aimed at producing absolute returns. Regarding the liquidity aspect, there should be a mandatory "lock-in" period of between six months to one year before an investor can sell his investments so that funds managers can maximize their investment freedom. Then, the cost of managing the hedge fund should be performance-related fees that investors pay if certain performance levels are achieved

vii)   Unit Trust Funds

These are pools of money invested in a portfolio that is fixed for the life of the fund; and its formation is done by a brokerage firm

(Sponsor) which buys a portfolio of securities that are deposited into a trust. The sponsor then sells to the public units/shares in the trust referred to as "Redeemable trust certificates". All income and payment of principal from the portfolio are paid out by the funds trustees to the unit/share holders. Most unit trusts hold long-term fixed-income corporate and government securities, equities, real property in the EAC region, but also off-shore investments, and expire at their maturity; thus, there is little active management of such funds since the portfolio composition is fixed. Investors who wish to liquidate their units may sell them back to the trustees for the net asset value. This is a more risk-averse method of playing the stock market. Unit trust funds and investment companies are the only pooled investment vehicles that have been operational in the EAC investment industry for a long time, though from 2014 a variety of many other such vehicles have been introduced such as the real estate investment trusts so as both to boost the real estate industry but also enjoy the enormous benefits in the housing sector.

viii)   Commingled Funds

Commingled funds are partnerships of investors that pool their funds. The management firm that organizes the partnership, for example, a bank or insurance company, manages the funds for a fee. Typical partners in a commingled fund might be trusts or retirement benefit schemes with portfolios much larger than those of most individual investors, but still too small to warrant managing on a separate basis.

Commingled funds are similar in form to open-end unit trust funds. Instead of shares, though, the fund offers "units", which are bought and sold at net asset value. A financial intermediary may offer an array of different commingled funds, eg, a money market fund, a bond fund, and a common stock fund.

ix)   Endowment Funds

These are permanent assets such as money, securities, or properties that are invested to earn income that is used to support an organization's activities for a variety of reasons as per the organization. An endowment is a portfolio of assets donated to a nonprofit institution to aid in its support, and in their medieval origins, endowments consisted of farmland donated to churches, which would earn rental income from the land's tenant farmers. In modern times, endowment assets are held in financial instruments, which may include real estate investments too and in an invested portfolio, the modern endowment can realize capital appreciation as well as current income.

Endowments are legal entities that have been funded for the expressed purpose of permanently funding the endowment's institutional sponsor (i.e., beneficiary). The intent is to preserve asset principal value in perpetuity and to use the income generated for budgetary support of specific activities of institutions such as: universities, hospitals, museums, and charitable. An endowment fund, is created when Board of Trustee or University Council or Donor, specify that a gift is to be invested and only the income earned from the gift investment, may be spent for a specific purpose. The gift amount is referred to as the principal or corpus. It is held in a fund that is managed by the Finance Department or Development Department of the organization or delegated to a Fund Investment Management Company. Endowment fund administration is well represented in the Laws of Uganda from the Trusts Act of 1950s during the colonial times.

OBJECTIVES OF ENDOWMENT FUNDS

The main objective of an Endowment fund is, to provide and guarantee greater financial sustainability and autonomy in all institutional programs.

Specific Objectives

- *Sustainability: to enhance the ability to plan for the long-term and to meet the future needs of the institutions in particular: infrastructure development, research & publication, business development, community service, etc.*
- *Autonomy: to increase an institution's independence from funding trends outside its control.*
- *Leveraging: to be used by the institution as a basis for acquiring additional funding from various organizations in the field of the organization's operations.*

How funds are sold to the public

Most of these funds have an underwriter that has exclusive rights to distribute shares to investors. They are generally marketed to the public either directly by the fund underwriter or indirectly through brokers acting on behalf of the underwriters. This could be done through: mails; offices of the fund; over the phone; over the internet; on financial pages of local newspapers; through the sales force.

Role/ Benefits of PIVs in the Financial System

Diversification of Risk: investors can secure a much wider diversification of risk, because these funds usually invest in different investments since studies have proved that the greater the diversification of a portfolio, the lower the risk in relation to the return

Access to a variety of financial assets: by investing a small sum (either in a lump sum or on a regular saving basis), an investor through the PIVs can achieve a personal portfolio spread over a diversity of financial assets.

Lower Transaction Costs: by investing in PIVs, investors incur lower costs than if they were to buy and sell a portfolio of individual securities directly. This is because transaction costs are generally inversely related to the size of the transaction, and investors benefit from the fund manager's ability to deal in larger quantities of shares at lower average dealing costs. Besides, fund managers can also allocate portfolios more efficiently than can individual investors.

Professional Management: due to the complexity of analyzing information regarding individual securities, most individuals do not have the professional skills to manage their own investments. PIVs provide full time professional management in a direct and simple form and this is especially important where market information is not widely available.

Investor Protection: PIVs have succeeded in developed markets due to an effective legal and regulatory framework. People need to have confidence that their money is protected from fraud, theft and other abuses. The Capital markets Act, the Retirement Benefits Act, the Collective Investment Scheme Act, among other regulations provides the desired regulatory framework that will protect investors.

Chapter 13

CENTRAL BANKING

"Ensuring price and financial stability are critical objectives of modern Central Banks."

i) Background information

Glance

Central banks are the most important players in financial markets world over since they are the custodians of the financial system soundness, the monetary authorities charged with the management of the credit control mechanisms, commonly referred to as the monetary policy. Their actions significantly affect not only: interest rates structures, the availability of credit, the money supply, and their impact on financial markets and other macroeconomic fundamentals; but also personal finance, corporate finance and public finance. Given the fundamental role, it is only prudent for us as finance students, analysts and practitioners to understand the regional Central Banks, their role as the custodian of the financial system, and also prudential management of the sovereign assets (basically the foreign exchange reserves) and their contribution not only to macroeconomic stability but to external-economy vulnerability management.

EAC CENTRAL BANKS

History of Central Banking & Islamic Banking

Bank of England (UK's central bank) was the first ever central bank in the world, founded in 1694. The others came much later, including the popular Federal Reserve System in the US in 1913, and the Bank of Japan in 1882.

The Sudan Currency Board was established in 1957, then later in 1959 the enactment of Bank of Sudan Act which consequently established the Central bank in 1960; becoming one of the first operational central banking institutions in Africa. In 1970s, the concept of Islamic banking appeared in the region and Sudan became a proponent of the same actually up to date since she is a major player in the Islamic financial system both in utilization and development of Islamic banking products. This, in fact, saw it convert its entire financial system in the 1990s into a Sharia-compliant model. But for South Sudan, even then, though part of the larger Sudan, it didn't fully embrace this system. In 2005, the signing of the Comprehensive Peace Agreement provided for a dualistic financial and banking system during the interim period. The Bank of Southern Sudan was established as a branch of the Central Bank of Sudan undertaking a conventional banking system while Sudan operated under an Islamic financial system; though both maintained one monetary policy but each supervising and chartering financial institutions in its jurisdiction.

Many central banks in the EAC were established in 1966 after the abolition of the East Africa Currency Board, which used to serve as the monetary authority (defacto Central Bank) for the following countries: Uganda, Tanganyika, Ethiopia, Eriteria, Somaliland, Zanzibar, and Kenya. It was established in 1919 to ensure prompt and timely convertibility of E.A shilling into UK pound sterling, and vice versa at a fixed rate but later from 1962, it also acted as a clearing agent for commercial banks. This was abolished due to huge imbalances in the level of economic development of the member states, which rendered its work pretty difficult to treat them equally, but also from a public financial management perspective of each state, the challenge was compounded by the differences in natural resources endowment of these economies. This necessitated the establishment of a Central Bank in each member state so as to foster both economic stability and financial soundness of each country. Bank of Uganda, Central Bank of Kenya, and Bank of Tanzania were consequently set up by the various Acts (according to their countries) in 1966 which empower them to foster macroeconomic stability and financial system soundness in their countries.

B.O.U Annual Report (2013) informs that the Constitution of the Republic of Uganda 1995 grants Bank of Uganda the mandate as the central bank of Uganda; and the Bank of Uganda Act (Cap 51) vests the authority of the Bank in the Board of Directors who should conduct its affairs with prudence, and accountability by ensuring the Bank's compliance with the law and business ethics. Both the Bank's Board of Directors and the management wing are headed by the Governor. Most EAC central banks' mission is "To foster price stability and a sound financial system"; and envisions "To be a centre of excellence in upholding macroeconomic stability".

Figure 3.11
Central Banking Performance in EAC Region
NB: Exchange rate used was as at 30th June 2015

Country	Banking Asset % to GDP	Banking Assets (USD)	Foreign Exchange Reserves (USD)	
			2014	2015
Burundi	29.10%	896,100,000.00	-	-
Kenya	64.10%	36,363,636,363.64	8,555,000,000.00	7,212,000,000.00
Rwanda	30.00%	2,801,120,448.18	992,700,000.00	885,700,000.00
Tanzania	29.50%	13,865,906,351.41	4,377,000,000.00	4,094,000,000.00
Uganda	29.50%	7,995,154,451.85	3,394,000,000.00	2,912,000,000.00
Average	36.44%	12,384,383,523.02	3,463,740,000.00	3,020,740,000.00

Source: EAC Central Banks; WBG (2015)

BANKING ASSETS

By and large, the total EAC banking assets have been steadily and significantly rising from 2012 at USD 45.2 Billion; yet in 2014 they had risen by 15% to USD 52 Billion; and furthermore by end 2015, EAC banking assets had grown by 17% (year on year) to approx. USD 62 Billion. Banking assets across the EAC region collectively grew more than 2.5 times faster than the regional GDP growth even before the global financial distress of 2015 that saw the IMF revise down wards the world economic growth (including the EAC region).

Kenya has the highest Banking Assets % to GDP at 64%. All other countries average around 29%. The same trend is reflected in the Banking Assets and Foreign Exchange Reserves, with Kenya having the largest amount. This is definitely because the Kenyan economy is larger than the various other economies within East Africa. Kenya remains the dominant banking market in the region, despite its banking supervision crisis that has so far seen at least three banks being closed by the Central Bank of Kenya within less than a year. It holds more than half of total banking assets, with growth outpacing even that of its original regional peers during the last 5 years period.

The EAC share of total Sub-Saharan Africa banking market is progressively rising though other markets like South Africa, Nigeria and Mauritius remain by far the most dominant banking markets currently.

Larger banking markets in the EAC region like Kenya and Tanzania enjoy larger economies of scale which result in higher returns to stakeholders across the value-chain compared to smaller markets like Uganda and Rwanda although they also enjoy higher margins than those in larger markets. Other EAC banking markets like Burundi and South Sudan need to work on their market fundamentals but also most importantly the access to available and reliable large samples of data that can facilitate rational analysis so as to gauge their performance along their EAC peers.

On the other hand, global studies that relate economic growth (GDP) to growth of the banking sector maintain that outstanding economic growth like that of the EAC regional bloc significantly provide a major stimulus for banks. Forecasts indicated that between 2013 and 2017: Uganda's banking sector would double in size; Rwandan banking system would follow closely behind; Tanzanian banking system would likely be 1.5 times larger; and Kenyan banking sector would also grow stronger at close to 75% larger than her current levels. It is imperative to note that though Kenya currently dominates the EAC banking space, the strongest growth in the near future are most likely expected to stem from the fastest growing economies such as Uganda, Tanzania, and possibly Rwanda.

FOREIGN RESERVES

Most central banks in the East African Community have been able to achieve both the IMF and EAC central banking requirements of maintaining an import cover for foreign exchange reserves of at least 4 months. This has seen the National Bank of Rwanda maintain a 4.02 months import cover as at June 2015; Kenya had a 5.7 months import cover in June 2014 but due to Central Bank of Kenya's intervention in forex markets in 2015, the import cover decreased to 4.6 months as at June 2015. And this is the same story for Uganda whereby the sovereign assets (forex reserves) were depleted due to the 2015 foreign currency volatilities and the Bank of Uganda's interventionist policy in the forex markets to preserve the financial system soundness but still it maintains the more than 4 months import cover as per the EAC macroeconomic convergence criteria benchmark. On the other hand, the Tanzania financial system was worst hit by global financial infrastructure woes because, with an import cover 4.2 months in 2014, the forex reserves were significantly exhausted to 3.6 months of import cover in 2015 which definitely expose the frontier market economy to adverse external shocks (vulnerability) and domestic macroeconomic flaws if not well managed.

Burundi has always been an outlier in most macroeconomic and financial system fundamentals due to political and financial system risks that have almost dragged her to nearly a "struggling" financial system. This saw her record foreign exchange reserves that can just cover 3.6 months of import cover in 2014; and this situation was further complicated in 2015 whereby Burundi was characterized by conflict and even ravaging the existing financial and political system infrastructure (compromising her forex reserves position further).

ii)   **Functions as Custodians & Controllers of the EAC Financial Systems** (Roles Played by EAC central banks in Development of EAC Region)

Governments use policies geared towards managing the macroeconomics of a country, and these measures are called Stabilization policies which are further broadly categorized as fiscal policy (largely governed by government spending and taxation); and monetary policy (credit control and money supply).

The following roles are outlined by the respective EAC Central Banks' Acts, and they are aimed at ensuring the financial soundness of the economy through its macroeconomic policies, and at the same time operate on a commercial basis by offering services to commercial banks. Among others, these are:

- *Currency Issuing & Management of Money supply; this is EAC central banks' prime role, which actually requires the highest degree of efficiency and trust, since it has the monopoly of issuing currency to match the resources accumulated by various sectors in the economy since the variables are highly correlated for macroeconomic stability. The supply of money should neither be too much nor too little so as to promote economic growth. Money issued by central banks is termed as legal tender, both in form of notes and coins, and it is empowered to settle debts. On the contrary, they keeps some resources to back the EAC domestic currencies but also to justify any new currency issuing in case the need arises, and these include: gold; silver; Special Drawing Rights (SDRs); foreign exchange reserves in currencies eg U.S dollars, Euros, Pound Sterling, Canadian dollars. Besides the above, the fiduciary issue of currency is backed by factors such as: government expenditures; balance of payment position; credit and foreign exchange transactions.*

- *Banker to the Government: well as commercial banks are bankers to the general public, they are bankers to the EAC governments in the following ways: transacts/ pays for the government; custodian/ receiver of government's finance in form of taxes & foreign aid; repayment of foreign loans; lender/ financier to government projects for short & long term basis.*

- *Advisor to the Government: this is in areas such as; economic policies, resource mobilisation (raising finance), management of private sector from financial management perspective (which project either the State or private sector should finance), management of inflation & value of the shilling.*

- *Manager of Public Debt: this is finance raised from citizens through the sale of government securities (treasury: bills, notes, and bonds) so as to finance different activities. EAC central banks do this by: receiving the finance; advising on interest rates, and the conditions for the sale of those securities.*

- *Banker to Commercial banks: EAC central banks do this role through roles such as: acting as a clearing house for receipts (inter-bank clearing facility); sole custodian of reserves & deposits from commercial banks' reserve ratio; short-term lending to commercial banks for liquidity problems; acts as arbitrator in* disputes among commercial banks; authorised to sell or discount promissory notes & bills of exchange for commercial banks; financial controller/ inspection of commercial banks' activities.

- **Creator of Financial Institutions:** they are charged with the responsibility of establishing a wide range of financial services given the needs of the financial system. This entails the development of financial markets, basically capital markets for long-term financing towards economic development, but also the money markets and possibly the derivative markets for a sound financial system.

- **Controller of Foreign exchange:** this is the finance that an economy earns through the sale of goods and services to foreign economies, and it is in form of foreign currencies such as; Euros, Dollars, Pound sterling, Yen, Francs, Yuan, etc. The management of foreign exchange is aimed at fostering Balance of Payment (B.O.P) surplus ie favourable balance between inflows from abroad (receipts) and outflows abroad (payments); EAC central banks will allow as little foreign exchange to leave the country so as to manage the macroeconomic stability of Uganda but also to hedge the economy against external vulnerability from the global financial system. Therefore, they are officially the sole sellers of foreign currencies in the EAC region and commercial banks can do this only with the approval of EAC central banks, and Bureaux de Change are only transact on behalf of the regional central banks that is why they are obliged to submit reports to BOU in a bid to compile statistics regarding the B.O.P position of the country but also the data is used in international trade decision-making process.

- **Financial Manager to Commercial banks:** banks are required by law to follow the guidance of EAC central banks in their activities and operations, according to Financial Institutions Act & EAC central banks' Acts. This could be in areas such as: investment areas for banks according to State's development plans; submission of *periodic reports for statistics to judge the financial soundness of the economy; corporate financial planning; advice in the process of credit creation; advice on expansion of bank branches.*

- **Lender of the last resort:** *despite its role as the custodian and regulator of the financial system, EAC central banks can also act as lenders of the last resort in the following scenarios: under high inflationary situations that could occasion a banking crisis; when commercial banks fail to raise requisite capital for huge investments due to liquidity constraints.*

Influencing the value of domestic currency through initiatives like intervening in currency markets, which all central banks actively did during the 2015 global foreign currency volatilities.

Providing a depositors' protection scheme for bank deposits, which partly insures depositors' funds in the event of closure of the bank and/or any other negative eventualities; a case in point is Kenya's banking system that witnessed the closure of at least three banks within a period of less than a year.

They are charged with **regulating the credit creation** capacity of commercial banks as part of the monetary policy by keeping it below the levels at which it would not increase money supply so much that it accelerates inflation.

iii)   EAC Central Banks & Financial Stability

"Ensuring financial stability is a collaborative effort of all regulators of the financial system: Ministries of Finance, Central Banks, Capital Markets, Retirement Benefits, Revenue Authorities, Insurance Regulators, Communication Regulators."

Financial stability is the resilience of the financial system to unanticipated adverse shocks while enabling the continuing functioning of the financial system intermediation process. A stable financial system contributes to broader economic growth and rising living standards. The financial system performs one of the most important functions in the welfare of citizens by supporting the ability of households and firms to hold and transfer financial assets with confidence. EAC central banks are committed to promoting the economic and financial welfare of East Africans by actively overseeing a stable and sound financial system through the provision of critical services such as: liquidity & lender-of-last-resort facilities; overseeing key foreign and domestic clearing & settlement systems; conducting & publishing analyses and research; collaborating with various domestic & international policy-making bodies so as to develop policy.

Financial stability is largely the product of interactions amongst the macroeconomy and the financial system; and the macroeconomy is basically interested in the following financial agents:
i) Households. ii) Corporations. iii) Government.
iv) Real estate prices

Financial stability is done through both micro-prudential and macro-prudential analyses: macro-prudential analysis is a system-wide analysis concerned with vulnerabilities that pose a risk for systemic stability rather than the failure of individual financial institutions. On the other hand, micro-prudential is the surveillance of individual financial institutions, payment systems, and markets separately so as to ensure their smooth functioning and compliance with regulations. Systemic vulnerabilities could usher in the following: loss of confidence in the financial system, increase in bad credit, falling asset prices, illiquidity in financial markets, lower investments, contraction of the economy, and disruption of payment systems.

On the other hand, financial system instability can also be defined as widespread distress in the financial system involving the failure of major financial institutions; and consequent failure of key functions of the financial system such as the payments systems, interbank market, and credit extension. However, systemic risk may build up and lead to a financial crisis even when individual financial institutions are complying with prudential regulations.

Therefore, financial stability ought to be viewed from a perspective of a balanced framework for supervision, and proper regulation of innovation that are crucial for stable economic growth. The challenge in all this, is to minimize the threats to systemic stability, while allowing for the requisite expansion and innovation for the growth of the financial system. Financial stability is a moving target and a sound regulatory framework is always a work-in-progress. The financial system comprises:

i)   Financial Institutions (Banks, pension funds, insurance). Financial institutions and processes underpin the functioning of any modern economy – through the role they play in:
- *Facilitating the allocation of capital/credit*
- *Price discovery*
- *Payment services and the exchange of goods and services*
- *Redistribution of risk*

ii)   Financial Markets and Assets (money, equities, foreign currency)

iii) Financial system Infrastructure, which provide the networks that enable transactions to occur, and interaction between international and domestic systems. But also financial system risk management

iv)   Financial Agents (households, businesses/organizations and government)

FINANCIAL SYSTEM RESILIENCE

It is very prudent to assess and also ensure financial system resilience, which is a function of financial system stress testing, tools of financial stability analysis. This can best be done using macro-prudential analysis by introducing system-wide or general equilibrium dimensions whose outcome depend on the size and nature of the initial shock, the buffers of financial institutions and their behavioral responses to the shocks.

There is need to embed stress tests into the financial stability policy frameworks across the EAC monetary authorities but keeping in mind that that macro-prudential stress testing is simply one of the many tools to assess systemic resilience. It ought, therefore, to be treated as a complement to other tools such as early warning indicators, and basically the ongoing supervision individual financial institutions (micro-prudential analysis).

NB: One of the EAC Central banks' Governors, Prof. Benno Ndulu (Governor, Bank of Tanzania) was awarded as "Central Bank Governor of the Year 2015 in Africa" by Africa Investor (Ai), an International Investment and Communications Group during its 8th annual CEO Investment Summit in New York, USA. But also closer to winning the same award were fellow EAC Central banks' Governors such as Uganda and Rwanda; the criteria includes: competence in their field and how that competence has benefited investments in their countries, and their contribution to developing a hospitable environment within their countries and/or their sub-regions such as EAC region for Prof. Ndulu. Central bank Governors are so instrumental in improving the EAC region's investment climate and also working to raise the region's investment profile.

iv)   EAC Central banks' Prudential Management of the Foreign Exchange Reserves

"Effective communication of macro-prudential policy is essential in ensuring the resilience of the financial system."

EAC central banks are guided by three cardinal objectives in sovereign assets (foreign reserves) management, which are chronologically followed in importance for macroeconomic vitality. These objectives are: safety of the funds (reserves); liquidity requirements of the financial system; and reasonable and consistent returns from investments, and these objectives influence, and are also influenced by both the investment philosophy of the economy and the development agenda of the country.

Objective 1: Safety of the assets (reserves)

EAC regional central banks are the custodians not only of the sovereign assets (national wealth) but also of the EAC financial systems, whose mission is majorly to "foster price stability and a sound financial system". The fact that the EAC economies are among the struggling Frontier market economies, the only option they have is being a very conservative investor given the volatility of the economies and the relatively low volumes of current assets under management (foreign exchange reserves). These central banks are guided by the old investment adage, "Better be sure but not sorry", as it manages the sovereign assets in volatile global financial markets.

Given both their custodial role and being a conservative investor, EAC central banks' reserve portfolio is divided into two portions: the internally & externally managed portfolios. The internally managed portfolio is mainly invested on short term (0-1 year) money market instruments, which are aimed at boosting and managing the level of economic activities in the country through: employment creation, equitable distribution of national income, boosting the GDP. The investment horizon is rather short (0-1 year) due to low absorptive capacity but majorly safety of the assets since this time period is quite predictable, but also the investment is purely in fixed-income securities of high growth companies with sound governance systems within the country. As at June 30, 2013, the internally managed portfolio of the Bank of Uganda amounted to US$ 1,864 B; this is according to strategic benchmarks by the Bank (B.O.U Annual Report, 2013).

Besides, externally managed portfolio was mainly invested in longer term (1-5 years) fixed income instruments, and it stood at US$ 1,036 B. This was prudently done with the help of internationally reputable fund managers because all the EAC central banks do not have the infrastructure and capacity to do active investment management due to huge assets under management, and heavy time resources required in investment research. JP Morgan, Strategic Fixed Income, and Goldman Sachs, and others were allocated the external portfolio to be invested in very stable economies of the Great 7 (G-7) for external-economy risk management.

Due to prioritizing the safety of the assets, EAC central banks' strategic asset allocation doesn't allow for investment in other asset classes regardless of their returns, and apparent safety and liquidity such as: listed equity; private equity; real property; real estate; debt instruments from both corporations and central banks (governments) which are not in the G-7 economic zone.

This is because these are not safe and some are highly illiquid which would cost not only the sovereign assets but the soundness of the financial system, and facilitate its failure to eradicate extreme poverty and hunger. The safety requirement doesn't permit investments in East African Community economies due to high volatility in these economies. It also requires issuers to be of a certain credit quality, backed by asset liability structures as core determinants: if any EAC economy has a liability in dollars, the respective central bank will buy asset denominated in dollars (as a currency).

Finally, though the EAC combined sovereign assets have grown to a tune of US$ 15.1 Billion as at end June 2015 (excluding Burundi & South Sudan) representing more 4.5 months of import cover for the EAC region, these assets under management are way below some of the small hedge funds in the U.S. Besides, these EAC central banks are very conservative due to fear of losing national wealth like the Colombian experience where Central bank tried to be an aggressive investor to the point of venturing in other asset classes like equity and more currencies but it lost 30% of its sovereign assets in 1990s; the governor and minister resigned, and they were later imprisoned.

Objective 2: Liquidity requirements of the financial system

EAC central banks are the bankers to the EAC governments: due to both the short-term and long-term obligations of these States such as debt management, public expenditure, and investments which are recurrent and some long-term in nature; and needs permanent cash flows, liquidity management is key in sovereign asset management. These central banks manage an internal portfolio which is invested in highly liquid financial assets of financially sound firms with: good governance systems; capacity to contribute to GDP; and employment creation in the country. Besides, the externally managed portfolio is also invested in highly liquid fixed-income securities in the strongest and safest G-7 economies such as: USA, UK, Germany, France, Canada, Australia, and Japan; due to their solid and expertise in operations. This is done in treasury bills, bonds and deposits with governments such as USA and other G-7s; deposits in liquid funds with Multi-lateral institutions such as the World Bank, Bank of International Settlements, and others; corporate bonds from highly rated corporate issuers by international standards (AAA rating) such as General Motors, Ford, among others. Besides, investment is basically done in foreign sound currencies like US dollar, Great Britain Pound sterling, Euro, and recently added Canadian dollar but also Chinese Renminbi since international assets tend to perform better than domestic assets when currency hedged.

NB: In 2015, the IMF approved the Chinese Renminbi to join its basket of Special Drawing Rights (SDR) currencies, thereby unofficially declaring this BRICS currency as a safe and liquid asset. In order to achieve this SDR status, the People's Bank of China (PBoC) had to demonstrate a commitment to let its currency be increasingly determined by market forces. This will serve to increase financial and exchange rate stability by reducing the USD dominance of many transactions. This arises from the fact that the USD index strengthened on an annual basis by 11% in October leading to an equal depreciation of 11% by the Euro and Japanese Yen; while the British Pound only depreciated by 5% annually.

As a liquidity management system, these central banks manage sovereign assets in tranches such as: liquidity tranche for in-house highly liquid assets in instruments like treasury bills and bonds; emergency tranche for in-house government expenditures; and investment tranche through both in-house and external companies. B.O.U Annual Report (2011) informs that by end-June 2011, US$77.91 million held in the liquidity tranche was managed in the form of repurchase agreements, overnight deposits and current account balances; US$50 million was held in the emergency tranche in the form of deposits and Treasury bills of up to 3 months; and the investment tranche had US$1,174.96 million held in bank deposits, Treasury bills, the World Bank Central Bank Facility (CBF), Equity at Afri-Exim Bank and US Treasury bonds under the Reserves Advisory and Management Programme (RAMP).

EAC central banks further manage public debt by using simulation software (program) and the optimizer tool that guides in crucial public financial management variables such as: short-term obligations; imports requirements; intervention in foreign exchange markets; risk budget analysis for decisions on efficient portfolios. Given the macro-prudential liquidity management, the EAC region has had a fairly stable economic growth averaging approx. 6% per annum (a result of good macroeconomic policies).

Objective 3: Reasonable and Consistent Returns

Despite the previous two objectives being of supreme importance, these central banks are equally mandated to grow the sovereign assets but with reasonable and consistent returns (national wealth creation) vis-a-vis sound macroeconomic stability. In effect, though the sovereign asset preservation objective takes precedent and significantly affects the strategic asset allocation, reserves managers have found themselves seeking instruments with higher yields in an effort to enhance returns. This objective explains why EAC central banks largely invest its assets in only: G-7 economies; highly-rated central and commercial banks' fixed-income instruments in those economies; fixed-income securities from AAA-rated corporate issuers. Besides, the regional central banks use international asset managers like JP Morgan which are highly experienced in global financial markets but it also gives them performance benchmarks, and advises on specific currencies as an asset class, and investments are basically in US and Euro denominated bonds.

By end-June 2015, the Net Foreign Assets owned by the Kenyan financial system declined from KSH 615.4 Billion from June 2014 to KSH 565.2 Billion; the fall reflects a drawdown of official forex reserves following CBK's interventions in the forex market. This saw forex reserves decrease from USD 8.5 Billion (5.7 months of import cover) in June 2014 to USD 7.2 Billion (4.6 months of import cover) in June 2015; besides, around the same period Kenya's banking system's total forex holdings were USD 9.4 Billion whereby commercial banks forex reserves were USD 2.2 Billion. These financials are rather good indicators of prudent sovereign asset management generally by the EAC Central banks' departments of Financial Markets.

Levy-Yeyati (2008), in their study on the trade-off between cost of holding reserves and their potential benefits, argue that foreign reserves act as implicit collateral against borrowing: a high level of reserves lowers the risk premium associated with financial vulnerabilities of emerging and frontier market economies. This signifies that a relatively aggressive investment philosophy that has led to the current reasonable and consistent returns in sovereign assets responds to: dealing comprehensively with the debt problems of developing countries through national and international measures in order to make debt sustainable in the long-term.

CRITICAL ANALYSIS OF EAC CENTRAL BANKS

It is the regulator of the financial and monetary system of the EAC countries, which is aimed at protecting the economy from both domestic and external shocks so as to achieve the national macroeconomic objectives.

It has a major resource mobilisation role which is aimed at availing financial and other forms of resource to the government to fund its annual budgets but also perspective plans in a bid to attain economic development.

The Central banks serve a critical role of lender of the last resort in the financial system for financial institutions basically banks so as to facilitate further capital formation and boost economic growth

The regional central banks also play an interventionist role in the financial system whereby, for matter of financial system soundness and macroeconomic stability, it intervene at time in the market forces that rule in the financial markets so as to influence and guide all financial players and intermediaries towards the government's desired economic objectives and outcomes. This is done the operations of the monetary policy instruments that affects most financial markets.

v) Limitations of Central banks as Custodian of Financial System

As already explained, the central banks, the custodian of the financial system works through fiscal and monetary policy instruments to foster prudent macroeconomic management and financial soundness in the EAC region. On the contrary, these policy instruments have limitations, and among others these are:

- *Large informal financial system whereby billions of money (large sums of money) are kept at home or hoarded by various people for various reasons eg fear of high taxation, negative attitude* towards & ignorance about banking services, but not kept in banks.

- Lack of cooperation between commercial banks and many EAC central banks, whereby banks are not transparent enough to disclosure all their transactions which hinder central banks from controlling money supply.

- Some policy instruments like selective credit control which directs banks to specific areas where to give credit facilities like agriculture or Karamoja region may not be of interest to banks due to both high risks and low returns; hence, frustrating the central banks' initiatives.

- Most banks don't get their credit/finance from central banks, and as such increases in bank rates may not affect the rates charged commercial banks. Besides, some banks charge different rates from those approved by regional central banks, which frustrates all the initiatives by the Central bank.

- Regional central banks have currently failed to synchronise/ streamline interest rates in financial markets: market rates don't change with Central bank rate (CBR). It is evident that the success of CBR depends on the extent to which other financial markets' rates change along with the CBR since the theory of bank rate policy presume that other rates of interest/ prices prevailing in financial markets change in the direction of the change in the bank rate. The failure of EAC central banks to satisfy this critical condition has partly catalysed its ineffectiveness in credit control measures.

- EAC central banks' custodianship role of the regional financial systems is complicated by the existence of a big number of non-bank financial intermediaries which are not directly under the control of the monetary authority yet they do a lot of funds mobilisation and financing activities basically in the capital markets.

- *Undeveloped financial markets: since money and capital markets in most EAC economies are rather undeveloped, with very few financial assets, and only traded by a few knowledgeable individuals who render central banks' initiatives of controlling the financial system fruitless.*

- *High liquidity preference by most East Africans: due to the alarming levels of financial illiteracy and also dubious dealings, majority of banks and individuals in Uganda enjoy keeping their money with themselves and so, they can't be influenced by monetary policies. They end up disorganising the commodities markets and consequently lead to macroeconomic disequilibria in the EAC region.*

- *EAC banking sector is over-saturated by foreign banks since most of the high performing banks are foreign owned; this can render central banks' monetary policy ineffective by either selling foreign assets or drawing money from their head offices even when central banks have put in place a tight monetary policy.*

- *Besides, the success of EAC central banks' monetary policy instruments like bank rate is greatly dependent not only on the elasticity of interest rates, but that of wages, costs and prices. This implies that when BOU changes its CBR; wages, costs and prices should automatically adjust themselves either to lower or higher levels depending on the CBR. On the contrary, given the inelastic (and of the CBR insensitive) wages and prices regardless of either inflationary or deflationary situations, the EAC Central banks can't effectively act as the custodian of the regional financial system.*

DEDUCTION OF PART 3:

With the banking system contributing the biggest portion of the overall financial system across the EAC region yet banking fundamentals and metrics are performing dismally in comparison to other African regions. This can be evidenced in: very few bank accounts compared to mobile money accounts; exorbitantly high interest rate regime that has led to financial distress in some EAC economies; limited geographical coverage and product range; and a curtail type of banking market structure across the EAC Bloc. On the other hand, the regional banking system has achieved relatively good performance in capital adequacy ratio, Non-Performing Loans, Private sector credit and also intermediation margin.

Most NBFIs are at nascent stages in most EAC economies, apart from Kenya which enjoys a long and rich history in the long-term investment industry that includes pensions, insurance, capital markets, and private equity. On the other hand, there is huge potential for activity, once integrated into one financial system and market for financial services, but also if well incentivized through rational and harmonized policy formulation.

Central banking operations are relatively good (monetary tightening saved the EAC regional macroeconomy from the 2008 and 2015 volatile global economic conditions). Other regulators of the financial system are also doing a good job although some are over-regulating the already small, nascent and constrained financial system, which is becoming a disincentive to growth and product innovation. A self-regulatory (deregulation) environment would be good, coupled to a Consolidated regulatory environment that is two-tiered in the EAC financial system but with efficient management of the financial system resilience by the proposed Central Bank of the East African Community.

PART 4
COMMODITY & FINANCIAL MARKETS

These are markets in which funds are transferred from financial agents (households, businesses, and government) who have a surplus of available funds to financial agents who have a shortage of available funds. Financial markets, unlike most other markets, serve the important role of linking the present and the future. Those who supply funds (savers) do so because they want to convert some of their current income into future purchasing power. Those who demand funds (borrowers) do so because they want to invest today in order to have additional capital in the future to produce goods & services. Thus, well-functioning financial markets are important not only for current generations but also for future generations who will inherit many of the resulting benefits.

A financial market is the place where financial assets (intangible asset whose value is derived from contractual claim such as bank deposits, bonds, and stocks) are created or transferred. These can be broadly categorized into: money markets, capital markets, derivative markets, foreign exchange markets, mortgage markets, and closely linked the commodities' exchange. The key functions are:

1. Assist in creation and allocation of credit and liquidity.
2. Serve as intermediaries for mobilization of savings.
3. Help achieve balanced economic growth.
4. Offer financial convenience.

Contemporary Financial Market Trends

Massive Regulatory Reforms: across all financial systems there is pressure from regulators and general investing public for transparency; trader must explain the market and the trade so as to leave no room for insider trading, market abuse but also money laundering tendencies.

Decreasing Equity Volumes: global stock markets are continuously posting substantially reduced commissions, execution and margin revenue. This is partly due anxiety amongst investors, risk aversion in the wake of the global financial crises (market crashes), etc.

Macroeconomic, Political and Cross Asset Impacts: Forces even domestic-only traders to track the global market since in the contemporary global financial system, global events significantly affect even small local firms due to increased exposures in foreign currency, investors and commodity prices.

Complex Market Structures: Venue proliferation significantly increases liquidity fragmentation which is a disincentive to corporate growth.

Automated Trading: A trader no longer needs the guidance of a broker so as to choose a financial asset thanks to technology whereby one can work on dozens of transactions; staying abreast of the news and events affecting those transactions is now possible.

Chapter 14

MONEY MARKETS

These are markets for short-term financial instruments that are close substitutes for money; they are highly liquid, easily marketable, and with little chance of loss (they are close to being money, hence the name "money market instruments). These markets (a network of markets that are grouped together for short-term finance) provide quick and reliable transfer of short-term debt instruments maturing in hours to not more than two years is used to finance the needs of customers, business, agriculture and governments. This is a market for short-term finances; funds to be used in business for a period ranging just hours to 2 or 3 years.

This is a segment of the financial markets in which financial instruments with high liquidity and short maturities, generally those with one year or less remaining to maturity are traded. Money markets should be instrumental in processing lending rates correctly so that the economy can take off due to efficiency in the flows of funds. Money market is dominated by commercial banks but with various other players in this segment with also a diversity of short-term instruments that are traded.

In the US and the West, money markets have been active since the early 1800s but have become much more important since 1970, when interest rates rose above historic levels, coupled with a regulated ceiling on the rate that banks could pay for deposits, resulted in a rapid outflow of funds from financial institutions in the late 1970s and early 1980s. This outflow in turn caused many banks and savings and loans to fail. The industry regained its health only after massive changes were made to bank regulations with regard to money market interest rates.

MONEY MARKET INSTRUMENTS

Treasury bills; these are short term securities that are issued by governments. These are non-interest bearing instruments (zero coupon instruments). Across the East African region, various Treasury bills (91-day, 182-day and 364-day) are issued every two weeks and each Member State has an annual issuance schedule that guides both the government in public resource mobilization but also the investment public in rational portfolio management. For the period ending December 2015, total stock of Treasury bills stood at UGX 3,282.9 billion in the Ugandan Treasury bills market. Below is the trend analysis of the 364-Day Treasury bills and the effect of inflation on the yields for the last 15 years.

Figure 4.1

TRENDS IN THE 364-DAY TREASURY BILL , INFLATION & USH/US $
(JANUARY 2000-DECEMBER 2015, %)

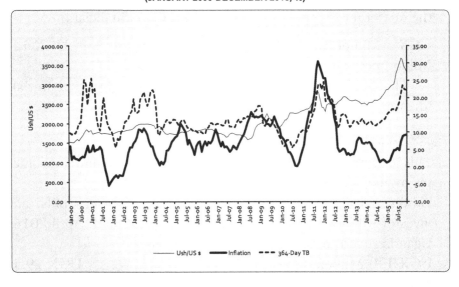

Source: CMA-Uganda (2016)

TBs vs Rental (property) Income

Due to the prevalent lack of financial information, many investors have been exposed only to one asset class that actually has a weakness of high liquidity risk (property/ real estate). Using a simple illustration, et me build a rationale for investments in the bond market (particularly Treasury securities) as opposed to earning rental income from owning property/building in an urban setting in Uganda.

Assuming that the initial outlay (investment) is UGX 130 Million.

Property cash flows:
An informal survey indicates that UGX 130 Million can roughly build 3 sets of 2 bedroom houses that are relatively well furnished; and such an investment can earn the investor a monthly rental income of approx. UGX 1 Million. Now we need to establish what the rate of return on investment is given these financial flows.

UGX 1 Million (monthly rent) * 12 months = UGX 12 Million per annum.
   Then, divide the annual rental income by the initial investment;

UGX 12 Million / UGX 130 Million * 100 = 9.2%

This 9.2% return on investment will be subjected to rental income tax by the tax body (URA).
However, UGX 130 Million investment in Treasury bills, an investor will receive 15% per annum (as per the 13th April 2016 Uganda government Treasury bond auctions);
UGX 130 Million * 15% = UGX 19.5 Million
Treasury bills earn UGX 19.5 Million per annum instead of just UGX 12 Million from rental income (of course, it will also be subjected to withholding tax).

Thus, for any rational investor who seeks to maximize returns on his/her investments given budget constraints, he will invest in Treasury bills since they offer higher real returns on investment as opposed to rental income. In this case, we are only considering rental income but not capital gains that come with sell of property.

NB: Treasury bonds give interest twice a year; and the interesting part of it, is that governments (world over) will always borrow because they will always be broke.

Term deposits (Certificate of Deposits- CDs): these are interest bearing bank deposits which can last for as long as 5 years. They are issued by banks in return for deposited money (tradable deposit accounts), since they can be bought and sold just like shares.

Inter-bank Lending: In Uganda, for instance, here has been a steady increase in the interbank turnover (fig 1) with a total of UGX 85.47 trillion traded since 2011 to date, representing an increase of 69.7% from 2011 to 2015.

Commercial paper is used mostly commonly by large companies,

i)   Types of money markets
Thus the money markets consist of the following sub-markets:

a) Call and Notice money market:

This is where money is traded for a period ranging from (just hours) one day to 14 days without collateral security.

b) Commercial bills market:

This is where bills of exchange, promissory notes, and invoices are traded, and /or discounted either with a broker or a bank.

c) Commercial paper market:

This is a market where highly rated companies raise short-term working capital requirements through the issuance of commercial papers for prospective buyers who could be individuals or corporate bodies.

d) *Treasury bills market:*

   This is where the central government through the Secretary to the Treasury of Uganda issues short-term government securities which are traded by commercial banks and dealers so as to bail out the liquidity position of the government of Uganda. In the first week of September 2015, the BOU offered 91 day, 182 day and 364 day T-bills for a total of UGX 10 billion, 25 billion and 135 billion respectively. The 91 day and 182 day issues were oversubscribed while the 364 day issue was undersubscribed. The 91 day received bids worth 34 billion and BOU accepted bids worth 24 billion. The 182 day received bids worth 33 billion and BOU accepted bids worth 29 billion. The 364 day on the other hand received bids worth 114 billion and the BOU only accepted a total of 68 billion

e) *Inter-bank Term market:*

   This type of money market is exclusively for commercial and cooperative banks which trade funds for a short period ranging from 14 days up to 90 days without collateral security. According to UAP Financial services, the interbank market (Uganda) was relatively liquid in the first week of September 2015, with the overnight rate remaining below 10% for most of the week. The o/n rate opened the week at 11.27% and hit a low of 6.76% on Wednesday and the 7 day rate averaged 16% over the week.

f) *Certificate of Deposits (CD):*

   This is a market where commercial banks issue such instruments at a discount on face value to prospective buyers (investors); and the discount rate is determined by market environment.

Players in EAC Money Markets

a)   This finance is issued/ sold by the following organizations: commercial banks; Government; Acceptance & discount houses; merchant banks; companies.

b)　　The following are the buyers of such finance: individuals; companies; institutional investors; Government; financial institutions. Both these categories of players are discussed below:

- *Ministry of Finance trades in this market through selling Treasury securities so as to fund the national budget.*
- *Central banks are key players that buys and sells EAC Treasury bills, notes and bonds as its critical mechanism of monetary policy.*
- *Commercial banks also buy Treasury securities; but also sell certificates of deposit, plus short-term loans; they also offer households accounts that invest in money market securities*
- *Corporations engage in these markets through buying and selling a variety of short-term securities as a part of their cash management system.*
- *Investment firms such as brokerage companies transact on behalf of their clients in these money markets.*
- *Finance houses (companies) also engage in money markets through lending funds to their customers (households) for asset-building purposes.*
- *Insurance companies basically non-life insurance firms trade in such markets so as to maintain the liquidity needed to meet unexpected demands.*
- *Pension funds are also players who maintain funds in money markets instruments anticipating investment in other capital markets instruments like stock and bonds.*
- *Households are also participants through the purchase of money market unit trust funds.*
- *Money market unit trust funds engage in such markets by facilitating small investors to participate in money markets by aggregating their funds to invest in a wide array of money market assets.*

Characteristics of such finance

- *Securities traded in this market are highly negotiable; they can be easily bought and sold.*

- *This finance is usually not secured and as such it depends upon the goodwill of the issuer or buyer.*

- *This finance is short-term and basically used to solve liquidity problems of issuers.*

- *This finance is usually very expensive; essentially because it is unsecured.*

- *Trading in this market is not a perfect market situation since the demand for such finance far exceeds its supply, and then the Bank of Uganda intervenes in this market through its central bank rate (CBR), so as to influence the price or interest rates on such finance.*

Chapter 15
CAPITAL MARKETS (OVERVIEW)

Globally, capital markets have been so instrumental in fostering economic development not only in developed economies but also in emerging economies; and, the value of the volumes of traded securities (market capitalization) of the capital markets in boosting the GDP (as a percentage of GDP) in various economies cannot be underestimated. Ssejjaaka (2011) argues that emerging stock markets grew by over 430% overall and volumes increased from US $ 4b to US $ 4 trillion between 1980 and 2000 and it can be noted that investment opportunities in Sub-Saharan Africa have been expanding greatly with over 522 firms listing on stock exchanges by end of 2007. Kenya is one of the emerging economies in the Sub-Saharan Africa that is reaping big in the capital markets investments since it has more than 50 listed companies and 45 mutual funds, whose total market capitalization has a significant impact on the economy's GDP.

PRIMARY MARKET

This market provides opportunity to issuers of securities, Government as well as corporate, to raise resources to meet their requirements of investment and/or discharge some obligation. The issuers create and issue fresh securities in exchange of funds through public issues and/or as private placement. When equity shares are exclusively offered to the existing shareholders it is called Rights Issue and when it is issued to selected mature and sophisticated institutional investors as opposed to general public it is called Private Placement Issues. Issuers may issue the securities at face value, or at a discount/premium and these securities may take a variety of forms such as equity, debt or some hybrid instruments. The issuers may issue securities in domestic market and /or global financial markets.

This is the market for new long-term capital; securities are issued by the company directly to investors. The company receives the money and issues new security certificates to the investors. Primary issues are used by companies for the purpose of setting up new business or for expanding or modernizing the existing business; a case in point is UMEME Ltd which did an IPO so as to raise finances to invest in pre-paid electricity cards facility and to scale down on its debts. The primary market performs the crucial function of facilitating capital formation in the economy.

Methods of issuing securities in the primary market are:
- *Initial public offer*
- *Right issue (existing company)*
- *Preferential issue*

Figure 4.2   Methods of Issuing Securities

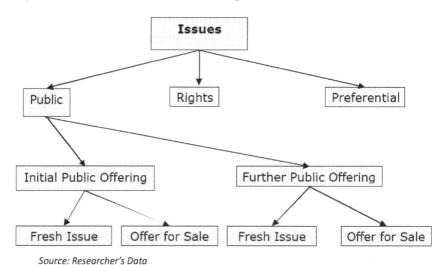

Source: Researcher's Data

Initial Public Offering (IPO) is when an unlisted company makes either a fresh issue of securities or an offer for sale of its existing securities or both for the first time to the public. This paves way for listing and trading of the issuer's securities.

Rights issue is where a listed company proposes to issue fresh securities to its existing shareholders. These are normally offered in a particular ratio to the number of securities held prior to the issue suited for companies which would like to raise capital without diluting stake of its existing shareholders.

Further Public Offer: is whereby an already listed company makes either a fresh issue of securities to the public or an offer for sale to the public.

Preferential issue is an issue of shares or of convertible securities by listed companies to a select group of persons which is neither a rights issue nor a public issue. This is a faster way for a company to raise equity capital. The issuer company has to comply with the Companies Act and the requirements of the CMA.

SECONDARY MARKET

It is a market in which securities are traded after the initial/primary offering gauged by the number of issues traded. In reality, majority of the trading is done in the secondary market, and it comprises of equity markets and the debt markets; whereby the over-the-counter market is the largest secondary market globally.

Functions of Securities Markets

- *Securities Markets is a place where buyers and sellers of securities can enter into transactions to purchase and sell shares, bonds, debentures etc.*
- *They perform an important role of enabling corporate bodies, entrepreneurs to raise resources for their companies and business ventures through public issues.*
- *There is transfer of resources from those having idle resources (investors) to others who have a need for them (business sector) is most efficiently achieved through the securities market.*

- *Securities markets provide channels for reallocation of savings to investments and entrepreneurship.*
- *Savings are linked to investments by a variety of intermediaries, through a range of financial products/securities.*

Africa's Capital Markets' Experience

Africa's capital market industry is growing stronger by the day, this is because funds raised in continent's capital markets in 2014 totaled to USD 10.9 Billion. This saw the highest level of activity in Africa's equity capital markets over the previous five years according to IPO Watch Africa 2014, a report by Pricewaterhouse Coopers. There were a total of 90 IPOs which raised USD 6.3 Billion between 2010 and 2014. Secondary offers raised USD 31.1 Billion, a representation of 83% of total capital raised. This is a great indicator of significant shift from commodity-based sectors to others particularly the financial services sector. Besides, there has been growth of regional stock exchanges outside South Africa, accounting for more than 55% of total IPO capital raised in 2014; which has seen an increase in money raised by companies on other African exchanges by 66% to USD 1 Billion. But by and large, Johannesburg Stock Exchange (JSE) remains the power house and dominant in Africa, since the World Economic Forum's 2014/15 Global Competitiveness Report ranked JSE first in the world for its regulatory framework.

Furthermore, international investors have been so active in African exchanges; between 2013 and 2015, a number of the top 10 IPOs were characterized by either foreign firms raising capital directly on African exchanges or African companies marketing shares through cross-listings and sales to qualified international institutional buyers. A whole USD 370 million and USD 107 million have been raised by nine (9) African firms listing outside the continent, and one (1) non-African firm listing in the continent respectively since 2010.

PERFORMANCE OF EAC CAPITAL MARKETS

These are markets for long-term financing; funds that will be available in business for a period between 7 years to 25 years and above. These markets are not well developed in the EAC region despite most EAC governments' initiatives to stabilize the macroeconomic climate but due to major short-term perspective of many East Africans, coupled with low levels of financial literacy on their part that have seen a sluggish growth of such markets compared to the rest of the world.

Nonetheless, a weak U.S Dollar, prospects of recovery in oil prices and also forecasts of extended monetary policy accommodation are continuing to pile risk appetite. And this has seen the global equities maintain an upward trajectory gaining 11.7% by the 1st Quarter of 2015; meanwhile the EAC equities continue to trade sideways as the banking sector has come under pressure (basically in Kenya) due to the closure of a couple of banks, that will likely trigger higher stringent supervision and weaker credit growth.

Capital markets have potential to provide well-functioning infrastructure such as electricity dams, reliable water supply, wide all-weather roads, airports and railways which are greater enablers of trade, investments and most importantly wealth creation. Capital markets regulators across the EAC region have undertaken a couple of measures to boost the domestic capital markets such as: nationwide education to increase the number of investors from the current dismal numbers. Besides, various stock exchanges have recently started Growth Enterprise Market Segment (GEMS) to provide opportunities for well-governed SMEs with growth potential to acquire long-term financing from the capital markets. Figures indicate that significant volumes have been raised in the EAC regional capital markets as follows:

Figure 4.3
Volumes raised in EAC Capital Markets between the year 2000 and 2015 (In USD)

Activity	Kenya	Uganda	Rwanda	Tanzania
Equity markets	11,802,828,282.83	176,862,507.57	116,666,666.67	
Bond markets	31,252,525,252.53	88,734,100.55	22,408,963.59	
IPOs	740,258,212.12	87,825,560.27	116,666,666.67	362,818,729.72
Rights issues	1,024,103,722.40	13,628,104.18		
Additional offers	70,580,451.46	75,408,843.13		
Government Bonds	-	2,725,620,835.86	177,871,148.46	1,934,631,432.55

Source: EAC CMAs & Securities Exchanges (2015)

Amounts exchanged at approximate Local Currency to USD rates as at 30th June 2015

On the contrary, all EAC capital markets are among the frontier market economies whose performance is not so impressive apart from Kenya's Nairobi Stock Exchange (NSE) that became operational in 1954 (so far 62 years old) with at least 64 listed companies on the NSE but other markets are relatively young capital markets with very few local listed equities and just a handful of cross-listed firms many of which are significantly illiquid. Majority of investors are foreigners who understand the workings and potential benefits of the market; there are very few products on the market, and more than 50% of the listed firms are illiquid. Most shares available to the market are held by institutional investors who don't trade them, for instance NSSF-Uganda alone has about 80% of the float on the Ugandan bourse yet it doesn't trade it. Besides, during the privatization move, a couple of firms had to be listed on the various stock markets across the EAC as a move to distribute the national wealth creation opportunities equally among citizens and institutions in region as the success story has been for those listed firm on the exchange. This implies that serious steps have to be taken by respective EAC governments to liven up the capital markets' activities, among others these are:

- *There is need to benchmark with the best capital markets in the world.*
- *Government should put up tax-free, high interest infrastructural bonds each year, after the country is still greatly deficient in real infrastructure.*
- *There is need to offer domestic investors inflation-adjusted bonds so as to absorb the monies/funds that are kept in pillows and under the mattresses (or pots and in house ceilings) but channel them into financing the real economy.*
- *The State should promote tax efficient alternatives during the process.*
- *There should strong stakeholder interactions that will serve to bridge the gaps/rifts amongst themselves.*
- *Governments should avail listed firms with tax reliefs for some period of time after listing on the USE.*
- *There is need to continually automate the exchange platform so as to increase accessibility even off web eg on phones.*

The capital markets are further sub-divided into the stock (equity) market and the bond (debt) market.

Chapter 16
EQUITY MARKETS

A stock exchange is an association of stock-broking firms; which grew out of a trading carried on in London's coffee houses by business men in the 17th Century.

It brings together lenders and borrowers; and the main lenders are: pension funds; life insurance companies; individuals; investment trusts; unit trusts; general insurance companies.

Private individuals were once the most crucial group but now investors prefer to invest through institutional investor firms.

The market for stocks is undoubtedly the financial market that receives the most attention and scrutiny since great fortunes are made and lost as investors attempt to anticipate the market's ups and downs. The investment world has witnessed an unprecedented period of volatility over the last decade which has had significant effects of both personal finance and corporate finance but also on the financial system at large.

World Federation Exchanges (WFE) indicate that total value of shares quoted on world stock exchanges was USD 60 Trillion by end 2014. Globally, NYSE is a largest exchange in the world with domestic market capitalization of over USD 19 Trillion by end 2014. This is followed by NASDAQ (also U.S) with nearly USD 7 Trillion ie the two New York exchanges account for a third of all exchange business; the 3rd is Tokyo Stock exchange with USD 4 Trillion; London Stock exchange is the largest in Europe, and Euronext. In Africa, JSE is the largest exchange, followed Nigeria Stock exchange, and Egyptian Stock exchange.

BIRTH OF STOCK MARKETS GLOBALLY

In 1553, the Muscovy Company which is the world's first joint-stock firm was founded in London. With the growth in such firms, there arose the need for shareholders to be able to exchange their holdings, leading to brokers acting as intermediaries for investors. In 1760, after being ejected from the Royal Exchange for rowdiness, a group of 150 brokers formed a club at Jonathan's Coffee House to buy and sell shares. Later, as the volumes of shares increased, the need for an organized market place to exchange these shares became necessary. Stock traders then decided to meet at a London Coffee house, which they used as market place. Later, they took over the Coffee house and in 1773 changed its name to the "stock exchange", this was the first ever exchange, the London Stock Exchange. The Exchange developed rapidly, playing a major role in financing UK firms during the Industrial Revolution.

This idea made its way to their American colonies with an exchange being established in Philadelphia in 1770. The market on Wall Street opened in May 1792 on the corner of Wall Street and Broadway; a total of 24 supply brokers signed the Buttonwood Agreement in New York City at Wall Street underneath a buttonwood tree. On the 8th March 1817, the group renamed itself as the New York Stock & Exchange Board, and moved off the street into 40 Wall Street. Today, the New York Stock Exchange (NYSE) is the largest and most powerful stock exchange in the world.

Wall Street Experience: As with many of the famous streets and roads in the world, Wall Street's origins have historical significance. Its name is a direct reference to a wall that was erected by Dutch settlers on the southern tip of Manhattan Island in the 17th century. During this time, a war between the English and Dutch threatened to spill over onto the island's American colonies. So the Dutch, located at the southernmost part of the island, decided to erect a defensive wall. Although this wall was never used for its intended purpose, years after its removal it left a legacy behind in the name Wall Street. This area didn't become famous for being America's financial center until the end of the 18th century, when 24 of the United States' first and most prominent brokers signed an agreement that outlined the common commission-based form of trading securities. Occurring under a "Buttonwood" tree, this marked the beginnings of the investment community of Wall Street and the creation of the New York Stock Exchange

The first African stock exchanges were founded in 1883 in Alexandria, Egypt; and in Johannesburg, South Africa in 1887; and are still currently the best stock markets on the continent both in volumes and sophistication of trading and financial assets.

History of Stock Markets in the EAC Region

Nairobi Stock Exchange

Trading equity in Nairobi begun way back in 1920s at the Café, Stanley Hotel in down town Nairobi as the venue for the less formal type of exchange. This witnessed transactions in which gentleman's agreements were made on the spot; physical settlement of shares happened later.

The official NSE opened in 1954, and now it hosts a couple of equities, government as well as corporate bonds, REITs, and it soon rolling out a diversity of other sophisticated securities like derivatives, ETFs, etc in 2016. Its market capitalization as of 2014 was USD 21.52 Billion (50% of GDP) but the goal is to boost it to USD 93.72 Billion (70% of GDP) by 2023. Kenya's capital markets is the largest and most visible in EAC; and currently the 3rd largest in Sub-Saharan Africa after South Africa and Nigeria. NSE is the 2nd demutualization (listing) of an exchange in Africa after Johannesburg Stock Exchange (JSE); and the process was completed in 2014. The IPO raised KSHS 627 Million off a subscription pool of KSHS 4.789 Billion (an over-subscription of 600%). NSE has 21 active trading participants; and it is a founder member and hosts the secretariat of ASEA (African Securities Exchanges Association).

The other EAC stock markets begun much later (actually more than 40 years after the establishment of the NSE); with DSE and USE opening in the late 1990s; RSE begun in the late 2000s; Burundi and South Sudan up to the present they don't have stock markets.

PERFORMANCE OF EAC STOCK MARKETS
Figure 4.4
Equity Turnover Trends for the EAC Markets

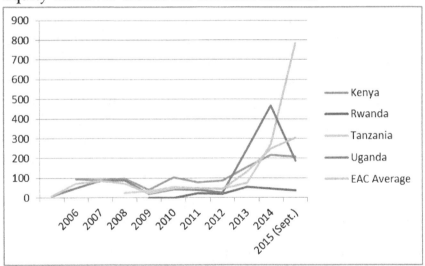

Source: EAC Securities Exchanges (2015)

a)   Rwandan Stock Exchange
It has had relatively stable growth in equity turnover since 2009. It has neither faced drastic drops nor realized drastic increases in equity turnover. RSE is driven by technology; it is an IT-based exchange with 90% automation & arguably the best in EAC region in automation which is fully linked to payment systems

(RTGS). There is good working relationship amongst key players in financial markets such as the stock exchange, Capital markets regulator, and the Central bank for rational policy formulation & conflict resolution.

Market Activity and Upcoming Developments

RSE expects to have full automation by the 1st Quarter of 2016.

Regional infrastructure to link EAC markets is also expected to be fully operational by the 1st half of 2016.

RSE is hopeful of more IPOs in 2016, and working on REITs products like Income REITs & Social REITs projects.

b)   Dar es Salam Stock Exchange

It had stable growth in equity turnover till 2013, when very sharp increases in equity turnover were realized. Such sharp changes are usually caused by extraordinary events like changes in regulations, an aggressive approach to attracting listings and activities on the bourse that are happening up to now in the Tanzanian financial system. The Dar Es Salam stock exchange is a very special case. Having realized very slow growth between 2008 and 2013, it suddenly picks up and spikes which is an indicator of some drastic action e.g. so many companies getting listed within the period the period in question such as a more aggressive marketing strategy from the Stock Exchange and the Capital Markets regulator.

Market Activity and Upcoming Developments

There are 21 firms listed on DSE and June – September 2015 saw at least 3 rights issues:

CRD Bank had TZSH 152 Billion rights issue which was all taken up.

Diamond Trust Bank had TZSH 29 Billion rights issue which was well subscribed.

Jubilee Insurance offered TZSH 30 Billion rights issue which was well subscribed.

There were 9 licensed brokerage firms & 23 investment advisors.

Most IPOs have been oversubscribed ie demand is there but supply side is lacking at the moment.

Bank of Tanzania increased capital requirement which has seen many commercial banks opting for the capital markets for resource mobilization (capitalization).

There was a corporate bond issue through mobile money ie Exim bank offered a TZSHS 10 Billion Bond in November. The law allows for a "Green shoe option" whereby a firm indicates in its prospectus that in case there is oversubscription of its issue, then it can retain a proposed percentage of it (Exim bank had requested for 50% retention of the oversubscription).

In 2014, Tanzania financial system opened up a 100% ownership of listed firms by foreigners ie the can buy up to 100% stake in a firm unlike the 60% regulation that was ruling then for foreign ownership of listed firms. This serves to boost liquidity and trading volumes that have increased significantly since then & more foreigners are showing a lot of interest in Tz which calls for more innovative products to accommodate such demand.

December 2014 saw the establishment of the option of an IPO through mobile money.

There is a University Capital markets challenge that is aimed at stimulating university students to trade in capital markets through mobile money. They had planned for only 2000 students but it was oversubscribed by 7000. This implies a positive trend towards rolling out capital markets products to students and interesting them in being active investors.

But a lot more activity was in the offing from December to at 1st quarter of 2016:

Mwalimu commercial bank (owned by Teachers' Association of Tz thru their economic wing was to list in early December. The IPO was to be done through Mobile money.

Yetu (Youth microfinance) was also preparing to list in December

Mufindi Community bank was also promising to list in December.

Bank M – one of the biggest and best performing banks in Tz was anticipating to do an IPO in the 1st quarter of 2016.

Unit Trust of Tz was planning to issue a corporate bond of TZSH 70 Billion (for its projects & infrastructural development). This proposal was under review by the time of my research.

DSE was in the demutualization process and hoped to complete it by the beginning of 2016.

c)   Nairobi Stock Exchange

It has been experiencing faster growth over the years than the Rwandan stock exchange, but relatively stable. Such indicates a market that has 'no surprises', no spectrum changing regulations, no serious new entrants that can change the investment landscape, etc. But the stock market is built on a strong financial system that is actually ranking high even on the international scale due to its global visibility, product innovation and stability.

NSE 2016 Outlook

This vibrant market anticipates to introduce new sophisticated financial products so as to give varieties (and exposure) to both regional and international investors, and these include: derivative instruments (whole product suite); Structured investment vehicles (Exchange-traded funds, Depository receipts, etc); and Islamic Capital markets products.

d) Uganda Securities Exchange

The market faced the same shocks as the Nairobi Stock exchange in 2009 (as revealed by the dip in the curve), but the Nairobi stock exchange picked up faster (majorly due to market certainty compared to its Ugandan counterpart), and thereafter growth continued to be suppressed. It took the USE, like the rest in East Africa, the period from 2009 to 2012 to start realizing increased growth in equity turnover. This could partly be attributed to the global financial crisis given the fact that the highest percentage of volumes and activity on all the regional bourses is on account of foreign institutional investors who practically control our stock markets. In 2012, there was a sharp rise in equity turnover in Uganda, a slower increase in Kenya and other countries. This sharp spike was on account of Umeme Ltd listing in November 2012 (apparently the most recent local listing on the Ugandan bourse) but also other secondary offering all through to 2014 including Umeme Ltd's additional offerings in 2014. In 2015, due to volatilities in the global macroeconomics (including currencies, commodities prices, etc) as a result of US economy rebound, and probably with anticipation of general elections in early February 2016, there was a sharp drop in equity turnover. Such drops are indicative of market anxiety and a risk aversion attitude by large institutional investors shying away from investing their money or having exposure to the Ugandan market. But investment theory has it that it may also have been simply a correcting measure, as the market sought to establish a new equilibrium. The fact that Kenya and Rwanda also realize a flattening or slight drop in this period indicates a likelihood of reduced trading in the region generally. Its just that Uganda got worse hit, possibly because it was more dependent on foreign direct flows into the market, or because it was more exposed to foreign exchange fluctuations, or mounting political risk as the country was nearing general elections.

USE 2016 Outlook

The bourse anticipates more activity in 2016 compared to 2015 which didn't have any issuance. This entails a possibility of financial restructuring with UCL likely conversion of its UGX 19.7 Billion (USD 5.76 million) debt into equity by their largest shareholder NSSF-Uganda. This has potential of reviving UCL's financial health to profitability after 2 years of losses characterized by close to 4 years of being highly geared (indebted).

Umeme Ltd is also likely to continue being the most active counter on the exchange.

NIC Holdings anticipates to cross-list to NSE given an approval from the shareholders at AGM 2014.

The CEO forecasts at least 4 IPOs in first ½ of 2016.

REITs Bill is before parliament and likely to be approved so that they can begin trading in 2016. This will boost USE activity since many investors are comfortable with real assets/ estates investments, and Uganda is still in huge deficiency of such (there is 500,000 housing deficit in Kampala). These will soon issue units/shares for investors to purchase & co-own investments in housing estates

Derivative products are also likely to begin trading in 2017 since the regulatory framework is being finalized. There is need to create awareness but many businesses are looking forward to their trading as a hedging mechanism to stay afloat & also making more profits.

Commodities exchange: initiatives are in place to establish systems efficient enough to facilitate trading amongst farmers, investors, USE, and traders in commodity derivative industry. USE is negotiating with URA to use their warehousing system & other efficient structural systems so as to synergize & together boost the commodities exchange. By 2018, CEO is optimistic that the commodities exchange will be fully operational & efficient.

By 3rd quarter of 2016, USE is going to demutualize & the Bill was before Parliament by 2015 awaiting approval. Then USE will issue shares and trade like the NSE, which will give both the exchange & listed firms & general public advantages through increased activity & efficiency.

Figure 4.5   Trends in Volumes of Shares Traded on EAC Stock Markets

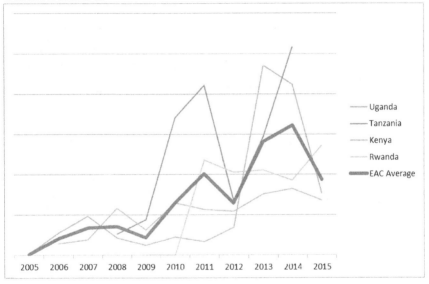

Source: EAC Securities Exchanges (2015)

Rwanda stock market which became operational in 2009 had a relatively consistent increase in volume of shares traded during the year due to major cross-listing of Kenya Commercial Bank (KCB) and the National Media Group (NMG) at the time. Thereafter, the volume of shares traded remained stagnant, indicating that the volume of shares traded was neither increasing nor reducing substantially. In 2014, we see an increase in the volume of shares traded. Remember that whereas the volume of shares traded is moving in this direction, the equity turnover remained relatively stable all through the years, indicating that not a lot of equity is normally traded in this market (relatively illiquid market).

The Shares Volume Traded for **Dar Es Salam stock exchange** speaks the same message with the equity turnover. A sharp increase was recorded in 2013, leading to a substantial increase in volume of shares traded. This trend has continued due to the factors already explained in the equity turnover and the general financial system landscape in Tanzania.

The Nairobi Stock Exchange is enjoying fast and stable growth in shares volume traded, just like its stable growth in equity turnover due to favorable investment climate in the 3rd largest capital markets in the Sub-Saharan Africa with an edge in product innovation, and the privilege of being the 2nd demutualized stock market in Africa.

The Uganda Stock Exchange, just like the Tanzania stock exchange, realized a sharp increase in shares volume traded in 2013. The Tanzanian one has maintained the upward climb, while the Ugandan counterpart dropped drastically in 2015 due to reasons already explained in the equity turnover analysis. For Uganda, the equity turnover dropped, and the shares volumes traded also dropped, indicating a presence of shares supplied into the secondary market, which supply is not matched with increased trading. This may be one indicator of capital flight, as investors sell and leave the market instead of selling one instrument to buy another instrument within the same market. O the other hand, the USE saw 2014 as a good year because an average 8.6 million shares were traded per day, which saw annual increase of 32% from 6.5 million shares traded in 2013 per day; and exceedingly higher than an average 350,000 shares traded in 2009.

Figure 4.6
Market Capitalization on EAC Stock Exchanges

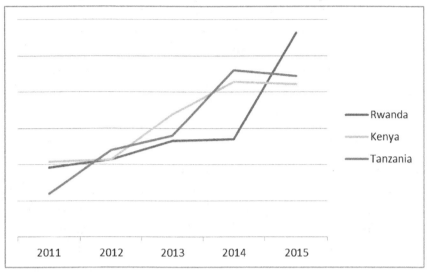

Source: EAC Securities Exchanges (2015)

Between 2011 and 2014, Rwanda recorded stable growth in market capitalization. Between 2014 and 2015, it experienced an exponential growth rate. This was as a result of the cross-listing of Equity Group Holdings Ltd in February 2015, and the listing of Crystal Telecom Ltd in July 2015 with share issues of 270,177,320; all this proved so incremental to the young bourse that it enjoyed a significant growth in 2015 unlike its EAC peers.

Kenya and Tanzania, between 2011 and 2014, experienced sustained high growth in comparison to their EAC peers which boosted their bourses in many market fundamentals. On the contrary, between 2014 and 2015, the figures for market capitalization almost stagnated for both stock markets. For Tanzania, the DSE had only one activity in 2014 which was the cross-listing of Uchumi Supermarkets in August 2014 but in 2015, majorly the second half of the year, activities picked up due to a couple of IPOs and other activities up to December 2015. On the hand, for Kenya, the NSE had relatively fewer activities in

2014 with only one IPO in September 2014 of the Nairobi Stock Exchange (NSE) itself issuing shares of 66,000,000; and just three rights issues from Diamond Trust Bank, NIC Bank, and Uchumi Supermarket. Then in 2015, market activity further slowed down with only one IPO from Stanlib Fahari REIT in October 2015 of share issues of 16,166,900,000; and still only one rights issue from HFCK. This definitely saw the market capitalization adversely more affected than ever before in the recent past.

U.S ECONOMY REBOUND & GLOBAL ECONOMIC DISTRESS

Rebound of U.S economy is due to reversal flows that were occasioned by increase in U.S interest rates. The giant economy for decades had been registering relatively poor results but in 2015, it recorded a recovery vis-à-vis other major economies. This was not just because of the recent oil production but the whole economic situation is responsible for the rebound including the Federal Reserve System lifting off rising interest rate that had been at almost 0% for decades to a 0.25%. This stimulated demand for USD due to increased investments in the U.S and a rebound in the U.S economy which has occasioned reversal flows to the strongest economy since it had become a profitable investment destination due to its being historically safe, and apparently offering high returns on investments. This, consequently, increased the demand for USD since all investors were channeling their savings/investments to the U.S economy so as to take advantage of rising interest rates as caused by the Federal Reserve System's macroeconomic policy stance. Some analysts believe that the USD appreciation was anchored on positive sentiments for recovery in U.S; leading to high USD demand on domestic markets against subdued inflows, particularly in struggling economies like EAC.

In 2016, major currencies and those of emerging markets were expected to be under pressure owing to the drastic appreciation of the USD. Besides, there was another fear of further increment in U.S interest rates but the Federal Reserve System had to rethink this position since it could likely crash the fragile markets like Japan, China, etc; whose stock markets almost crashed yet the U.S has lots of interest in these markets. There were lots of expectations among financial markets that the U.S Fed would increase its key interest rates at the beginning of 2016; and this saw many a financial institutions and markets price an interest rate hike into their existing rates. This has shifted capital from emerging markets to advanced economies, further encouraging stability in the global financial system.

Frontier markets (like EAC) are very weak and insignificant; that is why what they faced even in the 2007/2008 global financial crisis was largely a spill-over or secondary effects but not direct impact since these economies are not directly linked to the global financial system. These basically have their local financial woes like a huge current account deficit, which are further compounded by such spill-overs as USD appreciation in relation to domestic frail currencies. The U.S Quantitative Easing (Q.E) programs largely affected more liquid African markets that have seen considerable increase in foreign investments like South Africa since it is a more liquid emerging market; and possibly Nigeria, as a relatively liquid frontier market in the Sub-Saharan Africa. This is because EAC debt markets have not witnessed a great concentration of foreign investor participation, but this relative insulation of the EAC markets implies that long-term fundamentals continue to look favorable even for international investors.

HOW TO BOOST EAC SECONDARY MARKET PERFORMANCE

It is so critical to develop the secondary market so as to increase frequency & velocity of transaction (multiplier effect) and the attendant benefits all through the value-chain of securities transactions by the players such as the regulators, stock markets, financial services firms, investors, listed firms, and the financial system at large. This is owing to the fact that the more investors transact (sell/buy), it creates value for all the parties through fees & returns across the board. Besides, this exchange of stock creates "hypothetical & phantom" value on the underlying asset/ securities of a certain company which is so key in the development of any sector (example is the growth of technology firms & their stock valuation in U.S and Europe).

Thus, regulators & stock exchanges ought to deliberately do a lot of hype on the secondary market activities (reports) eg attracting the general public's attention to any new development on the stock market including captivating analysis on corporate performance (share prices, dividend payments & valuation) of good firms. This includes comparisons between profitability of financial assets (investments) and those of real assets (property) through return on investment and pay-back period analyses.

Regulators & stock exchanges ought to encourage investors to always transact on their SCD accounts for any simple activity (ranging from school fees payments, financing a house or mortgage, business trading; and social activities like marriage, etc). This is aimed at boosting the activity at the stock exchange so as to create value along the value-chain of financial investments; to further create "phantom" value/money. This will boost the multiplier effect in the economy (basically if there is a significant number of local investors in the financial markets); but also attract more attention of prospective investing public. This will serve as a remedy to the problem of low absorptive capacity in our financial markets that has led to huge institutional investors like NSSF-Uganda with a very huge float (approx. 80%) failing to offset some due to shallow capital markets; low levels of activity on stock exchange, and consequently failing to trade its float.

The model of stock markets that we have in the EAC is designed for developed financial systems, with well-established companies but not fit for most EAC economies that are still struggling. This model is a market where all firms: strong ones and very weak firms transact together under the same rules. There is need to tailor-make our capital markets to suit the size of firms that we have which are very small yet not strictly supervised; it is only strong firms that can supervise themselves not small ones. Thus, there is need for product engineering that suits our small capacity of firms.

GENESIS OF STOCK EXCHANGES & DEMUTUALIZATION DRIVE

Stock exchanges, simply put, were clubs/associations that brought some people of a certain class together for given objectives of mutual interest. This is why they were mutual organizations & normally registered as companies limited by guarantee; membership was so selective and dependent on those that the founding members could admit ie entry was highly limited and restricted even if someone had a lot of money and influence, this could not book him entry easily. This was largely for fear of taking over ownership/control of the organization by other people's interests.

London stock exchange was begun by an association of coffee dealers, and this is also true for most stock exchanges in EAC. Simply put, these were initiatives of groups of selected rich men or prominent traders in townships like the Kwagalana Group in Uganda, which were used as avenues for self-help in cases of financial distress and other social needs. That is why stock exchanges were mutual organizations whose membership and entry was highly restricted to those the members wanted; basically the high net-worth people. This is actually why up to the present, stock exchanges world over still suffer from this identity; whereby the lower class (majorly the unschooled) and poor view it as an investment for the rich and educated. In the U.S, it was not until Charles Merrill (a business man who believed in educating the public to become intelligent investors on the stock exchange) decided to bring it to the street. He strategized to make the lower class have access to the market & interest them in embracing it, thus adopting the name "Wall Street". Since then, global initiatives of making it pro-lower classes in a bid to embrace all prospective investors have been put in place. This raised the concern of whether stock exchanges should remain as "mutual organizations/ associations" yet there is need to render them a public good and give them the capacity of mobilizing resources themselves. This has seen a great need, but also pressure of "demutualizing stock exchanges" and the first ever stock exchange to do so was in Australia in the earlier 1990s; since then many have followed the trend including our own Nairobi Stock Exchange in 2014, which is the second exchange in Africa to demutualize, after JSE.

RATIONALE FOR DEMUTUALIZATION OF EAC STOCK MARKETS

When a mutual company owned by its users/members converts into a company owned by shareholders. In effect, the users/ members exchange their rights of use for shares in the demutualized company. Currently, my interactions with all the CEOs and technical personnel at the EAC stock exchanges indicate that all the bourses are working on demutualizing, and below are some of the reasons behind this world contemporary phenomenon:

Desire to monetize the value of exchange memberships

Concern about fair governance and desire to redistribute power among market participants:

- *Lack of independent governance in a public interest entity with rule enforcement or broader self-regulatory powers and responsibilities*
- *Lack of representative governance in most exchanges.*
- *Fairness of rule enforcement process*
- ` *Increased competitiveness and globalization, and this can be*

evidenced by the JSE and the Nairobi Stock Exchange that are highly competitive and global.

Resource demands of keeping up with market evolutions. In jurisdictions where the government owns the exchange: privatization would be the best remedy for rendering the exchange self-sustaining.

The advent of electronic platforms and their impact on the exchange business model has led to:
- *Interest in direct market access*
- *Interest in cross border access*
- *Lack of limitations of bricks and mortar firms*
- *Interest in non-owner access*
- *Increased market efficiency*
- *Resource demands of technology*
- *Ability to use extracted value to expand platform and to acquire other platforms*

Global Trend. Development of stock markets all over the world hasn't left East Africa aside, with a case in point being a number of companies far away from East Africa cross-listing in the East African market, trading at times in a more percentage as compared to locals. Furthermore, with trades done at finger tips, where investors now are in charge rather than the market intermediaries, hence need for more efficient which is achievable through demutualization

Enforcement Independence. A demutualized east African stock market will have a management which is freer to decide on operational issues. This type of management is perceived to be effective and fair in enforcement of rules and regulations.

Technology. With the current developments all over the world, where efficiency of its own essence, technological advancement which come with huge capital expenditure is inevitable. The buy in and ability of the members to fund expansion for technological upgradation and advancement in a mutualized exchange is rather limited. Contrary to that, demutualized East African market will have chance to make investment decisions faster and have access to funds from a large pool of investors

STOCK MARKET & REAL ECONOMY

Transactions on the secondary market help traders to get a lot of value & returns by escaping the tax system (nets) sine there is no capital gains tax in EAC. This was borrowed from the U.S where rich guys designed it in a way to help them make a lot of money without being taxed unlike the other real sectors of the economy which are heavily taxed.

Unfortunately for EAC, most of the float is owned by foreign institutional investors who exploit this loophole so as to get a lot of value/ returns from the financial system without practically contributing to the economy through taxation. This has seen a lot of capital outflows by means of capital gains being repatriated to developed economies due to that tax flaw. Foreign investors hold the highest value on our stock markets which robs locals of their chance of appropriating/acquiring that value so as to cause a multiplier effect in the domestic economy. This is why the stock markets have failed to transform the domestic economies in EAC & the various sectors because of foreign over-dominance; loopholes in the tax system; and very few local firms have resolved to access capital markets that would serve to return such proceeds/ returns in the real domestic economy. For instance, Stanbic Bank shareholders made a lot of money at IPO & subsequent issues but the biggest float is held by foreigners: funds are repatriated without going through the tax nets. Besides, reduction in foreign interest would cause substantial reduction in market turnover & revenues to intermediaries & exchanges but above all, EAC's exposure is very high due to this reality.

In South Africa, for instance, the equities markets are performing very well yet contrarily the real economy is going under. This is due to the "carry trade effect" but also loopholes in the tax system whereby the equity markets that are largely dominated by foreign investors do repatriate their money without being taxed (capital gains tax). The other problem that is characteristic of South Africa is the dual listing policy whereby firms are allowed to list domestically in South Africa and at the same time list on the London Stock Exchange (LSE). This brings a mismatch between the growth of stock market and that of the real economy.

That is why there is a strong reason for East Africans to get involved in investing in domestic financial markets so as to save their economies from being conduits for volumes of funds that are always repatriated by the large foreign institutional investors who are the most active in all EAC stock markets across the board. In the US, 65% of the 300 million Americans invest in their stock markets that's why the NYSE & NASDAQ are the largest exchanges world over (accounting for 33.5% of world exchange Business); and of course significantly contributing to US being the strongest economy in the world. In Uganda, only 0.2% of the 35 million invest in their stock markets; and ironically CMA (regulator) anticipates to make it to just 100,000 Ugandans by 2025 yet so as to match the growth of the stock market to that of the real domestic economy, there is need to incentivize as many locals as humanly possible to have investment exposure in financial markets.

CORPORATE DISCLOSURE

For equity markets to operate efficiently, there should be shareholder knowledge (information); shareholders ought to be availed with information that can empower them. This ought to be about financial information about the firm; directors' remuneration and other key costs that are likely to affect their return prospects.

Transparency in markets is very critical but in EAC, it is majorly the Kenyan financial system that freely shares its financial information to the international investor community.

There is need to do more research so as to attract foreign investors through information dissemination that will give investors exposure to EAC financial markets and facilitate their investment decision-making.

NB: Financial market crashes of 2007 – 2009 were induced by financial markets actions themselves: this was due to information asymmetry – thus, flow of financial information is very critical for both domestic and global financial systems.

EQUITY MARKETS WORK IN ALGORITHM PATTERN

When firms publish their financials, investors rush to buy stocks in high performing firms, and then equity markets get finances which are allocated to firms & the economy.

But now (since the GFC 2008/09), most markets no longer work like that because even if firms publish very good financials, investors no longer rush to buy their stocks; maybe because of mistrust in the market & high risk exposures.

CAPITAL GAINS TAX

This tax is economically good for equity markets due to its business concept yet bond markets especially for infrastructural bonds, if local capacity for resource mobilization is not existent then it would be logical that these bonds be exempted from capital gains tax so as to attract foreign capital to develop infrastructure which has a development (social) concept ie the case of Tanzania government of 100% ownership approval for basically bond issues.

ANIMALS ON WALL STREET (STOCK MARKETS)

Bulls, bears, pigs, and chickens on stock markets??!!

In the United States, basically during the Gold Rush era in California, miners used to actually pit bears and bulls together in a fighting ring. This bloody sport eventually was outlawed, but the symbolic strength of the two animals translated into modern Wall Street usage. As for the "up" and "down" parts, some claim this is a reference to the bull's tendency to slash upward and the bear's tendency to strike downward. The pigs and chickens are a modern addition by some unknown wit possibly to spice up the stock market vocabulary with a lot animals and risk/return profiles of various investors.

Pigs are loosely used to represent high-risk investors who want to make a killing in a short time but they are always led to the slaughter house. Due to their excessive appetite for returns which is not guided by prudent investment management and risk management, they end up losing almost everything.

Chickens are loosely used to represent risk averse investors who sit on their money. These are largely afraid of losing anything and so they invest in super-safe financial assets such as bonds and unit trust/mutual funds.

BULL MARKET

In a bull market, stocks show a tendency to go up in price over a period of time. This period can be weeks, months or years. It's not an exact term. Instead, it refers more to confident sentiment among investors. In practice, it means the market has more buyers than sellers: when demand exceeds supply, prices rise. Bull markets are most common when the economy is growing, unemployment is low and inflation is somewhat tamed. When someone says he is "bullish" on a single stock, he simply means he expects it to rise in price.

BEAR MARKET

Being in a bear market means stocks are headed down, in the analyst's estimation. This means sellers outnumber buyers; and a bear market can go on for years. If stocks go down for just a few days or weeks, the movement is usually called a "pullback" or a "market correction." Once stocks drop 20-to-30 percent in value, speculation may begin that it is a bear market, meaning it could drop a lot further before it comes back up. Some prudent investors actually make money in a bear market by buying stocks at cheaper prices in anticipation of them rising again soon.

STOCK MARKET INDICES

Indices are very crucial tools for investors in providing information on how markets are performing since they give a realistic benchmark against which the performance of a portfolio can be assessed.

These indices have the following uses:

Market barometer: by providing a comprehensive record of historic price movements so as to measure trends majorly by chartists, technical analysts and momentum investors in market timing (guiding decision-making on when to buy/sell securities.

Facilitate portfolio management research and asset allocation decisions.

Act as the basis for index tracker funds, exchange-traded funds, index derivatives, and other index-related financial products.

They help in performance measurement since they can be used as performance benchmarks for judging portfolio performance.

Figure 4.7
Data for constructing Stock Market Indices

Stock	Initial Price	Final Price	Shares (Million)	Initial Value of Outstanding Stock (UGX Billion)	Final Value of Outstanding Stock (UGX Billion)
Asante Capital	UGX 700	UGX 1000	7	10	110
Gracia Company	UGX 1000	UGX 1200	10	15	100
Total				25	210

Source: Researcher's Data

In the EAC, various stock markets have their local stock market indices that are used by investors to guide their rational investment decision-making, though there is a strong for a regional stock market index to clinically and comprehensive act as a regional markets barometer and also facilitate the standardization of performance measurement in the EAC region.

By and large, the stock markets performed their best during low interest rate environment across the EAC region; and they perform their worst, world over, in the course of high interest rates, and also bond prices decline. This saw rising interest rates from government borrowing shift investments equity markets to Treasury bill and bond markets which offer better returns in 2015 (this affects stock indices as well). This financial reality has led to bearish performance across EAC stock markets (as evidenced by all the stock market indices); and this has been attributed to largely the following factors: rising interest rates, the weakening of domestic EAC regional currencies, and dissatisfactory financial results from listed firms. For instance, the NSE All Share Index (NASI) hit a 20-month low in mid-October 2015, investor wealth (market capitalization) dropped to KSH 1.9 Trillion from KSH 2.3 Trillion the same period.

NAIROBI STOCK EXCHANGE
Figure 4.8
NSE 20 INDEX TRENDS JAN 2011- SEPTEMBER 2015

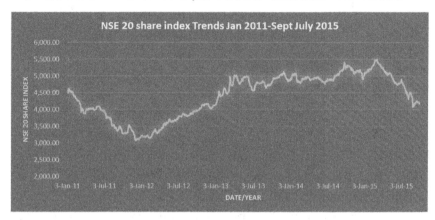

Figure 4.9
NASI INDEX TRENDS JAN 2011- SEPTEMBER 2015

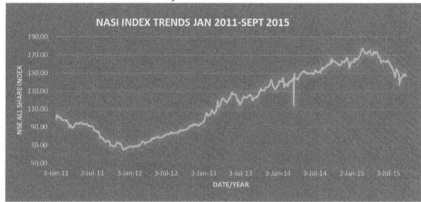

DAR ES SALAAM STOCK EXCHANGE

Figure 4.10

Tanzania Share Index (TSI) & All Share Index from January 2011 to June 2015.

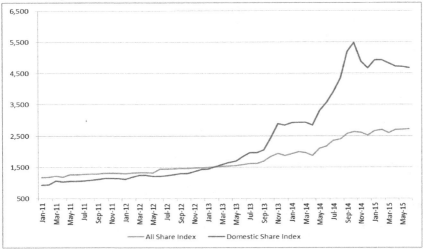

All Share Index: Includes all listed companies

Domestic Share Index: Includes only domestic listed companies

RWANDA STOCK EXCHANGE

Figure 4.11

RSI from January 2011 to June 2015.

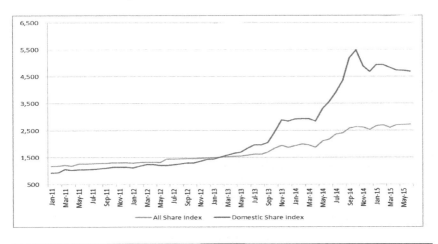

Figure 4.12
All Share Index

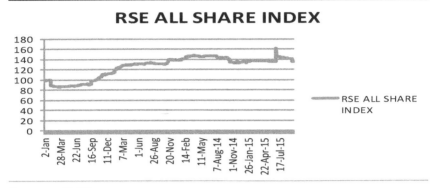

Source : RSE

UGANDA SECURITIES EXCHANGE

Figure 4.13
ALSI & LCI from January 2010 to December 2015

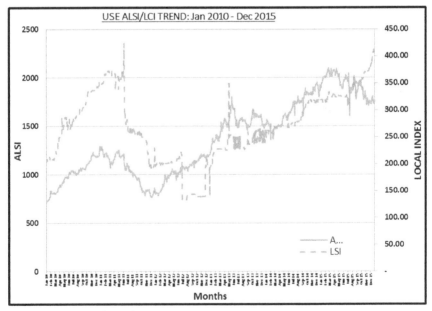

Figure: USE All Shares Index (ALSI); and USE Local Companies
Index (LCI)

INTERNATIONAL STOCK MARKET INDEXES

While the Dow is the best-known measure of the performance of the stock market, it is only one of several indexes used in the global financial markets to measure and analyze financial securities. The ever-increasing role of international trade and investments has made indexes of foreign financial markets part of the general news as well and also household vocabulary for the lovers of investments.

Dow Jones Averages

The Dow Jones Industrial Average (DJIA) of 30 large corporations has been computed since 1896. Its long history probably accounts for its pre-eminence in the public mind. Originally, the DJIA was calculated as the simple average of the stocks included in the index. Thus, one would add up the prices of the 30 stocks in the index and divide by 30; that is why it is called a price-weighted average. A percentage change in the Dow would then be the percentage change in the average price of the 30 shares. Since it corresponds to a portfolio that holds one share of each component stock, the investment in each company in that portfolio is proportional to the company's share price.

Standard & Poor's Indexes

The Standard & Poor's Composite 500 (S&P 500) stock index represents an improvement over the Dow Jones Averages since it is a more broadly based index of 500 firms; and it is a market-value-weighted index. It is computed by calculating the total market value of the 500 firms in the index and the total market value of those firms on the previous day of trading. A percentage increase in the total market value from one day to the next represents the increase in the index. The rate of return of the index equals the rate of return that would be earned by an investor holding a portfolio of all 500 firms in the index in proportion to their market values.

On the contrary, the sophistication in the global financial markets has occasioned the birth of many other indexes depending on the needs of various economies, and the construction has been championed by MSCI (Morgan Stanley Capital International. These can include: the Nikkei (Japan), FTSE (U.K.), DAX (Germany), Hang Seng (Hong Kong), and TSX (Canada).

Bond Market Indexes:

There are basically two most well-known bond market indexes that measure the performance of various categories of bonds, and these are: the Merrill Lynch; the Lehman Brothers; and the Salomon Smith Barney (which currently is part of Citigroup).

CORPORATE ACTIONS IN EAC STOCK MARKETS

This happens when a firm undertakes to do something that is likely to affect its share capital and/or bond. These are broadly categorized into three:

   a) *Mandatory actions, which requires no intervention from the shareholding or bondholders such as dividend payment since all shareholders (in particular) by default receive their dividends. Most listed companies in East Africa, at least, have been doing this consistently for the last two decades apart from some few cases like Uganda Clays Ltd that have not been able to, due to financial distress related problems.*

   b) *Mandatory actions with options, these have default options that may happen when shareholders don't intervene but are given opportunity to make a choice among options such as with the rights issue.*

   c) *Voluntary actions, which requires shareholders to make a decision, for instance, in the face of a looming takeover bid and/or merger, where a shareholder will have to choose whether to accept the offer or not.*

The following are among the available corporate actions in the East African financial system:

Rights Issues: this happens when a listed firm intends to raise more finance through the issuance of new shares for a variety of reasons such as debt servicing, expansion, etc, and this is provided for in the company Act that shareholders ought to be given the priority in such scenario. Normally, the price of such issues is set at a discount in relation to the market price of such stock, and shareholders have three choices in response to this happening: to take up the rights; to sell the rights to another investor; and to do nothing. The NSE, which is most visible and active exchange in the EAC region, recorded a total of 22 rights issues from various listed firms that were value at KSH 101,286,268,517 from January 2004 to September 2015. This implies an average 2 rights issue each year, which indicates a relatively good activity on the bourse given the inactive and highly illiquid markets in the frontier economies especially the Sub-Saharan Africa.

Bonus issues: these are also called capitalization/scrip issues where a firm gives existing shareholders additional shares without them having to pay for them; thus, increasing the numbers of shareholding across the board. This is at times done so as to boost liquidity of the firm's shares in the market and/or lower down the share prices; but also sometimes dividends can be paid in form of bonus issue so as to save the firm's liquidity position. In the EAC, Uganda Securities Exchange has seen some activities in this corporate action by firms such as Bank of Baroda Uganda, Umeme Ltd, DFCU Bank, and National Insurance Corporation that has served to reward their shareholders. On the other hand, the NSE has witnessed a whole 30 bonus issues by listed firms between 2004 and 2015 (which is an average of 3 bonus issues each year). This has significantly boosted both the corporate and market fundamentals in the Kenyan financial markets such as market capitalization, liquidity, and turnover and deals undertaken each year.

Dividends: this is a percentage of corporate profits that are shared out to the shareholders, and vary from company to company due to a diversity of underlying factors; and many a firms normally do this mandatory corporate action twice a year. It should be noted that investors buy shares so as to get the right to receive the next declared corporate dividends, and so "cum-dividend" refer to the opportunity by the investor to qualify for next declared dividends up to the day when the declaration is made. On the other hand, shares go "ex-dividend" in the period between the dividend declaration date and the dividend payment date; and so investors in shares during this period don't qualify for the declared dividends.

Stock split: this action is undertaken to reduce a share price that has increased so much that it has rendered its trading (liquidity) quite complicated; and this is done using a formula so as to subdivide it and render it easily tradable which alters the nominal value of the company shares. On the Uganda Securities Exchange, listed firms like Uganda Clays Ltd, Bank of Baroda Uganda, etc have witnessed a stock split for several times. Besides, the NSE has had 16 activities of listed firms in this corporate action between 2004 and 2015.

Open Offers: this is an opportunity given to company's shareholders to purchase more corporate securities in proportion to their holdings in a bid for the firm to raise more finance. However, special open offer may be designed to allow shareholders to apply for more than their pro rata holdings.

Mergers and Takeovers: these are designed to give firms opportunity to expand their operations; and this can either a friendly takeover or a hostile one where the bigger and/or more efficient firm (predator) seeks to acquire another one (target) using any measures possible. On the other hand, a merger is where two firms of similar size resolve enjoy economies of collective strategies (interests) and ultimately merge to form a bigger and/or more efficient entity.

Reverse Stock Split: this is also called a consolidation, and it is the opposite of the stock split whereby shares are consolidated (combined) so as to also to make them more marketable following a significant fall in share prices to rather low levels that are complicating their trading.

Pre-emptive Rights: this is an action by listed firms to convert dividends into more shares so as to dodge paying shareholders in form of money due to its riskiness on corporate liquidity position. So, the firm can decide to offer shares to shareholders for a given financial year instead of giving them dividends in form of money.

Extraordinary General Meeting: this is an AGM called to specifically discuss a prospective take-over or merger. This meeting requires at least 70% of the shareholding to be in attendance.

Chapter 17

THE BOND MARKET

A bond is a debt security; purchasing a bond is lending money to the corporation that has issued a bond. This corporation can be central or local governments, a municipality, a corporation, State agency or any other entity known as issuer. In return for the money, the issuer provides the buyer with a bond which is a promise to pay a specified rate of interest during the life of the bond and to repay the face value of the bond(the principal) when it matures (comes due).

The outstanding global bond market value exceeds USD 100 Trillion; of which domestic bond markets (firms and governments) account for 70%. The International bond market accounts for 30%, and these are issued by financially sound firms, governments, and supranational agencies like World Bank, African Development Bank, East African Development Bank, European Investment Bank, among others. South Africa has the largest bond market in Africa, and of course Kenya is the EAC regional giant in this market. Kenya's government has been successful in building its bond market, and has benchmark bonds with durations of up to 30 years that are traded on the stock exchange in contrast to most EAC peers that have bonds with duration of 15 years..

MAJOR CATEGORIES OF BONDS IN EAC

GEOGRAPHICAL CATEGORIZATION OF BONDS:

Domestic Bonds – these are bonds which are issued by domestic/local firm into the domestic market using the domestic/local currency, for instance, MTN-Uganda issues a UGX 50 Billion bond to be subscribed in Uganda.

Foreign Bonds – this is a situation whereby an overseas firm issues a bond in the domestic market denominated in the domestic currency, for instance, the African Development Bank issues a UGX 80 Billion to be subscribed in Uganda.

Eurobond – this is a situation whereby an entity (government, multinational firm) issues a bond denominated in a currency different from that of the financial/issuing center ie Kenya government issuing a KSH 500 Billion bond in US & UK financial markets.

Issuers' Categorization of Bonds:

Government bonds – these are bonds that are issued by national governments, and this is the major resource mobilization avenue for most governments world-over. EAC governments have different bond issuing schedules that are communicated to the investors (majorly institutional investors) so as to guide the governments' public financing programs but also the investing public's investment decision-making.

Corporate bonds – these are issued by firms, mainly large financial institutions, telecom firms, state-owned enterprises as part of their corporate financial management for various corporate objectives. In the EAC bond markets, a variety of corporate bodies have issued corporate bonds in most EAC economies that have been subsequently subscribed by investors (largely foreign institutional investors).

Supranational bonds – these are issued by supranational institutions (agencies) such as the East African Development Bank, African Development Bank, World Bank, etc. this is done for a diversity of objectives such as to aid and/or boost the domestic bond market like for the case of the EADB bonds in the EAC region, among others. The region has witnessed a couple of such bond listings that have since then been well subscribed due to their being super-safe investments given the credibility and financial soundness of the issuers (high credit rating).

BOND CATEGORIZATION ACCORDING TO ITS NATURE

Plain Vanilla Bonds: these are the fixed coupon bonds and they are the most prevalent in the EAC region due to various reasons.

Floating Rate Notes whose coupon changes over the life of the bond ie index-linked bonds.

Zero coupon bonds (zero doesn't mean no bond); this is a characteristic of infrastructural bonds or other bonds that are discounted upfront ie the investor doesn't receive any coupon during the life of the bond but receives all returns at the end (maturity). Normally, governments actually issue new bonds so as to raise funds to pay off such bonds at their maturity.

NB: Any discount instrument trades on yields; and there is an inverse relationship between bond price and its yield. If the yield goes up then the price will go down.

In the Uganda government securities market (bills and bonds), a total of UGX 14.15 trillion was traded in the secondary market since 2011 to early 2016, representing an increase of 87.6%. For the period ending Dec 2015, the stock of Treasury bonds stood at UGX 7,268.9 billion an increase from UGX 6,167.2 billion as at the end of December 2014.

A bond has two elements:
A Coupon (also called sweetener on bond) which is the interest on bond.

A Yield is a return on the bond.

A bond is a discount instrument: on which an investor takes the return upfront.

BOND PRICING VOCABULARY

Clean price is the bond price before any yields and coupon.

Dirty price is the bond price after the accrued yield and coupon.

Accrued value is determined by the time period that an investor holds the bond (days/ months/ years accrue different returns).

NB: Discount instruments – return is provided in the form of capital growth but not income growth like the case of bonds.

In financial markets, if the investor's need is capital growth, then he/she ought to buy ordinary shares; and he/she should establish a price at which to sell his equity holdings so as to take advantage of the capital growth lest the stock prices fall and then disappoints his investment objectives. On the other hand, if an investor's need is income growth, then he/she should invest in debt instruments and preference shares (most of these are discount instruments on which an investor takes the return upfront).

ix)   EAC Bonds Yields Comparison as at 31/12/2015

Figure 4.14

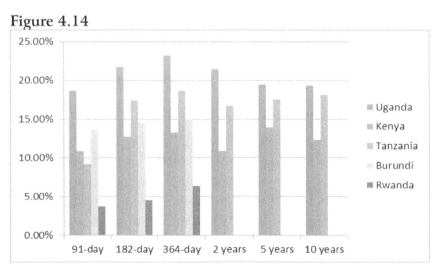

Source: EAC Central Banks (2016)

Regional Yields Comparison (source: EAC Central banks)

Uganda had the highest yields compared to its regional peers. Throughout 2015, well as Tanzania government securities were widely stable, Kenyan yields were largely unstable due to CBK's initiatives for more foreign currency inflows so as to cushion her local currency from further depreciation during the volatile year 2015 for the global financial system. This was largely caused by the rebound in the U.S economy that saw the USD becoming stronger at the hand of other global currencies across the board (including the emerging & frontier markets currencies).

Due to high levels of liquidity and fears of election financing towards the February 2016 General Elections in Uganda, Uganda bond yields were extremely high. This was partly a deliberate monetary policy measure to mop up excess (and, also projected additional) liquidity in the market that would lead to a repeat of the 2011 general election aftermath. This saw the government incentivize investments in the bond market by higher yields so as to prudently manage the macroeconomics of the frontier economy, but this equally present huge investment opportunity to institutional investors (majorly foreigners) who truly appreciated this unique happening.

UG GOVERNMENT SECURITIES 2015

Tight liquidity, Under-subscription, & Higher yields

The bond market reduced activity in 2015 due to tight liquidity both for short & medium term gov't debt. Uganda witnessed a high interest rate environment owing to the fact that Bank of Uganda raised its benchmark rate from 11% in January 2015 to 17% in December 2015 so as to stem inflation risks. This was compounded by the uncertainty related to the February 2016 general elections, and also the depreciating UGX that could potentially spur more inflation tendencies. All combined, were catalysts for the higher yield on government debt securities a case in point was the 23.6% yield on 1-year securities in October 2015. The government responded by Bank of Uganda mopping up liquidity in the markets through its monetary policy operations to mitigate further inflationary pressures. These consequently led to lower secondary bond market trading, and also under-subscription of many bond auctions that stimulated higher yields.

Bank of Uganda raised UFX 5.57 Trillion (USD 1.63 Billion) in 2015 throughout all auctions compared to UGX 6.63 Trillion (USD 1.93 Billion) in 2014.

NB: Government Securities Highlights 2015

Auction Amount Offered	UGX 6,630 Billion
	(USD 1,937 million)
Auction Amount Raised	UGX 5,570 Billion
	(USD 1,627 million)
Secondary Market Turnover	UGX 2,623 Billion
	(USD 766.80 million)

On the other hand, the Kenyan government had come up with austerity measures to reduce debt in the 3rd Quarter of 2015, supported by the issuance of a syndicated loan, which all combined successfully brought the Treasury yields down and back to a more affordable level by the end of 2015 (though the yields had peaked earlier on). Nonetheless, a shortage of investment options for liquid banks (mistrust in the banking system), institutional investors and a general flight to quality by the investing public has triggered massive appetite for government securities across the EAC. This, coupled with low inflation outlook, has exerted downward pressure on yields across the curve.

By and large, there is need to harmonize maturities, coupons and other features across the EAC so as to build a critical mass of issuance volumes for Government bonds but also create benchmarks for non-Government issuers. This is because, at the moment, the main features of Government bonds are largely different across EAC economies, and for Kenya given her better fundamentals and more developed investors' base, she has been able to issue debt securities at much longer terms (close to 30 years) and at lower rates compared to her peers like Uganda and Tanzania.

YIELD CURVE BASICS

The yield curve is a graph that depicts the relationship between bond yields and maturities; it is an important tool in fixed-income investing and investors use it as a reference point for forecasting interest rates, pricing bonds and creating strategies for boosting total returns. In the contemporary investment world, it has also become a reliable leading indicator of economic activity. The yield curve is a line graph that plots the relationship between yields to maturity and time to maturity for bonds of the same asset class and credit quality. A yield curve depicts yield differences, or yield spreads, that are due solely to differences in maturity. It therefore conveys the overall relationship that prevails at a given time in the marketplace between bond interest rates and maturities

Yield refers to the annual return on an investment. The yield on a bond is based on both the purchase price of the bond and the interest, or coupon, payments received. While a bond's coupon interest rate is usually fixed, the price of the bond fluctuates continuously in response to changes in interest rates, as well as the supply and demand, time to maturity, and credit quality of that particular bond. After bonds are issued, they generally trade at premiums (discounts) to their face values until they mature and return to full face value. The fact that yields are a function of price, changes in price cause bond yields to move in the opposite direction.

ANALYSIS OF BOND YIELDS:

Current yield: is the annual return earned on the price paid for a bond; and it is calculated by dividing the bond's annual coupon interest payments by its purchase price. For example, if an investor bought a bond with a coupon rate of 12% at par, and full face value of UGX 1,200,000, the interest payment over a year would be UGX 144,000. This would produce a current yield of 12% (UGX 144000/ UGX 1200000). When a bond is purchased at full face value, the current yield is the same as the coupon rate.

Yield to maturity: this reflects the total return an investor receives by holding the bond until it matures; it reflects all of the interest payments from the time of purchase until maturity, including interest on interest plus any appreciation or depreciation in the price of the bond. On the other hand, Yield to call is calculated the same way as yield to maturity, but assumes that a bond will be called, or repurchased by the issuer before its maturity date, and that the investor will be paid face value on the call date.

Since yield to maturity (or yield to call) reflects the total return on a bond from purchase to maturity (or the call date), it is generally more meaningful for fixed-income investors than current yield. By examining yields to maturity, investors can compare bonds with varying characteristics, such as different maturities, coupon rates or credit quality.

DETERMINANTS OF THE SHAPE OF YIELD CURVES

Most financial economists agree that three major factors affect the slope of the yield curve, which includes investors' expectations for future interest rates and certain "risk premiums" that investors require to hold long-term bonds. Below are the factors:

- *Pure Expectations Theory: this believes that the slope of the yield curve reflects only investors' expectations for future short-term* interest rates. Much of the time, investors expect interest rates to rise in the future, which accounts for the usual upward slope of the yield curve.

- Liquidity Preference Theory: this asserts that long-term interest rates not only reflect investors' assumptions about future interest rates but also include a premium for holding long-term bonds, called the "term premium" (liquidity premium). This premium compensates investors for the added risk of having their money tied up for a longer period, including the greater price uncertainty. Because of the term premium, long-term bond yields tend to be higher than short-term yields, and the yield curve slopes upward. On the contrary, the EAC bond yield curves represent the opposite since shorter-term bonds yields appear to be way higher than the long-term yields particularly in 2015 (but this can be partly attributed to the global foreign exchange volatilities and other domestic macroeconomic fundamentals in individual EAC economies.

- Preferred Habitat Theory: this states that in addition to interest rate expectations, investors have distinct investment horizons and require a meaningful premium to buy bonds with maturities outside their "preferred" maturity, or habitat. Supporters of this theory believe that short-term investors are more prevalent in the fixed-income market and therefore, longer-term rates tend to be higher than short-term rates.

Since the yield curve can reflect both investors' expectations for interest rates and the impact of risk premiums for longer-term bonds, interpreting the yield curve can be complex. Financial economists and fixed-income portfolio managers put great effort into trying to understand the exact forces that drive yields at any given time and point on the yield curve.

PLAYERS IN BOND MARKETS

- *Central government: this issues long-term notes and bonds so as to finance the national budget.*

- *Local and Municipal governments: these issue long-term notes and bonds to fund capital projects like roads, schools, sanitation and health facilities.*

- *Corporations: these issue a variety of corporate bonds for numerous objectives such as growth.*

- *Households: these are the largest buyers of bond securities which are done through their deposits in financial institutions that are used to purchase bonds in capital markets.*

ADVANTAGES OF INVESTING IN BONDS

- *Bonds provide regular income and act as a cushion against the unpredictable ups n downs of the stock market. Bonds do not move in the same direction as stocks.*

- *Bonds are predictable. One is able to know how much interest one is expecting to receive and how often they will receive it.*

- *The interest paid by short term bonds typically exceeds that paid by banks on saving accounts.*

DISADVANTAGES OF INVESTING IN BONDS

- *Although bonds are less volatile than stocks, they are not immune to price fluctuations.*

- *When a company defaults on bonds, this may result into total loss of principal for the bond holder.*

EUROBONDS IN EAC FINANCIAL MARKETS
EUROBOND ACTIVITY IN SUB-SAHARAN AFRICA

Kenya government issued the first foreign currency bond sale (Eurobond) in June 2014 that was in two tranches worth USD 2 Billion from international investors both with lower yields than initially thought. There was a 5-year bond worth USD 500 million with an interest rate of 5.875%; and 10-year note worth USD 1.5 Billion with a yield of 6.875%. This was the largest debut for an African economy in the sovereign bond market; and Kenya joined other SSA economies that have ever sold Eurobonds eg Nigeria, Ghana, South Africa, and our own Rwanda in 2013 worth USD 400 Million.

EUROBOND ISSUANCE FUNDAMENTALS FOR EAC

There is need to ensure that market fundamentals are favorable before kick-starting the process:

The U.S Federal Reserve Quantitative easing programs should be favorable so as to cause reversal flows (shift of funds to EAC/ Frontier markets).

Strategic and robust roadshows in the West (U.S & Europe) by meeting large numbers of investors to explain to them the structure of the economy, management of the projects to be financed by Eurobond.

The economy ought to be resilient and quite diversified for risk management reasons on the part of the foreign investors.

Macroeconomic fundamentals like debt sustainability management is so key in attracting foreign investors.

Rationale for Eurobond Issuance by corporations & governments

Eurobond market have the following merits over domestic bond market for debt issuers:

This is an innovative product that surely meets the issuers' needs.

It gives borrowers an opportunity tap prospective lenders globally in contrast to local investors who are normally financially constrained.

It gives investors the beauty of anonymity since this issuance is made in bearer form that protects their identity.

Investors enjoy gross interest payments since this transaction is under no jurisdiction that can subject it to significant taxation. There are lower funding costs due to the competitive nature and greater liquidity of the market.

Issuers have the opportunity to make bond issues at any short notice.

This market requires less regulation and disclosure, which would be so cherished by both government and corporate issuers.

PROPOSED NEW DEBT INSTRUMENTS FOR EAC FINANCIAL SYSTEM

Euro Commercial Paper: these are CP issues denominated in currency outside the country of issue eg Dollar commercial papers. These are better than bank credit especially when large firms have better credit ratings than banks.

Euro notes: these are instruments that large firms can issue to raise short-term funds. These are unsecured debt securities with interest based on interbank rates (rates that banks charge for lending wholesale funds to one another).

Repurchase Agreements (repos): a repo deal involves pledging collateral (usually government bonds or some low-risk instruments) in return for short-term wholesale funds. At a set date, the funds will be repaid and the collateral "released". This is a technique widely used by banks to facilitate liquidity in the money markets by allowing firms to raise short-term funds at wholesale rates by pledging longer-term financial assets.

Eurobonds: these have lower regulations and instead effectively self-regulated by the Association of International Bond Dealers.

Treasury Inflation-protected Securities (TIPS): these are index-linked bonds whereby the principal value of the bond is adjusted regularly following the consumer price index (CPI) to account for the impact of inflation. The coupon is fixed but payable on the inflation-adjusted principal amount.

Individual investor bonds: these can be structured for the high net-worth individuals with minimum funds in excess of ....

Bankers acceptances are short term credit investments created by non-financial firms and guaranteed by a bank. It is a negotiable type of time draft frequently used in financing,

Repos or repurchase agreements are a form of borrowing. A dealer, or holder of a government security, sells it under the terms and conditions of repurchase at an agreed price and date.

In reverse repos the process is reversed to that of a repo – the dealer buys securities from an investor and then sells them back at a higher price on a later date.

Disadvantage

These are only as good as short-term instruments, since historically they have underperformed most other asset types over the medium to long term. In the long run, their returns have often been barely positive given the effects inflation and taxation subjected to their returns.

i)   How Securities are Issued and Traded

When firms need to raise capital they may choose to sell or list securities. These new issues of stocks, bonds, or other securities typically are marketed to the public by investment bankers in what is called the primary market. On the contrary, trading of already-issued securities among investors occurs in the secondary markets like the Uganda Securities Exchange (USE). It is imperative to note that trading in secondary markets does not affect the outstanding amount of securities; but ownership is simply transferred from one investor to another.

In the primary market, there are two types of issues of common stock:

Initial public offerings (IPO): these are stocks issued by a formerly private limited company that is going public, ie, selling shares to the public for the first time eg UMEME Ltd had its IPO in November 2013.

Seasoned equity offerings: these are offered by companies that already have floated equity eg, a sale by UMEME Ltd of new shares of stock in 2014 was a seasoned new issue.

However for bonds, there is a distinction between two types of primary market issues (public offering Vs private placement):

Public offering refers to an issue of bonds sold to the general investing public that can then be traded on the secondary market. Once the CMA has commented on the registration statement and a preliminary prospectus has been distributed to interested investors, the investment bankers organize **road shows** in which they travel around the country to publicize the imminent offering. These road shows serve to: generate interest among potential investors and provide information about the offering; provide information to the issuing firm and its underwriters about the price at which they will be able to market the securities. Shares of IPOs are allocated across investors in part based on the strength of each investor's expressed interest in the offering. IPOs commonly are underpriced compared to the price at which they could be marketed. Such under-pricing is reflected in price jumps that occur on the date when the shares are first traded in public security markets. The most dramatic case of under-pricing occurred in December 1999 when shares in VA Linux were sold in an IPO at $30 a share and closed on the first day of trading at $239.25, which was a 698% return for simply one day.

Private placement refers to an issue that usually is sold to one or a few institutional investors and is generally held to maturity. The fact that private placements are not made available to the general public, they generally will be less suited for very large offerings. Moreover, private placements do not trade in secondary markets like stock exchanges; which greatly reduces their liquidity and presumably reduces the prices that investors will pay for the issue

Public offerings of both stocks and bonds typically are marketed by investment bankers who in this role are called **underwriters**. More than one investment banker usually markets the securities; but a lead firm forms an underwriting syndicate of other investment bankers to share the responsibility for the stock issue. These financial services firms advise the issuing firm regarding the terms on which it should attempt to sell the securities, and a preliminary registration statement must be filed with the Capital Markets Authority (CMA), describing the issue and the prospects of the company. This preliminary prospectus is known as a red herring because it includes a statement printed in red, stating that the company is not attempting to sell the security before the registration is approved; and upon acceptance and approval by the CMA, it becomes the **prospectus**. At this point, the price at which the securities will be offered to the public is announced.

In a typical underwriting arrangement, the investment bankers purchase the securities from the issuing company and then resell them to the public. The issuing firm sells the securities to the underwriting syndicate for the public offering price less a spread that serves as compensation to the underwriters, a procedure called a **firm commitment**. In addition to the spread, the investment banker also may receive shares of common stock or other securities of the firm.

ii) Listing Rules on the EAC Securities Exchanges (a case of Uganda)

There are three Market Segments:

a) Main Investment Market Segment (MIMS)
   Main quotation market segment with stringent eligibility; listing and disclosure requirements

b) Alternative Investment Market Segment (AIMS) or Enterprise Growth Market (EGM)
   Provides capital to small to medium size high growth companies that don't meet the eligibility of MIMS and is meant for institutional and high net worth investors

c) Fixed Income Securities Market Segment (FISMS)
   Provides a separate market for government bonds, corporate bonds, commercial paper, preference shares, debenture stocks and any other fixed income instruments

REQUIREMENTS FOR LISTING ON MIMS

- *The issuer shall be a company limited by shares and incorporated under the companies Act (cap 85) as a public limited liability or if it is a foreign firm, it shall be registered under part X of the company Act.*

- *The issuer shall have a minimum authorized, issued and fully paid up share of 50000 currency points and net assets of 100000 currency points before the public offering of shares*

- *The issuer shall have published audited financial statements for a period of at least 5 years complying with International Accounting Standards for an accounting period ending on a date not more than six (6) months prior to proposed date of the offer*

- *The issuer shall have prepared financial statements for the latest accounting period on a going basis concern*

- At the date of application, the issuer shall not be in breach of any of its loan covenants
- For the period of two years prior to the date of the application, no director of the issuer may be adjudged bankrupt, convicted of a felony; prohibited by court from acting as a director of a public issuer.
- The issuer shall have declared positive profits after tax attributable to shareholder in at least 3 years
- Allowing public shares offering, at least 20% of the shares shall be held by not less than 1000 shareholders
- Issuers shall comply with the detailed disclosure requirements

REQUIREMENTS FOR AIMS/ EGM

This segmented has been developed by most EAC stock markets in a bid to cater for the needs of a large informal sector across the East African Community which businesses have not yet tapped capital from the regional capital markets. This is an equity market specifically intended for small and medium enterprises (SMEs), and start-ups that are so prevalent within the Sub-Saharan Africa. This comes at the wake of liberalization of the EAC economies that has significantly stimulated entrepreneurship, thus progressively increasing the number of SMEs despite challenges in raising capital for such businesses. These are market segments within the organized and formalized EAC stock markets with less stringent issuance and listing rules compared to the main equities investment market segments. This renders the EAC regional equities markets two tiered (just like many developed financial systems world over), whereby: the AIMS/EGM being the less stringent, more easily accessible, and by default, more risky segment aimed at start-ups and SMEs; whereas the MIMS being the more stringent, less accessible and less risky market segment aimed at larger, more established firms. This alternative market is also expected to be the market segment on which firms can grow and mature so as to later list on MIMS.

All the EAC economies' perspective plans, embedded in their Vision (2020, 2030, 2040), have as a critical objective the creation of a conducive environment to the growth and development of entrepreneurship, SMEs and particularly the private sector. This, above all, entails enhancing and facilitating access to capital markets that will help firms to transition from the informal sector to the formal sector, given the incentives of this market segment. The current financial system which is largely characterized by commercial banking activities has not helped the situation given the fact that such banks are few, relatively small, extremely risk averse, highly conservative in their lending policies, and also the exorbitant interest rate regime. This renders this market segment as a healthy competition into the long-term financing industry and particularly a reliable alternative source of funding for SMEs. Besides, this market has potential bring dynamism and vibrancy to the equity market through a visible increase in issuances and listings; this should later translate into more investment choices for regional investors and more incomes, but also enhance the EAC regional savings culture.

Prior to submission of the application for the listing of an issuer on the AIMS a prospectus giving a summary of the nature of the issuer, its mode of operation, its business plan and its prospects shall be submitted to the exchange through a sponsoring broker.

The issuer shall be a body corporate or registered as a public issuer ltd by shares under the companies Act Cap 85

The issuer shall have minimum authorized, issued and fully paid capital of 10000 currency points and net assets of 20000 currency points before seeking listing

At the date of application, the issuer shall not be breach of any of its loan covenants

For the period of 2 years prior to the date of application, no director of the issuer may be adjudged bankrupt; convicted of a felony; prohibited by court from acting as director of a public issuer

The immediate number of shareholders immediately following initial listing shall be 100

The issuer shall have been in existence in the same line of business for a minimum of 2 years with good growth potential

Issuer shall have produced audited financial statements for a period of not less than 2 years

The accounts of the issuer shall not be older than 4 months before the date of listing and shall be audited.

The issuer shall not have suitably qualified senior management with relevant experience for at least one year prior to the application for listing

The issuer may not use the proceeds of a public issue to redeem any loans by the directors or the shareholders incurred prior to the listing

At least one third of the issuer's board of directors shall consist of non-executive and independent directors.

Issuers shall comply with the detailed disclosure requirements

NB: This segment is inherently risky for investors compared to the MIMS; therefore, investors are expected to be extra vigilant when investing their money. This call for prudent investors to carry out due diligence before investing, and it basically requires informed investors who can assess the market and make rational decisions about the companies they are investing in.

REQUIREMENTS FOR FISMS (OTHER THAN GOVERNMENT BONDS)

- *Issuer shall be a company, a government, a local government or any other body corporate.*
- *Issuer shall have net assets of 100,000 currency points before*

offering of the securities, if not so, the Issuer shall obtain a guarantee from a bank or other financial institution acceptable to the Committee.

- *Issuer shall have published audited financial statements for three years complying with International Accounting Standards for an accounting period not exceeding six months before the proposed date of offer.*
- *Issuer shall have prepared financial statements for the latest accounting period on a going concern basis.*
- *At the date of the application, the Issuer shall not be in breach of any of its loan covenants.*
- *Issuer should have made profits in at least two of the last three years preceding the issue of the Commercial Paper or the Corporate Bond; and if not so, the Issuer should obtain a guarantee form a financial institution acceptable to the Committee.*
- *Issuer wishing to issue or list debt securities shall not be insolvent within the meaning of the Companies Act 85 and any amendments thereto.*
- *Total indebtedness of the Issuer, including the new issue of the Commercial Paper or Corporate Bond shall not exceed 400% of the Issuer's net worth (or a gearing of 4:1) as at the date of the latest balance sheet.*
- *The ratio of the funds generated from the operations to total debt for the three trading periods preceding the issue shall be maintained at a weighted average of 40% or more.*
- *The directors and senior management of an Issuer shall have collectively appropriate expertise and experience for the management of the business; and their details shall be disclosed in the issue information memorandum.*
- *Issuer shall ensure that each director is free of any conflict of interest as provided under these rules.*
- *If the Issuer is subject by law to the regulations of a regulatory*

authority, the Issuer shall obtain a letter of no objection from the relevant regulatory authority or such form of approval that the regulatory authority deem appropriate.

iii) Rationale for going public/ listing on Stock exchanges

A listed company can raise permanent finance through issuing securities to the general public which can be invested in long-term ventures for company growth, such as: ordinary shares, convertible and irredeemable preference shares; and irredeemable debentures.

Such a firm is viewed as a credit-worth & established firm from the perspective of creditors, hence facilitating its obtaining finance on favourable terms since it can pay good and regular dividends, which are not a legal obligation.

These firms have access to cheaper finance that would significantly reduce on both the transaction costs and cost of capital; through the issuance of among other, rights issue.

Shareholders of a listed firm have access to ready secondary/ stock market for their shares, and through which they can gauge the value of their investments and also monitor their performance.

A quoted company has the opportunity to enjoy both national and global prestige, which will boost its goodwill & its ability to raise finance even globally.

It is only financially sound firms that the Uganda Securities' Exchange can approve for floatation/ listing, which serves as an assurance to potential shareholders that it is a viable investment.

Quoted firms will enjoy the privileges offered by the government to induce others to list on stock exchange such as tax allowances, and at times protection from competitors (Umeme Ltd).

These firms operate within specific ethical guidelines, which would help prevent such firms from engaging in unethical activities and practices during their operations.

A listed firm will be availed with information in form of feedback through the mechanism of share prices on the stock market infrastructure. This would reflect the public opinion regarding the corporate performance as embedded in changes in the share prices.

a) Types of Orders

There are two types of orders in the capital markets: market orders and orders contingent on price.

Market Orders: Market orders are buy or sell orders that are to be executed immediately at current market prices. For instance, Becky (an investor) might call her broker and ask for the market price of UMEME Ltd., and the broker might report back that the best bid price is UGX 500 and the best ask price is UGX 520, meaning that Becky would need to pay UGX 520 to purchase a share, and could receive UGX 500 a share if she wished to sell some of her own holdings of UMEME Ltd. Note that the bid–ask spread in this case is UGX 20.

On the contrary, the best price quote may change before her order arrives, again causing execution at a price different from the one at the moment of the order.

Price-Contingent Orders: this is a scenario where investors also may place orders specifying prices at which they are willing to buy or sell a security. A limit buy order may instruct the broker to buy some number of shares if and when UMEME Ltd may be obtained at or below a stipulated price. Conversely, a limit sell instructs the broker to sell if and when the stock price rises above a specified limit; a collection of limit orders waiting to be executed is called a **limit order book**.

FUNCTIONS OF SECURITIES EXCHANGES (SECONDARY MARKETS).

- In this market, securities are sold by and transferred from one investor or speculator to another. It is therefore important that the secondary market be highly liquid (originally, the only way to create this liquidity was for investors and speculators to meet at a fixed place regularly; this is how stock exchanges originated). In general practice, the greater the number of investors that participate in a given market, and the greater the centralization of that market, the more liquid the market.

- Fundamentally, secondary markets mesh the investor's preference for liquidity i.e., the investor's desire not to tie up his or her money for a long period of time, in case the investor needs it to deal with unforeseen circumstances with the capital user's preference to be able to use the capital for an extended period of time.

- Accurate share price allocates scarce capital more efficiently when new projects are financed through a new primary market offering, but accuracy may also matter in the secondary market because price accuracy can reduce the agency costs of management, and make hostile takeover a less risky proposition.

BENEFITS OF STOCK MARKETS IN EAST AFRICA

- In principle, the stock market is expected to accelerate economic growth by providing a boost to domestic savings and increasing the quantity and the quality of investment. The stock market is expected to encourage savings by providing individuals with an additional financial instrument that may better meet their risk preferences and liquidity needs. Better savings mobilization may increase the savings rate.

- Stock markets also provide an avenue for growing companies to raise capital at lower cost. In addition, companies in countries with developed stock markets are less dependent on bank financing, which can reduce the risk of a credit crunch. Stock markets therefore are able to positively influence economic growth through encouraging savings amongst individuals and providing avenues for firm financing.

- The stock market is supposed to ensure through the takeover mechanism that past investments are also most efficiently used. Theoretically, the threat of takeover is expected to provide management with an incentive to maximize firm value. The presumption is that, if management does not maximize firm value, another economic agent may take control of the firm, replace management and reap the gains from the more efficient firm. Thus, a free market in corporate control, by providing financial discipline, is expected to provide the best guarantee of efficiency in the use of assets. Similarly, the ability to effect changes in the management of listed companies is expected to ensure that managerial resources are used efficiently. Efficient stock markets may also reduce the costs of information. They may do so through the generation and dissemination of firm specific information that efficient stock prices reveal. Stock markets are efficient if prices incorporate all available information.

- Reducing the costs of acquiring information is expected to facilitate and improve the acquisition of information about investment opportunities and thereby improves resource allocation. Stock prices determined in exchanges and other publicly available information may help investor make better investment decisions and thereby ensure better allocation of funds among corporations and as a result a higher rate of economic growth.

- Stock market liquidity is expected to reduce the downside risk and costs of investing in projects that do not pay off for a long time. With a liquid market, the initial investors do not lose access to their savings for the duration of the investment project because they can easily, quickly, and cheaply, sell their stake in the company thus, more liquid stock markets could ease investment in long term, potentially more profitable projects, thereby improving the allocation of capital and enhancing prospects for long-term growth.

NB: It is important to point out, however, that, theory is confusing about the exact impacts of greater stock market liquidity on economic growth. By reducing the need for precautionary savings, increased stock market liquidity may have an adverse effect on the rate of economic growth.

DEMERITS OF STOCK MARKETS IN EAST AFRICA.

There are serious limitations of the stock market that have led many analysts to question the importance of the system in promoting economic growth in African countries; and among others these are:

- Critics of the stock market argue that, stock market prices do not accurately reflect the underlying fundamentals when speculative bubbles emerge in the market. In such situations, prices on the stock market are not simply determined by discounting the expected future cash flows, which according to the efficient market hypothesis should reflect all currently available information about fundamentals. Under this condition, the stock market develops its own speculative growth dynamics, which may be guided by irrational behavior. This irrationality is expected to adversely affect the real sector of the economy as it is in danger of becoming the by-product of a casino.

- Besides, stock market liquidity may negatively influence corporate governance because very liquid stock markets may encourage investor myopia. Since investors can easily sell their shares, more liquid stock markets may weaken investors' commitment and incentive to exert corporate control. In other words, instant stock market liquidity may discourage investors from having long-term commitment with firms whose shares they own and therefore create potential corporate governance problem with serious implications for economy.

- Moreover the actual operation of the pricing and takeover mechanism in well functioning stock markets lead to short term and lower rates of long term investment. It also generates perverse incentives, rewarding managers for their success in financial engineering rather than creating new wealth through organic growth. This is because prices react very quickly to a variety of information influencing expectations on financial markets.

- Thus, prices on the stock market tend to be highly volatile and enable profits within short periods. Additionally, because the stock market undervalues long-term investment, managers are not encouraged to undertake long-term investments since their activities are judged by the performance of a company's financial assets, which may harm long run prospects of companies. Furthermore, empirical evidence shows that the takeover mechanism does not perform a disciplinary function and that competitive selection in the market for corporate control takes place much more on the basis of size rather than performance therefore, a large inefficient firm has a higher chance of survival than a small relatively efficient firm.

- Such problems are further magnified in developing countries especially East African economies with their weaker regulatory institutions and greater macroeconomic volatility. The higher degree of price volatility on stock markets in developing countries reduces the efficiency of the price signals in allocating investment resources.

PROBLEMS FACING THE EAST AFRICAN STOCK MARKETS (FRONTIER MARKETS)

- Macroeconomic Factors: macroeconomic risks include inflation risk, interest rate risk, low foreign exchange reserves and thin financial market which all together affect the performance of a stock market since macroeconomic policy has a great impact on the performance of the stock market.

- *Corporate Governance: Coup d'états is quite famous in East African history. It appears that constitutional rule are present there and politicians are manipulating constitutions to either seek longer terms in office or perpetuate their stay. Thus, there is a lack of good corporate governance in the countries. In the absence of corporate governance, there is inappropriate policy taken by the government and regulatory frameworks. Moreover, there is no control of corruption, capacity building, and there is an ineffective, inefficient, no transparent and accountable system for mobilizing and allocating public as well as private resources.*

- *High unemployment: there is abundance of unskilled labor in the EAC region and this may lead to decline of the working class. The growth in demand for skilled labor does not match the decline of unskilled and semi-skilled jobs. The labour market is shifting towards more skilled workers, professionals and managers. There is looming unemployment in the region, which adversely affect household disposable incomes, and consequently frustrates the operations of investing in capital markets by many citizens.*

- *Trade Development: many East African economies are faced with a multiplicity of challenges that prevent them from participating in the global economy and reaping the benefits of increased globalization. East Africa is one of the most fragmented regions, with some countries being landlocked, the roots of the problem lie in chronic constraints to competitiveness including: poor infrastructure, small and fragmented markets, undeveloped financial markets, weak systems to facilitate trade, weaknesses in key institutions, and the lack of adequate human resources.*

- *Political Risk: political instability, institutional incapacity and social unrest restrain foreign capital inflows. These in turn lower investment appetites, and have a negative impact for economic opportunities and investment climate. Perceptions of political risk arising from particular events, such as those related to the recent elections in the EAC member states which generate market* volatility and discourage investment. Some countries are seen as zones of high political risk, and significant risk premium are demanded by equity investors, lenders and insurers.

- Currency fluctuation risk: the global economic slowdown in world growth has affected East African exports of agricultural products, minerals and other resources. East African's dependence on natural resource exports has made many countries vulnerable to commodity price shocks that are outside their control. Sudden increases in export revenues or import costs cause currency instability and budget uncertainty; and, there is strong evidence that currency depreciation has negative effect on the performance of the East African stock markets.

STRATEGIES FOR BOOSTING EAST AFRICAN CAPITAL MARKETS

- They ought to develop well-functioning capital markets regulatory, compliance and risk-monitoring systems. Pragmatic evidence has shown that a well-functioning stock market, along with well-designed institutions and regulatory systems, fosters economic growth. Improvements in the regulatory and economic environments in some EAC countries have led to improvements in the liquidity and capitalization of their stock markets.

- Economies should enforce disclosure rules, accounting standards and enforceability of contracts so as to improve transparency and boost investor confidence.

- They should enhance the privatization of state-owned entities since privatization provides promise for private equity as well as helping with increasing the number of listed shares on exchanges if the IPO option is chosen.

- States should shift to automated systems across EAC markets: It is important for these markets to promptly adapt to automation and electronic systems. Automation not only minimizes inefficiencies associated with manual systems, it also reduces the costs of transacting, increases trading activity, liquidity in the stock markets and speeds up operations.

- *Economies ought to demutualize their stock exchanges to improve governance as a result of separate ownership. Demutualization has become a global trend; in EAC region, demutualization can help deter undue government influence. In certain stock markets where demutualization occurred, there was a noted improvement in liquidity and foreign investment.*

- *Economies ought to amplify focus on pension reforms since often investor participation is directly or indirectly through pension plans, insurance policies, unit trust funds, etc. Reform for these collective investments vehicles will assist in increasing institutional demand for investments and improve the savings rates across the region and Kenya is a good example for this reality in contrast to the Ugandan pension system.*

- *The financial systems need to introduce measures that enable companies' growth from informal sectors into capital markets. This can be through the provision of incentives and assistance to grow the large number of small, medium and micro enterprises (SMMEs) to, at some stage, list on the stock exchanges or be considered for private equity investments.*

- *These economies ought to deliberately attract capital inflows and encourage foreign participation (FDIs) in these financial systems. Africa has been attracting positive attention driven particularly by improved regulatory, good economic fundamentals and empowering private initiative.*

- *Governments should develop comprehensive capital market databases to foster investment analysis and academic research. This will enable the capital markets to adopt best research practices that will lead to increased investor attention to the region.*

- *Capital Markets Authorities and other investments industry regulators should enhance education of the public regarding the benefits of investing in capital markets. This will serve to increase retail investing on stock markets and also assist in increasing* the number of unlisted companies that look to stock and bond markets for growth.

iv) Why Firms desist from Listing

Companies listed on most EAC stock markets (apart from NSE) are way lower than those on other bourses like Johannesburg Stock exchange yet hundreds qualify for floatation. So, among other reasons, these are:

- *Many firms have other cheaper sources of finance, which would have been the major reason for listing on stock exchange. Firms like Stanbic Bank are believed to have issued shares not basically to raise finance but to give Ugandans a chance to acquire ownership in the company.*

- *Listing can prove to be an expensive means of raising finance due to the high floatation costs, such as: underwriting & brokerage commissions; printing a prospectus; advertising, legal, audit & clerical fees.*

- *Some firms in Uganda have shunned away from going public due to fear of being exposed to corporation and other taxes, which they have either been avoiding or evading; thus it is logical to remain private.*

- *Many firms in Uganda are owned by families, who would not wish to lose their control due to these firms going public that can lead to dilution of their control by new shareholders.*

- *Going public is quite tedious a process since the firm as to: get permission from Capital Markets Authority (CMA); get permission from stock exchanges; organise to get an underwriter; prepare a prospectus; compile the firm's books of account for previous five years; etc.*

- *Many prospective firms fear the loss of secrecy to the public which is a requirement for listing on stock exchange; corporate details would be available to shareholders, and competitors who can use them to out-compete the firm.*

- *Many firms in Uganda are subsidiaries of multi-national companies which are already listed at home, and the original owners of the parent company may not be willing to sell their interest.*
- *Some firms in Uganda have certain core objectives which they can't compromise with in a bid for finance; such as cooperatives, which when listed, entails loss of members' interests for which they were formed to serve eg dairy cooperatives.*
- *Many firms may not have long-term interests in the country due to short-term needs of owners and nature of the market in question such as tour companies, construction firms.*
- *Most firms in the EAC region can't maintain proper books of accounts, which is not only a requirement by CMA but also a security to the investing public that would question the performance of such firms.*
- *The nature of many businesses in Uganda may be in high risk areas such as agriculture that is affected by volatile weather conditions and prices. Such firms may not attract potential investors if they were to list their shares.*
- *Besides, the stock exchanges and the regulators have not really created a favourable and enabling environment for many firms to go public: failure to boost the public's investment knowledge; failure to sensitize SMEs on financial opportunities in capital markets; inadequate professional activities in the capital markets industry; inadequate initiatives & funding in the area of investment research.*

v) Policy interventions & suggestions

- *The State should facilitate the establishment of commodities exchanges since most EAC economies are predominantly an agro-based and commodities-based economy yet farmers don't have access to markets. This would consequently boost the resource base of basically rural households that would also enable them to save/ invest their incomes on the stock market.*

- *The government should revise the conditions and costs required by the regulatory authorities to list securities since these would become disincentive to infant companies to issue securities in securities markets.*
- *Disclosure requirements of listed firms should be enforced so that information whether good or bad can be availed to all the companies and the general public that wishes to transact on the stock market.*
- *Regulators ought to up its sensitization drives to all East Africans about the advantages of saving inform of investing so that the financial system can raise the volumes required for financing by all corporations that have deficit budgets.*

Chapter 18
DERIVATIVES MARKETS

One of the most significant developments of financial markets in recent years has been the growth of futures, options, and related derivative market instruments. These instruments are sometimes called "Contingent claims" since their values are contingent on the value of other assets.

A derivative is a financial instrument (or more simply, an agreement between two people) that has a value determined by the price of something else. For example, a sack of beans is not a derivative; it is a commodity with a value determined by the price of beans. However, you could enter into an agreement with a friend that says: If the price of a sack of beans in one year is greater than UGX 300,000; you will pay the friend UGX 100,000. If the price of beans is less than UGX 300,000; the friend will pay you UGX 100,000. This is a derivative in the sense that you have an agreement with a value depending on the price of something else (in this case, beans).

Though many folks may argue that this is not a derivative but just a bet on the price of beans, derivatives can be thought of as bets on the price of something. Of course, we can't absolutely rule out the element of betting in the derivative operations because: let us presume your family grows beans and your friend's family buys them for their restaurant. The bet provides insurance: you earn UGX 100,000 if your family's sack of beans sells for a low price; this supplements your income. Your friend earns UGX 100,000 if the sack of beans his family buys is expensive; this offsets the high cost of a sack of beans. Therefore, this bet hedges the two parties against unfavorable outcomes; and the contract has reduced risk for both parties. In fact, many investors use this kind of deal simply to speculate on the price of a sack of beans. On the contrary, the context in which this dealing is done determines everything; since this contract is neither insurance nor the contract itself, but how it is used, and who uses it, which determines whether or not it is risk-reducing.

a)   Uses of Derivatives

The following are some of the reasons why derivatives are becoming popular in their usage:

Risk management: Derivatives are a tool for companies and other users to reduce risks. The beans example above illustrates this in a simple way: The farmer/ seller of beans enters into a contract which makes a payment when the price of beans is low. This contract reduces the risk of loss for the farmer, who we therefore say is hedging: and this is not a complex transaction, just as many other derivatives are simple and familiar. As a matter of fact, every form of insurance is a derivative in the real sense. Automobile insurance is a bet on whether you will have an accident or not.

Speculation: Derivatives can serve as investment vehicles since derivatives can provide a way to make bets that are highly leveraged (that is, the potential gain or loss on the bet can be large relative to the initial cost of making the bet) and tailored to a specific view. For example, if you want to bet that a liter of Petrol will be between UGX 3500 and UGX 4500 one year from today, derivatives can be constructed to let you do that.

Reduced transaction costs: Sometimes derivatives provide a lower cost way to effect a particular financial transaction. For example, the manager of a unit trust fund may wish to sell stocks and buy bonds; and doing this entails paying fees to brokers and paying other transaction costs. But it is possible to trade derivatives instead and achieve the same economic effect as if stocks had actually been sold and replaced by bonds; hence, lower transaction costs than actually selling stocks and buying bonds.

Regulatory arbitrage: It is sometimes possible to dodge regulatory restrictions, taxes, and accounting rules by trading derivatives. Derivatives are often used, for example, to achieve the economic sale of stock (receive cash and eliminate the risk of holding the stock) while still maintaining physical possession of the stock. This transaction may allow the owner to defer taxes on the sale of the stock, or retain voting rights, without the risk of holding the stock.

b)   Perspectives on Derivatives

How a player thinks about derivatives depends on his position/ interest in the derivative markets, and so the following are the three distinct perspectives on derivatives:

The end-user perspective: These are the corporations, investment managers, and investors who enter into derivative contracts for the reasons listed in the previous section: to manage risk, speculate, reduce costs, or avoid a rule or regulation. End-users have a goal (such as, risk reduction) and care about how a derivative helps to meet that goal.

The market-maker perspective: These are intermediaries, traders who will buy derivatives from customers who wish to sell, and sell derivatives to customers who wish to buy. In order to make money, market-makers charge a spread. They buy at a low price and sell at a high price, just like shop/ market vendors who buy at the low wholesale price and sell at the higher retail price; and their inventory reflects customer demands rather than their own preferences. Market-makers typically hedge this risk and thus are deeply concerned about the mathematical details of pricing and hedging.

The economic observer: After a clinical analysis of the use of derivatives, the activities of the market-makers, the organization of the markets, the logic of the pricing models; then there is need to make sense of everything. This is the activity of the economic observer/ regulators who must often be guided in deciding whether and how to regulate a certain activity or market participant.

Early derivatives introduced an element of certainty into commerce and attracted much popularity; this led to the opening of the world's first derivatives exchange in 1848, the Chicago Board of Trade (CBOT). In fact, modern commodity markets trace their roots in trading of agricultural products; several African countries have established commodities exchanges but the Ethiopian Commodity Exchange (ECX) is remarkably one of the most active. However, Africa's first futures (derivatives) exchange opened in Alexandria, Egypt firstly dealing in cotton transactions in 1885. Derivatives came into existence due to the need to hedge risks. This begun from farmers who wanted to mitigate their risks or speculate on prices.

Today, derivatives trade also in financial instruments, indices, metals, energy and a diversity of other assets. These trading can be either over-the-counter (OTC) ie directly between intermediaries/ players or exchange-traded when it takes place on an organized exchange.

VOCABULARY IN DERIVATIVES TRANSACTIONS

Fair value is the actual value of products in the market.

Arbitrage is the pricing differently in various markets

Equity derivatives are called warrants and these are so popular on JSE.

TYPES OF DERIVATIVES

Derivatives can be broadly categorized into two, over-the-counter derivatives and the exchange-traded derivatives, and below is the break-down of each sub category:

Exchange-traded Derivatives

These have standardized features which renders them tradable on organized exchanges so as to guarantee settlement of such sophisticated financial products like index derivatives. This is done through a market intermediary called "central counterparty" between the parties in the transaction. Globally, there are many exchanges that deal in derivative instruments such as the Chicago Mercantile Exchange (largest derivative exchange), London Metal Exchange (that trades in non-precious metals), JSE (largest African derivative exchange that majorly deals in financial, commodity and currency derivatives. On the other hand, as the EAC, this year (2016) our own Nairobi Stock Exchange is rolling out derivative instruments, though also Dar es Salaam Stock Exchange and Uganda Securities Exchange are optimistic that by 2017 derivatives transactions will be operational.

The future, which is a legally binding agreement between a buyer and a seller whereby a buyer agrees to pay a pre-specified amount for the delivery of a particular pre-specified quantity of an asset at a pre-specified future date. On the other hand, the seller agrees to deliver the asset at the future date, in exchange for the pre-specified amount of money. The buyer is said to go long of the contract and the seller is said to go short of the contract; and entering into the transaction is called opening the trade yet the delivery of the commodity/instruments will close-out the trade.

The Options, this gives a buyer the right but not the obligation to buy or sell a specified quantity of an underlying asset at a pre-specified exercise price, on or before a pre-specified future date or between two specified dates. The seller in exchange for the payment of a premium (money paid by the buyer to the writer at the beginning of the options contract – non-refundable) grants the option to the buyer.

Equity derivatives

Equity futures and options on broad equity indices are perhaps the most commonly cited equity derivatives securities. Index futures contract enable an investor to buy a stock index at a specified date for a certain price. It can be an extremely useful hedging tool. For example, an investor with a stock portfolio that broadly matches the composition of the Umeme Ltd share index, he will suffer losses should the Umeme Ltd index record a fall in market value in the near future. Since he means to hold the portfolio as a long term strategy, he is unwilling to liquidate the portfolio. Under such circumstances, he can protect his portfolio by selling Umeme Ltd index futures contracts so as to profit from any fall in price. Of course, if his expectations turned out to be wrong and the Umeme Ltd index rose instead, the loss on the hedge would have been compensated by the profit made on the portfolio. Other commonly traded equity derivatives are equity swaps

Commodity derivatives

Basically on Commodities exchanges, the earliest derivatives instruments have been associated with commodities, driven by the problems about: storage, delivery and price volatility. The resulting price volatility in the spot markets gave rise to demand of commodity traders for derivatives trading to hedge the associated price risks. This saw for example, the popularity of forward contracts on Brent and other grades of crude in the 1970s following the emergence of the Organisation of Petroleum Exporting Countries.

Over-the-Counter Derivatives

These are negotiated and traded privately between parties without the use of exchanges; and this is the largest market for derivative instruments.

Swaps, these are agreements to exchange one set of cash flows for another; and they are negotiated between different parties so as to meet their different needs

Interest rate derivatives

Interest rate swap is one of the most popular interest rate derivatives in developed financial systems. It may involve a bank agreeing to make payments to a counterparty based on a floating rate in exchange for receiving fixed interest rate payments; thus providing an extremely useful tool for banks to manage interest rate risk. Given that banks' floating rate loans are usually tied closely to the market interest rates while their interest payments to depositors are adjusted less frequently, a decline in market interest rates would reduce their interest income but not their interest payments on deposits. By entering an interest rate swap contract and receiving fixed rate receipts from counterparty, banks would have hedged interest rate risk.

Foreign exchange derivatives

Essentially in the foreign exchange markets of the global financial system, the increasing financial and trade integration across countries have led to a strong rise in demand for protection against exchange rate movements over the past few decades. A very popular hedging tool is forward exchange contract: a binding obligation to buy or sell a certain amount of foreign currency at a pre-agreed rate of exchange on a certain future date.

For currencies of those economies with restrictions on capital account transactions, the profit or loss resulting from the forwards transaction can be settled in an international currency called non-deliverable forwards contract, and often traded offshore. Another type of foreign exchange derivatives are cross-currency swaps which involves two parties exchanging payments of principal (based on the spot rate at inception) and interest in different currencies.

Credit derivatives

A credit derivative is a contract in which a party (the credit protection seller) promises a payment to another (the credit protection buyer) contingent upon the occurrence of a credit event with respect to a particular entity (the reference entity). A credit event in general refers to an incident that affects the cash flows of a financial instrument (the reference obligation). The fastest growing type of credit derivatives over the past decade is credit default swap (CDS). In essence, it is an insurance policy that protects the buyer against the loss of principal on a bond in case of a default by the issuer. The buyer of CDS pays a periodic premium to the seller over the life of the contract. In the event of a credit incident, the buyer has a right to demand compensation from the seller.

WHY EAC STOCK EXCHANGES SHOULD EMBRACE DERIVATIVE INSTRUMENTS

i.   Derivatives allow the sharing or redistribution of risk. They can be used to protect (hedge) against a specific exposure of a business (e.g. exchange or interest rate, default of a creditor etc.) or can be used by market participants to take on risk and speculate on the movement in the value of underlying assets, without ever owning the assets.

ii.   Derivatives can allow businesses to manage effectively, exposures to external influences on their business over which they have no control. An example of this type of usage is in the Airline industry in which Airline companies hedge fuel prices exposure through the use of derivatives, which allows the company to focus on its core business. By taking out a futures derivative to purchase some fuel in advance of receipt at a fixed price, airlines get protected against an increase in fuel prices. If prices fall below the level set in the contract, the loss made on the derivatives contract is offset by the lower cost of fuel that they buy in a conventional manner.

iii.   Derivatives allow parties to speculate on the values of underlying assets, without necessarily having any actual interest in the asset itself. This use of derivatives for speculating on prices, is not necessarily bad. However, if it is coupled with a lack of transparency in the derivatives market as a whole, can lead to parties taking on too much risk and potentially destabilizing the financial system.

iv.   Derivatives also catalyze entrepreneurial activity and increase savings and investment in the long run, thus increasing the volume traded in markets because of participation of risk adverse people in greater numbers.

v.   Price Discovery. Futures market prices depend on a continuous flow of information from around the world and require a high degree of transparency. A broad range of factors climatic conditions, political situations, debt default, refugee displacement, land reclamation and environmental health, for example, impact supply and demand of assets commodities in particular and thus the current and future prices of the underlying asset on which the derivative contract is based. This kind of information and the way people absorb it constantly changes the price of a commodity. This process is known as price discovery.

vi.   Derivatives Also Help Reduce Market Transaction Costs - Since derivatives are a form of insurance or risk management, the cost of trading in them has to be low or investors will not find it economically sound to purchase such insurance for their positions.

FUNDAMENTALS OF DERIVATIVE TRADING FOR OUR SHALLOW FINANCIAL MARKETS

1.   Traders: There are 3 types of traders in the derivatives markets; namely, hedgers, arbitrageurs, and speculators. They ensure the flow of trades back and forth and bring balance to the market

2.   Electronic Trading Platforms: these enable exchanges to operate on a global scale, providing a steady level of speed, access and transparency.

3.   Clearing Houses: these stand at the center of every trade, acting as the buyer for every seller and the seller for every buyer, ensuring that each side can make good on the terms of the trade and protecting the integrity of the market.

4.   Liquidity: this is the ability for every buyer to find a seller, and every seller to find a buyer, so that trading activity can remain consistent and reliable.
   - *Public Education,*
   - *Improvement of market infrastructure in terms of technology,*
   - *Integration of information platforms*
   - *Buy in from regulators*

c)   Players in Derivatives markets

Derivatives markets are investments markets that are geared toward the buying and selling of a certain type of securities, or financial instruments. The following are the players or participants in derivatives markets;

Hedgers:

These are investors with a present or anticipated exposure to the underlying asset which is subject to price risks; and they use the derivatives markets primarily for price risk management of assets and portfolios. Hedger is a user of the market, who enters into futures contract to manage the risk of adverse price fluctuation in respect of his existing or future asset. Among hedgers are stockists, exporters, and producers: these have an underlying interest in commodities/ financial assets and use futures market to insure themselves against adverse price fluctuations

Speculators:

These are individuals who take a view on the future direction of the markets: whether prices would rise or fall in future and accordingly buy or sell futures and options to try and make a profit from the future price movements of the underlying asset. A trader, who trades or takes position without having exposure in the physical market, with the sole intention of earning profit is a speculator. Speculators are those who may not have an interest in the ready contracts but see an opportunity of price movement favorable to them. They are prepared to assume the risks, which the hedgers are trying to cover in the futures market; and they provide depth and liquidity to the market. They provide a useful economic function and are an integral part of the futures the market and their absence may at times lead to the collapse of markets

Arbitrageurs:

These take positions in financial markets to earn riskless profits. The arbitrageurs take short and long positions in the same or different contracts at the same time to create a position which can generate a riskless profit. Arbitrage refers to the simultaneous purchase and sale in two markets so that the selling price is higher than the buying price by more than the transaction cost, resulting in risk-less profit to the arbitrageur.

Day-traders:

Day traders take positions in futures or options contracts and liquidate them prior to the close of the same trading day.

Floor-traders:

A floor trader is an Exchange member or employee of a member, who executes trade by being personally present in the trading environment. The floor trader has no place in electronic trading systems.

Market makers:

A market maker is a trader, who simultaneously quotes both bid and offer price for a same commodity throughout the trading session. Some of the commodities have liquid market and some have either less liquid or illiquid markets. To bring the liquidity in the market of particular commodity, the exchange gives privileges to certain market players who are "market makers". As they normally belong to the class of speculators, they quote both rates for sale and purchase simultaneously

d)   Instruments & Markets in Derivatives Industry

There are four types of derivatives contracts and markets: forwards, futures, options, and swaps. And they are discussed below with the help of some specific examples of these instruments.

1.   Forwards contracts Market

A forward contract is an agreement to buy or sell a specified quantity of an asset at a specified fixed price with delivery at a specified date in the future. The value of the contract at inception is zero and typically does not require an initial cash outlay. The total change in the value of the forward contract is measured as the difference between the forward rate and the asset's spot rate at the forward date.

2.   Futures contracts Market

Futures contract is a contract between two parties; to buy or sell an asset for the price agreed upon today with the delivery and payment occurring at a future point (the delivery date) because it is a function of an underlying asset. Like forward contracts futures are;

- *Traded on an organized exchange*
- *The exchange clearing house becomes the intermediary between the buyer and the seller of the contract*
- *Contracts are standardized versus customized*
- *An initial deposit of funds is required to create a marked to market each day*
- *Represent current versus future monetary value therefore eliminating the need for discounting*
- *The party that writes the contract is said to be the short and the owner of the contract is said to be the long*

3.   Options contracts Market:

Options contracts can be either standardised or customised. There are two types of option: call and put options.

Call option: these contracts give the purchaser the right to buy a specified quantity of a commodity or financial asset at a particular price (the exercise price) on or before a certain future date (the expiration date).

Put option: these are contracts that give the buyer the right to sell a specified quantity of an asset at a particular price on or before a certain future date, based on the American-style option. But for a European style option, the contract can only be exercised on the expiration date. In options transaction, the purchaser pays the seller an amount for the right to buy or sell called the option premium. An important difference between options contracts; and futures and forwards contracts is that options do not require the purchaser to buy or sell the underlying asset under all circumstances.

4.   Swaps Market

Swaps are agreements between two counterparties to exchange a series of cash payments for a stated period of time. The periodic payments can be charged on fixed or floating interest rates, depending on contract terms. The calculation of these payments is based on an agreed-upon amount, called the notional principal amount or the notional. Swaps are a type of forward contract represented by a contractual obligation arranged by an intermediary that requires the exchange of cash flows between two parties. For example, a company with a loan payable with a fixed (variable) interest rate of interest expense for a variable (fixed) rate of interest.

In conclusion, derivatives are invented in response to some fundamental changes in the global financial system. If properly handled, they should help improve the resilience of the system and bring economic benefits to the users. In this context, they are expected to grow further with financial globalisation. However, past credit events exposed many weaknesses in the organisation of derivatives trading. The aim is to minimise the risks associated with such trades while enjoying the benefits they bring to the financial system. An important challenge is to design new rules and regulations to mitigate the risks and to promote transparency by improving the quality and quantity of statistics on derivatives markets particularly in the frontier market economies such as the EAC.

Chapter 19
FOREIGN EXCHANGE MARKETS

Glance

In the early 1970s, Ugandan commodities (both goods and services) were less competitive with their EAC counterparts; this saw many Ugandan traders and consumers spend a lot on importation of commodities from economies like Kenya, including simple household commodities like agricultural products which were even domestically available. Record has it that not only was the economy doing well but the value of Uganda shilling was slightly lower than the US dollar, and of course, better than other EAC currencies, hence making domestic commodities more expensive than imported ones. By the 1990s and early 2000s, after a couple of financial crises in Uganda, the value of the Ugandan shilling had fallen significantly from its highs in the 1970s, Ugandan commodities cheaper and domestic businesses more competitive regionally. This was evidenced by significant increases in the agricultural exports, influx of EAC and other foreign students in Ugandan education institutions, the growth in GDP, among other economic metrics

The foreign exchange market is one financial market that is characterized by high levels of volatility; and the exchange rates affect our daily life as households, the business sector, and the economy at large. This is because when the domestic currency like UGX (Uganda shilling) becomes more valuable relative to foreign currencies, foreign goods become cheaper for Ugandans and consequently Ugandan goods become more expensive for foreigners. On the contrary, when the UGX falls in value, foreign goods become more expensive for Ugandans and Ugandan goods become cheaper for foreigners. This has actually seen China in a situation of managing its Yuan so as to favourably compete in the global commodities markets but which is against the IMF policies of free market economy where the price mechanism should determine the foreign exchange rates amongst economies.

Most EAC economies adopted a free-floating exchange rate regime in response to the macroeconomic instabilities in the early 1980s and 1990s to ensure a consistence path towards economic development. This implies that the EAC central banks permitted the free market forces of demand and supply to determine the exchange rates. On the contrary, this has exposed these economies to great macroeconomic shocks (domestic and external) due to the high volatility in the exchange rates. The public, basically traders and consumers have always wondered why their governments do not come to their rescue by intervening in the foreign exchange market during hard times which has continually proved to be a thorn in the States' flesh and the Central banks have at times failed to have full control over the macroeconomic movements as compared to the free market forces.

Nonetheless, while addressing the business community on the 10th Private Sector Foundation Uganda International Trade Expo on why the Uganda Shilling is falling, Prof. Emmanuel Tumusiime-Mutebile (Governor, Bank of Uganda) made informative remarks. Uganda's exchange rate has faced repeated bouts of pressure since the first half of 2014; and on the trade weighted basis, the exchange rate has depreciated by around 23% since August 2014. The basic reason for this was that Uganda has suffered external shocks that have adversely affected her exports, tourism, and foreign direct investments yet actually the imports have remained quite strong. It is imperative to note that depreciation of the exchange rate has implications for the country's macroeconomics and the different sectors of the economy. Besides, given the flexible exchange rate regime, EAC central banks do not attempt to control the level of exchange rate because it is neither feasible in small open economies subject to external shocks nor desirable but monetary authorities restricts their intervention in the foreign exchange market to dampening volatility when the exchange rate becomes excessive. The exchange rate depreciation is a negative supply shock for the economy since it raises the cost of supplying goods and services in the economy; because many of these commodities are either directly imported or are produced locally but required imported inputs during their production (the case of most EAC economies). Thus, such shocks will inevitably raise inflation though it may take up to a year for the full effect of an exchange rate depreciation to be felt on the domestic prices.

From a theoretical perspective, any increase in demand for foreign currency or increase in supply of the local currency has in most cases been followed by escalation in the exchange rates.

FOREIGN EXCHANGE MARKETS

These are the largest financial markets with a daily global turnover in excess of USD 5 Trillion. The exchange rate basically measures the strength of one currency in relation to another, and the rate at which the two are exchanged (exchange rate) is largely determined by the forces of demand and supply. The foreign exchange market is an over-the-counter (OTC) market where traders/brokers negotiate directly with each other, without a central exchange or clearing house. These transactions used to be arranged over telephones but now electronic trading is trendy.

Of old, currencies were backed by gold (intrinsic value of money), which prevented the value of money from being debased and managing inflation. Later, the gold standard was replaced by the Bretton Woods Agreement after the Second World War, which aimed to prevent speculation in currency markets by fixing all currencies against the US Dollar and rendering the USD convertible to gold bullion at a fixed rate of USD 25 per ounce. This arrangement prohibited the devaluation of countries' currencies by more than 10%; but the growth of international trade and finance later undermined this agreement leading to its abandonment in the 1970s. Henceforth, currencies were permitted to freely float against each other ushering in the development of sophisticated financial assets in the foreign exchange markets.

This market is largely dominated by the UK, US, Japan, Eurozone and Singapore whereby transactions are done on 24/7; but trading in Africa has been quite thin largely due to exchange controls in many economies. On the contrary, the South African rand (ZAR) is the most liquid and visible African currency, followed by the Nigerian naira, and (the East Africa counterpart) Kenyan shilling

In the Ugandan market, foreign exchange turnover (between banks, forex bureaus, institutional and retail clients) averaged US$ 96.68 million in 2015 up from US$ 91.68 in 2014 and US$ 89.23 reported in 2013. A flexible exchange rate regime is pro-development but it could at times result in higher inflation and tightening of the monetary policy that would consequently lead to rising commercial bank lending rates. This was evidenced globally (but in particular East African Community) all through 2015 that actually led to escalating yield in both the debt markets across the board.

EAC Exchange Rates as at mid-May 2016

	KSH	TZS	UGX	RwF	BIF
KSH	-------	21.78	33.16	7.4	15.54
TZS	21.77	--------	0.66	2.96	2.09
UGX	33.29	1.52	-------	4.28	2.16
RwF	7.70	0.35	0.23	--------	0.50
BIF	15.55	2.1	2.16	0.49	

Source: EAC Central Banks (2016)

UGX has been rising against the USD since the relatively peaceful elections in Uganda that led to increased investor confidence; but also a tighter monetary policy by the Bank of Uganda. This has seen the local currency significantly appreciate in value vis-à-vis the USD compared to its record lows in September/October 2015.

KSH has equally been strengthening against the USD and of course other EAC peers due to Central Bank of Kenya's tighter monetary policies; coupled to the sale of a 9-year infrastructure bond that has been drawing in USD from off-shore investors.

RwF has also been relatively rising though by May 2016, it had failed to beat the negative predictions that that effects of the country's poor export earnings and a strong USD in 2015 would spill-over even in the bigger part of 2016.

TZS has equally been steadily strengthening despite some mild pressures from the domestic and global financial systems; but it is hopeful that USD inflows from firms that are seeking to meet their tax obligations and also payment of salaries would later usher in the desired stability.

"CARRY-TRADE" IN FOREX MARKETS

This is the borrowing of money from an economy with low interest and invest it in an economy with high interest rates to make a gain ie in Japan, there is a negative interest rate (government incentivizes people to borrow at almost 0% rate). So, some Japanese borrow from their economy so as to lend/invest in the U.S which has a 2% interest rate; and ultimately make a clean gain of 2% so as to later repay in Japan the money.

NB: This is why the equity markets don't really represent the economy because many foreign investors do this kind of trade & invest in emerging and frontier markets (hot money) to make huge gains.

The Instruments of Foreign Exchange Markets

Forward: it is an agreement established between two parties wherein they purchase, or trade an asset at a pre-agreed upon price called a forward contract. Normally, there is no exchange of money until a pre-established future date has been arrived at. Forwards are normally performed as a hedging instrument used to either deter or alleviate risk in the investment activity.

Future: this is a forward transaction that contains standard contract sizes and maturity dates are. Futures are traded on exchanges that have been created for that purpose exclusively. Just like with commodity markets, a future in the foreign currencies market normally designates a contract length of 3 months in duration; and interest amounts are also included in a futures contract.

Option: these are derivative instruments wherein the owner has the right to, but is not necessarily obligated to exchange one currency for another at a pre-agreed upon rate and a specified date. When referring to options in any form, the foreign exchange market is the deepest and largest, as well as the most liquid market of any options in the world.

Spot: where futures contracts normally employ a 3-month timeframe, spot transactions encompass a 48-hour delivery transaction period. There are four characteristics that all spot transactions have in common, namely:
- *A direct exchange between two currencies*
- *involves only cash, never contracts*
- *No interest is included in the agreed upon transaction*
- *Shortest of all transaction timeframes*

Swap: currency swaps are the most common type of forward transactions. A swap is a trade between two parties wherein they exchange currencies for a pre-determined length of time. The transaction then is reversed at a pre-agreed upon future date. Currency swaps can be negotiated to mature up to 30 years in the future, and involve the swapping of the principle amount. Interest rates are not "netted" since they are denominated in different currencies.

PLAYERS IN THE FOREIGN EXCHANGE MARKET

There are many parties that trade on the foreign exchange market for completely various reasons than those in other financial markets. Therefore, it is very important to identify and understand the functions and motivations of these main players in the foreign exchange market.

Governments and Central Banks

The most influential participants involved in the forex market are the central banks and government bodies. In most countries, the central bank is an extension of the government and it conducts its policy in unison with the government objectives. However, some governments feel that a more independent central bank is more effective in balancing the goals of managing the country's macroeconomics and achieving a sound financial system that are critical towards economic growth. Central banks are often involved in maintaining foreign exchange reserves in order to meet certain economic goals.

Banks and Other Financial Institutions

Along with central banks and governments, other largest participants in foreign exchange transactions are banks for people, who need foreign currency for small-scale transactions. Banks also make currency transactions with each other on electronic brokering systems that are based on credit; and only banks that have credit relationships with each other can engage in transactions. The larger banks tend to have more credit relationships, which allow those banks to receive better foreign exchange prices yet the smaller the bank, the fewer credit relationships it has and the lower the priority it has on the pricing scale.

Hedgers

All financial agents, regardless of their size, are appreciably affected by the volatility of foreign currencies; whether a business is selling to an international client or buying from an international supplier; and foreign exchange risk is a big problem for many multinational corporations. Since the exchange rate can fluctuate in any direction over the course of a year, any company that transacts in the global financial system has no way of knowing whether it will end up paying more or less foreign currencies at the time of delivery. One choice that a business can make to reduce the uncertainty of foreign-exchange risk is to go into the spot market and make an immediate transaction for the foreign currency that they need.

In the world of business, hedgers are entities (individuals or businesses) wanting to reduce their risk of loss from price changes. Their risk naturally occurs because they are doing business with economic goods and/or financial instruments. In broad terms, there are two types of hedgers: short hedgers and long hedgers; i.e., hedgers who either want to protect against a price decline or a price rise, respectively. Because hedgers have one foot in the money markets, they tie future prices to present prices. Thus, as we move into the future, future prices become present prices (convergence).

Because the various FOREX markets tend to move parallel to one another, it is possible to hedge currency risk. While there are both long and short hedgers providing liquidity to one another, hedging is also facilitated by speculators who provide the bulk of liquidity that makes for ease of entry and exit for hedgers.

Speculators

Another class of participants in foreign exchange markets is speculators. Instead of hedging against changes in exchange rates to finance international transactions, speculators attempt to make money by taking advantage of fluctuating exchange-rate levels. Speculators assume risk in the pursuit of profits, and their risks are calculated to maximize profit potential. They might speculate that prices will rise, decline, go sideways or that price differentials will widen or narrow

Arbitrageurs

Arbitrageurs buy and sell the same currency at two different markets whenever there is price discrepancy. The principle of "law of one price" governs the arbitrage principle. Arbitrageurs ensure that market prices move to rational or normal levels. With the proliferation on internet, cross currency, cross currency arbitrage possibility has increased significantly.

SWIFT

In an interbank forex transaction, no real money changes hand. All transactions are done electronically through SWIFT. Banks undertaking forex transactions simply transfer bank deposits through SWIFT to settle a transaction. SWIFT is the Society for Worldwide Interbank Financial Telecommunication is a cooperative organization headquartered at Belgium. The Swift network connects around 8300 banks, financial institutions and companies operating 208 countries. Swift provides a standardized messaging service to these members. As and when two counterparties undertake a transaction, SWIFT transports the message to both financial parties in a standard form. As the forex market is mainly an OTC market, SWIFT message provides some kind of legitimacy to the transactions. It is solely a carrier of messages, and it does not hold funds nor does it manage accounts on behalf of customers, nor does it store financial information on an ongoing basis. As a data carrier, SWIFT transports messages between two financial institutions. This activity involves the secure exchange of proprietary data while ensuring its confidentiality and integrity. For every participating member, SWIFT assigns a unique code which is used to transport messages.

Big Multi-National Corporations

Big multinational companies earn their revenue and incur expenses in various currencies eg, Switzerland-based Nestle operates in 86 countries across the globe. To hedge their foreign exchange risk these multinational companies directly participate in the wholesale market.

Hedge & Unit Trust Funds

Hedge funds are also major player in this market since they collect huge sums from high net-worth individuals and undertake speculative trades in equity, debt, forex and derivatives market. Mutual funds with international equity portfolio are also major players in this market because they can't escape the volatility of foreign currencies, and their effects on the fund's risk/return profiles.

Chapter 20
MORTGAGE MARKETS

PROPERTY & MORTGAGE MARKET

As an asset class, property has at times offered positive real long term returns, low volatilities and a reliable flow of income. Therefore, an exposure to property investments particularly in EAC economies like Uganda and Kenya (which have property/land tenure systems that promote absolute private ownership) can provide diversification benefits owing to its low correlation with both traditional and alternative asset classes. This can be either through direct private investment in this asset class or institutional investing within a diversified portfolio opting for indirect exposure via real estate investment trusts (REITs), etc.

Investments in these markets, especially housing sales, have a powerful effect on the economy since homeowners tend to fill up their dwellings with a couple of consumer products like furniture, electronics, dishwashers, among other household consumables. On the other hand, investment in huge infrastructural projects have among the highest and longest-lasting economic multiplier effects since they lead not just to jobs but to shortage of labor. Such shortages of labor have potential to drive up wages and consequently increase savings, which will later significantly boost the financial system.

EAC property markets are some of Africa's best performing markets for investors, and their prices have been increasing drastically. For instance, figures from the Kenya Property Developers Association indicated that investment returns were in excess of 28% by early 2015. Returns are, in fact, believed to possibly go as high as 35% in some major cities across the EAC though also the risk package is equally high in this asset class in many parts of the EAC region due to poor or no regulation at all. On the other hand, with the introduction of REITs by Kenya's capital markets, and later prospectively by Uganda, Rwanda and Tanzania (according to interactions with securities markets' CEOs), this will provide a means to tap the dormant liquidity stored in banks, insurance and pension funds through an attractive mechanism of securitizing developments across the EAC region.

Currently, statistics indicate a huge housing deficit within the EAC, for instance Kenya's deficit has grown to 2 million housing, with an annual deficit of 150,000 homes. Across the EAC, just like many African markets, financing in the residential property has significant blockages; in Kenya the regional giant economy with a relatively better developed mortgage market, there were just 22,000 mortgage accounts by early 2015. Statistics show that only 11% of Kenyans earn enough to support a mortgage; this has led to very low levels of mortgage uptake partly due to high commercial banks interest rates such as Uganda (24.4%), Kenya (17.8%), Tanzania (16.0%), Rwanda (17.0%), and Burundi (16.3%) as at March 2016.

Large pools of long-term capital are available in pensions and investment funds although these are not prepared to invest in mortgages. The MD of NSSF-Uganda decries the poor regulation of the mortgage industry, coupled with the diverse land tenure systems across the EAC (but Uganda in particular).

Mortgage: is a debt instrument, secured by the collateral of specified real estate property that the borrower is obliged to pay back with a predetermined set of payments. Mortgages are used by individuals and businesses to make large real estate purchases without paying the entire value of the purchase up front. Over a period of many years, the borrower repays the loan, plus interest, until he/she eventually owns the property.

Mortgage market: is a market for loans to people and organizations buying property or market for mortgages that have been bought by financial institutions and are then traded as asset-backed securities.

CLASSIFICATION OF MORTGAGE MARKET

Primary mortgage market. The market where borrowers and mortgage originators come together to negotiate terms for mortgage transaction. Mortgage brokers, mortgage bankers, credit unions and banks are all part of the primary mortgage market. After being originated in the primary mortgage market, most mortgages are sold into the secondary mortgage market. Unknown to many borrowers is that their mortgages usually end up as part of a package of mortgages that comprise a mortgage-backed security (MBS), asset-backed security (ABS) or collateralized debt obligation (CDO).

Secondary mortgage market. The market where mortgage loans and servicing rights are bought and sold between mortgage originators, mortgage aggregators (securitizers) and investors. The secondary mortgage market is extremely large and liquid. A large percentage of newly originated mortgages are sold by their originators into the secondary market, where they are packaged into mortgage-backed securities and sold to investors such as pension funds, insurance companies and hedge funds. The secondary mortgage market helps to make credit equally available to all borrowers across geographical locations.

MORTGAGE LOAN TYPES

There are many types of mortgages used worldwide, but several factors broadly define the characteristics of the mortgage. All of these may be subject to local regulation and legal requirements.

1. *Interest: Interest may be fixed for the life of the loan or variable, and change at certain pre-defined periods; the interest rate can also be higher or lower.*

2. *Term: Mortgage loans generally have a maximum term, that is, the number of years after which an amortizing loan will be repaid. Some mortgage loans may have no amortization, or require full repayment of any remaining balance at a certain date.*

3. *Payment amount and frequency: The amount paid per period and the frequency of payments; in some cases, the amount paid per period may change or the borrower may have the option to increase or decrease the amount paid.*

4. *Prepayment: Some types of mortgages may limit or restrict prepayment of all or a portion of the loan, or require payment of a penalty to the lender for prepayment.*

The two basic types of amortized loans are the fixed rate mortgage (FRM) and adjustable-rate mortgage (ARM) (also known as a floating rate or variable rate mortgage). In some countries, such as the United States, fixed rate mortgages are the norm, but floating rate mortgages are relatively common. Combinations of fixed and floating rate mortgages are also common, whereby a mortgage loan will have a fixed rate for some period, for example the first five years, and vary after the end of that period.

1. *Fixed Rate Mortgage. The interest rate remains fixed for the life (or term) of the loan. In case of an annuity repayment scheme, the periodic payment remains the same amount throughout the loan. In case of linear payback, the periodic payment will gradually decrease.*

2. *Adjustable Rate Mortgage. The interest rate is generally fixed for a period of time, after which it will periodically (for example, annually or monthly) adjust up or down to some market index. Adjustable rates transfer part of the interest rate risk from the lender to the borrower, and thus are widely used where fixed rate*

funding is difficult to obtain or prohibitively expensive. Since the risk is transferred to the borrower, the initial interest rate may be, for example, 0.5% to 2% lower than the average 30-year fixed rate; the size of the price differential will be related to debt market conditions, including the yield curve.

Balloon Mortgages

These last for a much shorter term and work a lot like a fixed-rate mortgage. The monthly payments are lower because of a large balloon payment at the end of the loan. The reason why the payments are lower is because it is primarily interest that is being paid monthly. Balloon mortgages are great for responsible borrowers with the intentions of selling the home before the due date of the balloon payment.

The charge to the borrower depends upon the credit risk in addition to the interest rate risk. The mortgage origination and underwriting process involves checking credit scores, debt-to-income, down payments, and assets. Jumbo mortgages and subprime lending are not supported by government guarantees and face higher interest rates. Other innovations described below can affect the rates as well.

3   Interest Only Mortgages

The borrower only pays the interest on the mortgage through monthly payments for a term that is fixed on an interest-only mortgage loan. The term is usually between 5 and 7 years. After the term is over, many refinance their homes, make a lump sum payment, or they begin paying off the principal of the loan. However, when paying the principal, payments significantly increase. If the borrower decides to use the interest-only option each month during the interest-only period, the payment will not include payments toward the principal. The loan balance will actually remain unchanged unless the borrower pays extra.

Players in the mortgage market

- *Deposit Taking Microfinance-Institutions (DTMs)*
- *Private Equity Firms*
- *The Government*
- *Investors.*
- *The banking sector*

Challenges to Developing the Mortgage Market in the EAC Region

Lack of Long-term Funds: Uganda's financial system still lacks sufficient long-term liabilities, owing to an undeveloped pension industry and limited life insurance funds.

The commercial banks, which play the dominant role, have mostly short-term deposits and are therefore inclined to provide loans only for periods not exceeding two years.

Infrastructure Provision and Costs: the Domestic EAC regulation empowers local authorities to control development and provide urban services. However, delivery of the vast bulk of infrastructural services (access roads, water, sewerage and electricity connections) has been pioneered by developers and individual builders, to make their housing estates more attractive to end buyers. Infrastructural investments are estimated at between 15 and 25 percent of the price of the house depending on the location of the site on top of the existing infrastructure services.

Land Provision and Cost: EAC region land tenure systems have presented a major hurdle to the supply of decent housing stock, especially in urban areas.

The Land Act provides that land is held under four tenures; mailo3, customary4, freehold and leasehold. However, terms set on how they are exercised (other than leasehold) do not adequately respond to changes in urbanization5. For example, in the case of the mailo tenure, the Act separates ownership of land (title holder) from occupancy or ownership of development by 'lawful' occupants.

Affordability: The lack of affordability is a combination of factors which includes the low levels of income (especially in rural areas), and the high and volatile level of inflation and relatively high mar¬gins charged by banks. Issues on the supply side also create a price barrier for many, where the cost of even the most basic new house is out of reach for the vast majority.

Risk Management: Deficiencies in a lender's ability to capture or understand risks mean that lend¬ers have to charge a high 'risk premium'. This is due to the fact that credit bureaus do not yet offer comprehensive credit histories, there is a high level of informality, and the value of collateral is tem¬pered by deficiencies in the foreclosure process, resale market and the valuation process.

Financing: This is ranked as the biggest obstacle but the facts suggest a relatively liquid banking sec¬tor with a low loan to deposit ratio. The issue is the availability of long term funds and the mismatch between short term deposits and the longer term mortgage loans. However, the current ratios sug¬gest that banks could engage in further maturity transformation before hitting limits. Some of the large lenders however are constrained and certainly if current levels of growth continue, the rest of the sector will be also.

Economic growth: Periods of economic growth exhibit key characteristics that influence the mortgage market. Growth generates positive consumer and investor expectations of continued economic development. The added confidence in economic performance encourages consumer spending and business investment. Higher levels of spending and investment increase the demand on the money supply moving through the economy. Higher demand for money puts upward pressure on interest rates throughout the economy.

Inflation: this places upward pressure on prices resulting in the erosion of purchasing power for both consumers and investors. During periods of economic growth where the demand for money grows, competition for money increases, pushing interest rates continually higher. The result in the mortgage markets is that financing costs increase while home values decrease.

Economic Decline: periods of economic decline can have negative consequences for the mortgage market. When the economy shrinks, consumers and investors spend less money. The decrease in spending shrinks the demand for money. With less competition for money, interest rates are pushed downward. For prospective home buyers, lower interest rates during periods of low economic growth can help decrease the long-term cost of home ownership.

Unemployment: this is one of the most significant developments in Uganda during periods of economic decline. Higher unemployment rates decrease the levels of consumer spending as incomes are reduced. For the mortgage market, lower incomes for potential homeowners and overall economic uncertainty helps decrease the demand for homes and mortgages.

DEVELOPING THE EAC MORTGAGE MARKETS

The following measures seek to address the challenges and barriers which prevent the development of EAC mortgage market:

Expand the stock of mortgage-able properties: The supply of land for housing and having a functioning secondary market for housing sales are essential elements of an efficient mortgage system. This requires a more streamlined and cost efficient property registry system; and a unified and simplified mortgage law.

Provide Affordable Finance: the current cost of mortgage financing is prohibitive for the vast majority of the population. The urban population could consider taking out a mortgage loan which represents just 2 or 3 percent of the national population however, Mortgages are completely out of reach for the entire rural population but steps could be taken to improve affordability such as new products design

Improve Risk Management: As the market grows in size, some economies of scale will arise, but efficiency gains and lowering of the risk premium can also help to bring down the cost of loans. Thus, improvements such as: expanding coverage of the Credit Reference Bureau to have fuller credit histories, as well as to non-bank finan¬cial intermediaries; standardization of documentation; fortifying confidence in the sector by introducing prudential standards for loan underwriting

Development of a secondary mortgage market: there is need to develop a mortgage liquidity facility which would benefit the sector as a whole, while also pursuing the development of a mortgage covered bond framework for the larger lenders. This will target institutional investors, but it would be important to review investment rules of Pensions Funds and Insurance Companies.

Chapter 21
THE EAST AFRICAN COMMODITIES EXCHANGES

Introduction

A commodities exchange can be defined as an entity, usually an incorporated non-profit association that determines and enforces rules and procedures for the trading of commodities and related investments, such as commodity derivatives. Commodities exchange also refers to the physical center where trading takes place.

The exchange carries out its commodity derivatives transactions on the basis of an open and free market system, and it also facilitates the procurement system of standardized commodities by identifying warehouses. Ancient commodity markets began with the trading of agricultural products, such as: corn, cattle, wheat and pigs. In fact, the first commodity exchange in Africa was initiated via Egypt through the Alexandria Stock Exchange that was dealing in food crops which brought participants from the whole world though it collapsed in 1961; but Ethiopia established the first modern commodity exchange on the continent. Contemporary commodities markets trade many types of investment vehicles, and are often utilized by various investors from commodity producers to investment speculators. For example, a corn producer could purchase corn futures on a commodity exchange to lock in a price for a sale of a specified amount of corn at a future date, while at the same time a speculator could buy and sell corn futures with the hope of profiting from future changes in corn prices.

Commodity Markets.

A commodity is the generic term for a good for which there is demand, but is also supplied with no material differentiation across a market. This means that most commodities are fully, or at least, partially fungible (ie, uniform, interchangeable, and substitutable). A commodity is a raw, or primary, product. A strict definition means that a commodity is a basic good that is used in commerce and is interchangeable with others of the same type. Commodities are most often used as inputs in the production of other goods or services. The quality of a given commodity may differ slightly, but it is essentially uniform across producers.

The main types of commodities include:

- *Agricultural (dairy products and livestock, coffee, sugar, corn and wheat, etc).*
- *Energy (oil and gas).*
- *Metals and natural resources (copper, aluminium, rubber).*

In commodities markets, the categories of soft and agricultural commodities are used interchangeably, since, by definition, both refer to commodities that are grown and not mined. Commodities markets include both over-the-counter (OTC) and cash markets, as well as a range of global exchanges.

Energy markets are those commodities markets that deal specifically with the trade and supply of energy. Oil is one of the most traded commodities in the world. Oil is traded in a wide range of products. This ranges from the different grades of oil contracts and gasoline futures that are traded on exchanges. Crude oil has many uses in many different markets and industries.

GENESIS OF COMMODITIES EXCHANGES

Commodities (Futures) trading dates back to 17th Century Japan with rice as the major commodity. Future trading is a natural progression of things in response to the difficulties of maintaining a year round supply of products which are dependable on seasons like agricultural crops. In ancient Japan, rice used to be stored in warehouses for future consumption by the rice merchants. To raise funds, these merchants would then sell their "rice tickets" (receipts of the stored rice). Later, these rice tickets came to be regarded as a sort of all-purpose currency. As trading in rice tickets became more widespread, rules to standardize the trading of these rice tickets were introduced. In a way, these rules were akin to the current rules of the US Futures trading.

Futures trading began in the US only towards mid 1800s and the Chicago Board of Trade (CBOT) was setup in 1848; and currently, there are ten commodity exchanges established in the US, with the CBOT being the largest.

COMMODITY DERIVATIVES

These were originally developed as a method for farmers to lock-in the value of their crops and avoid the risk of it going below its cost price. Derivative contracts were offered on various agricultural products, such as cotton, rice, coffee and wheat.

The first organized exchange, the **Chicago Board of Trade** (CBOT), with standardized contracts on various commodities was established in 1848. The trading of commodities derivatives takes place in both the OTC and on a number of global exchanges. Exchange-traded commodity derivatives have seen a significant increase in trading volume since 2000. This was largely a result of the growing attraction of commodities as an asset class and the development of different types of derivative contracts, which has made it easier to access this market. Trading on exchanges in China and India has gained in importance in recent years due to their emergence as significant commodities consumers and producers.

China now has the fourth largest commodities derivative exchange (the Dalian Commodities Exchange). As the BRIC (Brazil, Russia, India, and China) economies continue to grow and the income of their population rises, demand for a wide range of commodities is expected to also rise. This, in turn, will support demand for commodity derivatives, as price volatility is forecast to remain high.

CURRENT SITUATION IN EAC ECONOMIES (OPERATIONS)

In spite of being fully liberalized, the marketing of agricultural products continues to face problems particularly in the non-traditional export crop sector, where markets are poorly structured, and transaction costs are high. There is a paucity of market price information on these crops upon which producers can make appropriate marketing decisions and this coupled with an almost complete absence of inventory finance results in large fluctuations in price throughout the two annual marketing seasons.

The commercialization of agriculture in Uganda is a slow but ongoing process; commodities such as coffee and cotton are predominantly small holder produced for the export markets and as such are cash crops. The small holders producers for these commodities are integrated into the marketing chain and as such benefit from greater access to market information and financial instruments such as inventory credit from the processors and exporters of these commodities.

Regional buyers and sellers, as well as international producers and consumers can participate in the commodity trading activities on these Commodities Exchanges, and these could carry out commodities derivatives (futures and options) transactions on the basis of an open and free market system.

RWANDA

Rwanda's commodity exchange called "EAX" (East Africa Exchange) trades in beans, maize. It begun in 2013 & it operates thru auctions but uses automated trading system. It is self-regulated but draft legal framework is with parliament that will make it be regulated by CMA. The Warehousing receipt system is in place & plans are underway for it to deal commodity derivatives in gold, and precious metal that are existent in the country.

UGANDA NATIONAL COMMODITIES EXCHANGE

Formerly Uganda Commodities Exchange (UCE), has the mandate of operating a commodities exchange; this has stakeholders like: the farmers' federation, Uganda Development Corporation (development arm of gov't), Grain Council of Uganda, and Uganda Co-operatives Alliance. It is now being regulated by CMA through giving licenses to players, and regulating trading but the instrument that is used "warehousing receipt" is regulated & issued by Uganda Warehousing Receipt Systems Authority (UWRSA).

The commodities exchange envisions, "establishing a market that brings value to its members and the general trading public". Its mission is "to provide market information and services to buyers and sellers of commodities by establishing and operating a commodity exchange of the highest integrity available to Ugandans as well as regional and international buyers and sellers, based upon an open and free market system for the mutual benefit of the sellers and buyers; and to facilitate the procurement of and marketing of any commodity provided or desired by any consenting parties through the auspices of the exchange".

TANZANIA MERCANTILE EXCHANGE (TMX)

This first ever commodity exchange in Tanzania was launched on 30th October 2015 so as to promote agricultural development and also the capital markets. This is to serve as a new centralized marketplace where commodity producers will be able to sell and market their products internationally but also regional markets thus adding value to the global food security requirements. The TMX seeks to promote transparency, reduce transaction costs via natural price discovery; and it is initially begin with the following commodities: coffee, cashew nuts, cotton, rice; but will later on include a diversity of other commodities and trading is expected to begin in June 2016 after numerous trainings of rural districts. It is imperative to note that the agricultural sector significantly contributes to the Tanzanian GDP a whole 30% yet this initiative has potential of even doubling this percentage, and thus bettering the per capita income and productivity for rural dwellers (in particular, farmers in rural Tanzania).

The TMX (Plc) is an entity formed under Public Private Partnership comprising of shareholders from the Government of the United Republic of Tanzania and Public sector Institutions (49% ownership); and Private sector Institutions such as cooperative societies and farmers-based organizations (51% ownership). The exchange is licensed under the Commodity Exchange Act, 2015 and regulated by the Capital Markets & Securities Authority. This initiative comes as the result of farmers' fragmentation in Tanzania but also EAC region that has adversely affected national development yet cooperatives can serve as a major channel for many farmers to sell goods at a competitive market rates from smallholder farmers. Besides, the development of agricultural value-chain is poised to be a catalyst towards poverty eradication across the EAC region where such organized marketplaces greatly lack. This exchange will operate in a similar way via the warehouse receipt system just like the structure in Ethiopia and Ghana; seeking to provide market integrity that promotes price transparency, price discovery and reduced costs. Thus, empowering farmers to receive the best possible prices for their agricultural production.

PARTICIPANTS IN THE EAC COMMODITIES EXCHANGE

Efficient commodities markets require a large number of market participants with diverse risk profiles; but ownership of the underlying commodity is not required for trading in commodity derivative (just like for all derivative markets). The market participants simply need to deposit sufficient money with brokerage firms to cover the margin requirements; and market participants can be broadly divided into hedgers, speculators, arbitrageurs, and regulators.

Hedgers: drive prices down. One could take a short position, for instance, in maize futures, and if prices fall, one could then buy back the futures at a lower price than had previously sold them (this is a risk management system). Of course, if prices rose, one would lose money on the futures transaction, but the idea is to use futures as a hedge.

Speculators: They are traders who speculate on the direction of the futures prices with the intention of making money. Thus, for the speculators, trading in commodity futures is an investment option. Most Speculators do not prefer to make or accept deliveries of the actual commodities; rather they liquidate their positions before the expiry date of the contract. A speculator, including individual investors and professionals such as hedge funds or managed futures traders, could take the opposite side of the hedger's futures transaction. That participant would bear the risk that prices are going to rise in hopes of generating a profit on the long futures position. Most likely, this type of speculator has no actual stake in the business, other than futures trading.

Arbitrageurs: These are traders who buy and sell to make money on price differentials across different markets. Arbitrage involves simultaneous sale and purchase of the same commodities in different markets; it keeps the prices in different markets in line with each other (normally such transactions are risk free).

Regulators: These are government bodies which regulate transactions in this industry, and they include majorly Capital Markets and Securities Authorities across the EAC region but also Warehousing Receipt System Authorities. These set the guidelines to be followed in commodities trading, license the players, and promote the whole industry.

The Exchange: This is the platform or the infrastructure that links the various players in this market and ensures efficiency, integrity and transparency in the commodities transactions.

Prospective Instruments to be traded on the EAC Commodities Exchanges

- *Agricultural produce*
- *Mineral fuels, oils, distillation products, etc.*
- *Electrical, electronic equipment*
- *Machinery, boilers, etc*
- *Vehicles other than railway, tramway*
- *Plastics and articles thereof*
- *Optical, photo, technical, medical, etc. apparatus*
- *Pharmaceutical products*
- *Iron and steel*
- *Organic chemicals*
- *Pearls, precious stones, metals, coins, antiquity, etc*

NB. Agricultural commodities are the major commodities to be traded in the EAC commodities exchange and these include coffee, grains, food and fiber as well as livestock and meat.

INITIATIVES TO DEVELOP THE EAC COMMODITIES EXCHANGES.

Clear Objectives. These commodities exchanges needs to make a clear plan with a well-defined scope. The exchange must have a detailed business plan, operating budget and strategy to engage productively with stakeholders basically the private sector.

Good Governance. Any commodity exchange must have a well-thought-out governance structure that emphasizes and responds to membership needs while maintaining an effective board and advisory structure that upholds business standards and meets performance targets. The board should include representatives from government, banking, storage/warehousing and the agricultural sector (e.g. traders, processors, input suppliers, etc.). The exchange employees must be committed to the exchange's mission and understand/promote the benefits of the exchange for all users and potential users.

Stakeholder Buy-In: The exchanges' leadership must meet with farmers, traders, processors, banks, the Central Bank, Ministry of Agriculture, Ministry of Finance, and development partners/ relief agencies to generate support for the exchange. It is essential that each constituency understands the function of the exchange, their role in the process and the expected benefits so as to rally the requisite usage, trust, support and recognition from all stakeholders.

Economic and Legal Infrastructure: EAC countries need to have legislation in place that consistently addresses agricultural, financial, trade and legal policies. However, legislation specific to a commodity exchange is not necessary for it to operate. Policies should allow for free market tendencies. There is also need for sound infrastructure such as payment systems, brokerage services, storage, and transport. While legislation governing the functioning of the exchange can evolve over time, the rigidity it imposes up front can impede the development and limit the exchange's flexibility to address changing market needs.

Well-Designed Trading and Clearing Systems: The exchange must develop a system that is appropriate to the environment in which it is operating. This can include open outcry (shouting and the use of hand signals to transfer information), electronic or a combination of the two. Electronic systems allow for longer trading sessions, greater flexibility and greater freedom for members. An exchange must have graded products that meet quality standards, but it should not limit what grades and type of product can be traded.

Clear Rules, Consistent Enforcement: The EAC regional exchanges should have clear, consistently applied and balanced rules and regulations designed to protect the integrity of the exchange. The rules must govern all parties to the exchange: members (including their employees and clients), brokers, arbitrators, exchange employees, and other relevant parties. The rules should stipulate capital requirements for members, acceptable conduct of all parties, performance and sanctions for infractions. Trading rules need to include delivery guarantees or a means of alternative dispute resolution that ensures performance by all parties. The exchange must develop a transparent surveillance and monitoring system and act decisively when breaches in rules occur.

Accurate Contracts: The exchange should work with members and the industry to develop an agreed contract to facilitate trades and more detailed commodities-specific contracts that contain standard information on quality standards, analysis, delivery and weights, demurrage, force majeure and arbitration, among others.

Extensive, Continuous Education and Training: The regional commodities exchanges must carry out training and certification of members and brokers to ensure the integrity of the exchange. The exchange should develop training and testing materials for this purpose and require certification of all parties trading through the exchange.

Relevant and Adaptable: An exchange serves the market; and therefore, it must constantly re-evaluate its performance, regulations, systems and membership to ensure that it is delivering value and maintaining its integrity. Exchanges must understand that they will make mistakes but the important lesson is to learn from those mistakes and be willing to adapt and change whenever necessary.

Large Volumes of Commodities Traded: To stay viable, the EAC commodities exchanges must attract large volumes of commodities across its trading floor. The commodity exchange planning phase must research trade volume potential. If the potential doesn't exist, neither should the exchange.

WHY EAC SHOULD ESTABLISH COMMODITIES EXCHANGES?

1.   Pricing

Commodities exchanges allow the trading of agricultural products, livestock, foreign currencies, oil, precious metals and other products and establish prices for products around the world. Commodities prices are determined by the market forces of supply and demand in the trading pits of the exchanges by public open outcry. What appears chaotic actually is well-organized, as brokers, buying and selling for themselves and their clients, use hand signals to trade. Prices reported from the commodities exchanges are communicated around the world and are used as the basis for numerous economic and political decisions.

2.   Organizing markets

Futures exchanges such as the New York Mercantile Exchange and the Chicago Board of Trade fulfill an essential economic function by providing organized marketplaces with standardized contracts. Without this function, futures transactions would be negotiated independently with no structure at all. Each futures exchange maintains its own clearinghouse that fulfills all transactions. This provides stability to the market, as the clearinghouse acts as the other party in all transactions. Because traders are buying and selling contracts throughout the day, their buys and sells may not be equal when trading ends. Traders settle any imbalances once at the end of the trading day with the exchange rather than settling each trade separately.

3.   Hedging

Merchants, farmers and international firms use the futures exchanges to hedge future transactions. When a farmer plants his crop of coffee, for example, he does not know what the price will be at harvest time. To remove the risk of price changes, he sells coffee futures contracts at planting time. When he sells his crop a few months later, he buys back the futures contacts. If coffee prices have fallen, he is protected because the futures contracts he buys at harvest cost less than the ones he sold at planting. An importing firm can use financial futures contracts in the same manner to lock in a price for the goods it will be importing later in the year.

4.   Speculation

Speculators fill the important economic function of providing liquidity to an exchange. With the money that speculators bring to the exchanges, the spread between bid and ask prices is much narrower than it otherwise would be; commodity prices would fluctuate more erratically without the participation of speculators. When hedgers buy and sell contracts to cover their risks, it is the speculative commodity traders who assume those risks, thereby helping stabilize prices.

5.   Collecting Information

In an active futures market, the demand for information by traders is enormous. Futures exchanges tend to become collection centers for statistics on supplies, transportation, storage, purchases, exports, imports, currency values, interest rates, and other pertinent information. These data, which are compiled and distributed throughout the exchange community on a continuous basis, are immediately reflected in the trading pits as traders digest the new information and adjust their bids and offers accordingly. As a result of active buying and selling of futures contracts, the market determines the best estimate of today and tomorrow's prices for the underlying commodity. In effect, prices are discovered at futures exchanges. Prices determined via this open and competitive process are considered to be accurate reflections of the supply and demand for a commodity, and for this reason they are widely used as today's best estimate of tomorrow's cash market prices for a standardized quantity of a commodity.

Apart from other many advantages of commodity exchange, one major distinguishing factor for east Africa is that majority of its citizens depend on agriculture. Agriculture is among important sectors of the Tanzanian economy. It provides three quarters of merchandise exports, contributes about 95% of the country's food demand, 26.8% of GDP, and 30.9% of foreign currency and provides employment to over 75% of Tanzanians. Government budget allocation to agriculture has been increasing annually which is at 6.2% of the national budget for the year 2015.

Currently there are few commodities under Warehouse Receipt System (WRS) that has been quite helpful to farmers, warehouse operators and other players in the agricultural sector, but still the system is weak due to the absence of a commodity exchange. Hence the commodity exchange being a missing link is of vital importance.

Chapter 22

MODEL FOR DEVELOPING COMMODITIES SPOT AND MULTI-ASSET DERIVATIVES EXCHANGE IN EAC

1. Introduction

'EAC Visions 2020, 2030 & 2040' state that agriculture is the main stay of the EAC regional economies employing an average of 65% of the labour force and contributing 25 percent to the GDP. In addition, by early 2015 the sector accounted for an average of 60 percent of total regional export earnings. Its contribution to the GDP has been declining but remains very important to provide a basis for growth in other sectors, given the linkages (backward and forward).

Agriculture Reforms

East Africa aspires to transform the agriculture sector from subsistence farming to commercial agriculture. This will make agriculture profitable, competitive and sustainable to provide food and income security to all the people of the EAC region. It will also create employment opportunities along the entire commodity value-chain of production, processing and marketing. Specific emphasis will be put on promotion of aqua-culture and livestock farming.

Governments will reform the extension system in the country to increase information access, knowledge and technologies to the farmers; ensure that land fragmentation is reversed to secure land for mechanization; collect adequate agricultural statistics; improve weather information and its dissemination and intensify environmental control measures to halt the decline in soil fertility.

Governments of EAC member States will strengthen and harmonize the legal, regulatory and institutional framework and ensure the sector client charter is developed, popularized and enforced. Appropriate human resource in agriculture will also be developed, retooled and motivated.

Commodity Exchanges

In order to achieve some of the aforesaid objectives, the EAC region should develop an Integrated Commodity Spot & Multi-asset Derivatives Exchange (the Exchange), and a Central Counterparty Clearing House (the Clearing House).

This step by the EAC economies will also complement existing efforts by seeking partnerships, bringing to these markets enhanced trading methodologies, technologies, expertise, capacity-building and management of the physical commodity, plus the pan-African overlay which provides the channels and procedures to offer a broader customer base than Africa's fragmented national boundaries would otherwise not allow.

2. OBJECTIVES OF THE EXCHANGE

The objectives of the EAC Integrated Exchange would be -

- *To ensure that the EAC bloc's position as a pivotal supplier of raw and processed commodities delivers maximum employment and income benefits to the African economy and people;*

- *To unleash the entrepreneurial energies of all stakeholders in the commodity and financial ecosystem of the EAC region, including the smallest and most marginalized among them;*

- *For risk management entailing hedging risk of different underlying assets,*

- *For price discovery of the commodities produced in the country, and*

- *To facilitate advantageous engagement with globalizing commodity and financial markets, removing barriers to expanding, equitable and sustainable trade.*

3. BENEFITS FOR EAC REGION

Thus, the Exchange will deliver critical structural gains for entities throughout the commodity and financial ecosystem of the EAC region:

a) *Transparency to level the playing field for all commodity chain participants;*

b) *Pricing that is closer to and fairer for African commodity chains;*

c) *An efficient procurement and delivery platform;*

d) *Rule-based trade and investment with improved market access and reduced counter party risk;*

e) *A mechanism for business risk management;*

f) *A forum for hedging in Africa's notoriously volatile markets;*

g) *Increased access to economical sources of finance for market participants;*

h) *Promotion of pan-African economic integration especially Exchanges;*

i) *Introduction of a flagship financial centrepiece;*

j) *Capacity-building to empower market participants; and*

k) *Significant job creation, incomes, and world class infrastructure.*

4. THE EXCHANGE PERSPECTIVE

A commodity exchange is an organized marketplace where buyers and sellers come together to trade commodity related contracts following rules set by the exchange. There is a wide variety of ways in which the market can be organized, but exchanges tend to have the following elements in common:

- *An exchange provides a trading platform, either a physical location (a trading floor) or, preferably, an electronic trading system, in both cases with an intricate set of trading rules. With the advent of high-end technology, an electronic trading system is preferred.*

- *Except in its simplest form (trading fairs, bulletin boards), an exchange provides standard contracts, rather than letting buyers and sellers determine all contract provisions themselves. The extent to which the contracts are standardized in terms of quality, quantity, delivery location, delivery time, etc. can vary – in their most evolved form, exchanges set all the contract conditions except for the price.*

- *An exchange will not deal with most of its users directly, but through brokers. Brokers act as the agents for buyers and sellers, not just for placing transactions, but also for managing the related payment and information flows, and for managing the delivery process. Exchanges deal with the implicit agency risks in two ways. First, there are strong controls on the ways that brokers execute their clients' orders, to make sure that brokers do not abuse their clients. Second, the exchange has the broker assume liability for his clients, in terms of payment obligations, delivery processe etc.; this ensures that a broker will exercise due care in approving clients for trading on the exchange.*

- *An exchange provides security on the quality and the quantity of the commodity traded. It will normally set grades and standards, and license those who are permitted to issue grading certificates. It may use warehouse receipts, which guarantee the physical presence of the goods. It may have a mechanism to settle quality disputes. A fully-developed exchange guarantees the delivery; if there is a problem, it will either procure goods on the market for delivery to the buyer, or compensate him financially.*

- *Exchange trading is tightly regulated, with the exchange as frontline regulator. Regulations may be simple – e.g., arbitrage procedures to deal with conflicts between buyers and sellers – but in an advanced stage of development, there are several layers of regulation involving different regulatory agencies.*

The world's largest commodity exchanges are futures markets - trading futures and option contracts that are meant as risk management tools rather than tools to buy or sell the underlying commodities. In emerging markets, however, commodity exchanges can play a useful role for physical trade, including in the financing of commodity inventories. By providing a transparent, disciplined marketplace they can reduce the discovery costs of physical trade and the counterparty risks in commodity transactions.

The trading systems of the Exchanges have different regulatory implications. The regulatory implications should be seen in the light of the need to regulate – governments should refrain from unnecessary intervention. There are just three possible reasons: to protect the integrity of the operation of the exchange; to protect customers from abuse; and to protect the wider financial sector from systemic risk.

5. OPPORTUNITIES FOR INTERNATIONAL PARTICIPANTS

The Exchange will provide significant opportunities for international market participants: an integrated commodity spot and multi-asset derivatives platform; central counterparty clearing house, efficient and secure trading environment; gateway to African opportunities; Portfolio diversification; enhanced sales and procurement strategies, all involving substantial foreign investments which Uganda needs.

6. REQUISITES FOR SETTING-UP THE EXCHANGE

The necessary pre-requisites for setting-up the Exchange and Clearing House are listed as under:

i) **Demutualized Exchange.** *In a demutualized environment, management and ownership are fully separated from trading interests, leading to good governance of the Exchange.*

ii) **Strong Governance.** *The Exchange should have well-structured governing framework (Board of Directors and Advisory Board) that upholds business standards and meets performance targets. The Management should be committed to the Exchange's mission and promote the benefits to all users.*

iii) **Regulatory environment.** *This should have prudential regulation, market integrity regulation, business conduct regulation and market stability protection.*

iv) **Capital Adequacy Norms for the Member-Brokers.** *Capital Adequacy Norms should consist of Minimum net-worth requirement and Security Deposit (pre-defined by the Exchange and Clearing House) for the Member-Brokers.*

v) **Transparency in Operations and Decision Making.** *The Exchange should maintain transparency in all its operational activities and decision making, while dealing with its Member-Brokers, Clients and other users.*

vi) **Strong Rules and Regulations for Consistent Enforcement.** *As a Self-Regulatory Organization, the Exchange must have well defined Rules, Regulations and Procedures for managing the Exchange, its operations and compliances to protect and maintain the integrity of the Exchange and its participants.*

vii) **Extensive Education and Capacity-Building.** *Training and capacity building of the market participants is critical to ensuring the wider participation on the Exchange platform. Broader* education and awareness campaigns targeting potential users across Uganda must be included in the annual operating budget to drive more business.

viii) **Online Trading System**. The Exchange should provide fully automated screen based trading, using a modern, fully computerized trading system designed to offer market participants and investors across the length and breadth of the continent a safe and easy way to transact.

ix) **Accurate Contracts**. The Exchange should work with member-brokers and the industry to develop an agreed contract to facilitate trades and more detailed commodities-specific contracts that contain standard information on quality standards, analysis, delivery and weights, demurrage, force majeure and arbitration, among others.

x) **Focus on Market Information dissemination**. The Exchange should focus on online dissemination of trade information to different market participants across the country for better and quick decision.

xi) **Robust Risk Management System**. The Exchange should develop robust risk management system, to also include collaterals from Member-Brokers, daily price circuit filters for each commodity contract, trading limits, margining system, and settlement guarantee fund.

xii) **Efficient Clearing and Settlement System**. The efficient system should provide shorter settlement cycle, delivery based transactions, Central Counter Party Clearing (every seller to buyer and every buyer to seller), and timely settlement of all trades.

xiii) **Warehouse Receipt System**. A system of negotiable warehouse receipt should be developed by the Exchange to ensure better price discovery, delivery process, credit delivery and its recovery. The Exchange to interact with the Government for developing *appropriate regulation that will enable the warehouse receipt system to be opened up to all the participants.*

These requisites are drawn from extensive knowledge of and hands on experience with African, Asian and international Exchanges.

Following the aforesaid requisites, the Exchange should also work to achieve the objectives laid down by **International Organization for Securities Commission** (IOSCO):

a)   To ensure the market to remain fair, efficient and transparent,

b)   To minimize the systemic risk and

c)   To protect the interest of the participants.

7.   COMMODITIES FOR TRADING

a) Initially, the Exchange will launch trading in spot commodities (for immediate delivery of the physical commodity), in select commodities. Trade will be offered in those commodities (viz., maize, cotton, sorghum, coffee etc.) which are of crucial importance to the local markets, so as to secure buy-in and participation from important market participants and other stakeholders in those countries.

b) After launching spot commodity contracts (i.e., phase 1), the Exchange will offer trading in commodity-based futures for risk management and hedging purposes, with later introduction of options trading. Commodity Sectors will include agriculture, metals, minerals and energy.

NB: Since some EAC economies like Uganda and Kenya are net producers of electricity this can become a major energy commodity basically when the electricity market is liberalized. If there are many suppliers of electricity in the EAC region (a function of EAC Ministries of Energy), an open spot market can result in a better price discovery mechanism and more attractive pricing. Nonetheless, such energy markets need to be adequately regulated to ensure that there is real competition between suppliers and the cheapest priced electricity is provided to consumers both within the EAC region and outside.

c) *Trading in financial derivatives products (like currencies, indices, carbon credits etc.) can also be launched on the Exchange platform later on.*

8. Features Of Exchange And Clearing House

The basic features of the Exchange and its Clearing House will be –

Exchange	Clearing House
• Demutualized Exchange	• Efficient Clearing and Settlement
• Capital Adequacy Norms for the Trading Members	• Capital Adequacy Norms for the Clearing Members
• Online Trading System	• Automated Clearing and Settlement
• Transparency in Operations and Decision Making	• Transparency in Operations and Decision Making
• Dissemination of Real Time Price and Trade Information	• Efficient Delivery System
• Central Counter Party System	• Settlement Guarantee
• Impartial Management	• Central Counter Party System
	• Impartial Management

9. Competitive Edge

These are:

- *Integrated Automated Commodity Spot and Multi-asset Derivatives Exchange;*
- *Africa's first Multi-asset Derivatives & Commodity Spot Exchange, and Central Counterparty Clearinghouse (outside South Africa);*
- *State of the Art, end-to-end technology solutions to support exchange, clearing house and brokerage activities;*

- *Trading platforms offering multi-asset class (agriculture products, metals, minerals, energy products, currency and index) and multi-instrument (spot, futures and options) functionality;*
- *Advisory board, board of directors and management team;*
- *Multiple layers of Risk Management in the Exchange;*
- *Ecosystem-approach that develops not just an exchange but also provides the tools and incentives for organizing and upgrading the commodity and financial sectors across the EAC region;*
- *To associate with Pan-African Multi-asset Derivatives & Commodity Spot Exchange, and Central Counterparty Clearinghouse.*

10. FINANCIALS

Capital Expenditure for setting-up the Exchange and Clearing House would include Pre-launch Expenditure, Exchange Technology, Hardware-Servers and Datacenter, Network Connectivity, Furniture and Fixtures.

The Exchange will generate revenues through four distinct mechanisms: transaction fees, membership subscription, interest income on security deposit, and technology hosting and supply. The Clearing House will generate revenues through distinct mechanisms: clearing/delivery fees, membership subscription, interest income on collaterals. Other revenue sources for the Exchange are likely to include info-vending, training and capacity-building, etc. The Exchange shall maintain strategic control over the long term sustainability of its revenue streams through: ownership of relationships with important customers and market participants, strategic partnerships with pivotal ecosystem stakeholders, high barriers for entering the exchange and clearing business.

NB: It is worth noting that commodity derivative markets can only develop successfully if there is real end-user demand for their products for hedging purposes. Many derivatives markets fail as they are set up to appeal more to speculators and there is no local trading in the underlying physical products. The success of agricultural futures markets in China, Ethiopia, and South Africa is evident because these economies are major producers of specific agricultural products and so the derivative products are used by farmers, trading houses and end-users. Therefore, their success comes thanks to the existence of a real underlying physical market supported by a full-bodied warehousing receipt system.

Chapter 23

REAL SECTORS & FINANCIAL SECTOR

The EAC region is an agro-based economy with agriculture and its value-chains contributing significantly to the regional economies: 26% of the Kenyan GDP by June 2015; but 65% of Kenya's total exports; 60% of employment; and 80% of rural livelihood in Kenya. The example is befitting the EAC regional contribution since these economies have a lot of similarities, and so it can simply generalized to represent the regional bloc. There is need to develop a model of both producer cooperatives and chain stores eg Shoprite to link commodities exchanges and capital markets whereby farmers are connected to Shoprite thru Warehousing Receipt System; which consequently links them to the financial markets and the financial system. All these will be linked to the EAC real domestic economic; thus creating value-chains but also forward and backward linkages throughout the flow of resources. There is high level of product duplication due to many retail outlets concentrated in one area; which has led to fragmentation of returns/ profits leading to all retailers earning small. Hence, no impact on both small holders' welfare and the economy at large. There is need for product innovation & adoption of international business model of chain stores that will provide forward & backward linkages to the economy at large.

Figure 4.15

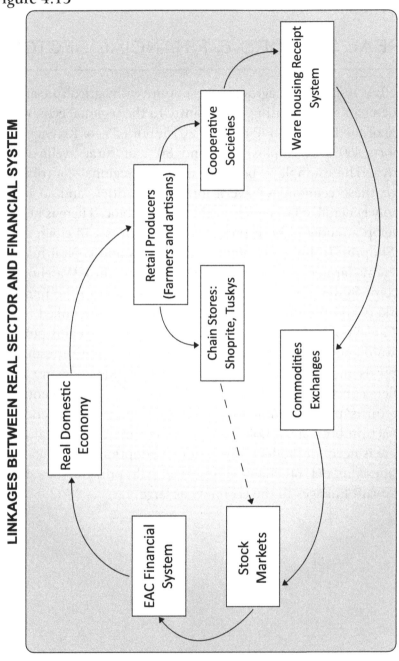

LINKAGES BETWEEN REAL SECTOR AND FINANCIAL SYSTEM

Source: Researcher's Data

DEDUCTION OF PART 4:

Despite their relative growth at the present, EAC financial markets are far from being efficient, they are characterized by: being shallow, high transaction costs, limited activity and financial instruments, high information asymmetry, very low local participation, low absorptive capacities of funds, and macroeconomic risks. That is why most are not even fit to be called "Frontier markets", but once they are integrated into one large market, EAC financial markets will be very visible and competitive globally, more efficient avenues for financing and investment but also with better capacity to attract foreign investments. Once integrated, money markets can efficiently process lending rates correctly so that EAC economies can take off due to funds allocation efficiency; capital markets can turn into efficient resource mobilization avenues for households, governments and corporations (all financial agents) but also safe investments for financial agents across EAC Bloc; derivative markets would further render the financial system into a developed and sophisticated environment for both regional and global investors. Other financial markets would significantly develop and incrementally facilitate both cheap financing and rational investments. But this would require the establishment and operationalization of some regional financial institutions to regulate and also incentivize the desired growth; need to boost the current financial skills set across the EAC region; need to work on the political and financial system risks in the regional economies; monitor corporate governance systems of institutions; further integrate the financial system infrastructure across the EAC Bloc; boost financial literacy across the board; and further work on the macroeconomic convergence variables so as to smoothen the way to a unified EAC currency.

PART 5
FINANCIAL ASSETS
Chapter 24
REAL ASSETS VS FINANCIAL ASSETS

Real assets are those resources that are used by the company in its normal line of business to produce goods and services so as to generate profits. They are categorized into tangible and intangible assets. Tangible real assets are those that physically exist such as: land, equipments, machinery, buildings, plant, and furniture. On the contrary, intangible real assets are those that don't physically exist such as: goodwill, trademarks, brand names, technical know-how, technological collaborations, copyrights, etc.

Financial assets are claims/securities to the income generated by real assets or claims on income from the government; and these assets are a store of value to their owners. They include securities (stocks and bonds); derivative contracts; currencies; and alternative assets eg infrastructure, unit trust funds, hedge funds, private equity, commodities, and specialized real estate.

Financial securities can be classified as debt or equity: whereby debt securities are promises to repay borrowed funds while equity securities represent ownership positions in a firm. Publicly traded securities on exchanges or through securities dealers are subject to regulatory oversight nonetheless private securities are not traded in public markets and they are often illiquid and not subject to regulation.

Derivative contracts have values that depend on the values of other assets. Financial derivative contracts are based on equities, equity indexes, debt, debt indexes or other financial contracts and are traded on securities' exchanges. Physical derivative contracts derive their values from the values of physical assets e.g. gold, oil, coffee, wheat, among others and are traded on commodities exchanges.

Figure 5.1
Product Structure (present and proposed)

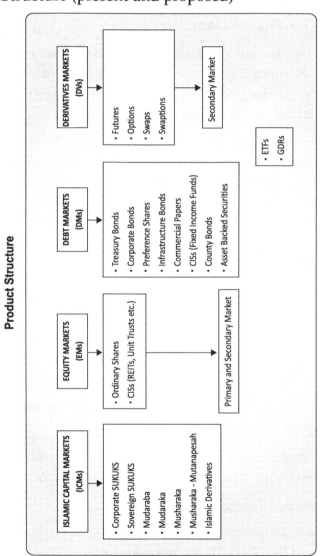

Source: Researcher's Data

1. Securities

These can be classified as fixed income or equity securities, and individual securities can be combined in pooled investment vehicles. Corporations and governments are the most common issuers of individual securities.

a)   Fixed income securities

Debt securities are promises to repay borrowed money in the future: short-term generally have a maturity of less than one or two years; long-term are 5yrs-10yrs and intermediate term maturities fall in the middle of maturity ranges.

Bonds are long-term; notes are intermediate term; commercial papers refer to short-term debt issued by firms. Governments issue bills yet banks issue certificates of deposit (CDs). In repurchase agreements, the borrower sells a high-quality asset and has both the right and obligation to repurchase it (at a higher price) in the future; repurchase agreements can be for terms as short as one day in the interbank money markets.

Convertible debt: this is where an investor can exchange for a specified number of equity shares of the issuing firm with a debt instrument.

b)   Equity securities

These represent ownership in firms; include common stock, preferred stock and warrants, among other as discussed later.

Warrants are similar to options in that they give the holder the right to buy a firm's equity shares (usually common stock) at a fixed exercise price prior to the warrant's expiration.

c)   Pooled Investment Vehicles

These include unit trust funds, mutual funds, real estate investment trusts (REITs), depositories and hedge funds. The term refers to structures that combine the funds of many investors in a portfolio of investments, and investors' ownership interests are referred to as shares, units, depository receipts or limited partnership interests.

- *Unit trust funds are collective investment vehicles in which investors can purchase shares either from the fund itself (open-end funds) or the secondary market (closed-end fund).*

- *Exchange-traded funds (ETF) and exchange-traded notes (ETN) trade like closed-end funds but have special provisions allowing conversion into individual portfolio securities or exchange portfolio shares for ETF shares that keep their market prices close to the value of their proportional interest in overall portfolio. These funds are sometimes referred to as depositories and their shares called depository receipts.*

- *Asset-backed securities represent claim to a portion of a pool of financial assets e.g. mortgages, car loans or credit card debt. The return of the asset is passed through to investors with different classes of claims (called tranches) having different levels of risk.*

- *Hedge funds are organized as limited partnerships with investors as limited partners and the fund manager as the general partner. Hedge funds utilize various strategies and purchase is usually restricted to investors of substantial wealth and investment knowledge. Hedge funds often use leverage and their managers are compensated based on the amount of assets under management as well as on their investment results.*

2. CURRENCIES

These are issued by the central bank and some are called reserve currencies, which are those held by governments and central banks worldwide. These include the dollar and euro; secondarily the British pound, Japanese Yen and Swiss franc. In spot currency markets, currencies are traded for immediate delivery.

3. CONTRACTS

These are agreements between two parties that require some action in the future; for example exchanging an asset for cash. Financial contracts are often based on securities, currencies, commodities or security indexes (portfolios). They include futures, forwards, options, swaps and insurance contracts.

a) *Forward contract is an agreement to buy or sell an asset in the future at a price specified in the contract at its inception. An agreement to purchase 100 ounces of gold 90 days from now for $1000 per ounce is a forward contract. These are not traded on exchanges or in dealer markets*

b) *Futures contracts are similar to forward contracts except that they are standardized as to amount the asset characteristics and delivery time and are traded on an exchange (in a secondary market) so that they are liquid investments.*

c) *Swap contracts: two parties make payoffs that are equivalent to one asset being traded (swapped) for another. In simple interest rate swap, floating rate interest payments are exchanged for fixed rate payments over multiple settlement dates. A currency swap involves a loan in one currency for the loan of another currency for a period of time. An equity swap involves the exchange of the return on an equity index or portfolio for the interest payment on a debt instrument.*

d) *An option contract gives its owner the right to buy or sell an asset at a specific exercise price at some specified time in future. A call option gives the option buyer the right (but not obligation) to buy an asset. Sellers or writers of call (put) options receive a payment called the option premium when they sell the options but incur the obligation to buy or sell the asset at a specified price if the option owner chooses to exercise it. Options on currencies, stock, stock indexes, futures, swaps and precious metals are traded on exchanges but also in the Over-the-Counter markets.*

e) An insurance contract pays a cash amount if a future event occurs. They are used to hedge against unfavourable, unexpected events; examples include life, liability and automobile insurance contracts. Insurance contracts can sometimes be traded to other parties and often have tax-advantaged pay outs.

f) Credit default swaps are a form of insurance that makes a payment if an issuer defaults on its bonds. They can be used by bond investors to hedge default risk. They can also be used by parties that will experience losses if an issuer experiences financial distress and by others who are speculating that the issuer will experience more or less financial trouble than is currently expected.

4. COMMODITIES

These trade in spot, forward and futures markets and include precious metals, industrial metals, agricultural products, energy products and credits for carbon reduction.

Futures and forwards allow both hedgers and speculators to participate in commodity markets without having to deliver or store the physical commodities. Rather than buying the physical assets that are highly illiquid and would require substantial due diligence before investing; and coupled high costs of managing them. Investors may choose to buy them indirectly through an investment such as Real Estate Investment Trust (REIT). Besides, an investor can also buy the stock of firms that have large ownership of real assets.

NB: Investment/capital budgeting decisions relate to decisions on what real assets the firm should invest in; while financing decision relate to how the cash for investment should be raised. Financial analysis in capital budgeting involves bringing together estimates and ideas from a variety of disciplines: marketing, technology, accounting, law, tax; in order to reveal the financial implications of different possible courses of action.

The following can be called financial assets available to the investors in such instruments; or can also be sources/types of finance available to the issuers such as corporations and government bodies:

Chapter 25
EQUITY FINANCE (ASSETS)

This is the largest source of finance to any company, and forms the base on which other finances are raised. Among the features of this type of finance, these are:

- *These shareholders are endowed with voting powers which empowers them to control policies and the kind of management that will achieve their interests in the firm.*

- *This finance can only be raised by limited companies according to the regulations in the country.*

- *This finance is permanent in the company which can only be refunded to its providers during liquidation of the firm.*

- *This finance positively affects the gearing level of the firm and it can't lead the firm into liquidation; on the contrary, it lowers down the firm's debt liability.*

- *This finance is the single largest source of capital to limited companies, on which other kinds of finance are raised.*

- *It is the only type of finance that grows with time as a result of retention called "growth in equity."*

- *Ordinary shares carry no nominal cost to the company since ordinary dividends are not a legal obligation to the firm.*

- *This finance carries a variable return meaning that in a good year, a shareholder might get higher dividends depending on the firm's profitability; unlike debt finance that has a fixed rate of return regardless of the level of profitability of the firm.*

- *Ordinary shareholders are the third-class claimants (residual claim) in the event of liquidation after all other finance providers have claimed their dues; this finance poses the highest risk in the company.*

Equity finance is a function of the following sub-categories:

Ordinary Shares: these are share of ownership and also finance to the company that is provided by the real owners of the firm. Ordinary shareholders have full rights to vote at Annual General Meetings; they are entitled to dividends and surplus revenue in the event of liquidation. However, dividends are not a legal obligation and this ordinary shares carry the highest risk in the firm since they are paid after all classes of claimants have been settled.

Preferred Ordinary and deferred ordinary shares: the former rank for payment of an agreed rate of dividends before the latter receives anything. Mutual agreements may also permit the preferred holders to a share in the corporate profits after they have received their priority percentages.

Non-voting Shares: such shares are used to raise equity finance without losing control over the firm which most family-managed and private limited firms fear. Nonetheless, these share holders can't influence policies and the executive management of the firm the fact that they don't have voting rights to either vote out or in favor of any policy.

Retained Earnings: this finance arises out of undistributed profits over and above dividends paid to shareholders. It is normally a company policy to put aside (into a fund) a certain percentage of annual profits.

It is a cost free source of finance and the opportunity cost to the investors is just the money that ordinary shareholders who have taken home as additional dividends for their consumption expenditures. This finance constitutes "growth in equity", and many firms find the following advantages in retained earnings: acts as stabilizer for future dividends during unprofitable years; it is a cost free finance unlike fresh capital form financial markets; it serves to cover contingencies to the firm; it lowers the company's gearing level; it positively affect the company's share price on the stock exchange.

Capital Reserves: these are funds which can't be classified as normal trading profits arising out of the firm's ordinary trading activities. For instance, if Asante Capital Hub Ltd (a financial services firm) intended to sell its share to the public at UGX 200 per share; then maybe due to oversubscription of the IPO (Initial Public Offering) and the price mechanism, the share goes to UGX 250 above the par value, then the UGX 50 is a profit/share premium to the firm. Lets hypothetically assume that the firm had offered 500, 000,000 shares; the share premium would be (500,000,000 shares × UGX 50 = UGX 25,000,000,000). And this UGX 25 Billion would be credited to the capital reserves to offset some expenses like those involved in the IPO.

Founders' Shares: with such finance/assets, dividends are paid only after all other categories of equity shares have received their rates of dividends. Much as they carry the highest returns in case of a good/profitable year, they have the highest risk in the firm, especially, in years of low/no profitability.

Golden Shares: (in newly privatized industries) these are held by the government following a privatization, and they give the State certain rights such as voting rights and veto rights on certain critical and strategic issues.

Share Warrants: these are entitlements to buy a stated number of shares at a specific price up to a certain date; and often attached to loan stocks (available in derivative markets).

Shares with multiple voting rights.

Islamic financing: this is an equity-based form of finance that works to obey Islamic law (Shariah law – not interest-based financing). Some bankers and finance companies are currently seeking to tap this market in Uganda by engaging in home-owning "partnerships" with the Muslim and some non-Muslim customer, since according to the Islamic faith; Shariah forbids paying or receiving interest.

Its primitive stage is traced back in the 15th Hijira Century (Islamic calendar) in the mid 1970s; but it was not until 1974 that the world's first development bank in compliance with the Sharia laws was established called "the Islamic Development Bank". The system emerged as an alternative financial system that neither gave nor took interest, thereby introducing a fair system of social justice and equality while fulfilling the financial needs of people and maintaining high standards of ethics, transparency, and a sense of responsibility.

It helps financial agents to build tangible and appreciating assets for themselves; founded on a solid economic base but also encouraging the spirit of entrepreneurship amongst its customers. It is based on a unique concept of profit and loss sharing by way of Sharia-compliant financing and investment tools. It is the first where financial agents are not just customers but partners with the financial institution; since both share risks, as well as profits of such partnership or ownership. This system offers a portfolio of innovative, Sharia-compliant financial models such as: Murabaha, Musharaka, Mudaraba, Istisna, Salam, and Ijara that are formalized and arranged uniquely between a customer and a financial institution.

Chapter 26
PREFERENCE SHARES (QUASI-EQUITY)

This finance is contributed by quasi-owners or preference shareholders; it combines characteristics of both equity finance and debt finance. It is termed "preferred" due to the preferential treatment accorded to owners of such finance over other equity sub-categories such as: sharing in dividends; and sharing of assets in the event of liquidation.

Features of Preference Share capital are as follows:

- *These shares are only sold by limited companies but not sole traders and partnerships.*

- *If these shares are not redeemed after their maximum redemption period (normally 7 years), then they turn into creditors who can actually sue the firm.*

- *These shares carry fixed dividends as return except the participative preference shares that are given more accommodation during dividend distribution.*

- *Holders of these shares are referred to as "second-class claimants" on the company assets during dissolution or liquidation ie before ordinary shareholders but after debt finance providers.*

- *Cumulative preference shareholders have a benefit of claiming their dividends in arrears in the event of a good year after non-profitable years.*

- *Convertible preference shares have an advantage of being convertible to ordinary shares which renders their holders real owners of the firm.*

This kind of finance is classified into majorly four sub-categories:

Classification according to dividend payment: cumulative preference shares their dividends in arrears if a firm takes like five years without earning profits but on the sixth year it earns profits, then they would get dividends for the years they missed their dividends due to unprofitability of the firm. However, the non-cumulative preference shareholders are not treated in that way; if they miss dividends in any year, they can't claim it in arrears.

Classification according to convertibility: convertible preference shares can be converted into ordinary shares upon the approval/request of the firm, shareholder or both parties. Conversely, non-convertible preference shares can't be converted into ordinary shares.

Classification according to redemption: redeemable preference shares must be bought back from their holders normally at the minimum period of time (5 years) or at the maximum period of time (7 years) beyond which they will turn into company creditors. On the other hand, irredeemable preference shares are permanent finance to the company and they can only be redeemed in the event of liquidation or they can be transferred to other parties through the stock exchange infrastructure.

Classification according to participation: participative preference shares are entitled to more than their fixed rate of return during high profits seasons or high asset value along with the ordinary shareholders. In opposition, non-participative preference shares can't claim anything over and above their fixed claim of dividends.

Chapter 27
DEBT FINANCE (ASSETS)

Debt finance has the following characteristics:

- *It has a fixed rate of return: interest on debt instruments is fixed regardless of the level of the firm's profitability.*
- *Debt instruments don't carry voting rights, which cripple their holders' ability to influence policies and choice of management for the company.*
- *Interest on debt finance is a tax-allowable expense to companies.*
- *Interest on debt securities is a legal obligation on the part of the firm to pay, and failure to pay may lead to either receivership or liquidation at extreme cases.*
- *Debt finance is always refundable except for irredeemable debentures.*
- *Debt finance is usually given on conditions and restrictions basically bank loans.*
- *Debt securities carry a first claim on profits and company assets before any other provider of finance (first-class claimants).*
- *Debt finance negatively affects the firm's gearing level.*
- *Most types of debt finance are secured against the firm's assets.*

LONG-TERM DEBT

i) **Debentures**: these are secured loan stocks or corporate bonds issued by financial sound corporate bodies to raise finance for their operations. It is a legal document showing the right to receive interest and a capital repayment; they are often negotiable. The following are the types of Debentures:

Fixed-charge Debentures: (also called mortgage debentures) these have fixed assets nominated as security for this debt finance.

Floating-charge Debentures: for these debentures, all the present and future assets of the firm are held as security for the loan stock.

Zero Coupon: with these debentures, no interest is paid, but there is a large difference between initial payment for the bond and its redemption value.

Among the merits of using Debenture financing, these are:

> *The use of debenture doesn't entail dilution of the company's control since they don't carry voting rights as do ordinary shares.*
>
> *Interest on debenture is tax-allowable expense, and as such it lowers down the firm's tax liability.*
>
> *They are not expensive to raise as they entail less formalities in comparison to equity capital raising.*
>
> *They are used without preconditions and restrictions, hence making them flexible to use in flexible company financing initiatives.*
>
> *If they are redeemable, both interest and principal are reduced in real monetary terms due to the effect of inflation on the value of money.*
>
> *Irredeemable debentures can form permanent finance o the company which can be invested in long-term ventures like and fixed assets.*

ii) Unsecured Loan Stock: it is a legal document showing the right to receive interest and capital repayment. Such loan stocks are positioned low down in pecking order for payment in the event of liquidation. Coupon/ interest payment is higher than debentures due to also higher risk involved in their transactions.

iii) Floating-rate Notes (FRN): it is a bond on which the rate of interest is linked to short-term interest rates basically in the interbank money markets.

iv) Convertible Unsecured Loan Stock: these are loan stocks which can be converted into equity capital at the option of either the holder, the firm or both parties. These have lower interest rates than debentures, and are normally cheaper to the firm. Interest is a tax deductible expense and they are often self-liquidating.

v) Bank Loan: this can either be term lending at fixed rate or floating rates. This type of debt finance has administrative fees; it is usually secured; and guarantees by directors. Covenants are usually required, that is, target interest cover ratios or limits on further borrowing.

vi) Syndicated Lending: this is a situation where a group of banks provide a large loan to either a retail borrower or an institutional borrower that would otherwise have been hard for a single bank to offer such a debt facility.

MEDIUM-TERM DEBT

i) Bank Loans: these are the same as the details above for bank loans except the period is one to seven years (1 – 7 years).

ii) Medium-term Notes (MTNs): this is a promise to pay a certain amount of money on a specific date. This type of debt finance is unsecured and its maturity is 9 months to 20 years, and normally sold in financial markets. This can either be fixed, floating or zero interest rates debt facility.

iii) Floating rate Notes (FRNs): these are promissory notes with a floating interest rate traded basically in the Interbank markets; but mostly used in the Euromarkets.

iv) Leasing: this is whereby an equipment owner conveys the right to use the equipment in return for rental payments over an agreed period of time. This saves firms from up-front lump-sum payments that would be quite huge for smaller firms; and this kind of finance is available when other sources have been exhausted. Besides, it has tax advantages to the firm since leasing expenses are tax deductible costs; and it can classified into:

Finance (capital) lease: this covers the whole useful life of an asset, and the finance house receives back the full capital investment plus interest over the lease period.

Operating lease: this only covers a proportion of the useful life of the asset such as machinery, vehicles, concrete mixer, etc.

v) Hire Purchase: this happens when a hire purchase company buys an asset which is used by the hirer; who after a series of payments becomes the owner of such an asset. This type of debt finance is so convenient and it is normally available when other sources of finance are either expensive or not quite available. This kind of finance is more expensive than bank loans, and a firm needs a guarantor since it doesn't call for collateral securities to raise it. The hirer must honor all the terms of the agreement ie if it fails to pay any installment before it clears 2/3 then the hiree may repossess the asset.

Below are the circumstances under which it is an ideal type of finance:

- *If the asset is so expensive that there is hardly a single source of financing eg purchase of aircrafts.*
- *If the asset will meet the company's future expansion programs despite current financial constraints.*
- *If the firm is highly geared and can't afford borrow so as to finance the asset's purchase.*
- *Under conditions of restrictive credit control by the Central bank and the only option is purchase through hire purchase.*
- *If the firm doesn't have enough real assets to cover a loan as collateral security.*
- *If the asset is not very sensitive to technology that it would become obsolete soon.*

SHORT-TERM DEBT

i) Trade Credit: this is the most popular type of debt finance available basically to small business units in the EAC region due its lower conditions for its access as a source of finance. It is all about delaying payments for goods received; as a source of finance, it is so convenient and informal though not necessarily free. The only (opportunity) cost it has is the loss of the discount that the trader would have received as a result of cash/ spot payment.

Below are some of the reasons why Trade credit is popular in the EAC regional bloc:

- *It is a cheap source of finance because the only cost involved is the discount lost.*
- *This type of finance is rarely misused and many firms are willing to give it due to lower risks in its misuse.*
- *Many a firms in East Africa lack collateral securities which are a necessity to raise other debt finance from financial institutions.*
- *This finance doesn't require a firm to be so financially sound so as to be eligible to acquire it unlike other finance sources.*
- *This finance hardly affects the gearing level of the firm and such it can't lead the firm into liquidation.*
- *Due the credit control measures of the Central bank, the only resort for firms is the trade credit which is not at all affected by the monetary policies of the Central bank.*
- *It is quite flexible in that it may be the only way how firms can get their commodities sold and this boosts the firm's sales' volumes.*
- *Most businesses in East Africa are not known to financial institutions, which makes trade credit the most sought after kind of finance due to its lower qualification criteria for this finance.*

ii) Overdraft: this is a facility that commercial banks offer to its known clients of drawing a lot more funds than the balance they had on their accounts. Such finance is easy to arrange, flexible, unsecured, and repayable on demand. Its challenge is the it is way too expensive and it can a only be used as working capital but can't be used for the purchase of fixed capital requirements of a firm.

iii) Factoring: this is the outright purchase of the firm's debtors, normally the Factor Company pays the firm 80% of the value of its outstanding. And in confidential invoice factoring, the customer is unaware that the debts have been sold; so, he continues sending payments to the firm but not the factor.

In Uganda, there is only one major factoring company called Oscar Associates but Kenya has a couple of such institutions given its developed financial system. Here are some of the key necessities for establishing a factoring business:

- *One should have good background knowledge in legal issues: contractual knowledge and its application.*
- *One should have basic knowledge in accounting.*
- *There is need for wide sources of finance since there are many clients but very few players in the sector.*
- *Thorough background in liquidation of assets, discounting techniques and principles are all required.*
- *There is need to network with a couple of law firms for risk management and legal interpretation (litigation).*

iv) Invoice Discounting: this type of finance is closer to factoring though for it, it has stages such as: (1) the firm sends its invoices to the finance house, and the firm guarantees that its invoices will be paid. (2) the finance house pays up to 80% of invoice amount to the firm. (3) three months later, the firm collects debt from customer and pays financial house. The costs are normally variable depending on the financial requirements of the firm and the financial capacity of the finance house.

v) Deferred tax payments: this arises as a result of intervals between earnings of profits by the firm and its payment of tax liability that produces cash availability.

vi) Commercial Paper: this is a legal document expressing loan terms with a maturity that ranges from 1 week to 2 years.

vii) Bills of exchange: it is an unconditional order in writing addressed by one person to another signed by the person giving it, requiring the person to whom it is addressed to pay on demand at a fixed or determinable future date a certain sum of money to the bearer; most of these mature between 90 – 120 days. An accommodation type of bill of exchange is that type where two parties X and Z are such that X has no finance and is not known to banks but Z is known to banks as a client. The two enter into an agreement whereby X draws a bill on Z, and Z accepts it and thereafter X can either discount the same bill or endorse it to another party to get finance which X will have to refund later to Z

viii) Bank Bills (Acceptance credit): this is type of finance whereby a bank promises to pay out the amount of a bill of exchange at a future date, which empowers the firm to sell the bill. On maturity, the bank pays the bill holder and later the firm pays the bank.

ix) Revolving Underwriting Facility (RUF): this is a kind of finance whereby a bank underwrites the borrower's access to funds at a specified rate in the money markets throughout an agreed period of time.

Chapter 28
HYBRID TYPES OF FINANCE (ASSETS)

i) **Mezzanine finance:** (closer to preference shares and convertible loans) this is a fusion type of finance that is characterized by high-yielding loans, usually with equity warrants attached to this finance. They are low security finance that implies high risk; and are useful for corporate restructuring, buyouts and leveraged takeovers. They are normally sold in the primary financial markets; and these include among others junk bonds.

ii) **Venture Capital:** this is a type of financing for new businesses or management buyouts (as already discussed under "Private Equity investments"). Financial institutions are the major suppliers of such finance and normally looking for exit route between 5 years to 10 years; due to high failure rates, high returns are required.

iii) Sale and leaseback: this is a situation whereby firm A, due to its financial requirements, decides to sell its property so as to raise the requisite finance and then after agrees with the party that has bought it to lease the same property to firm A for its continuous production processes

iv) **Mortgaging:** this is a type of finance which is available to firms with freehold and leasehold real assets such as land and buildings. It works as an arrangement where the mortgagee agrees to give a specific sum of money to the mortgagor on the strength of the real asset acting as collateral security for the finance. This finance is good for firms due to its long-term orientation towards financing which serves for the acquisition of fixed assets that are so critical for long-term growth and sustainability of the firm.

v) **Eurobonds:** these are international bonds sold outside the jurisdiction of the country of the currency in which the issue is denominated. Some of the characteristics of Eurobonds: there is no formal regulatory framework; interest is paid before tax; normally cheaper than domestic bonds; and they give borrowers access to international investors. Eurobonds are commonly issued by governments, corporations, and international organizations; and since the 1950s, it has been possible to arrange with investment banks for debt facilities to be issued to investors without it being affected by the legal or tax jurisdiction of any country. The market for this type of debt is called the Euro-market, though incidentally it is not confined to Europe. In fact, Eurobond issues can be made in almost any currency including the "euro" but most Eurobond issues are denominated in dollars. Among the types of Eurobonds, these are:

Straight Eurobonds: *these are bonds with fixed rate of return and fixed redemption.*

Subordinated issues: *these are bonds where the bondholder's right to payments (principal and interest) is subordinate to the right of creditors.*

Assed-backed issues: *these are bonds where the credit of the securities depends on segregated assets.*

Convertible bonds. *These can be exchanged for shares, at a predetermined price.*

vi) Securitization: this is a kind of finance whereby a package of financial claims such as the right to receive payments from 500 mortgage holders for 20 years is sold as a derivative instrument. Among the assets that can be securitized include: mortgages, commercial papers, car loans, credit card receivables, etc.

vii) Export finance: this entails documentary Letters of Credit (LCs) whereby the trader's bank undertakes to pay at maturity on a bill of exchange. This means that the exporter's bank discounts the bills of exchange so that international trade can be facilitated.

viii) Forfeiting: this type of finance involves the bank purchasing a couple of sales invoices or promissory notes from an exporting firm; and normally the importer's bank guarantees the invoices.

ix) Project finance: this kind of finance is a medium-term borrowing for a particular purpose and the bank's security is the project itself. There are high risk/return profiles for lenders; and many Islamic banks are into such transactions eg the Arab Investment Bank , and Afri-exim Bank (Egypt). This kind of funding has been so instrumental in boosting infrastructural projects basically in the emerging economies and frontier-market economies that have high growth potential but resource-constrained.

x) Bull dog Bond: this is, for instance, a TZS-denominated bond that is issued by an overseas borrower in the traditional Tanzania bond market, and its trading occurs on the stock exchange, unlike the Euro-bond whose trading occurs through investment banks.

Chapter 29
INVESTMENTS & VALUATION

Individuals make investments because they want to enjoy the benefits of wealth in the future rather than at the present. This is particularly in pensions where people choose not to spend all of their income as soon as they receive it but they invest a portion of it now, with a view to spending in retirement. Investments thus represent a trade-off: consumption is foregone now so that it can be placed in the future. The value of an investment must therefore be equal in some way to the value of consumption. If consumption in retirement is valued more highly than current consumption, then there is an incentive to increase the level of investment, and thereby reduce current consumption. This incentive will continue until the point at which the benefit of investment is judged to be almost the same as the benefit of current consumption. In a way, therefore, the value of an investment is a highly personal and subjective assessment (this is more analyzed in behavioral finance). Of paramount importance is how a given investor chooses to define the trade-off between current and future consumption; which is a function of a diversity of factors among which are, the investor's future earning capacity and his perspective of the future.

Marginal rate of substitution is the rate at which investors are willing to trade-off current against future consumption; while marginal rate of transformation is the rate at which the economy/ financial system is able to convert current investment into future consumption. The interest rate is determined at the point where these two marginal rates are equal, since this point represents the optimal trade-off between current and future consumption. The aggregation of all individuals' trade-off decisions will determine the market rate of interest, and the prices of individual assets must themselves be determined relative to the overall market rate of interest. The value of all assets and investments is normally assessed relative to all other assets regardless of the type of asset; and the value of any financial asset therefore depends upon the value of all other financial assets available. This renders Valuation to be a relative concept due to a direct comparability of financial assets, since no asset or investment can be valued in isolation (this is the bottom-line of valuation theory).

In equilibrium, the price of any financial asset will equally depend on two fundamentals: expected return and risk. Whereby the return on the asset/ investment is also comprised of three factors:

- *The amount of money that the asset is expected to generate;*
- *The point in time when the money flows are expected to occur;*
- *And, the effect of inflation on the forecasted returns.*

On the other hand, risk is a measure of the estimated range within which the future returns are likely to fall (measure of dispersion of estimated future returns around their expected value). Risk and return profiles differentiate one financial asset/ investment from another, and consequently form the basis of investors' choices between alternative assets/ investments regardless of how sophisticated both the investors and the investments may be in a given financial system.

Historically, equity investments have outperformed bonds and cash equivalents over the longer term ie a period of ten years and more; however the realities today are less clear due to reverse trends in the stock market logarithm (necessitated by stock market crashes, market anxiety, and improved yield from the bond issues). Rational investors will always compare a certain dividend paid on a company's shares with alternative investments available like shares of other companies, bonds (corporate & government), money market instruments, real property; which is technically termed as calculating the "dividend yield".

INVESTMENT POLICY GUIDELINES

i)   Investment Policies

In the investment world, three terms are so critical yet somewhat confusing in the field of portfolio management, though they ought to be handled by different people so as to maximize the risk/return profiles of the investors, and these are: investment management, investment policy, and investment strategy. In effect, investment management refers to the actual practice of selecting financial assets and placing them in a portfolio (collection of assets); while an investment policy (IPS) is a statement outlining the expectations of the portfolio manager and the constraints under which the manager must operate to achieve investment targets. On the contrary, an investment strategy is a series of short-term activities that are consistent with established investment policy and that will contribute positively toward obtaining the portfolio objective.

In the pursuit of making the most profits out the investments, there are some constraints, risks and huddles that must be scaled before getting to the ecstasy of investment profits. To be a successful investor, one should put sound policies and plans in place to ensure that he/she is not taking undue risks or making disastrous investment decisions.

Asset allocation refers to the allocation of the portfolio across major asset categories such as: Money market assets (cash equivalents), fixed-income securities, equities (both listed and private equity), real estates, real properties (precious metals and other commodities), and derivative assets. Only after the broad asset classes to be held in the portfolio are determined can one sensibly choose then specific securities to purchase. Investors who have relatively high degree of risk tolerance will choose asset allocation more concentrated in higher-risk investment classes, such as equity, to obtain higher expected rates of return. More conservative investors will choose asset allocation with a greater weight in bonds and cash equivalents

Retail Vs Institutional investors

Whereas households need not concern themselves with organizational efficiency, institutional investors with large amounts to invest must structure asset allocation activities to decentralize some of the decision making. A common feature of large organizations is the investment committee that includes top administrators, senior portfolio managers, and senior security analysts. The committee determines investment policies and verifies that portfolio managers and security analysts are operating within the bounds of specified policies. A key responsibility of the investment committee is to translate the objectives and constraints of the organization into an "asset universe", which is an approved list of assets for each of the organization's portfolios.

ii)   Investment Decision-making

But by and large, investment decisions for any financial agent are sub-divided into: investment objectives; investment constraints; and investment policies. And below is a tabular representation of these three investment basics from a portfolio management perspective:

Figure 5.2

Investment objectives	Investment Constraints	Investment Policies
	Liquidity needs	Asset Allocations
Return	Investment horizon	Diversification possibiliti€
Requirements	Regulations on investments	Risk positioning
Risk Tolerance	Taxes (tax liability)	Tax positioning
	Unique needs of investors	Income generation

Source: Researcher's Data

NB: Investment horizon refers to the final time to fund or the planned liquidation date of the investment. And **regulations** refer to universal investment laws like the prudent man's rule (all investments evaluated from a portfolio perspective); whereby an investment professional is held accountable for the IPS (investment policy statement) even in courts of laws; among other local laws that govern/ affect investments in a given financial system. The prudent investor rule requires a fiduciary to "cautiously" invest clients' assets as if they were his own, based on the knowledge the fiduciary has at the time and considering only the needs of the beneficiaries.

The prudent expert rule requires that the fiduciary manage the portfolio with the care, skill, prudence, and diligence, under the circumstances then prevailing, that a prudent investor would use. It extends the prudent investor rule beyond prudence by suggesting a higher level of expertise.

Investment objectives are basically centered on the risk/return profiles (trade-off), and so both investors and their investment managers ought to know the factors that govern each investor categories. Below are some of the established investor categories:

- *Retail (household) investors and personal trusts*
- *Unit trust funds and other CIVs*
- *Pension funds & Retirement benefits schemes*
- *Endowment funds & Foundations*
- *Life Insurance companies*
- *Banking institutions*
- *Non-Life Insurance companies*

Below is an analysis of the underlying determinants of the investment objectives & constraints vis-à-vis the investor categories:

Figure 5.3

Investor Category	Return Requirement	Risk Tolerance	Liquidity	Horizon	Regulation	Taxes
Retail investors & personal trusts	Life-cycle needs such as education, caring for their children, retirement needs etc.	Life-cycle risk profiles: younger investors are more risk tolerant in contrast to older folks.	variable	Life-cycle	None	Variable
Unit trust funds & CIVs	Variable (depending on underlying composition)	Variable (depending on underlying composition)	High	Variable	CMA & Pension laws	Yes
Pension funds & Retirement Benefit funds	Dependent on presumed Actuarial rates	Dependent on proximity of pay-outs.	Variable due to age.	Long	Pension laws	None
Endowment funds & Foundations	Based on current institutional income needs and asset growth.	Generally conservative.	Low	Long	Few/ none	None
Life Insurance companies	Above periodical money market rates so as to meet expenses & actuarial rates.	Relatively conservative.	Low	Long	Composite	Yes
Banking institutions	Based on the Interest spread.	Slightly below Average	High	Normally short	Changing	Yes
Non-life Insurance firms	No benchmarks	Relatively conservative.			Few	Yes

iii)   Asset Allocation Strategies

Besides, in investment management, one of the key policies that ought to be prudently designed is the asset allocation policy since some investment gurus have established that asset allocation decisions explain about 90% of the variability of returns over time (Ibbotson and Kaplan, 2000). And globally, various asset allocation systems have been developed from 1952 when Harry Markowitz established his seminal work on Modern Portfolio Theory (MPT) that introduced the science of the risk-efficient portfolio. So, among them are:

- *Single asset allocation.*
- *Static asset allocation guided by the MPT.*
- *Strategic asset allocation guided by the CAPM (capital asset pricing model).*
- *Tactical asset allocation that was championed by Wells Fargo in the late 1970s after the market declines at that time.*
- *Risk-focused asset allocation (CAPM Tangent Added theory) introduced by Mellon Capital in 1989.*
- *Pine Bridge CML Approach introduced by Pine Bridge Investments research team in 2000.*
- *Risk-focused & Risk parity in the wake of the 2008 Global financial crisis.*

Generally, designing asset allocation policies requires a four stages process:

- *Specifying asset classes to be included in the portfolio, such as: money market instruments; fixed-income securities; stocks; real estate; commodities, etc. institutional investors are basically interested in the first four unlike retail investors.*
- *Specifying capital markets expectations using historical data and economic analysis.*
- *Deriving the efficient portfolio frontier: the portfolio achieving maximum expected returns for any given level of risk.*

- *Finding the optimal asset mix: one that best meets investors' risk/ return objectives while satisfying the constraints they face.*

iv) Investment Policy Statement (IPS)

The IPS content largely includes the following as set by financial regulators of institutional investors across the EAC region:

i.   Investment Objectives

ii.   Types of investments to be held and percentages to be in various classes.

iii.   Risk and return appropriate to the scheme

iv.   Liquidity

v.   Realization

vi.   Asset/ liability matching

vii.   Performance Benchmarks

viii.   Diversification

ix.   Performance monitoring and review

Figure 5.4 Allowable Classes of Investments:

	CLASSES OF ASSETS	MAXIMUM % LIMIT
1	Cash & demand deposits	5%
2	Fixed deposits, time deposits	30%
3	Commercial paper, corporate bonds	30%
4	Government securities	80%
5	Listed shares	70%
6	Immovable property/ REITS	30%
7	Private equity	15%

Source: URBRA (2016)

NB: Pensions and Capital markets regulators across the EAC region may approve "other investments" but normally they would be limited to 5% of total scheme/ institutional fund.

PART 6
AGENTS/PLAYERS OF THE FINANCIAL SYSTEM

FINANCIAL AGENTS IN THE FINANCIAL SYSTEM

In a synopsis, there are three major financial agents (players) in the financial system:

Firms as net borrowers: they raise capital now to pay for investments in plant and equipment. The income generated by those real assets provides the returns to investors who purchase the securities issued by the firm. They receive their incomes from remuneration of capital, transfers from the government and the rest of the world plus net capital transfers from households; and they pay corporate tax to the government which is a proportion of their incomes.

Households as net savers: they purchase the securities issued by firms that need to raise funds, thus providing them with finance for their operations. They receive their incomes from primary factor payments, transfers from the government, and also from the rest of the world but they pay income tax that is proportional to their incomes

Governments can be borrowers or lenders, depending on the relationship between tax revenue and government expenditures. Since most economies globally run budget deficits, meaning that their tax receipts are been less than its expenditures. The government, therefore, has had to borrow funds to cover its budget deficit. Issuance of Treasury bills, notes, and bonds is the major way that the government borrows funds from the public. In contrast, in the latter part of the 1990s, the government enjoyed a budget surplus and was able to retire some outstanding debt.

In the real financial world, government revenue is composed of direct taxes from households and firms, indirect taxes on domestic activities, domestic value added tax, tariff revenue on imports, factor income to the government, and transfers from the rest of the world.

Corporations and governments do not sell all or even most of their securities directly to individuals. For example, about half of all stock is held by large financial institutions such as pension funds, mutual funds, insurance companies, and banks. These financial institutions stand between the security issuer (the firm) and the ultimate owner of the security (the households).

In the financial environment, we classify majorly three agents due to their demands on the financial system, and how they can be addressed: the household sector; the corporate/business sector; and the government sector. The corporate sector has been made to comprise of also the not-for-profit agencies and the hybrid organizations such as the unincorporated or family-run businesses for simplification purposes.

In the financial environment, we classify majorly three agents due to their demands on the financial system, and how they can be addressed: the household sector; the corporate/business sector; and the government sector. The corporate sector has been made to comprise of also the not-for-profit agencies and the hybrid organizations such as the unincorporated or family-run businesses for simplification purposes.

Figure 6.1

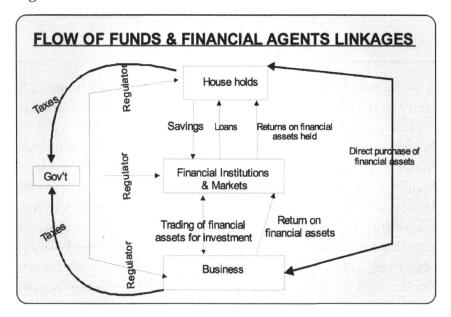

Source: Researcher's Data

Chapter 30

BUSINESS SECTOR
(CORPORATE FINANCE)

A household is, among all other financial agents, an imperative factor in the operation of any business venture since he furnishes his resources to the running of a business. These resources can be in form of: human (both mental and physical capacities); financial (monetary and otherwise); physical (land, machinery and buildings); among other resources for the production processes. Hence, it is upon his discretion to invest these resources in any line of business which will definitely affect the form of business organization he needs to set up so as to realize his business objectives. This critical investment decision has significant implications for growth and development of the chosen form of business, basically in: the way it can raise capital, enjoyment of benefits like profits and decision-making; but also on liability in form of debts and law suits; among other consequences that come with a particular ownership form.

Business financial decisions are concerned with the need to raise finances for investment in real assets such as plant, equipment and technology. But also invest surplus funds in either financial and/or other real assets. There are two major ways that are available for businesses to raise funds: equity financing by taking on new shareholders through issuing stock/shares of ownership in the firm; or debt financing through borrowing from banks and directly from households by issuing bonds.

i)   **Forms of Business Organisations in EAC Region**

e) SOLE PROPRIETORSHIP
This is a form of business owned and run by one person. The sole trading business has no legal requirements before it is

established. With little capital or skill, a household can start a sole trading business. This form of business is the oldest and commonest type in EAC bloc. Many factors have made people to start a sole proprietorship on their own; these factors include inheritance of business from a relative, desire to be independent, desire to build a fortune, unemployment and exploitation of ideas. It is basically run on family grounds and members of a family manage such business for profit. This type of business was necessitated by the fact that there was surplus of production over and above the need of a certain household; and this surplus had to be sold to those with deficiencies/ shortages. It begun initially as a barter system, then the monetization of societies transformed the whole setting; whereby money was later used as a medium of exchange. Such business undertakings are usually short-term and they can live as long as the owner still lives; and so, legally there is no difference between the business and the owner. Hence, the owner has full liability; and his sources of finance remain the traditional ones: owner's savings, loans from relatives and friends, trade credit, and may be short-term loans from financial institutions.

Advantages

- *It is easy to start with minimum cost and no legal formalities.*
- *All profits belong to the entrepreneur.*
- *Sole trading does not pay tax like statutory companies. They only pay personal income tax.*
- *The business can be liquidated easily if the need arises just as it was started.*
- *Decision can be taken quickly since the owner need not consult anybody.*
- *The owner enjoys top secrets and privacy in the matters of his business affair.*
- *The sole trader can give his personal attention and touch to his customers due to the small size of the business.*

- He can supervise all the employees more closely and try to motivate them to work more efficiently.
- This type of business is highly adaptable and flexible form of business due to changes in: customer preferences, seasons, social changes, and regulatory environment in the society.

Disadvantages

- Unlimited liability of the owner, all loses are the responsibilities of the owner and if he fails to bear the losses his property may be forfeited.
- The business lacks originality in that the owner may not be able to get expert ideas that may be required in running a modern business.
- There is no continuity in the business as it may die with the owner.
- Insufficiency of capital is one of the major drawbacks to this form of business.
- The success of the business depends upon the judgment and managerial capacities of its owner: with rational judgment, it will thrive.
- Due to its being confined to only traditional sources of finance, the profitability levels will be rather low.

Conditions Favorable For Establishing a Sole Proprietorship Business

- When capital is small and there is a desire to go into business
- When there is a need to start the business quickly and urgently in order to exploit an advantage.
- When the skill of the owner is an important consideration in the operation of the enterprise
- Where the business is operating in a high risk area and thus needs prompt decision-making to counter any possible catastrophes.

- *In situations where the customers need special attention due to the nature of services rendered such as: medical, legal and consultancy services.*

F) PARTNERSHIP

When two or more persons come together to conduct a business enterprise, a partnership is said to exist. These people come together with the sole aim of sharing profits and losses arising from the partnership. It is formed to boost capital base of a business and benefits from the contributions of the owners. The nature of partnership is such that the partners are co-owners of the business. Partnership can operate under different degrees of formality ranging from an informal oral understanding to a formal written state.

Formation of Partnership

Common law provisions and other statutes guide formation of partnership in East Africa, and this could be in the following ways:

- *Oral agreement*
- *Simply by the actions of the persons concerned: if they are acting as if they were partners*
- *By a simple written agreement*
- *By a deed: an agreement under seal, signed by persons who have committed to become partners.*

On the contrary, if partners wish to run their business under a certain name registered by the Registrar; they must furnish the Registrar with the following particulars:

Some provisions in the partnership agreement include the following:

- *The business name*
- *The general nature of the business*

- *The principle place or location of the business*
- *The Christian and surnames, and any former name of each partner with their usual residence*
- *The nationality of each partner*
- *Any other occupation of each partner*
- *The date of commencement of their business*

Forms of Partnership

i) General Partner (Active Partners): Unless otherwise stated, all partners are regarded as general partners. Such partners have unlimited liability and may personally bear the responsibility of the debt of the business, especially in cases where others could not meet up with their liabilities.

ii) Special Partners: These are partners whose liabilities are limited by the agreement. Such partners do not normally involve themselves in the management of the business.

iii) Sleeping or Dormant Partners: These partners are not known by the public to be actively involved in the business. They are silent partners and do not involved themselves in the daily management of the business.

Features of a Partnership Business

- *Business is formed by a minimum of two members and a maximum of twenty members.*
- *Partners have unlimited liability status: in the event of dissolution of the business, personal assets of partners can be attached if the business fails to clear its creditors' claims.*
- *Each partner is treated as part and parcel of the business except for limited partners.*
- *Each partner may act as an agent of the business.*
- *Ownership of any one partner can't be transferred without the consent of other partners.*
- *Admission or dismissal of any partner must have the consent of others.*

- Books of account of a partnership business are not audited.
- The death or bankruptcy of any one partner leads to dissolution of the business.

Conditions Favorable for the Operation of Partnership

- When a moderate amount of capital is required and where diversified managerial talents could be got from partners.
- Professionals who specialized in different areas could find an opportunity in partnership agreement for better performance and efficiency such as: legal and auditing professions
- When risk is relatively low and could be borne by the partner.
- Where there are clear boundaries of a business and each partner can be identified to a specific area such as engineering field.
- In case the would-be partners have a common bond that they are not willing to sacrifice by inviting other parties such as relatives, family members, professionals, and parties with long association.

Advantages of Partnership

- Partners could have diversified skills, which could be put to the business advantage.
- The business has the opportunity of securing more capital in that there is more than one owner.
- The operation of the business is relatively free from government control.
- It is easy to form and organize in that there are no complicated legal requirements to meet before starting.
- Decision-making process is done by unanimous position of all partners, which can lead to rational decision-making. This would lead to efficiency, high profitability and sound business policies.

Disadvantages

- Inability to transfer ownership in partnership business poses a drawback to this form of enterprise.

- *The partners are jointly and separately liable for business debt. This means that if a partner is unable to meet the claims resulting from the liquidation of the partnership, the remaining partners must take over the unsatisfied claims, drawing on their personal assets if necessary.*
- *It may be difficult to find compatible partners who could work together peacefully, especially in a situation where people do not trust each other.*
- *Uncertainty of the lifespan of the business. If a partner withdraws or dies, the withdrawal or death of the partner dissolves the partnership.*
- *There is a like-hood that partners may not pool their talents equally and this may lead to indifference amongst partners during the general running of the partnership business and frustration on the part of the others.*
- *Some active partners may use the partnership assets to achieve their personal gains at the expense of the interests of the dormant partners.*
- *There may be lack of mutual trust amongst partners: each viewing the other with suspicion; this may create friction among partners and consequently lead to dissolution.*

g) Joint Stock Companies (Limited Liability)

These are advanced forms of partnership where a group of people pool their resources together and contribute to the capital base of such corporations through the purchase of shares of such firms. They are governed by an Acts of respective EAC Parliaments called the Companies' Act; which lays down their formation and general conduct.

For formation, the promoters of a company will have to register it with the responsible regulatory bodies in the EAC; but for Uganda's case, it is with the Registrar of Companies under the Ministry of Trade, Investments and Co-operatives so as to become a legal entity, and it will be issued with a Certificate of Incorporation after the submission of the following documents:

The Memorandum of Association, which contains: the objectives of the company; the authorized share capital; and the types of accounts the company should maintain.

The Articles of Association, which entails: the issue of share capital; borrowing powers of company's directors; appointment, remuneration and powers of company's auditors; meetings and their schedules; voting powers of shareholders; appointment and remuneration of company directors; but also dividend policy to shareholders.

The company's registered office

A list of members who have been appointed directors; their names, qualification, age, occupation, and share holding in a company.

The limited liability companies are usually divided into two basic types across the EAC; and these are:

a) **Private limited liability companies** whose shares are not quoted on the stock exchange market that is, the public do not subscribe to their shares but sell their share privately to interested members of the pubic, which is called private placement.

Such companies are very many across the EAC region, and they are largely run on family grounds with no intentions of going public so as to safeguard their secrets and control.

b) **Public limited companies** are those whose shares are quoted on the stock exchange and subscribed to by the public through the sale of ordinary (common stock) or preference shares. These companies normally raise large sums of money from the public after being granted permission from: the Capital markets Authorities across the EAC which are normally under the East African Ministries of Finance; and also approval from the various EAC Securities Exchanges which manages the stock exchange infrastructure. The exchanges would consequently appoint/ propose a financial services firm called investment/wholesale/ merchant bank or an underwriter to advise that company on how to go about the issuing of financial securities (underwriting process).

Advantages of Limited Liability Companies

- *The company enjoys continuity in that the company is expected to exist forever unless it is dissolution by the law.*
- *Liabilities of owners are limited to the amount of capital contributed. This means that in event of liquidation, if creditors' claims exceed the value from company's assets then shareholders' assets will not be attached.*
- *It is easier to raise additional capital on identity of the company either by issuing shares or borrowing.*
- *Shares can easily be transferred.*
- *Shares of such companies can be used as collateral security for loans, as long as the company is financially sound.*
- *It gives wide scope to different investment.*

Disadvantages of Limited Liability Companies

- *Limited liability companies suffer too much control from government.*
- *There are great difficulties in starting the company because of the legal requirements.*
- *They suffer from double taxation for example, companies pay tax on profit, dividend, properties, etc.*
- *The growth of bureaucracy can bring slow decision-making.*
- *Possibility of impersonal relationship between management of the company and its workers.*

- *The requirement to publish audited accounts and shareholders access to corporate books leads to loss of privacy/secrecy on the part of the company, and competitors can use such information to out-compete the company.*

H) CO-OPERATIVE SOCIETIES

This is a form of enterprise which fosters cooperation among its members with the view to enhancing mutual and self-help; promote economic interest and welfare of the participating members. A cooperative society derives its strength from the interest and patronage of its members who provide nearly all its finance, own, manage and control its operations.

They are usually guided by statutes and sponsored by government especially because of their aim, which is to make life better for people in terms standard of living.

Types of Co-Operative Society across East Africa

i) Producers' Co-operatives: This form of co-operative society involves co-operation in production area to facilitate greater output, economies of scale, better pricing and improved marketing of product to minimized members' exploitation like Bugisu Cooperative Union in Uganda.

ii) Consumers' Co-operatives: This co-operative society is based on consumer ownership and control. Consumers' co-operative society involves co-operation in retail distributive trades. The society purchases consumer goods in bulk and at wholesale prices and sell to its members. Their objective is to eliminate intermediaries in the distribution of goods thereby enabling members to buy at lower cost. These are not so popular across the EAC due to: poor policies on consumer protection; individualism/self-centeredness; and lack of knowledge on the advantages of economies of collective strategies among many EAC consumers.

iii) Saving and Credit Co-operatives: These co-operatives societies are formed with the aim of promoting culture of long-term perspective towards life among members; members save money in the association based on their ability. The major objective of the saving and credit or saving co-operatives is to discourage the habit of living from hand to mouth and encourage the habit of saving among members. Funds pooled together through savings are given as loan to members at lower interest rates than those of money markets, but there is need to integrate them into the formal financial system possibly through the mobile money systems.

Members of these co-operatives are often drawn from the low-income people, and these are the commonest organizations across the EAC but there are either loosely regulated or not regulated at all in various member States. This renders the informal financial system so large with huge volumes of funds through savings vehicles exchanging hands almost every day without the supervision and oversight of the monetary and financial system authorities. Their number are absolutely not known by any regulator in the EAC, and so is the value of net assets but they have so incremental and outstanding in bettering people's livelihoods and also community-asset building basically in the rural areas.

Advantages of Co-Operative Societies

- *They facilitate easy access to some external sources of finance ie these funds serve to leverage other funds.*
- *Members enjoy economies of both scale and collective strategies.*
- *They serve as useful agents of economic development in that through the societies, incomes of members are raised and more businesses are established by obtaining capital from the cooperatives.*
- *The saving and credit societies have encouraged saving habit among people.*

- *Co-operative societies enjoy less tax burden from government since they act as agent of development for the government.*

Disadvantages of Co-Operative Societies

- *Co-operatives suffer from the lack of adequate finance which put severe limitations on their development and expansion in the range of activities they can offer to the society.*
- *Many of these organizations soon or later turn in political grounds for political parties and personal egos, which compound their poor management skills set.*
- *Co-operative societies are mostly run by inexperienced managers who are not well equipped with modern managerial techniques.*

i) Public Corporation (parastatals)

Public Corporation is a business organization whose ownership is vested in the government who also owns the capital as a trustee for the people. The corporation has its own legal existence and; it is usually organized along a business line but normally a not-for-profit organization. There are many such corporations in the EAC, though their numbers significantly reduced during the 1990s as a result of the World Bank's Structural Adjustment Programmes (SAPs) that was commonly known as privatization. For each corporation, there is an Act of the Parliament that determines the scope of its activities and the broad policies that governs its operations; outlines the format of the organization; and formulates the financial structure and other basic features. It is worth noting that the management and control of a parastatal is vested in a Board of Directors whose members are appointed by a Commissioner/Minister of the Central Government. In many economies, regardless of their economic systems, parastatals are undertaken in areas of public utility such as electricity, telecommunication, water, oil and gas, steel development, television authority, etc. And so among the EAC has a couple of surviving parastatals (list the surviving parastatals in the EAC)

Justification for Government Ownership of Parastatals

- *Some corporations provide services that cannot be left in the hands of private individuals. Examples are the services Central banks, Water and energy corporations, among other parastatals that provide strategic and sensitive services.*

- *The capital requirement for some projects is so enormous that an individual may not be able to afford it.*

- *The desire for rapid economic development may necessitate the government to provide (through ownership), long-term capital projects such as infrastructures and basic services which require huge sums for their investments and which cannot, therefore, be profitably attractive to/and undertaken through private investment.*

- *Government's ownership in business is necessary because, provision of certain goods and services by private enterprises may not be adequate in a way that can promote social justice.*

ii)   Goals/ objectives of business organisations

Promoters of business organisations initiate them for a variety of objectives/ goals, depending on the nature of the business, its prospective clientele, and long-term vision. Some of these objectives overlap each (achievement of one will, by default, embed that of some other objective) while others are absolutely conflicting with each other (achieving one will entail a hindrance to the achievement of some other objective), as my reader will later make a critical analysis of them all. These objectives can be broadly classified into financial objectives & non-financial objectives, as discussed below:

a)   Financial Objectives;

- *Profit maximization: many a firms are established to gain as much profits as humanly possible so as to give a return to their owners; offer attractive salaries and benefits to employees; but also to use these profits to contribute to social causes.*

- *Wealth maximization: some firms aim at maximizing the net-worth of both the business but also of the shareholders through avenues such as retaining and consequently re-investing their profits in viable long-term ventures and capital formation.*

b) Non-Financial Objectives

- *Welfare maximisation of employees: some firms appreciate the value of human resources, and so they strive to boost their welfare since it significantly correlate with high corporate productivity through sales and profits. This can be done through giving reasonable and commensurate salaries; transport and medical facilities; but also assurance of terminal benefits, and recreation facilities for relaxation and managing work-related stress.*

- *Welfare of the Society: businesses have a social responsibility to community were they operate and earn profits. This can be through ethical practices such as; maintaining good relations with communities, avoiding harmful production processes, and also companies contributing to social causes eg MTN Marathon that raises funds for provision of clean water to remote rural areas.*

- *Fair dealing with Suppliers: a business can aim at having a good dealing with its suppliers of goods and services through meeting its obligations in due time; avoiding double dealings in procurement process.*

- *Customers' Interests: organisations ought to be mindful of their customers and seek to retain them by; providing quality products, ensuring the provision of value for money transactions, avoiding ill-treatment of the customers.*

- *Duty to the Government: in modern mixed economies where governments no longer lead production, their role is basically regulatory and provision of public goods & services. Given that fact, businesses should pay corporation taxes & other taxes; they should operate within the government's development plans; but* also operate within a legal system that control their production processes.

- Some firms seek for growth and diversification in the industry.
- Other firms aim at improving productivity and becoming market leaders in the industry.
- Companies seek to survive autonomously from their mother companies.
- Some firms seek to maintain a competitive labour force.

iii) Finance Functions in the Corporate Sector

Finance functions in a corporate body are greatly intertwined with other business operations such as production, marketing, strategic management, and others. They require skilful planning, control and execution of the company operations since these functions affect the size, profitability, growth, value of the firm and its risk management systems. Thus, the following are the major finance functions/decisions in a given firm:

Investment Decision (long-term asset-mix)

Corporate investment decisions greatly entail capital expenditure analysis, and so these are referred to as capital budgeting decisions: decisions of allocation of capital to long-term assets that would yield benefits in the future. Investment decisions are a function of: evaluating the prospective profitability of new investments; and, measuring/comparing the cut-off rate against the prospective returns of new investments. This further entails aspects of risk management due to uncertainty, and also replacement decisions of less productive real assets of the firm.

Financing Decisions (capital mix)

Corporate financial managers should be skilled enough to make rational decisions on when, from where, and how to acquire finances to meet the business' investment needs. This leads to an important element in corporate finance "capital structure": the appropriate mix of debt and equity long-term financing of the firm. They must endeavor to obtain the best financing mix called the optimum capital structure which is achieved when the market value of the company's shares is maximized. Despite its challenges, on the contrary, debt financing is so critical in corporate financing in variety of ways.

Dividend Decision (profit allocation)

This decision is quite imperative to firms, and so corporate financial managers ought to prudently decide whether the business will distribute all its profits; retain some profits; distribute a certain percentage of profits and then retain the remain portion. The fraction of profits distributed as dividends is called the dividend-payout ratio, while the retained fraction of profits is called the retention ratio. An optimum dividend policy is one which maximizes the market value of the firm's shares since a dividend policy should be determined in terms of its effect on the shareholders' value.

Liquidity Decision (short-term asset-mix)

Liquidity is so critical in corporate financial management due to its contribution either to corporate liquidation or survival in operations. And it is significantly affected by investment decision in current assets; these must be managed efficiently so as to safeguard the firm against liquidity risks. In corporate finance, profitability management and liquidity risk management normally clash basically in context of investment in current assets due to need to keep enough funds for recurrent operations of the firm yet some idle current assets don't earn profits to the firm. Thus, the profitability-liquidity trade-off advocates for sound techniques of current assets management by the finance department through estimating the firm's currents financial requirements so as to make available such funds when need arises.

IV) INVESTMENT OPTIONS AVAILABLE FOR CORPORATE

TREASURIES

As already emphasized, corporate treasurer have a wide array of investment avenues available to them not only to safeguard the corporate funds or provide for the liquidity requirements of the firm but also create more value (returns) for the firms from any funds that are not currently in use. These have been thoroughly discussed in "Financial Assets", but among others, these are:

Deposits at banks (current accounts): these are instantly withdrawn, highly liquid but low returns.

Time deposit at a bank: a notice is required to withdraw the funds; interest rate is slightly higher than for current account but still close to the rate of inflation which actually almost washes away the supposed return.

Certificate of deposit (CDs) offered by banks

Treasury bills: these are sold by the government for its liquidity requirements but also monetary policy instruments. These are tradable in the secondary market.

Bank bills: also called acceptance credit (as discussed in earlier)

Local Authority deposits: this is an avenue of lending to local governments/ authorities through instruments like municipal bonds, infrastructural bonds, etc. County governments in Kenya, Kampala Capital City Authority (KCCA) in Uganda, among other local governments across the EAC have shown interest in issuing infrastructural bonds so as to boost its infrastructural development projects.

Discount market deposits: these are deposits normally repayable at call (on demand) or made for a very short-term basically in Inter-bank money markets.

Government treasuries: this is the purchase of EAC governments' bills, notes and bonds in the secondary market.

Corporate bonds: this entails the purchase of bonds/ debentures issued by firms but in the secondary market.

Eurobonds and Bull-dog bonds: this is about lending on an international bond market.

Commercial papers: these are unsecured promissory notes usually 60 days or less to maturity.

Shares: as already discussed for public limited companies.

Derivatives: such as futures, swaps, options, etc. Unfortunately, the derivative industry in the whole East African Community has not had any trial or activity for a variety of reasons.

Chapter 31
HOUSEHOLD SECTOR/ INVESTORS
(PERSONAL FINANCE)

These make decisions regarding activities such as: work; job training; retirement planning; savings versus consumption. Most households are interested in a wide array of assets that are attractive; these can vary considerably depending on: one's economic situation; the tax liability and its management; coupled with the risk elements in the available assets and their hedging possibilities. These financial decisions are aimed at boosting the net-worth of each household through prudent investment, and are the driving forces behind financial innovation, so as to accommodate all investor categories, their tax management and risk and return profiles.

IV) PERSONAL ASSET-BUILDING

Investment research has shown that a person's age and level of responsibility affects the kind of investments he makes at each stage in life. Nonetheless, the most critical investment decision for most households concerns education in early life and interestingly this constitutes a perpetual investment in human capital development. It is imperative to note that any investment in human training is golden and life-long. In labor economics, we believe that human beings working in an organization are its most important assets (actually for me, I normally refer to them as "human assets", when discussing about personal and community asset-building). On the contrary, for them to be called human resources but not laborers they must be educated, trained, skilful and productive otherwise it could be amassing a population of people with no value to add to an organization or an economy.

This is because the major asset most people have during their early working years (after their education or training) is the earning power derived from their skills. At this point in the life cycle, the most important financial decision (asset) concerns insurance against the possibility of disability or sudden death before retirement.

Secondly, the first economic asset many people crave to acquire is their own house. Across the EAC region, for instance, it is an element of pride and prestige to live in owner-occupier property since this is viewed as a hedge against two types of risk: increase in rent payables annually; and the risk availability of that property for one to always occupy it since soon or later the landlord may give you a quit notice. The more interesting economics of owning one's own house is that landed property (land and building) are the only real assets, in theory and practice, that appreciate in value as time passes-by and as the locality where the house is located develops and gets more densely populated.

Towards old-age, as a household accumulates savings to provide for consumption during retirement, the composition of personal assets shift from human assets to financial assets. At this point, portfolio choices become progressively more important with shorter investment horizons unlike during middle age, when most households will be willing to take on a meaningful amount of portfolio risk in order to increase their returns.

RISK AND RETURN PROFILES

In the investment world, all investors would like to preserve their principal capital and make sure that it is always safe and free from any risk, and whenever they invest, to maximize the rate of returns on their investments (net of tax and inflation). Unfortunately, these two objectives are always in conflict since, in Finance, we believe that: the higher the risk in an investment, the higher the anticipated returns (risk-return trade-off) so as to compensate for the probability of a loss. However, practical investment results have shown that, in the great majority of cases, less risky investments earn more income than high-risk investment, and there lies the dilemma of risk-return assumptions in investment. In practice therefore, increased investment risk does not always guarantee a higher return on investment.

Chapter 32

GOVERNMENT SECTOR
(PUBLIC FINANCE)

i)   Its role as financial agent

Government also need finance for their expenditures due to their deficit budgets. Unlike corporations, governments can't issue equity securities and so they are confined to borrowing as a means of raising funds since normally tax revenues are not sufficient to cover expenditures. On the contrary, they can also print more money, though this source if excessively used has inflationary implications that can adversely affect the financial system soundness of a country. States are advantaged in the debt market due to their taxing power that makes them credit worthy and so they can borrow at low rates and for long-term.

ii)   Public finance & its Constituents

Public finance is the science that studies avenues through which government sources for revenue and how it spends the funds. It refers to the total amount of money a government receives from a variety of both domestic and foreign sources in a given period for its expenditure, and this includes: public revenue; public expenditure; public debts; financial administration; fiscal policy management.

Public Revenue: this is the total income acquired by the government through its taxation and non-taxation measures. Among the taxation sources are: the direct taxes (income tax, property tax, corporate tax, land tax, among other taxes); while the indirect or expenditure taxes (sales tax, excise and custom duties, sumptuary tax, octroi tax, and value added tax). On the other hand, the non-taxation avenues are: collection of fees, market dues, road tolls and rates; acquisition of gifts and grants; borrowing internally and externally; sale of licences; government investments; deficit financing).

Public Expenditure: this is the total amount of money which the government and its institutions spend on provision of public services and development projects such as infrastructure, health, education. This can be classified into: consumption expenditure on daily administrative activities like paying civil servants, and maintaining law and order; capital expenditure on medium and long-term State projects for economic development like establishing industries and infrastructures; and transfer payments such as grants, donations, bursaries, subsidies, pensions, and re-distribution of wealth.

Public Debt: this is total amount of resources borrowed directly or indirectly by local governments and parastatals; from both internal and external sources. This can further be categorized into: reproductive debt which is invested in productive activities like infrastructure; dead weight debt whose returns can't cover the debt like financing wars and State functions; funded debt whose repayment period is not specified; floating debt whose repayment period is fixed and usually short term.

Financial Administration: this is the process involving preparation of the budget and auditing of all government ministries, departments, and entities.

Fiscal Policy Management: it is the use of taxation, borrowing and government expenditure to finance State activities and to bring about economic stability for proper growth and development.

Public Financial Management (South Sudan Experience)

In the South Sudan (a young nation & new entrant into the EAC bloc), the public financial management systems are still weak and fiduciary risks are substantial due to weakness in Public Financial Management (PFM) systems. But positive trajectory and PFM reforms are being implemented such as:

The use of IFMIS

The introduction of South Sudan Electronic Payment System (SSEPS)

The enactment of the PFM & Accountability Bill

The Taxation Act

The Public Expenditure & Financial Accountability

iii) Need for public finance

Governments, as a financial agents, perform a wide array of functions which must be financed; thus, below is the rationale for public finance:

- *Public revenue is used by the State to carry out investments that are aimed at efficiently allocating resources for national benefit.*

- *In mixed economic systems where resource are largely owned by individuals, public finance is used as a tool to direct private investments in a variety of ways: taxation to stimulate/discourage production in certain sectors and regions; public expenditure on infrastructure to attract private investors in a certain region.*

- *It helps government in provision of public services like road construction, establishing schools and universities, security, and communication facilities.*

- *Public finance is rather critical in undertaking risky and expensive ventures that can't be undertaken by private sector such hydro electricity power generation.*

- *It is used to give relief to vulnerable groups and also in overcoming catastrophes such as the following in Uganda: Bududa landslide victims, Kasese floods victims, but also the poor, displaced and war victims in Nakivale, Rwamwanja and other refugee settlement camps.*

- *Public finance through the prudential management of EAC Central banks serve to ensure economic stability through the use of fiscal and monetary policies so as to achieve macroeconomic stability and financial system soundness.*

- *It can be used as an instrument for the government to fight poverty through government expenditure on infrastructure that provides incomes to citizens who subsequently better their livelihood.*
- *The State uses public finance mechanisms to foster equitable distribution of incomes and also regional balances basically through the instrument of taxation and government spending.*
- *It can be used as a tool for public debt management through taxation and other revenue sources that help the economy in debt servicing.*

iv) Objectives of Fiscal policy

- *EAC governments aim at accelerating private-sector led economic growth.*
- *Maintain macro-economic stability, including low inflation close to the medium term target of 5% per annum according to the EAC prudential standards, and a stable exchange rate.*
- *Improve domestic revenue mobilization and optimize a mix of financing sources such as PPPs, equity financing, less concessional external loans and other debt market financing instruments to implement critical priority infrastructure investments.*
- *Improve expenditure efficiency through public finance management reforms to ensure effectiveness of scarce resources.*
- *Support increased production and productivity as well as skills training to create jobs.*
- *Fiscal policy serves to regulate economic activities through government expenditures and taxation patterns that either boost or trim aggregate demand according to the need of the economy.*
- *Governments use taxation (which is part of fiscal policy) to protect the health of her citizens through over taxing demerit commodities (goods & services) such as toxic drugs, gambling, among others.*

- EAC governments use fiscal policy to promote economic development by either direct investments using government expenditure or through the provision of tax incentives to private investors and this has seen a drastic growth in FDIs across EAC from USD 2 Billion in 2005 to USD 6 Billion in 2015..

- The regional governments aim at equitable distribution of income through the progressive taxation device that renders high-income earners' tax liability to be higher than low income earners, and consequently redistribute those tax funds to low income earners through service provision.

In a bid to accelerate economic growth, increase per capita income to middle income country status by most EAC economies, and reduce poverty faster; priority should be given to improving domestic resource mobilization, expenditure efficiency and diversifying sources of financing, including exploring new financing options available on the global financial markets like Sovereign Sukuks, Eurobonds, Bull-dog bonds, syndicated loans etc; and this should be an integral part of the fiscal strategy of all EAC governments in this decade.

v)   The National Budget

This is a statement/account outlining anticipated government revenue and expenditure together with measures to boost economic development in the forth coming financial year. This outline unearths the following fundamentals: economic, social and political objectives to be achieved; revenue expected and its sources; nature and allocation of expenditures; summary of economic performance; contribution of different sectors to GDP; among others.

PUBLIC RESOURCE MOBILIZATION

EAC governments use both domestic and external avenues to mobilize resources for their annual budget. Domestic tax revenue is the most crucial source of resources for funding the national budget; this is under the docket of the Directorate of Economic

Affairs (EAC Ministries of Finance) that is tasked with shaping the tax policy. This has far reaching implications across the government system, and this is compounded by the dwindling donor aid, due to a variety of reasons, which has rendered the collection of adequate taxes by most EAC governments more instrumental than ever before. For the government of Rwanda, in her bid to manage the country's fiscal vulnerability, it plans to enhance revenue mobilization and pursue expenditure rationalization with the objective of reducing reliance on donor funding. This comes at a time when donor support declined from 9.2% in 2014 to 7.3% in 2015, and it is projected to fall further in 2016.

Diversified Public Resource Mobilization avenues

Sovereign Sukuk (Islamic bonds): EAC governments can make use of the currently popular Islamic sovereign bond market to raise cheaper long-term finances for their expenditure.

Entering the Yen market

Launching a Diaspora bond for EAC in EAC currencies since most nationals in the diaspora are still so much interested in the growth of their home economies plus the fortunes therewith.

Issuing a Syndicated Loan: Kenya got a Syndicated loan of USD 600 million from a trio of foreign banks eg Citigroup of U.S; the UK's developing-markets-focused Standard Chartered Bank; and Standard Bank Group of South Africa.

GLIMPSES INTO EAC TAX PERFORMANCE: A CASE OF UGANDA

The total revenue collections for FY2013/14, registered a drop in nominal growth from an average of 19.4% in the previous consecutive three fiscal years to 12.4% that amounted to UGX

8,031.03 Billion. This decline is a function of: lower than projected GDP growth; lower performance in telecommunication and banking sectors; government not meeting tax obligations on behalf of some companies with tax holidays; tax avoidance by some telecommunication firms; volatile exchange rate; and also a number of policy measures aimed at increasing taxes but not approved by Parliament. Total direct taxes amounted to UGX 2,624.45 Billion against the projected UGX 2,873.57 despite a nominal year on year growth of 7.8% in that fiscal year.

Figure 6.2

Comparative Analysis of Performance of Selected Direct Taxes.

Corporation Taxes

SECTOR	FY2012/13	FY2013/14	% CHANGE
Banking Sector	80.32	31.73	-60.50
Telecom. Sector	115.02	91.06	-20.82
Beer Sector	33.2	4.32	-47.75
Cigarette Sector	9.1	7.86	-13.58
Withholding Tax Growth (Billions)			
Government Payment	53.25	59.06	10.92
Management & Professional fees	33.11	36.10	9.05
Dividends	46.73	29.20	-37.51
General Supplies	195.38	236.71	21.15
Foreign Transactions	64.70	45.30	-29.99
Total	393.17	406.37	3.36
Treasury Bills & Bond Payments (Billions)			
Tax on bank interest	67.66	68.66	1.48
Treasury bills/ bond	153.94	178.44	15.92
Total	221.59	247.10	11.51

Source: URA Databases; MoFPED (2014)

The underperformance of the banking sector was largely due to higher provisioning for bad debts which are deductible for tax purposes and hence reduce the taxable income of banks. This saw at least three financially strong banks (Stanbic bank, Citi bank, and Diamond Trust bank payment decline by UGX 10.12 Billion. Besides, regarding the withholding tax, poor performance basically stems from lower profits among the main tax payers and a decline in offshore loans from parent companies by 30% (UGX 19.40 Billion) which led to lower dividends especially in the banking and insurance sectors.

a) Types of National Budget

There are basically three types of national budget, these are:

Balanced Budget: this is a budget whose expected annual revenue is equal to the estimated expenditure in a given fiscal year.

Deficit Budget: this is a budget whose estimated annual expenditure is greater than the estimated annual revenue. This is characteristic of most LDCs which run deficit budgets that necessitate supplementary funds through: internal and external borrowing; using foreign exchange reserves; issuing more money; seeking for grants; among other avenues.

Surplus Budget: this is a budget whose estimated revenue is greater than the estimated expenditure in a given fiscal year. This kind of budget is aimed at: reducing money circulation in the financial system; raising more revenue for debt financing; encouraging hard work and strengthen the private sector; increasing national foreign reserves.

b) Functions of National Budget

- *A national budget serves to regulate and allocate resources through the exploitation of certain resources and subsidizing some activities but also discouraging some production processes.*
- *It is used as an instrument of social and economic policy to mobilise citizens towards designed economic targets.*

- *It serves to foster appropriate monetary and fiscal policies to influence money supply, government expenditure and economic development that is desirable in a given fiscal year.*
- *It is used in bringing about regional balances by allocating more resources and subsidies to the less developed regions and sectors in an economy.*
- *A national budget is used as a mechanism to stabilize the balance of payments through boosting domestic production and exportation, and equally discouraging unnecessary importation.*
- *It is used to reduce income inequalities in the country through highly taxing the wealthy so as to subsidize the poor and provide equal income opportunities.*

c) Rationale for Drawing a Deficit Budget across the EAC

- *Deficit budgets are used as an avenue for stimulating aggregate demand in an economy, and consequently stimulate domestic investments.*
- *It serves to reduce unemployment through government's expansionary fiscal policy in a way of huge government expenditure in infrastructure and public service.*
- *It serves to reduce income inequality and regional imbalances through both taxation and government expenditures.*
- *Deficit budgets can be used as a remedy to low government revenue in most EAC countries which is so crucial to public financing.*
- *There are circumstances when government borrowing can be a cheaper and quicker source of financing for its projects than revenue from other avenues like taxation.*

d) Effect of Budget Deficit on Macro-economic Stability

The national debt is the amount of money that the government owes those from whom it has borrowed, and this varies from year to year depending on the macroeconomic objectives of the economic and its needs for financial system soundness. In a year when government spending is less than tax collections, the difference is the government surplus. The national debt shrinks by the amount of the surplus. In a year when government spending is greater than tax collections, the difference is the government deficit. The national debt grows by the amount of deficit.

A government spending more than it collects in taxes (including the inflation tax) must borrow the difference in order to finance its spending. A government borrows through the facility of the Open Market Operations: sale of treasury securities to its citizens and foreigners, which are promises that the government will repay the principal it borrows with interest. These accumulated promises to pay make up the national debt. The government budget deficit is equal to purchases minus net taxes while the fiscal policy measures purchases and taxes. The government's budget balance is a measure of the fiscal policy but the budget deficit is not the right measure of the government's actual deficit (or surplus)

Economists are interested in the deficit for two reasons.

- *The deficit is a convenient and often handy, though sometimes treacherous, measure of fiscal policy's role in stabilization policy. It is an index of how government spending and tax plans affect the position of the IS curve.*

- *The deficit is closely connected with national savings and investment: rising deficit tends to depress capital formation, and it lowers the economy's long-run steady-state growth path; besides reducing the steady-state GDP per worker. High national debt means that taxes in the future will be higher to pay with high interest charges. Such high tax liabilities are likely to further discourage economic activity and economic welfare of the citizens*

The Budget Deficit and Stabilization Policy

An increase in government purchases increases aggregate demand, which shifts the IS curve out to the right, increasing the level of real GPD for each possible value of the interest rate. A decrease in government tax collection also increases aggregate demand, and shifts the IS curve out, as demonstrated in the following Curve.

Figure 6.3

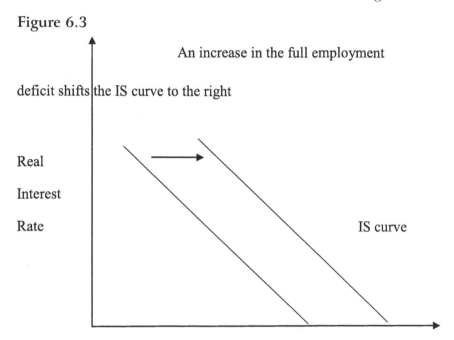

An increase in the full employment deficit shifts the IS curve to the right

Equilibrium Real GDP

The cyclically-adjusted budget deficit is a good measure of the impact of the government's taxing and spending on aggregate demand. When the cyclically or full employment adjusted budget deficit rises, the IS curve shifts right as government policy becomes more stimulative. When the cyclically-adjusted budget deficit falls, the IS curve shifts left as government policy becomes more contractionary.

However, most EAC economies' productive capacity is low where most of the purchases are from abroad (imports), the increase in government purchases does not stimulate local production and demand to bring about an outward shift in real GDP. In this case, increase in government purchases has led to increase in resource outflow leading to slow economic growth and subjecting the economy to persistent high real interest rate as a result of the crowd-out effects.

In addition, most of EAC governments purchases are not productive investments, coupled with increase in capital expenditures such as Universal Primary Education, buying Fire arms and choppers to promote domestic security, interstate highway system, and improvement in the national parks. All these bring about benefits only in the future; it is hard to see any long-run dividing line between government investment and government consumption expenditures that would be sustainable from a political point of view. Thus, critics regard capital budgeting as simply too difficult to implement in a helpful way, nonetheless, supporters point out that not doing capital budgeting at all is, in a sense, worse than even the least helpful implementation.

DEFICITS: SHORT –RUN CONSEQUENCES

In the short run, a deficit produced by a tax cut stimulates consumer spending yet a deficit produced by an increase in government spending increases government purchases. Either way, it shifts the IS curve out to the right: Any given interest rate is associated with a higher equilibrium value of production and employment. If the monetary policy is unchanged to bring about a change in the LM curve, then output and employment rise in response to the tax cut. If the Central Bank does not want inflation to rise, it will respond to the rightward expansionary shift in the IS curve by tightening monetary policy and raising interest rates, neutralizing the expansionary effect of the deficit. J. Delong, the American

Economist indicated that the decision making and policy implementation cycle for monetary policy is significantly shorter than the decision-making and policy implementation cycle for the discretionary monetary policy and it's the role of the central Bank to keep legislative actions to change the deficit from affecting the level of production and unemployment. The central Bank should try its best to guide the economy along the narrow path without excess unemployment and without accelerating inflation.

EFFECTS OF BUDGET DEFICIT ON THE OPEN- ECONOMY

Such an increase in the government budget deficit also leads to an increase in the trade deficit. The outward shift in the IS curve pushes up interest rates: higher interest rates cause appreciation of the domestic currency and depreciation in the foreign currency which causes imports to rise and exports to fall. It is implicitly assumed that the composition of aggregate demand has no effect on the productivity of industry. Business sector is implicitly assumed to be equally happy and productive whether they are producing consumption goods, or capital goods for household use, or goods and services that the government will purchase, or commodities for the export market.

As large deficits that increase interest rates raise the value of the exchange rate, export industries that are highly productive shrink as exports shrink. This presumably reduces total productivity, though; nobody has a reliable and concrete estimate of how large these effects might be to the economy/financial system.

THE EFFECT OF BUDGET DEFICIT ON ECONOMIC GROWTH

High full employment deficits lead to low investment; on the IS –LM equilibrium, a deficit whether from more government purchases or lower taxes, shifts the IS curve to the right. In any run long enough for the full-employment flexible-price model, large full-employment deficits lead to lower aggregate savings, higher real interest rates, and lower investments. In a flexible-price context analysis, the analysis of persistent deficits is straight forward; and such deficits reduce national savings. Flow-of-funds equilibrium thus requires higher real interest rates and lower levels of investment spending.

Figure 6.4

High Full-Employment Deficits Reduce Investments

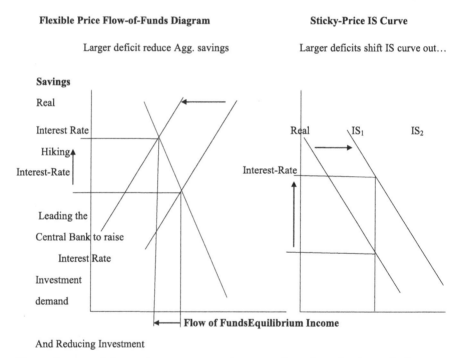

Flexible Price Flow-of-Funds Diagram   **Sticky-Price IS Curve**

Larger deficit reduce Agg. savings   Larger deficits shift IS curve out...

And Reducing Investment

Even in a sticky-price context, it may be that higher deficits reduce investment. The central Bank can change the monetary policy to neutralize the effect of higher deficit on real GDP. The central Bank chooses its baseline monetary policy in order to try to strike the optimum balance between the risk of the higher-than-necessary unemployment and the risk of rising inflation.

The central Bank does not want this balance disturbed by shifts in the IS curve, so it is highly likely to use monetary policy to offset the effect of the deficit- driven shift in the IS curve on the level of real GDP and employment.

A higher deficit means a higher debt, which means that the government owes more in the way of interest payment to bondholders. Even if the level of deficit is kept constant, the rise in interest rates will require tax increases and these tax increases will discourage entrepreneurship and economic activity. In addition to the reduction in output per worker resulting from the lower capital-output ratio, there will be an additional reduction in output per worker: the increased taxes needed to finance the interest owed on the national debt will have negative supply-side effects on production.

Figure 6.5
EAC Current Account Balance (% of GDP)

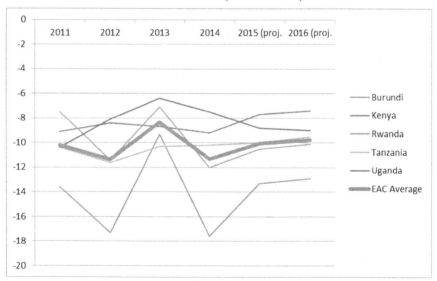

Source: EADB; EAC Central Bank (2015)

Generally, the Balance of Payments summarize all the transactions between one country and the rest of the world (majorly representing the relationship between exports and imports), and this can indicate BOP surplus or deficit. This reality is appreciated in the three components of BOP:

Trade balance, which is also categorized into visible trade balance (difference between value of imported and exported physical goods); and invisible trade balance (difference between value of imported and exported services eg tourism, banking, education, and financial services). The economy can have either a trade surplus or a trade deficit.

Capital account, this records international capital transactions related to financial securities, real estate, investment in business, ownership and sale of fixed assets. This can be further categorized into foreign direct investments; portfolio investments; and other investments.

Current account, this calculates the total value of goods and services that flow into and out of the country. My major interest is in this measure because, it is a function of trade balance figures for both visible and visible commodities, plus other receipts like dividends from sovereign (overseas) assets and remittances from nationals in the diaspora. This is of a unique importance because sovereign assets, and also remittances from nationals abroad are so significant in the East African financial system due to their increasing volumes each year and also contribution to the local resource basket in the region.

All EAC economies have been experiencing a current account deficit for a long period because they are net importers of foreign commodities, and this is particularly worse off for member States like Burundi (in deep waters), Rwanda, and Tanzania that are faring comparatively poor in this indicator; and of course South Sudan with -27% in 2012, though the year after she was relatively improving. This has significantly affected the EAC average but it recorded a spike of an improvement in 2013, later to decelerate in 2014 and even all the projections are underlining a progressive deceleration in this indicator. On the other hand, this progressive current account deficit across the board can be corrected by stimulating net inflows of capital from overseas like remittances from EAC national in the diaspora, boosting our financial markets so that they can attract a lot of foreign participation and activities but also boosting the real sectors such as agriculture, services and manufacturing geared towards the export market.

vi) Forms of Public Expenditure

There are majorly three forms of public expenditure, as discussed below:

Operational/Recurrent Expenditure: this is the total amount of resources spent by governments on funding its administrative or daily activities such as enforcing law and order, paying civil servants, financing foreign trips, etc.

Capital/Development Expenditure: this is money spent by governments on medium and long-term state projects which significantly contribute to economic development such as: establishment of industries, transport and communication infrastructure; but also social systems like schools and hospitals.

Transfer Payments: these are funds that States spend on non-profitable initiatives such as: giving grants, donations, bursaries, pension payments, scholarships, etc.

Roles of public expenditure

Public expenditure can be financed through either taxation financing, debt financing or both as already discussed earlier on. And below is the contribution of public expenditure to the financial system:

- *It serves to boost economic development through huge expenditure in sectors like agriculture that can stimulate the private sector activities which are normally limited and resource constrained.*

- *It stimulates the economy's purchasing power and attraction of investors when governments spend on recurrent activities and transfer payments that boost aggregate demand in the country.*
- *Public expenditure is used to invest in projects that the private sector can't afford to invest in due to huge capital requirements such as electricity, oil refinery, and others.*
- *States use public expenditure to invest in non-profitable and public ventures that are so critical for economic development such as social and economic infrastructure.*
- *It serves to foster regional balance since governments expenditures ensures equal regional distribution of the national cake (resources) in form of investment and enabling atmosphere so as to facilitate balance economic growth.*
- *This also serves to maintain governments in power through the provision of services and delivering their mandate especially through good administration, health care provision and investment in internal and external security.*

VII)   PUBLIC DEBT

a)   Classification of Public Debt

Public debt can be specifically classified according to the following criterion:

Debt Sources: whereby there are internal debts – funds borrowed by the government within the economy through the sale of government/treasury securities like bills, notes and bonds to the public while external debts are funds borrowed by the State from outside the economy such as: international aid, high net-worth individuals, other governments through securities like Eurobonds.

Debt Utilisation: some debts are reproductive debts – funds borrowed and invested in productive activities like infrastructure and parastatals; while dead weight debts are funds borrowed for financing activities that can't be used to repay debts like financing wars, State functions, etc.

Debt Repayment: a funded debt is one whose repayment schedule is not specified and such debts are secured; while an unfunded debt is debt whose repayment schedule is fixed and on short run basis like sale of treasury securities.

EAC GOVERNMENTS DEBT LIABILITY

Figure 6.6

Total External Debt Stock as at June 2015

EAC Country	Uganda	Kenya	Rwanda	South Sudan	Tanzania
External Debt Stock	USD 4,877.2 Million	KSH 322.7 Billion	USD 1,851.54 Million	SSP 7.802 Billion	USD 15,320.1 Million

Source: EAC Central Banks (2015)

b)   **Rationale For Public Debt**

Although some governments have enough capacity to levy taxes so as to cover their budgetary expenditure, there are concrete reasons as to why many a governments opt for debt financing in the form of internal and external borrowing. Among other bases, these are:

- *Economic stability: borrowing, basically domestic debt through issuing treasury instruments (bills, notes, and bonds), helps to regulate the circulation of money. Consequently, this can reduce on inflation rates, but also direct both investments in target sectors and aggregate demand.*

- *Lessening the tax burden: public debt can serve to reduce on the effects of high taxation such as: deflationary situation whereby households' disposable incomes are way below the aggregate supply of commodities in the market due to high tax liabilities. Besides, taxation may discourage people from working hard (progressive tax system).*

- *Generating more government revenues: in reality, most frontier market economies like EAC economies are characterized by high prevalence of tax evasion, corruption, tax avoidance, high informal sectors, and low taxable capacities. These render governments automatically to opt for debt financing due to the unproductiveness of taxation.*

- *Remedy for recession: economies that are facing economic depression normally borrow in a bid to boost aggregate demand, domestic investments and production for economic revitalization.*

- *Fixing the balance of payment position: LDCs are characterized by high operational expenditures, and this can only be financed through external borrowing.*

- *Public debt financing is sought for basically as the last resort in case of emergencies and disasters like famine, epidemics (Ebola, typhoid), wars that befall countries and many LDCs are not prepared enough to handle such eventualities. Hence, economies resort to foreign aid.*

- *Due to high debt burden in Frontier economies, at times they go into the debt market so as to clear/pay old loans that are chocking their economies.*

- *Political capital: many governments go in for borrowing like dead weight debt so as to render their regimes popular through the provision gifts (unstructured hand-outs) to people in a bid to mobilise support for the government.*

- *Debt financing can serve to redistribute incomes among the residents of a country in a bid to fight poverty.*

c) Managing Public Debt

Public debt management are systems, mechanisms and policies through which the central bank contracts debts on behalf of the government, and services/clears both internal and external debts guided by the macroeconomic policies of an economy. This is primarily a function of the central bank since it is the custodian of the financial system and should ensure macroeconomic stability. Managing public debt entails the following roles:

- *Determining when to contract the debt*
- *Determining the volumes of funds required*
- *Determining the source of debt (domestic or foreign)*
- *Determining the nature of the debt (treasury securities, euro-bond, bull dog bond, etc)*
- *Determining the means to service the debt (taxation, foreign exchange reserves, another loan, etc)*
- *Determining the mode of servicing the debt*

d) Methods of Public Debt Management

Public debt management, as already discussed, is a function of the country's central bank; and to achieve this macroeconomic goal, there is need separate between domestic debt management and external debt management so as to facilitate the process.

Managing Domestic Debt can be through the following methods:

- *The State can seek for grants and donations from foreign sources to help clear internal loans to the government.*
- *The government can resort to a tax system that levies extra taxes on wealthy individuals and financially strong corporations*
- *Governments can opt for surplus budgets in a bid to mobilize additional resources for servicing domestic debts.*
- *Some economies use the avenue of privatisation of State parastatals so as to raise finances to clear domestic loans.*
- *There is also the opportunity of obtaining fresh debts from the public through the issuance of more government securities in a bid to either service or clear outstanding debts.*
- *In economic systems where the State still engages in production, accumulated profits from government parastatals can be used to service domestic debts.*
- *There is yet another monetary policy instrument that a State can exploit; that is running national rotaries like Jadah in the 1990s so*

as to extract excess liquidity from the public for macroeconomic equilibrium (domestic debt management).

On the contrary, systems of external debt management are as follows:

- *The State might resolve to borrow further in the international financial markets so as to service and/or clear her foreign debts; through issuing Sovereign Sukuks, Eurobonds, Bull-dog bonds, and also from the IMF and World Bank.*
- *The government may use its foreign exchange reserves to service/ clear outstanding debts since they are actually used to manage the external economy vulnerabilities such as B.O.P alignment and debt servicing.*
- *There is also the option of seeking for foreign grants so as to service the country's outstanding debts.*
- *The economy can deliberately pursue policies that promote production for exports and also import substitution so as to better her B.O.P position and scale down on the debt liability.*
- *Besides, the government can use a wide array of mechanisms such as: debt rescheduling, barter negotiations, debt repudiation and debt cancelling in a bid to service/clear her outstanding debts.*
- *The State can also deliberately increase tariffs on international trade so as to mobilise funds for debt servicing/ clearing.*

j)   IFMS (Financial Administration)

The Integrated Financial Management System (IFMS) has been adopted and implemented by most EAC governments since the early 2000s with a view to improve efficiency in budget preparation, execution and financial reporting. Its design was based on a centralized architecture which enables central processing and storage of financial transactions done in the data centre of the Ministries of Finance, connecting all Ministries, agencies and Local/County governments over a Wide Area Network (WAN) and accessing it through a web browser.

Since its inception in the EAC, it has been extended across many ministries and central government agencies; but also implemented in many local/county governments, which has enabled EAC governments: to address many of the fiduciary issues faced before; greater expenditure control and discipline in budget management due to oversight ad enforcement of internal controls. Besides, there has been a reduction in taken time to process payments; improvement in account reconciliation; and more accurate & reliable financial reporting. Upon full implementation, the following transactions should be covered: all government transactions like revenue receipts, debt, expenditures (including transactions financed by donor or other agencies); and all government units (ministries, agencies, sub-national units, and projects). This will enhance implementation of common control regime and comprehensive fiscal reporting since the IFMS interfaces with the tax bodies, Central banks, and other agencies.

Figure 6.7
Key IFMS COMPONENTS

IFMS Component	Role
Public Sector Budgeting	Enables vote holders to prepare & submit budgets electronically. Consolidation of transactions on the system
General Ledger	Enables electronic & automated posting of transactions on system.
Payables	Receiving & processing supplier invoices are linked electronically & validated in real time.
Purchasing	Links purchase orders to the online cash limits thus enhancing commitment controls.
Cash Management	Enables cash forecasting & bank reconciliation to be done online in real time. An interface with Central banks is in place to facilitate automated reconciliation.
Revenue/ Receipting	Links EAC Treasury with EAC tax bodies in respect of tax returns. Invoicing & collections of non-tax revenues can be managed online.

Chapter 33
PUBLIC PRIVATE PARTNERSHIPS (PPPS)

Public Private Partnership is defined as an arrangement between a State department or agency, Government Corporation or local/ county government (contracting authority) and a private party, where the private partner performs a public function or provides a service on behalf of the contracting authority and receives a benefit for it either in the form of compensation from a public fund and /or charges to consumers and generally liable for risks arising from the performance of the function. This arrangement applies to the financing, construction, operation, equipping or maintenance of infrastructure projects; and other dealings.

Public Private Partnerships (PPPs) are a form of financing that usually involves the use of private resources to provide a public good, especially infrastructure. They are a critical tool for fiscal control and management of public debt since budgetary commitments in respect of infrastructure and provision of services provided under the PPP arrangements are known in advance. The PPP Act 2013 in Kenya, and PPP Act 2015 in Uganda, and similar Acts of Parliaments in Tanzania, and Rwanda are fully operational. These projects often require guarantees or allocate some risks to the State: retaining risks and issuing guarantees create contingent liabilities, which increases as the stock of PPPs increase. In response to this, most EAC governments are developing tools which will carry out an assessment of the level of exposure of risk and *contingent liability*. By 2013/14, explicit contingent liability arising from PPPs in Uganda stood at 0.23% of GDP over the medium-term. Governments, world over, believe that employing these PPP projects can procure the following to a given financial system:

- *Mobilization of the private sector resources and development.*

- *Better utilization and allocation of public funds.*
- *More efficient development and delivery of the requisite public infrastructure.*
- *Achievement of value for money from public resources.*
- *Ensure good quality public services.*
- *Efficiency through healthy competition*

In Uganda, the government has currently committed to explicit contingent liabilities through seven on-going PPPs though in FY 2014/15 no contingent liability was called upon from the existing PPP projects. Therefore, the summed estimated contingent liabilities on Government that may arise from these on-going PPP projects for FY 2015/16 fiscal year stood at UGX 123.6 Billion, equivalent to 0.15% of GDP. And below is the status of the PPP programs since 2003 and an analysis of the progress of on-going projects:

- *Kalangala Infrastructure Services Project: it is a 20 year multi-sectoral project undertaking by Kalangala Infrastructure Services Ltd since 2009 under the Build, Own and Operate (BOT) modality. So far, among the deliverables: the ferry is operational and solar power and water supplies are readily available; the road component is 70% complete and Resettlement Action Plan (RAP) is substantially complete.*

- *Umeme Electricity Distribution Project: in 2004, Umeme Ltd was awarded a concession to distribute and supply electricity for a period of 20 years. Thus far, power outage has significantly reduced; connection to power grid increased; and power losses reduced from 38% initially to 24% currently.*

- *Kampala Serena Hotel Project: it is a 30 year concession contract signed between Tourism Promotion Services Ltd and Nile Hotel International Ltd on January 15, 2004. Despite the volatility of the tourism sector, the project has transformed Nile Hotel Ltd into a 5 Star Hotel and rebranded to Kampala Serena Hotel.*

- *Eskom Electricity Generation Project: it is a 20 year concession agreement between Eskom Uganda Ltd and Uganda Electricity Generation Company Ltd, which took effect in April 2003. Currently, the project supplies over 67% of Uganda's electricity energy.*
- *Kenya-Uganda Railway Project: in 2006, Kenya and Uganda signed a 25 year Kenya-Uganda Railway concession to improve transport conditions through restoration of railway operations. The railway comprises a total track length of 2,350 Km, of which 1920 Km is in Kenya and 430 Km in Uganda.*
- *Kilembe Mineral Project: it ia s 25 year concession arrangement between Kilembe Mines Ltd and Tibet Hima Automobile Industry Company Ltd executed in 2013 to further explore and develop minerals; hence creating jobs and preserving the natural environment.*
- *Bujagali Hydroelectric Project: it is a 30 year Build, Operate and Transfer (BOT) contract signed in 2005 between Bujagali Energy Ltd and Uganda Electricity Generation Company Ltd for the development of a 250MW hydroelectric plant, at an estimated construction cost of USD 902 million. The project was commissioned on 15th June 2012 and is currently operational.*

in Kenya, the government is struggling to bridge an infrastructure deficit estimated at USD 35 Billion over the next 6 years; and it is looking to develop public infrastructure through PPPs. Kenya currently has published 59 high priority projects in energy, roads, ports, health, and housing.

There is need to set to set up a PPP unit under the EAC Ministries of Finance with roles of reviewing proposals, identifying priority projects from all sectors, and prepare them for private sector investments. Before undertaking any project, a contracting authority must first assess the advantages of a PPP over developing the facility or providing the service itself based on the following core indicators: value for money; affordability for the contracting authority and end-users; and appropriate transfer of risks to the private party. PPP projects may be undertaken either by solicited bids or by private initiated proposals

SOLICITED BIDS

In such bids, a contracting authority conceptualizes the projects it wishes to undertake and submits the project to the PPP Unit, which reviews the project lists submitted to it and makes its recommendations to the PPP committee, which will then compile and forward a national priority list for approval. This will be followed by the contracting authority conducting a sector diagnostic study covering technical issues, legal and regulatory framework, institutional capacity and commercial aspects of the project to later submit a project proposal for approval to the PPP Unit.

PRIVATELY INITIATED BIDS

Unsolicited bids can be submitted by a private party to a contracting authority, which would not be subject to a competitive bidding process in the following circumstances:

Where there is an urgent need for continuity of a certain public initiative;

Where the costs relating to intellectual property rights in relation to the project design are substantial;

Where there exists only one person capable of undertaking the project;

In such as case, the contracting authority must submit a proposal to the PPP Unit for approval, and thereafter negotiations can begin with the private party.

THE PUBLIC INVESTMENT OUTLOOK & EAC COUNTRIES VISIONS

In this decade, the government has progressively continued to promote the private sector as the engine of economic growth; and attracting increased investment both foreign and domestic is a key priority in the EAC governments' strategy to accelerate employment, productivity and socio-economic transformation of the country as envisaged in the various EAC countries perspective plans as evidenced in (Vision 2020, 2030 and 2040).

A 2016 report by Making Investments Work for the Poor indicated a significant growth in FDIs from USD 2 Billion in 2005 to USD 6 Billion in 2015. But there is mismatch because despite the astronomic growth in investments, the biggest percentage of locals in EAC region remain very poor. These have been witnessed in basically the oil & energy as well as the manufacturing sectors but also the multinational corporations, and the recent massive USD Billions projects to expand the EAC regional railway network to standard gauge by Chinese firms. This strong increase in FDI reflect international investors' confidence in the EAC region's long-term growth prospects, and will continue to underscore the regional bloc's economic development. Besides, more investment inflows are expected from trade summits like China-Africa, Euro-Africa, Turkey-Africa, Japan-Africa, US-Africa and Hong Kong-Africa. On the other hand, financial outflows have also reached unprecedented levels with developing economies being the net losers: more money flows out of African countries than actually into them rendering the hypothesis that multinationals' influx is just an onslaught to exploit the natural resources more valid now than ever before. The Global Financial Integrity (GFI) estimates that, for each USD 1 developing economies receive in foreign aid, USD 10 in illicit money flows abroad; facilitated by secrecy in the global financial system. The outflow is equivalent to the Africa's current GDP, and its about four times Africa's current external debt according to African Development Bank (AfDB) estimates.

On domestic investments, more private investment will require a larger share of credit channelled to production in the economy. Since the beginning of this decade, credit to the private sector in the EAC region has, on average, expanded by more than 120% in constant terms though this has not yet translated into similarly high growth; and this weak link between private-sector-credit and growth implies that credit is predominantly channelled to consumption rather production with just 21. 4% channelled to productive sectors like agriculture and manufacturing.

Interest rates in advanced economies have been exceptionally low in response to low inflation and very low growth, and many central banks have been stimulating their economies through unconventional monetary policies code-named monetary easing. As those economies recover, central banks will have to reabsorb large amounts of liquidity, if not, this may lead to quickly accelerating inflation in those economies forcing their central banks to aggressively raise interest rates. For the EAC region, this is of particular concern, as more than 40% of credit to the private sector is denominated in foreign currency.

PUBLIC INVESTMENT MANAGEMENT AND HIGHER SOCIAL RETURNS

According to World Bank's Uganda Economic Update (2016), Public investment management has the potential to help East Africa address its current constraints on growth, particularly the country's infrastructure deficit. Leveraging on the current strategy of building the EAC region's capital stock in energy and transport infrastructure, these investments priorities can drive faster economic growth and improve households' socio-economic welfare. Besides, this could also facilitate delivery of public services, connect citizens and enterprises to economic opportunities, improve productivity, and create jobs for the country's large and growing population. On the other hand, experts believe that the success of this strategy hinges on getting the anticipated dividends from the current huge infrastructure investments so as to support a faster growth of incomes, and also raise the capacity of Government to invest in social services.

The perspective plans of most EAC economies as enshrined in their respective National Visions and National Development Plan, EAC countries' fiscal policies prioritize investments in capital development although reports have indicated that the returns on these investments often falls short of the expected returns. Thus, converting investments into productive assets requires an effective management of public investments at all stages of the project cycle, from when a project idea begins, to the management of the completed asset.

Regional governments ought to deliberately initiate institutional reforms aimed at strengthening review process by establishing a new department responsible for project appraisal and public private partnerships, which will be responsible for formulating standards and criteria for project appraisals, but also ensuring that any project that is submitted for public financing meets the minimum standards.

The World Bank Economic Update (2016) recommends that governments should sustain the momentum of reforms to strengthen Public Investment Management. The focus of these reforms could include:

- *Institutional strengthening – There is a need to build capacity of institutions across the entire project cycle to prepare quality projects, carry out rigorous appraisal, construct the assets efficiently and at minimum cost, and monitor and maintain these assets. This will require training to undertake appraisals and manage projects more effectively.*

- *Standardization – Harmonization of standards and guidelines is critical for quality control, greater tracking, and monitoring of results. A shared understanding is needed across institutions related to identification, appraisal, implementation, evaluation of projects. Developing manuals on various aspects of public investment management will be important in harmonising standards across all ministries as it would allow for more effective and continuous monitoring, data collection, and to be able to carry out evaluation.*

- *Strengthening the legal and regulatory framework – A robust legal and regulatory framework underpins an efficient and successful Public Investment because it strengthens mandates of various institutions involved, and creates incentives for agents to program. Gaps in the current legal framework would need to be addressed if the reform effort is to succeed.*

DEDUCTION OF PART 6:

Financial agents (players/agents in the financial system) are basically the key decision-making units in a financial system since they make crucial financial decisions that affect not only their welfare but also that of the overall financial system. It is incumbent upon them to appreciate rights, duties, mandates and regulatory environment that affect their rational financial decisions but also a thorough knowledge of the wide array of cheap financing for their objectives and also investment options available to them. In a special way, the government as a key financial agent whose duty is to ensure a sound financial system, it is prudent for governments to better understand how to make rational public financial management and also public investment management decisions so as to stimulate the activity and productivity of other financial agents. Besides, EAC governments ought to set efficient structures under the PPP units (in the respective Ministries of Finance) so as to stimulate private sector investments in infrastructure and other priority sectors in a bid to boost the investment climate of the EAC Bloc. The EAC organs by June 2016 were in the process of creating an EAC PPPs policy and the corresponding Directives aimed at harmonizing this sector. There is need to convert the EAC Bloc's large investment programs into productive assets through strengthening the public investment management systems across the EAC region to ensure maximum value from public investments and eliminate wastage.

PART 7
FINANCIAL INFRASTRUCTURE, RISKS &
INTERMEDIATION

Chapter 34

FINANCIAL INFRASTRUCTURE

"An efficient & safe payment system provides an enabling environment
for economic growth and financial system soundness."

PAYMENT & SETTLEMENT SYSTEMS

These provide practical mechanisms for money to be transmitted and received quickly and reliably. It is an essential prerequisite for commercial activities to take place and for participation in regional trade and investment. Access to these payment systems is a vital component of financial inclusion for households.

Central Securities Depository (CSD) – this is a key part of the financial system infrastructure and it plays the following roles:

It provides a secure central record of the ownership of securities;

It enables the owners of securities to enjoy the benefits of ownership like voting and income rights (through company registrars);

It provides the means for the secure transfer of ownership of securities;

This is the security settlement system process:

An investor places an order with a broker (member of a stock exchange), who then executes the trade using the exchange's trading system. Once the trade is executed, details of the trade are put into the settlement system by the broker or sent automatically from the trading system. Then, the settlement system checks whether the two sets of instruction agree and, if it is so, the trade is matched and made ready for settlement on the intended settlement day. On this day, the seller's account is credited with proceeds of sale and the securities are delivered to the buyer.

Below is the security settlement system process:

An investor places an order with a broker (member of a stock exchange), who then executes the trade using the exchange's trading system. Once the trade is executed, details of the trade are put into the settlement system by the broker or sent automatically from the trading system. Then, the settlement system checks whether the two sets of instruction agree and, if it is so, the trade is matched and made ready for settlement on the intended settlement day. On this day, the seller's account is credited with proceeds of sale and the securities are delivered to the buyer.

Automated Trading Infrastructure

This infrastructure which is automatically linked to the Central Securities Depositories (CSD) and the Real Time Gross Settlement (RTGS) at EAC Central banks. This ensures real time gross settlement for securities traded on stock exchanges; mitigates all possible transaction risks; fosters efficiency in securities trading. This payment system works through the Central banks' RTGS via SWIFT messaging technology that is aimed at achieving efficiencies in Delivery versus Payment (DvP). This was first introduced by the Rwandan financial system (RSE) which has made a record of no transaction failure or complaint in RSE's five years of existence due to its high levels of efficiency & elimination of risk exposures by the players. The four EAC economies with stock exchange infrastructure have adopted this model and are implementing it though their central banks. Reality, coupled with empirical research indicate that it will be a huge enabling facility for an integrated EAC stock market, which will serve to reduce securities settlement & delivery time to three (3) working days to match international standards.

Regional Inter-Depository Transfer Mechanism

This facility was put in place to simplify movement of cross-listed securities and provide new possibilities for investors seeking cross-border trade opportunities. This was debuted by Umeme Ltd through its cross-listing on NSE in August 2013; followed by Uchumi Supermarkets which cross-listed from Kenya to USE & RSE. Investors can now enjoy proficient movement of securities across the region, and sufficiently reduce the exchange rate risks and price movement arbitrage. By 31st December 2014, a total of 50,598,824 shares had been transferred through this mechanism.

MOBILE MONEY REVOLUTION IN EAC

Its revolution in EAC in 2011 led to inflationary pressures across the board due to its practical application of the multiplier effects (drastic & instantaneous increase in purchasing power everywhere due to high mobility& quick transfer of funds. Hence affecting effective demand & commodity markets. This caught Central banks unaware. Mobile money expedites the velocity of money thus creating value & making financial services so good & interesting.

Facility for tapping into informal Financial system

In Zimbabwe, people keep their money in their beds, cupboards, gardens; and lots of money because they fear that banks may either be nationalized one time or there could be a systemic failure and they lose their money. Hence, lots of funds are blocked from being channeled to productive use in the real economy so as to stimulate economic growth. However, the facility of mobile money can serve to integrate such volumes of funds in the informal financial system into the formal financial system to create value across the value-chain.

Mobile Money Transactions EAC

Cross-border mobile money transactions are so critical for EAC integration and key growth areas for even regional telecoms but also to business.

NB: Tigo Rwanda & Tigo Tanzania launched the first ever cross-border mobile money in February 2014. But there was great need for harmonization of payment platforms policy and currency conversion by majorly regional Central banks through issuance of licenses & guidelines. Many telecoms have now successfully rolled out these services.

Statistics on Cross-border Transactions:

According to National Bank of Rwanda, transactions between Rwanda & Tanzania on Tigo cash platform were at 6,245 valued at RwF 248 Million for 2014. But USD 2 Billion was the whole mobile money services.

In Kenya, close to USD 25 Billion was pushed through mobile money in 2014 up from less than USD 20 Billion in 2013.

In Uganda, close to USD 7 Billion in 2014 was transacted from just over USD 5 Billion in 2013. Besides, 2015 saw a huge growth in mobile money services whereby a whole UGX 24 Trillion was transacted; accounts for almost a third (1/3) of Uganda's GDP that is worth UGX 76 Trillion.

In Tanzania, more than USD 15 Billion was transacted through mobile money in 2013 in cross-border transactions. On the other hand, there were 41,380,791 mobile money accounts; and a total value of mobile payment transactions worth TZS 40.8 Trillion was achieved by end 2014.

Therefore, these national mobile money transfer services indicate the potential of the sector as more people prefer these platforms to banks due to convenience in service provision; historically high liquidity preference amongst EAC; high levels of mistrust in the banking system. Besides, mobile money expedites the velocity of money, thus, creating value and making financial services rather good and interesting.

Challenges of MM services

There is need for multi-sectoral participation in this financial product so as to enjoy the benefits & accelerate financial intermediation at the national level.

Security on the platforms is very key since many customers have lost/ been robbed of their since MM services were introduced in EAC.

There is urgent need for Policies & regulations to keep platforms safe & free from fraud & laundering which are quite rampant world over.

Monetary authorities across the EAC region ought to address monetary issues and conversion ratios across different currencies which mobile operators are facing that hinder efficient and safe transactions. This intervention should be done at the policy level, preferably by the Monetary Affairs Committee of the EAC (which comprises of Governors of the six Central banks).

Figure 7.1
East African Payment Systems (EAPS) Dec. 2014 – July 2015

	Inward Messages		Outward Messages	
Currency	Volume	Value	Volume	Value
FrW	12	181,601,612	20	274,524,012
UGX	16	391,849,474	34	322,630,372
KES	14	22,901,888.7	30	21,896,208
TZS	6	4,400,000	0	0

Source: EAC Central Banks (2015)

Chapter 35
EAC POLITICAL & FINANCIAL SYSTEM RISKS

"What we know about the global financial crisis is that we don't know very much..."

Best's Country Risk Tiers:

This ranges from CRT-1 for economies with: predictable & transparent legal environment, legal system and business infrastructure; sophisticated financial system regulation with deep capital markets, and mature insurance industry framework. This ends with CRT-5 for countries with: unpredictable and opaque political, legal and business environment characterized by limited or non-existent capital markets; low human development, and social instability; emerging insurance industry.

A.M Best defines Political risk as the likelihood that government or bureaucratic inefficiencies, societal tensions, inadequate legal system or international tensions will cause adverse developments to/for an investor. This comprises of the stability of the government/society, the effectiveness of international diplomatic relationships, the reliability and integrity of the legal system and of business infrastructure, the efficiency of government bureaucracy, and the appropriateness & effectiveness of the government's economic policies.

On the other hand, Financial system risk is the risk that financial volatility may erupt due to inadequate reporting standards, weak banking system or asset markets, and/or poor regulatory structure. It also includes an evaluation whether the financial services industry's level of development & public awareness; transparent and effective regulation; reporting standards & sophisticated regulatory body will contribute to a volatile financial system, and compromise the ability of an investor to get his expected value (return on investment) projected at a given time period.

NB: Kenya and other EAC economies rank at CRT-5 (basing on A.M Best's rating) given a history of low GDP per capita, ethnic tensions, high levels of government debt, and political instability.

Much of the EAC region continue to suffer from low levels of wealth and high levels of poverty; income inequality, corruption, exchange rate volatility, high inflation rates, high unemployment levels (especially the youth demographics), insufficient infrastructure, ineffectual government institutions.

Increased terror attacks from Al Shabab & internal/political unrest have led to decreased investor confidence, and have negatively impacted FDI flows.

Kenya is a regional hub for trade & finance, but it its development is limited due to relative volatility in the region, domestic political challenges, and the economy's reliance on primary goods.

KENYA

Political risk has been high but now it is improving since the post-election violence in 2007-2008 that saw changes in its institutional system including a new constitution in 2010. Besides, the ICC cases against Kenyatta & Ruto for inciting 2008 elections violence have been called off. But still a third of Kenya's GDP is lost due to corruption according to State Prosecutor's office.

Financial system risk: financial sector is still vulnerable to government influence & weak supervision. Government debt burdens are high with about half of total revenues going to finance the wage bill. Therefore, reduction in the wage bill and increased tax revenues are anticipated to lower the deficit.

EAC Sovereign Debt Rating

Sovereign credit rating institutions paint a positive outlook on the EAC which is favorable to the region in general as a good investment destination compared to many other Sub-Saharan African (SSA) economies. These rating agencies included: the Standard & Poor (S&P), the Moody, and the Fitch; which put EAC economies between "B+ to B stable" positions in general. These stress that the continued infrastructure investments and the solid-medium term growth prospects in EAC partly offset the risks from fiscal and external imbalances. Below is a representation of some of the EAC economies ratings by these agencies, and a comparison with some peers in the Sub-Saharan Africa:

Figure 7.2
ISSUER RATING (Long-term) between 2013 and 2015

	Burundi	Kenya	Rwanda	South Sudan	Tanzania	Uganda	Zambia	Ghana
S & P	-	B+ Stable	B+	-	-	B Stable	B+	B
Fitch	-	B+ Stable	B+	-	-	B+	B Stable	B Stable
Moody	-	B1	-	-	-	B1	-	-

Source: WBG; EAC Central Banks (2015)

NB: By June 2016, Tanzania was in advanced stages of hiring international Credit rating agencies so as to carry out the necessary ratings; but Burundi and South Sudan had no information in this line.

Moody Rating Guiding Questions

These questions guide informed investment decision-making in financial markets (esp. bonds)

Will the country be able to repay debt?

If the economy is not growing, how is it going to repay debt?

Is the economy resilient enough to take shocks from the global economy?

EAC credit ratings are positive & good since the future outlook is good enough; though most currencies are weak but credit ratings are more fundamental than currency values (which are largely spot valuations but don't really at times take into consideration macroeconomic fundamentals).

IMF maintains that most East African countries are relatively high on growth, low on inflation and they have adequate internal reserves (way above EAC and IMF benchmarks), with sustainable external debt and above all sound financial systems.

GLOBAL FINANCIAL CRISIS OF 2007 & FINANCIAL
SYSTEM RISKS

The GFC drove many industrialized & emerging economies into recession & resulted into systemic failures. It highlighted the imperative of financial system regulators (charged with financial stability) to strengthen their analysis and surveillance of systemic risks to the financial system, and also devise policy instruments so as to mitigate them.

Quote:
"What we know about the global financial crisis is that we don't know very much....."
Paul A. Samuelson (Economist)

Figure 7.3

EAC Financial Systems Positions in the Global Financial Sector Competitiveness Ranking (Score is out of 140 economies)

Country	2010/2011	2015/2016
Burundi	139	140
Kenya	27	42
Rwanda	69	28
Tanzania	90	101
Uganda	72	81
Nigeria	84	79
Malawi	64	100
Ghana	60	76
South Africa	9	12

Source: The Global Competitiveness Report 2015 – 2016; and 2010 – 2011. And World Economic Forum

At least 2 of the EAC economies rank in the first half of the 140 economies; and still Uganda and Tanzania, though lying in the 2nd half, they appear way competitive in the face of many African middle income economies like Ghana and Nigeria. Thus EAC, due to its positive outlook and promising macroeconomic fundamentals, is likely to attract more foreign capital in the future than many other African peers and Asian economies.

Chapter 36
FINANCIAL INTERMEDIATION
"Narrow banking could throw the baby (intermediation) out with the bathwater (crisis)"

Households want desirable investments for their savings, but their small financial assets makes direct investment pretty hard. These investors seeking to lend money to businesses in need of huge capital investments don't have any medium/ link to the willing and desirable borrower. Besides, such a small holder would not be able to diversify across a wide variety of borrowers as a risk management system. Thus, it is at this stage that financial intermediaries come into the investment picture, basically to act as a "conduit" that links lenders (those with surplus funds) to borrowers (those with deficit budgets). These include: banks, investment companies, insurance companies, and credit unions, who issue their own securities to raise funds to purchase the securities of other corporations. They are institutions that serve to connect the financial agents (households, business, and government) so that: households can invest their surplus incomes; businesses can finance production; and government can carry out its mandate to its citizens.

Figure 7.4:

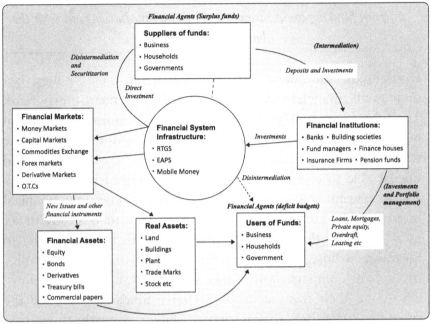

OVERVIEW OF FINANCIAL SYSTEM

Source: Researcher's Data

Despite the fact that many households can invest directly in securities of business firms and government agencies, many households prefer investing indirectly through the financial system facility of financial intermediaries who do financial transactions on their part. Thus, financial intermediation is the process by which individual savings are accumulated and mobilized by financial services firms, and in turn lent out or invested in a productive and prudent manner. It is the process of indirect financing using financial intermediaries as the primary route for moving funds from net lenders to net borrowers. And research has proved that financial intermediaries are a far more important source of financing for corporations than securities markets.

Financial intermediaries stand between buyers and sellers, facilitating the exchange of assets, capital and risk. Their services allow for greater efficiency and are vital to a well-functioning economy; and below are a tabular representation of some of the financial intermediaries in a financial system.

Figure 7.5

Structure of the EAC Banking System
Comparisons & Indicators of Financial Intermediation
across the EAC

EAC Economy	No. of Commercial Banks	No. of Microfinance Institutions	No. of Forex Bureaus	No. of Money Remittance	No. of Credit Reference Bureaus	No. of
Burundi	7	N/A	N/A	N/A	N/A	N/A
Kenya	43	12	86	14	3	1
Rwanda	12	493	88	9	1	1
South Sudan	10	6	79	N/A	N/A	N/A
Tanzania	34	15	254	N/A	2	1
Uganda	26	47	226	N/A	2	1

Source: EAC Central Banks (2015)

Kenyan Banking System: It is the 4th largest in Sub-Saharan Africa behind South Africa, Nigeria and Mauritius; it includes 44 commercial banks with 12 foreign banks; very active cross-border linkages with 7 Kenyan banks having at least 14 subsidiaries in the EAC regional peers.

Tanzanian Banking System: It has grown significantly since 2003, and includes at least 34 commercial banks with 16 foreign banks.

Ugandan Banking System: It expanded significantly since a moratorium on licensing new banks was lifted in 2005; 9 new banks have been licensed since then, bringing the number to 26 by early 2016.

Rwandan Banking System: There are 12 commercial banks, with 3 foreign banks.

Burundian Banking System: It includes 7 commercial banks and two financial establishments; the privately owned banks account for more than 75% of the banking assets.

South Sudan Banking System: It comprises of 10 commercial banks; and more than 80% is foreign owned.

Figure 7.6
Types of Financial Intermediaries

Type of Intermediary	Source of Funds (Primary Liability)	Uses of Funds (Primary Assets)
1. Depository Institutions		
Commercial Banks.	Deposits	Business & household loans; mortgages; treasury securities; municipal bonds.
Credit Institutions & MDIs (credit & savings assoc.)	Deposits	Mortgages.
Savings Banks.	Deposits & individual savings.	Mortgages.
Credit Unions.	Deposits.	Household loans.
2.Finance Firms		
Finance companies.	Commercial paper; stocks; bonds; other financial intermediaries.	Household & business loans.
Mortgage banking firms.	Stocks; deposits; other financial intermediaries.	Real estate; real property; mortgage.
Factoring companies.	Stocks; commercial paper.	Company & bank debtors; bills of exchange; invoices; real estate.
3. Securities Firms		
Investment companies (unit trust funds).	Unit trusts/ shares; individual savings.	Stocks; bonds; real estate; real property; money market instruments.
Securitizers & Wholesale/ merchant banks.	Stocks; bonds; other intermediaries.	Stocks; bonds; other debt facilities.
Brokerage firms.	Stocks; bonds; other financial intermediaries.	Stocks; bonds; other equity & debt instruments.

4. Contractual Saving firms		
Retirement benefit schemes; pension funds; government retirement funds.	Employers & employees contributions.	Mortgages; corporate & treasury bonds; stocks; real property.
Life & Health Insurance firms.	Premium paid on policies.	Treasury & corporate bonds; mortgages; stocks; money market instruments.
Property & Liability Insurance firms.	Premium paid on policies.	Treasury securities; municipal bonds; corporate bonds & stocks.
5. Other Intermediaries. Alternative Trading Systems (ATS).		
Arbitrageurs. Clearing houses. Custodians.		

Source: Researcher's Data

DEPOSITORY INSTITUTIONS

Depository institutions are financial intermediaries that accept deposits or savings from individuals and institutions and then lend these pooled savings to all financial agents (households, businesses, and government). These institutions include commercial banks and the thrift institutions such as: credit institutions; Micro-finance Deposit Taking Institutions (MDIs); savings banks; etc, these accumulate individual savings and provide credit for asset-building such as machinery, automobiles, houses, education, among others.

These funds can further be invested by these depository institutions in a wide array of investment avenues such as: business and household loans; mortgages; treasury securities (treasury bills, notes, and bonds); and municipal bonds for profitability purposes.

CONTRACTUAL SAVINGS FIRMS

These firms collect premiums and contributions from their clients so as to provide them with retirement benefits and coverage against major losses in life. Among these are: insurance companies that provide financial protection to households and businesses for life, health, property and liability uncertainties. This is done through the payment of premiums by the insurance policy holders which are invested in treasury securities, corporate bonds and stocks, and money market instruments until the insured claims must be paid. On the other hand, retirement and pension funds are mobilized as contributions from employees and/or their employers periodically and proceeds are invested on behalf of the employees. Schemes such as Occupational (private) benefits scheme, National Social Security Fund (NSSF), government/ public service retirement funds are actively involved in financial intermediation by investing their contributors' funds in basically long-term financial assets such as: mortgages; corporate & government bonds; stocks; real property; etc.

In the developed and developing economies the pension sector (contractual saving) has drastically grown, since people are progressively realizing that they cannot rely on their children to care for them in their retirement. In rural settings, families tend to stay together on the farm; and property passes from generation to generation with an implicit understanding that the younger generations will care for the older ones. Contrarily, when families become more dispersed and move off farms, both the opportunity for and the expectation of extensive financial support of the older generations from the younger one significantly declines.

Types of Pension Plans

There are a variety of pension plans globally depending on factors such as the economic system of a country, level of economic development and civilisation, among others. The following are some of the popular types well known:

- *Defined-benefit plan: is a pension plan whose retirement promise is framed according to benefits to be paid to participants. Benefits are often calculated by a formula related to years of service, rate* of pay over some specified time period, or a combination of both such as the government pension system.

- *Cash balance plan*: is a hybrid defined-benefit plan that maintains individual account records for plan participants showing their current value of accrued benefit. The difference with traditional defined-benefit plans is that an account, rather than an actual fund, is maintained for each individual.
- *Profit sharing plan*: is a defined-contribution plan whose contributions are established somewhat by the profitability of the plan sponsor.
- *Defined-contribution plan*: is a pension plan whose retirement promise is framed according to the contributions made to the plan by the plan sponsor. The liability to the sponsor is only the contribution, not the benefit ultimately received by the participants.

PENSION PLAN FUNDING

Among the pension plan funding world over, there are:
- *Funded status*: is the relationship between the present value of the pension plan assets and the present value of the pension plan liabilities.
- *Fully funded*: means the present value of the pension plan assets is greater than or equal to the present value of the pension liabilities. When the present value of plan assets becomes much greater than the present value of plan liabilities, sponsors can at least temporarily stop making contributions to the plan's asset base.
- *Surplus*: is the difference between the present value of pension plan assets and the present value of pension plan liabilities.
- *Underfunded*: means the present value of pension plan assets is less than the present value of the pension plan liabilities. Underfunded plans may require the sponsors to make special contributions to the plan in addition to the usual, regular contributions.

SECURITIES FIRMS

These firms accept and invest individual savings; but also facilitate the transfer of securities among investors. They mobilize funds by selling unit trusts/shares, stock; individual savings; issuing bonds; and using finances from other financial intermediaries, which they prudently invest in a diversified portfolio of corporate and government bonds, stocks, real estate and property, and money market instruments

Unit Trust funds allow shareholders to pool their resources so that they can take advantage of lower transaction costs when buying large blocks of stocks or bonds. Thus, allowing them to hold more diversified portfolios than they otherwise would afford; shareholders can redeem their shares at any time. On the other hand, wholesale/merchant banks despite their name, are not banks but financial intermediaries that help corporations issue securities through: advising on which type of securities to issue (stocks or bonds); then helping sell (underwrite) the securities by purchasing them from the corporation at a predetermined price and reselling them in the market. Besides, brokerage firms assist households who want to purchase new securities issues or who want to sell previously purchased securities.

Much as, wholesale banking and brokerage activities are often combined in the same firm in the contemporary financial world; wholesale banking is fundamentally a merchandising role (new issue) yet brokerage services are about marketing existing or seasoned financial assets.

Securitizers, however, are intermediaries that pool large amounts of securities or assets and then sell interests in the pool to other investors; the returns from the pool (net of the securitizers' fees) are passed through to the investors. By securitizing assets, these intermediaries create a diversified pool of assets with more predictable cash flows than the individual assets in the pool.

This creates liquidity in the assets, and economies of scale in the management costs of large pools of assets, and potential benefits from the investment manager's selection of assets.. assets that are often securitized include: mortgages, car loans, credit card receivables, bank loans, and equipment leases.

FINANCE FIRMS

These firms provide finance, basically loans, directly to households and businesses, but also help borrowers obtain mortgage loans on real property. This could be through financing installment purchases of durable assets like cars, homes, machinery but also provision of small loans to those financial agents. Some of these firms are actively engaged in the outright purchase of company and banks' debtors at an agreed discount with the client, which is termed as factoring/ debt factoring.

Among the finance firms, there are: finance companies; mortgage banking firms; factoring companies; among others that mobilize their funds through issuing commercial papers, stocks, bonds, but also make use of funds from other financial intermediaries. They then invest such finances in a diversified portfolio of assets that include: household and business loans; purchase of real estates, real property and mortgages; purchases/ discounting of corporate debtors, bills of exchange, and invoices.

Other Intermediaries

ALTERNATIVE TRADING SYSTEMS (ATS)

These systems serve the same trading function as organized securities exchanges but have no regulatory function; they are also called Electronic Communication Networks (ECNs). There is one such system that is currently becoming popular in Uganda, it was developed by two students (at that time) and it deals in trading of foreign currencies and some equities/ stocks that are also traded on the Uganda Securities Exchange; it is called FX Trades.

ARBITRAGEURS

These intermediaries buy financial assets in one market and resell it in another market at a higher price. By so doing, they provide liquidity to participants in the markets where the asset is purchased and transferring the asset to the market where it is sold. Arbitrageurs try to exploit pricing differentials for similar assets, for example, a dealer who sells a call option will often also buy the stock because the call and stock prices are highly correlated. These intermediaries use complex models for valuation of related securities and for risk management reasons.

CLEARING HOUSES

These act as intermediaries between buyers and sellers in the financial markets, and they provide the following services:

- *Escrow services of transferring cash and assets to respective parties.*
- *Guarantees of contract completion (surety bonds)*
- *Assurance that margin traders have adequate capital (surety bond)*

Through these activities, clearing houses limit counterparty risk: the risk that the other party to a transaction will not fulfill its obligations.

CUSTODIANS

These intermediaries improve market integrity by holding clients' securities and preventing their loss due to fraud or other events that affect the broker or investment manager.

INTERMEDIARIES' ECONOMIES OF SCALE & UNIQUENESS

They are able to invest in financial assets of corporations at lower rate of return due to the following economies of scale:

- *Efficiencies in gathering information on riskiness of purchasing a certain security: this is because individuals don't have easy access to such data sources (financial soundness) and/or expert analysis in that way.*

- *Risk spreading: intermediaries are able to spread funds in a wide portfolio of financial assets, thereby reducing the overall risk, which retail investors can't easily do.*
- *Transaction costs minimization: there is reduction in search, agreement and monitoring costs that would be incurred by retail investors in direct transaction. The reduced information costs, convenience and passed-on benefits from the economies of operating on large scale mean that retail investors are motivated to use the intermediation of such institutions.*
- *Liquidity & price risk: they provide financial claims to households with superior liquidity attributes and lower price risk.*
- *Maturity intermediation: intermediaries can better bear the risk of mismatching the maturities of their assets and liabilities.*
- *Transmission of monetary supply: depository institutions are the conduits through which monetary policy tools by the Central banks impact the rest of the financial system and the economy.*
- *Credit allocation: intermediaries are often viewed as the major, and sometimes only, source of financing for particular sectors of the economy such as agriculture, SMEs, and residential real estate.*
- *Payment services: the efficiency with which depository institutions provide payment services like checks, directly benefits the financial system.*
- *Denominational intermediation: intermediaries like unit trust funds allow small investors to overcome constraints and costs which are not borne by large institutional investors, and so they facilitate the pooling of small savers funds so as to help them enjoy economies of collective strategies.*
- *Intergenerational wealth transfers: intermediaries like insurance firms and pension funds provide savers the ability to transfer their wealth from one generation to the next one (children/ beneficiaries).*

ROLE OF FINANCIAL INTERMEDIARIES IN THE FINANCIAL SYSTEM:

- *To channel household savings to the business sector: this is the most crucial role of financial intermediaries, also referred to as the "social function". This is done by banks, unit trust funds and other intermediaries pooling the resources of many small investors, and then lends considerable sums to large borrowers like business organisations.*

- *To lend to many borrowers, whereby intermediaries achieve significant diversification, by giving loans that might be too risky from an individual point of view.*

- *Intermediaries build expertise through the volume of business they do and can use economies of scale and scope to manage credit risk.*

- *They lower the transaction costs of both investors and users of finance through their expertise in financial intermediation. Hence, facilitating an efficient, cheap and reliable way of allocating and transferring funds from one party to another.*

THE ADVANTAGES OF INTERMEDIARIES

Financial professionals help channel savings from individuals into investments; an important service since individuals want opportunities to grow their savings, and it stimulates economic growth and development. Financial intermediaries can help manage investment risk with their specialized knowledge and experience. Below are the advantages of using financial intermediation in a financial system:

Risk management advantage: Intermediaries help to manage investment risk by providing professional advice on investment opportunities. However, the advice they give may increase overall risk because of the nature of the investments, the potential rewards also increase. They also provide expertise and the technology to carry out investment transactions easily and quickly, and while intermediaries often steer their clients to certain investments that may be managed by their company, they are obligated to act in the client's best interest rather than their own or that of their employer.

Fiduciary duties: They have a legal duty: to act in the best interest of the individual investor client; to disclose material information about their business that could affect the client; and they must refrain from activities that cause conflicts of interest with clients. Any self-dealing activities that involve clients are violations of fiduciary duties legally owed to clients. For example, an adviser should not unload unwanted securities on unsuspecting clients, or push a stock because of a higher commission even though it does not fit the client's portfolio.

Liquidity management: They help their clients sell their investments when the client needs or wants to sell. They make a market for the client by finding willing buyers, and this usually happens immediately using the stock exchange infrastructure.

Professional information: Financial intermediaries have a team of professionals that provides research and analysis on various investment opportunities. Such information is usually made available at no additional cost to the individual investor. In fact, providing this type information free is a marketing strategy used by financial intermediaries to attract clients. The better the information, the more competitive the financial intermediary will be when attracting clients.

Highly regulated trading environment: The Capital Markets Authorities (CMA), EAC regional stock markets, and other regulators of the financial system regulate financial intermediaries. Although the stock exchanges are not government agencies, they have established rules that must be followed. If a financial intermediary does not follow these rules, no trading on the particular exchange involved will be allowed. There are licensing requirements that must be complied with and violations of laws, rules and regulations can result in severe fines, sanctions and even criminal charges. Individual investors can register complaints with any of the regulators that will be investigated since the role of the government is to protect its people and their assets.

Chapter 37
FINANCIAL DISINTERMEDIATION

The Sub-Saharan African financial systems remain under-developed: this huge region is highly concentrated and generally inefficient at financial intermediation; the banking system is characterized by small and low intermediation despite little barriers to entry and exit, as evidenced by dominant market share of foreign banks; competition is still limited. Access to finance in Sub-Saharan Africa is among the lowest in the world, and presents one of the key obstacles to the activity and growth of enterprises – which constrains the region from achieving its fully growth potential. The EAC financial sector, in particular, is still shallow compared to other African regions like the South and the North. This low level of financial intermediation indicates that although the EAC regional banking system accesses more resources through deposits, the resources are only partly extended to the private sector. Besides, World Bank (2007) complements that generally the EAC bloc is intermediation constrained rather than savings constrained. On the other hand, the EAC region enjoys a relatively stable macroeconomic and financial environment coupled to current reform momentum and the expected strong growth GDP growth across the EAC regional bloc.

Financial Disintermediation can be referred to as the investing of funds that would normally have been placed in a bank or other financial institutions directly into financial assets issued by the ultimate users of the funds. Investors and borrowers transact business directly and thereby bypass financial intermediaries.

Besides, disintermediation can also be defined as the elimination of intermediaries between the first class providers of capital (basically the household sector and other collective investment vehicles) and the ultimate users of capital; withdrawal of funds from financial intermediaries such as banks, savings and credit institutions, and life insurance companies in order to invest directly with ultimate users.

Disintermediation: these are business to business financial transactions (lending) that eliminates the banking intermediary. It is a process whereby firms borrow and lend funds directly between themselves without recourse to banks and other financial institutions.

Securitization: it is the capitalization of a future stream of income into a single capital value that is sold on the capital markets for immediate cash. It is the development of new financial instruments to meet ever-changing corporate needs (financial engineering). This involves a credit rating agency assessing the issue and giving it a credit rating. It can also mean the process of unbundling and repackaging a debt offering from traditionally separate institutions to be handled through a single intermediary. For instance, this can be illustrated by a conventional debt with many elements, each traditionally handled by a different institution eg loan origination, credit status evaluation, financing and collection of interest & principal. This same debt offering can be done by one institution with an aim of lowering the cost of the loan, and bringing in convenience to the client. However, this was one of the major causes of the 2007 Global financial crisis.

Securitization and disintermediation have facilitated large firms to create more flexible alternative forms of corporate financing. This era has seen new developments of outlandish securitization eg collections at pubs; gate receipts from a particular sports club; future income from a pop star's recordings; popular book series sales; and even the football World Cup competition for 2006, 2010, and 2014.

How Securitization Works
Securitizing Jose Chameleon's music:

Let us assume that Asante Music Records strike a deal with EAC pop star Jose Chameleon to unlock USD 10 million over 10 years against the future value of his music publishing catalogue. It is worth noting that music publishing is a separate business from recorded music; comprising the rights to the written composition of a song; performance rights; from use in advertisement or movies. Such securitization can be sold as a bond, equity or mezzanine finance issues; such sophisticated financing can help Jose Chameleon to get a good share of the publishing rights of his compositions but also share value with others who are willing to embrace the riskiness of the security offering.

Figure 7.7

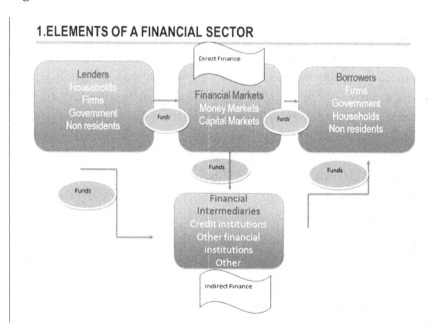

Source: Researcher's Data

While there has been a general trend toward bank disintermediation and a greater role for financial markets in many countries, the pace has differed and there are still important differences across financial systems. Therefore, differences in financial structures do affect how households and firms behave over the economic cycle.

In financial systems characterized by a greater degree of arm's length transactions (liberal economies), households seem to be able to smooth consumption more effectively in the face of unanticipated changes in their income, although they may be more sensitive to changes in asset prices. On the other hand, financial systems that rely less on arm's length transactions, firms appear to be better able to smooth investment during business cycle downturns, as they are better positioned to access external financing based on their long-term relationships with financial intermediaries.

However, when faced with more fundamental changes in the environment that require a real-location of resources across sectors, financial systems with a greater degree of arm's length transactions appear to be better placed to shift resources to take advantage of new growth opportunities. Evidence has shown that cross-border portfolio investors appear to allocate a greater proportion of their holdings in countries where the arm's length (laissez-faire/ non-interference/liberal) content of the financial system is higher, which may contribute to the financing of current account deficits.

Disintermediation can then be referred to as the removal of intermediaries from a process, supply chain or market. The disintermediation of capital markets is particularly important in an investment context, and it has become increasingly important in financial markets, largely as a result of the increasing use of securities to raise capital from capital markets, rather than from banks.

Banks usually act as financial intermediaries for debt, borrowing from depositors and lending to borrowers. By selling securities such as bonds, instead of borrowing, a borrower can borrow directly from investors, by-passing the banks. The greater use of a wider range of financial instruments such as asset-backed securities and convertibles (in addition to the bonds and debentures) has encouraged this. High levels of disintermediation reduce the amount of business available for commercial banks. It also increases the size of capital markets and generates more business for investment banks (advising on the issue of securities) and, indirectly, for other investment businesses (brokers, fund managers, stock exchanges etc.).

Borrowers can hope to borrow at lower cost as a result of disintermediation. Investors lose the safety of bank deposits but then they also should get better rates of return. Investors take on some extra risk which can be controlled through the usual mechanisms of diversification and the selection of appropriate investments. At the same time disintermediation eliminates the banks' interest margin and this benefit is shared by investors, borrowers and financial market intermediaries.

Financial disintermediation is gaining momentum in the modern economy: the advent of the Internet as well as the development of electronic exchanges has facilitated an efficient and effective way of buying and selling financial instruments. These phenomena also have contributed to less prominent roles for financial intermediaries in the economy. For examples, individual investors no longer need to call brokers before placing trades. They can log into a secure Web portal and make traces quickly, seamlessly and anonymously.

CAUSES OF FINANCIAL DISINTERMEDIATION:

During my interview with the Bank of Uganda – Director of Financial markets on the growth of the Asset/fund management sector, he commissioned me to equally do a research that establishes why some key players in the financial system deliberately dis-intermediate the financial system. And below are some of the causes/ reasons:

Money market funds : this is due to competition for bank deposits from investment banks, many investors have chosen to invest in unit trust funds other than deposit their money with banks.

Junk Bonds (downgraded bonds): currently, bond market competes with commercial banks for corporate borrowing yet before 1980s, only investment grade bonds were issued whose requirements are very strict. Therefore, only well-established companies had access to the bond market; and small, medium, lesser known, younger firms could not issue bonds, they had to go to a bank for a commercial loan which is no longer the case.

Commercial paper: this is an alternative form of disintermediation to short-term bank credit that was made possible by information revolution, and it is easier to assess credit risk. Pension funds and money market funds provide the supply of credit for commercial paper, and these two assets grew together. Money market funds started getting lots of funds to invest; commercial paper provided the ideal short term money market instrument features of liquidity, low riskiness, and short-term asset.

Securitization: this is disintermediation (financial innovation) resulting from information technology's capacity to lower transaction cost, and transforming illiquid financial assets into standardized, liquid, marketable securities. This is about banks and mortgage companies packaging mortgage loans in large bundles/portfolios, and selling ownership interests in the portfolios as securities in specific amounts. Securitization also developed in other areas such as: car loans, credit cards, computer leases, etc.

Regulatory flaws: some players in the financial markets make use of loopholes in the legal framework that governs the financial system so as to profit from such weaknesses and thus dis-intermediate the financial flows which render some institutions irrelevant in the process.

Large informal financial system: this is characterized by a diversity of institutions which are not monitored and regulated such as SACCOs, money-lenders, ROSCAs, Women groups, NGOs, CBOs. These have financial transactions that total to hundreds of Billions weekly but the regulators of the financial system have apparently failed to integrate them into the formal system. These organizations use such funds in ways they feel will protect their value, hence, aiding the disintermediation in the financial system.

EAC banking system is characterized not only by low levels of intermediation but also by relatively high interest rates, wide intermediation spreads, and substantial bank profitability. High lending interest rates, whether caused by inefficiency or lack of competition, do more than add to borrowers' costs.

High interest spread and limited depth and breadth of the financial systems are closely related to each other. Countries with higher interest rate spread have lower levels of credit to the private sector as share of GDP and deposits in the financial system as share of GDP

If high interest spreads and margins and limited depth and breadth of financial services are the result of underlying deficiencies and impediments in the financial systems, then in order to increase access to financial services and reduce spreads and margins, these underlying causes have to be addressed.

Chapter 38

KEY CHALLENGES AND RISKS OF THE FINANCIAL SYSTEM

"Monitoring risks to the stability of the financial system from majorly the real estate sector is a critical element of policy formulation."

Among the challenges of the financial system, these are:

- *Volatile and reversible capital inflows that characterize bank consolidation exercise.*
- *Major weaknesses in the business environment.*
- *Failure in corporate governance in banks and financial institutions.*
- *Inadequate disclosure and transparency in financial reporting.*
- *Engagement in/of multiple financial activities that increase the complexity of their operations.*
- *Uneven supervision and enforcement.*
- *Inadequate risk management frameworks for identifying, measuring and controlling risk associated with the activities of deposit money banks.*
- *Lack of investor and consumer sophistication (protection).*
- *The EAC regional population is significantly under-banked, with only few million accounts as compared to other systems like mobile money services.*
- *EAC region has a bank dominated financial system whereby very few top foreign banks accounted for more than 45% of banks' total assets as by 2013.*
- *There is wide gap between the formal financial system and the informal financial system which has led to excessive levels of liquidity amongst the household sector while the financial markets are struggling with liquidity problems.*

- *The levels of domestic savings are so low; and many EAC economies rank high among Sub-Saharan Africa economies with the lowest savings to GDP ratio.*

- *Poor households in rural settings are largely excluded from the formal financial system; leaving them to the mercies of informal financial institutions which are weak and not regulated. This doesn't only increase the risk to poor households' savings but also threatens the domestic financial system.*

- *The financial system is characterized by limited financial instruments such as treasury securities, corporate bonds, commercial papers, a few stocks/equities. This limits the choices of the would-be investors in financial assets since securities like derivative instruments, hybrid assets, and a wide array of actually more debt and equity assets would attract more to such investments.*

- *The banking system is characterized by very low returns on savings due to high liquidity in banks and also the effect of donor-funded wholesale funds for on-lending.*

- *Shallow capital markets in most EAC economies also constrain domestic resource mobilisation on the part of both the corporate and the government sectors which forces them to look for external sources of financing.*

- *There is also the problem of lack of information and confidence about contracts due to huge loopholes in the legal framework but also the absence of commitment to enforce legal and formal business processes.*

- *There is a poor savings culture which is propagated by low levels of financial literacy, limited access to safe and sound institutions, and scepticism about the domestic financial system (due to local currency volatility, alarming levels of corruption, desperation, among others).*

- *EAC's financial outflow is quite high ie for Uganda it is over 13% of the total government revenue, approximately UGX 2.2 Trillion majorly through: tax evasion, bribes, trade mis-invoicing from fraudulent over-and under-invoicing of trade transactions from anonymous companies, and subsidiary companies overstating commercial loan interest payment to parent companies.*

Among the key risks to the financial system, these are:

- *Slowdown in the economy: this is basically caused by high non-performing loans (NPLs) for banks, unemployment and inflation.*
- *Prices of assets: Securities, real estate prices could fall or change abruptly, creating uncertainty on the financial markets, with the result that investors may lose money.*
- *Concentration risks by banks: Banks could grant large loans to a specific industry and then find that they are vulnerable to any downturn in that industry.*
- *Concentration risk for investors: Investors could make large-scale investments in stock or bond markets and then become vulnerable to falling prices in those markets.*
- *Principal /agent problem: agents taking on excessive risk taking or some not taking enough risk which both jeopardizes the value of investors.*

The following are the regulatory remedies to such risks and challenges:

- *Prudential regulation: these are rules that financial institutions have to comply with in order to ensure effective risk management and the safety of depositors' funds), accompanied by the disclosure of information so as to promote market discipline. These are embedded in the operations of all central banks and other regulators.*
- *Governments should prioritize mobilization for revenues; in this, much as there should be flexibility across countries, taxes ought to be simple, broad-based, and administered effectively; coupled to transparency in extractive industries.*

- *Furthermore, these resources should be efficiently and effectively used in pursuit of development and supported by strong public financial management.*
- *Prudential supervision: ensuring that financial institutions follow these rules as stipulated by the EAC central banks.*
- *A deliberate introduction and embracing of the Islamic financial system (banking, markets and insurance).*
- *An efficient and independent central banking system that will implement sound macroeconomic policies such as containing inflation, boom-bust cycles, and public debt; and that will maintain health fiscal positions and adequate foreign exchange reserves for external-economy vulnerability management.*
- *Financial engineering for both governments and corporations as a tool for both resource mobilization, and developing/deepening the domestic financial markets (financial assets diversification)*
- *Seeking for international partnerships/cooperation since all financial systems are interdependent on each other through a global financial system. This would usher in responsible policymaking that promotes global economic and financial resilience.*
- *Besides, financial literacy and inclusion are the real lever to developing any financial system world over.*
- *Monitoring and assessment activities, which identify vulnerabilities and risks in the financial system as a whole; this is the responsibility of all regulators of the financial system.*
- *The private sector is an essential partner for development: developing the financial system by protecting creditor rights can expand access to basic financial services for households and small enterprises. This calls for carefully designed tax and trade regimes that can help attract foreign investment that are k for vital development payoffs.*

- Greater transparency in financial transactions contracts and thorough due diligence is key to improving and managing financial inflows and outflows in the financial system.
- The tax body ought to double crackdown on tax evaders (both domestic and foreign firms); and further train its officers to better detect international mis-invoicing and other trade transactions malpractices.
- The State needs to ensure proper central and public registries of meaningful beneficial ownership information for all companies formed in the country to combat the abuse of anonymous companies like EUTAW.
- Commercial banks ought to know the true identity of the final beneficiary of any account opened in their financial institutions to avoid paying off anonymous companies.
- Besides, the EAC Bloc needs to subscribe to international codes of practice like the Extractive Industry Transparency Initiative (EITI) to stamp out malpractices in the exploitation of natural resources.

DEDUCTION OF PART 7:

Despite the fact that mobile money systems have done an outstanding job in boosting financial inclusion across the EAC region: there is need to further integrate all mobile money platforms across the region; incentivize multi-sectoral participation; and also beef up the security and safety on these platforms; and finally address the monetary issues and conversion ratios across EAC region's different currencies.

For payment and settlement systems, much as stages are at high levels of integrating these systems across EAC for a functional single market in financial services, political will on the part of EAC governments and also business sense on the part of the business community are so key in facilitating the achievement of this grand initiative. Integrating the Real Time Gross Settlements,

Central Securities Depositories, Credit Reference Bureaus, and also adopting common Automated Trading Systems would go a long way in boosting the drive to an integrated financial system. Much as the Sovereign credit ratings paint a positive outlook on the EAC region as a favorable investment destination compared to many of its African peers, the political risk is quite high given the violent electioneering in most EAC countries; terrorist attacks/ threats in the major EAC economies; social and political tensions; and inadequate legal systems. Besides, the financial system risks prevalent in the region that need urgent attention from policymakers include: weak supervision in the financial system (especially Kenyan banking system where 3 banks were closed in barely 9 months); worsening government debt burden; and in some economies the financial sector is vulnerable to undue government influence.

Regarding financial intermediation, much as the EAC region has made good strides towards intermediations through the banking system and other financial system infrastructure and institutions; the financial system remains under-developed and shallow compared to other African regions like Southern and North. The EAC is intermediation constrained rather than savings constrained, it implies that EAC regional banking system accesses more financial resources through deposits but these resources are only partly extended to the private sector.

Part 8
INTEGRATED EAC FINANCIAL SYSTEM

"Policymakers should focus on the effectiveness of the financial system"

Chapter 39
EAC MONETARY UNION

EAC Fact Sheet

The EAC Bloc is a function of six sovereign economies which comprise of: Burundi, Kenya, Rwanda, South Sudan, Tanzania, and Uganda. It is only in February 2016 that a new entrant South Sudan was officially integrated into the EAC bloc, among other background information about the region, these are:

Figure 8.1

Area (exclude. South Sudan)	182 million square Km
Population	Approx. 170 Million.
GDP (current market prices)	USD 161.17 Billion.
EAC Headquarters	Arusha, Tanzania.
First formerly established	1967
Re-established	7th July 2000.
Official language	English.

Other Critical Information

1977	EAC dissolved.
30th November 1993	Signing of Agreement for establishment of Permanent Tripartite Commission of East African Cooperation.
14th March 1996	Secretariat of the Permanent Tripartite Commission of East African Cooperation launched, and full cooperation operations begin then.
30th November 1999	Treaty for establishment of EAC signed.
7th July 2000	EAC treaty enters into force.

18th June 2007	Rwanda & Burundi accede to EAC treaty.
1st July 2007	Rwanda & Burundi become full members.
2013	EAC Monetary Union Protocol signed & ratified.
March 2016	South Sudan becomes full member of EAC.
2024	EAC anticipates to attain Common currency & unify fiscal management.

Source: EAC Secretariat; The East African (2016)

HISTORY OF EAC COOPERATION

Initiatives of integration date back further than independence in 1917 when Kenya and Uganda established a Customs Union; this was followed by the short-lived formal EAC from 1967 to 1977; but later revived in the 1990s by the Presidents of Uganda, Kenya and Tanzania. The driving notion for integration is that together, these economies present a larger and more attractive market for foreign investors. EAC currently has a population of approx. 170 Million people; a GDP of over USD 161.17 Billion; and a 6.1% GDP growth by early 2014; a single digit inflation averaging 6.9 by 2014; and a relatively huge current account deficit.

EAC monetary union was signed in 2013, and it sets out a 10-year road map to a single currency for EAC. This provides for fiscal, financial and monetary policy harmonization. The partners States have agreed on critical macroeconomic convergence criteria; and work on fiscal, financial and monetary harmonization is ongoing.

The EAC economies since then have put in place macro convergence criteria to guide and hasten the monetary union though the progress in aligning individual economies to the set benchmarks is still not harmonized as yet given the discrepancies in institutional mechanisms, social and economic structures.

This has seen up to now a failure to standardize the tax system, maintain currency convertibility, and modernizing and integrating the financial infrastructure fully (payments & settlements systems), synchronizing the trading practices and rules in the financial markets. But by and large, the regional bloc has achieved significant strides in realizing this grand objective through establishing the requisite committees, harmonizing policies and ensuring a coordinated oversight of the implementation process, and fulfilling some of the requirements of the macro convergence criteria.

The operationalization of an East African Monetary Union is premised on the aforesaid macroeconomic convergence criteria as establishment by the EAC Monetary Affairs Committee, which framework is comprehensively made of primary and secondary criteria whose implementation would then usher in the single EAC currency. This EAC macroeconomic convergence criteria is centered such as areas as: price stability, exchange rate stability, strengthening the level of foreign exchange reserves, fiscal restraints (controlling public debt and deficits), and also encouraging policy coordination among the EAC member States. Below are some of the criteria, many of which the EAC has made serious strides in implementing them but also a lot needs to be desired:

Figure 8.2   Macroeconomic Convergence Criteria

Primary Criteria

Budget deficit/GDP	< 5%
Foreign exchange reserves (months of import cover)	> 4 months
Annual inflation rate	< 5%

Secondary Criteria

Exchange rates	Stable
Interest rates (market based)	Maintain
Real GDP growth	> 7%
National savings/GDP	> 20%
Reduction in current account deficit	
Sustained pursuit of debt sustainability	

Source: EAC Secretariat

Implementation of 25 core principles of bank supervision and regulation based on the agreed action for harmonization of bank supervision.

Adherence to core principles of systematically important payment systems by modernizing payment and settlement systems.

Figure 8.3

Some Macroeconomic Indicators of the EAC Region

EAC Economy	Population (Million)	GDP (USD)	GDP per Capita (USD)	Projected Annual Average Inflation	Gross Domestic Savings (% of GDP	Debt to GDP ratio
Burundi	10.82	3.09 Billion	330.12	5.70%	2%	14.2%
Kenya	44.86	60.94 Billion	1461.12	5.50%	3.9%	46.26%
Rwanda	11.34	7.89 Billion	619.93	--	10.9%	29.4%
Tanzania	51.82	49.18 Billion	768.27	5.10%	20.6%	39.9%
South Sudan	11.91	13.07 Billion	144.64	150%	N/A	10.23%
Uganda	37.78	27.00 Billion	685.75	5.60%	22.1%	31.5%

Source: EAC Central Banks; IMF; WBG; EADB (2015)

The projected annual inflation average for the EAC region is promisingly favorable within the EAC macroeconomic convergence criteria at 5% target, and it proves that the regional bloc is making good strides towards its desired integration.

Regarding the Gross national savings, only two economies (Tanzania and Uganda) have achieved the 20% target as proportion to GDP, and other regional economies still lagging way behind the macroeconomic convergence criteria. But there is a lot of hope that this will be achieved soon as well to facilitate the de integration.

Concerning debt sustainability within the EAC bloc, using the public debt to GDP metric (below 50%), we realize that all the EAC economies are faring well apart from Kenya whose debt proportion is an outlier in the EAC region with 46.26% debt/GDP ratio. This implies that for 1 KSH value produced in Kenya, 46.2% is in form of debt; which if not checked might plunge the EAC regional giant economy in a debt crisis like Greece currently in the European Union.

For the current account deficit as a convergence criteria, at least most EAC regional economies represent a very small part of GDP below 12% apart from Burundi (an outlier in the EAC region) due to the political crisis in the country but also South Sudan. This implies that, by and large, the EAC bloc has been able to score highly in this EAC macroeconomic convergence criteria, hence facilitating regional integration.

The following additional macroeconomic convergence criteria have been discussed thoroughly in the Book under their specific areas, so please refer to those topics for an understanding of how various EAC economies are faring as regards these indicators:

i)Exchange rate criteria

ii) Forex Reserves criteria

iii) Real GDP growth

iv)Interest rates

v)Payment systems

CHALLENGES TO ACHIEVING THE EAC M.U

Development of the requisite institutions to manage a monetary union at the regional level such as the Statistics body, a fiscal surveillance body, a monetary institute, and also a unified EAC Central bank.

Ensuring that all the partners States meet the macroeconomic criteria underline in the protocol so as to smoothly lead to the attainment of the long desired regional monetary union.

Chapter 40
EAC REGIONAL INTEGRATION DEVELOPMENTS

Globally, an economic integration comprises of largely a four stages of development: a Free Trade Area; a Customs Union, a Common Market; and a Monetary Union. The EAC regional bloc has undergone most of these stages but currently working on the final one, monetary union, that would climax the whole initiative to fully integrate the EAC economically. Regional integrations involve the growth of linkages and transactions derived primarily from economic activity but involving social and interconnectedness; besides, in integration, supranational institutions replace national ones in importance.

EAC REGIONAL FINANCIAL SECTOR INTEGRATION OBJECTIVES

In a bid to oversee a deliberate and harmonized regional integration in the financial subsystem of the EAC regional Bloc, the EAC Secretariat along with the World Bank, instituted a project code-named "Financial Sector Development Regionalization Project". This project has majorly five objectives (components) on which the regional integration is built, and these are:

1. *Financial Inclusion and Strengthening Market Participants: this is aimed at improving access to financial services by the underserved communities and businesses in a bid to promote equitable market driven economic growth across the EAC region. This comes at a backdrop whereby financial inclusion across the EAC is very low; financial systems are largely dominated by the banking sector which serves a select clientele and also a very limited range of products; and also exorbitantly high interest rate regimes in most EAC economies. This project aims at establishing a single market for financial services in the EAC, diversify the clientele and also*

financial providers, increase competition in this industry to drive prices down, and also facilitate capacity building programs to all market players.

2. *Harmonization of Financial Laws and Regulations: this is geared towards harmonizing legal and regulatory frameworks in the banking, securities markets, insurance, pensions, payments and investment funds to further facilitate the efficient functioning of a single financial services markets in the EAC region. The EAC Secretariat and the Council Structure has been working on this since 2011, along with the various financial system regulators across the EAC, and also aligning these laws with the Common Standards in the global financial sectors and later submit them as Bills to the EAC Council of Ministers who would facilitate their enactment into law; and these include among others:*

   Microfinance & SACCOs: *Development of EAC Microfinance and SACCOs Bill.*

   Branchless Banking: *Development of EAC Mobile banking Bill; Development of EAC Agent banking Bill.*

   Banking Sector: *Development of EAC banking sector legal and regulatory Bill;*

   Development of EAC Corporate governance for banking institutions Bill;

   Development of EAC Depositors protection mechanisms Bill.

   Securities Markets: *Development of EAC Securities legal and regulatory Bills.*

   Pension Sector: *Development of EAC Pension system legal and regulatory Bill.*

   Insurance Sector: *Development of EAC Insurance sector legal and regulatory Bill.*

   Investment Funds: *Development of EAC UCITS Bill; Development of EAC Private Equity Funds Bill.*

3. *Mutual Recognition of Supervisory Agencies: this objective seeks to streamline EAC regional supervision in the financial subsystem, in the way that, a financial institution and/or market intermediary licensed by the supervisory authority in one EAC Partner State will be permitted to operate in all Partner States upon a simple notification to the supervisory authority of the host State. Achieving this objective is a tricky one which require the EAC to develop and implement comprehensive action plans for effective supervision of financial intermediaries for mutual recognition across the EAC. What makes this objective quite hard to easily achieve is the fact that, currently, financial system development (various financial subsectors) amongst the Six Partner States are at different levels of development and sophistication. A practical example is that of Capital markets whereby various EAC economies have very divergent levels of experience and sophistication: Kenya (62 years), Tanzania (19 years), Uganda (18 years), Rwanda (7 years), Burundi (no stock exchange), and South Sudan (no stock exchange). Besides, various EAC supervisory agencies would have to assess their compliance with global regulatory and supervisory agencies in their line of operations.*

4. *Integration of Financial Market Infrastructure: this is aimed at streamlining all the financial system infrastructure across the EAC such as the Real Time Gross Settlement (RTGS), Central Securities Depositories (CSD), Trade Reporting System (TRS), among others. This is basically because an efficient market infrastructure that is compatible at the EAC regional level is critical to the creation of a vibrant and competitive regional financial market environment in the EAC and globally. The EAC Secretariat and the FSDRP has been working on these forms of financial markets infrastructure integration since 2011, along with the various financial system regulators across the EAC; and these include among others:*
   ***Securities Exchange**: Advocating for the Demutualization of EAC stock exchanges;*

Facilitating the establishment of a Regional stock exchange;

Aiding the establishment of equity market and also Capital Market Development Authority in Burundi to enable integration with regional stock market;

Separation of CMA and Rwanda Stock Exchange to enable integration with Regional stock market;

Facilitating the development of a regional commodities/ futures market in the EAC.

Central Securities Depositories (CSD): Facilitating the integration of CSD;

Aiding the creation of governance, operational and risk management systems;

Facilitating the process for the PPP framework for the EAC regional CSD;

Aiding the integration of regional CSD with the regional RTGS in the EAC Bloc.

Payment, Remittances & Securities Settlement Systems: Aiding the Payment System harmonization and the integration of the RTGS systems;

Development of a centralized database for capturing payment flows within the EAC;

Building of regional capacity on payment systems issues.

Automated Trading System (ATS): Aiding the adoption of common ATS platform;

Licensing of existing ATS in EAC Partner States;

Facilitating the establishment of backups for ATS.

Credit Reference Bureau: Aiding the interconnection of credit bureaus across the EAC.

5. Development of the Regional Bond Market: this is intended to allow bond issuers in all EAC economies to have access to a deeper pool of liquidity but also the establishment of a Government bond yield curve with liquid benchmarks that could serve as a reference

for the pricing of even non-Government debt securities. This is aimed at broadening avenues for mobilizing long-term resources on domestic bond markets for the financing of investments in specific strategic sectors such as extractive, infrastructure, housing industries and SMEs

6. *Capacity Building: this objective seeks to create capacity for regional policy formulation and coordination at the level of the EAC Secretariat through preparation of EAC Acts and Regulations by the EAC Authorities. Besides, it would also serve to strengthen financial sector supervisory capacity in Partner States in addition to the support provided by national –level projects through strengthening financial skills set and delivering capacity building curriculum for regulatory agencies and market players.*

The Regional Bloc has since then achieved a degree of legal and institutional capacities which are very indicative of a real potential for regional integration. These include among other: the EAC legislature (which adopts laws and harmonizes policies over-riding national laws); the EAC Judiciary; and the EAC Secretariat. But, in order to sanction EAC Acts, there is need for co-decision between East African Legislative Assembly (EALA) and the Summit of Heads of Partner States, then everything would be harmonized and further implemented. Furthermore, the integration schedule is managed by the Council of Ministers and the Sectoral Councils in the following sectors: Trade, Finance, Investment, and Industry. Nevertheless, there are three top level committees and their subcommittees that provide additional support in the whole initiative, and these are: the Monetary Affairs Committee (MAC), which is composed of Governors of all Central Banks ; the Fiscal Affairs Committee (FAC), which is a function of senior officials from the Ministries of Finance charged with the harmonization of taxes and duties; and finally, the Capital Markets Insurance and Pensions Committee (CMIPC), which brings together securities, insurance and pension regulators across the EAC region.

There has been a couple of regional integration initiatives in the financial sector through:

East Africa Securities Exchange Association (EASEA). This brings together the regional securities exchanges (stock markets & commodities exchanges) for a harmonized regulation and trading environment so as to facilitate the desired financial system integration in East African Community.

Capital Markets, Insurance & Pensions Committee (CMIPC). These officials normally meet from all the member States to deliberate on issues of common interest such as progress of capital market infrastructure project (CMI); its legal framework and also the development of the Securities Industry Training Institute (SITI East Africa) but also to get updates from the EAC Financial Sector Development Regionalization Project (FSDRP). This is aimed at supporting regional integration. Technical Working Groups (TWG) of the EAC have been established such as:

Capital markets Infrastructure project (CMI), and the TWG on the Capital markets Directives.

One of their undertaking is to put in place the trading and settlement infrastructure; and by 2015, they had also developed and published at least seven (7) legal framework/ regional integration directives; besides another set of 13 directives had been developed but being subjected to stakeholders' review in each partner State before approvals by relevant authorities so as later to be published. The 7 published Capital markets Directives include:

- *EAC Directive on Public Offers (Equity)*
- *EAC Directive on Public Offers (Debt)*
- *EAC Directive on Collective Investment Schemes*
- *EAC Directive on Public Asset-Backed Securities*

- EAC Directives on Corporate Governance for Securities intermediaries.
- EAC Directives on Admission to secondary trading.
- EAC Directive on Listing.

East African Insurance Supervisors' Association (EAISA) established in 2008 by all insurance regulators in EAC to synergize in insurance supervision but also harmoniously develop the insurance industry.

East African Pension Supervisors' Association (EAPSA) which is charged with harmonization of pension supervision in EAC to increase efficiency & facilitate cross-border transactions within the EAC bloc.

Monetary Affairs Committee of the EAC is composed of Governors of the six EAC Central banks mandated with coordinating the harmonization and cooperation in Central banking activities and ensuring financial system soundness within the EAC region. This committee has subcommittees covering the banking integration issues and also monetary union.

KEY ECONOMIC ACHIEVEMENTS OF THE EAC

By the early 2016, below is a summary of the economic achievements of the EAC regional bloc since its formal revival in 2000:

- Establishment of the EAC Customs Union;
- Establishment of the EAC Common Market;
- Convertibility of currencies of Kenya, Tanzania and Uganda; agreed to open reciprocal accounts for each of the other AC Partner State currencies to facilitate local currency convertibility.
- East African Payment Systems was launched in November 2014; plus capital account liberalizing among all EAC Partner States to facilitate free flow of capital among Partner States

- *Capital Markets development and Cross-listing of stocks;*
- *Implementation of Preferential tariff discount;*
- *Free movement of stocks;*
- *Harmonizing operations of Ministries of Finance and Central Banks during national budget preparation and presentation.*

Chapter 41
FINANCIAL HUB & CENTRES FOR EAC REGION

Historically, the financial world experienced substantial changes prior to 1914, which created an environment favorable to an increase in and development of international financial centers and hubs. Principal among such changes were unprecedented growth in capital flows and the resulting rapid financial center integration, as well as faster financial and communication infrastructure. Before 1870, London and Paris existed as the world's only prominent financial centers and hubs; soon after, Berlin and New York grew to become major financial centers. Henceforth, an array of smaller financial centers and hubs became imperative as they found market niches, such as: Amsterdam, Brussels, Zurich, and Geneva. London remained the leading international financial center in the four decades leading up to World War I.

Globally, financial hubs and centers have been so outstanding in promoting financial system developments and global competitiveness for respective economies. This has seen various world economies become global financial hubs such as: Switzerland is a hub for private banking; Luxembourg is a hub for bond market; Malaysia is a hub for Islamic finance; but also NASDAQ is a hub for listings of technology firms yet NYSE is a hub for listing of other traditional companies

For EAC to be able to establish and progressively sustain the long desired integrated financial system, there is need to identify a financial hub for the region but also to assign (establish) financial centers within the EAC bloc guided by rational financial realities and competitive advantage. Besides, there should be an enabling environment (legal framework that foster this) and above the business sense that facilitates all the interactions across the region.

Business sense: the concept of integrated EAC financial system must make business sense for firms and investors (financial agents) to opt for this ideal. Currently, there is still a lot that needs to put in place; it is quite hard to find an EAC currency in another EAC economy forex bureau (apart from KSHS), and EAC member States seem to be more integrated with the global market than EAC regional markets. USD are all over EAC and many transactions are done in USD but very few done in another EAC currencies; USD accounts are way too many compared to EAC local currency accounts. Many forex bureaus in EAC hardly even trade another member State currency because it doesn't make economic sense (less/ no transactions with it). Intra-EAC trade amongst Member State is very low & currently it doesn't call for integration but the EAC regional governments and institutions can work on this so that the region can enjoy benefits and economies of collective strategies within the region but above all in the global economy.

On the other hand, the status for a financial hub must be earned: everything must be in place that facilitates financial transaction that investors/ traders are looking for such as money/funds, fund management; expertise in doing sophisticated financial analysis (key characteristics of a financial hub). No EAC economy has all these financial requirements but Kenya is comparatively faring well and the fact that its Vision 2030 development plan strategically is aimed at this, then it has a competitive and comparative advantage amongst its peers. But given the fact that all EAC economies fall short of the financial hub status, there is need to establish regional centers that are also based on the theory of competitive advantage and also revealed comparative advantage (regionally) though also centers evolve with time and they should also be earned by a certain economy. By and large, Kenya somewhat qualifies to earn the financial hub status due to the following reasons:

It is more developed economically and with relatively better infrastructure in the region.

The financial markets industry is way developed as compared to its regional peers, with the introduction of sophisticated financial products from 2015.

It has enjoyed a long history of banking and financial services, with very many firms in this industry in comparison to its regional peers.

For purposes of simplification, I'm going to highlight the four fundamentals of Competitive advantage that are squarely based on resources:

- *These resources should be very different from those of the competitors, and they should be immobile lest they are acquired by the competitor.*
- *They should add value: they should be valuable so as to create value strategies.*
- *These resources should be rare to get; and they should not be copied/ imitated.*
- *There should not be substitutes that can deliver the same benefits that your resources can. This is because competitors can capitalize and develop strategies on the substitutes which has been a winning strategy world-over.*

Besides, the revealed comparative advantage is an index used in international economics for calculating the relative advantage or disadvantage of a certain country in a certain class of goods and services as evidenced by trade flows (country's total exports divided by total world exports in that good/service. A comparative advantage is "revealed" if this ratio is larger than 1; but is it is less, then it is a comparative disadvantage. Most EAC economies don't have any revealed comparative advantage in any good or service but once integrated as a Single financial system or economic bloc, then both the EAC regional bloc and also individual economies will be rather competitive and highly visible. Besides, the usage of revealed comparative advantage is on the EAC regional basis analysis (in my study) but not global basis; hence, various EAC economies can position themselves and also take advantage of revealed comparative advantages in various goods and services

PREREQUISITES FOR AN INTEGRATED EAC SECURITIES MARKET

Regional financial integration can serve to address several issues associated with the small and fragmented financial markets across the EAC region; these small financial systems tend to have fewer players which consequently renders them less competitive and operationally inefficient since they lack systemic scale economies. Players are quite constrained in diversifying their investments and operational risks, and the regulatory infrastructure of such small financial systems tend to be of higher costs and lower quality as compared to larger financial systems. Besides, other key components of the financial infrastructure like credit information services are widely unavailable and inaccurate but also too expensive to operate.

A huge securities market is good for all EAC members; it is easier to diversify. There is need to establish centers within EAC member states based on both their respective revealed comparative advantage & also competitive advantage such as:

1) *Rwanda: center for compliance, automation & governance. Thus, those processes of the stock market ought to be managed in Rwanda due to those advantages. World records have it that Rwanda was:*

   The most compliant State on MDGs in the world; and she ranks 3rd best country in the world in Ease of Doing Business (it takes only six hours to register a business).

   The most developing country for the ¼ Century based on Human Development Index.

   The 7th most efficient government in the world. Its vision 2020 projects attaining a middle-income economy with per capital income of above USD 1300.

2) *Kenya: Financial hub & center for listings & derivative assets trading due to sophisticated skills in financial analysis, high efficiency levels; very long history in financial markets; biggest number of listed firms & stock activities; creativity & hard-working nature; but also home to most manufacturing industries (which attracts listings).*

3) *Tanzania & Uganda: centers for commodities exchange & infrastructural development projects due to high potential in agric. production because of vast fertile lands & infrastructural space.*

4) *Uganda: center for stock exchange due to her people that are very accommodative & receptive to foreigners since time immemorial.*

5) *Burundi & South Sudan: these still need to develop their political & financial systems so as to earn any center status on the EAC stock market infrastructure.*

Figure 8.4   `EAC Financial Hub

EAC FINANCIAL HUB AND CENTRES

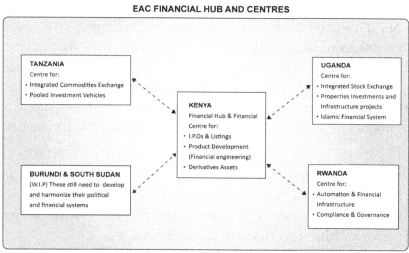

Source: Researcher's Data

All the individual securities markets would become microcosm of the EAC securities exchange but facilitating the access of securities by their local people in the whole EAC region.

EAC FINANCIAL SYSTEM

Challenges

Integration of EAC financial system begun in 1997 when EASRA was established, and then re-energized in 2010 when a road map towards an integrated financial markets was put in place. EASRA is committed to having a unified/ integrated financial markets environment by 2017 under an "East African Stock Market". Below are some of the challenges to this:

EAC Monetary Union is so desirable (including a one currency policy) but it has lots of challenges basically discipline in fiscal policy amongst the six member States;

Most EAC businesses are micro and the region doesn't have the absorptive capacity of the funds available; this means that generally the bloc is producing at excess capacity of her resource and financial endowment. As a matter of fact, if the domestic resources were fully exploited, EAC governments would not need to get financing outside the EAC regional sources. A case in point is NSSF-Uganda biggest pension fund in EAC region and largest financial institution in Uganda) which who asset size reached USD 1.9 Billion as at March 2016; this asset holding is actually way larger than Rwanda's foreign exchange reserves as at June 2015. These resources can be efficiently channeled and allocated to productive sectors which would be so incremental to the EAC bloc.

There is still a great need for local content: good local financial services firms in a bid to enjoy but also maximize benefits of multiplier effect in the EAC region, and also the growth of local capacities within EAC leveraging on technology.

EAC has a whole nine (9) Central depositories which is ridiculous in such a relatively small market; whereby some Member States have more than one Central Securities Depositories (CSD) such as Uganda with one for Bank of Uganda – government securities & also for Uganda Securities Exchange – corporate securities. This is absolutely expensive, duplicative & uncalled for in such a frontier market economy; there is need for one EAC CSD system linked to regional Central banks for improved efficiency and convenience in securities transactions.

Disharmony in major macroeconomic drivers: there is need for harmonization of key macroeconomic indicators such as: interest rates, inflation, currency differences.
Centralized securities clearing and settlement.

Differing capital adequacies among the six (6) financial systems: this significantly constrain resource mobilization within the region because the banking system in some EAC member states is stringent in comparison with other peers.

Improved liquidity is a huge requirement for most financial markets in the EAC, apart from the Kenyan financial system that has relatively liquid, developed and sophisticated markets. Most other financial markets are largely illiquidity due to constrained activities, poor disclosure tendencies, and among other reasons.

Political will of each Member State to the implementation of the policies, directives, and regulatory framework designed to facilitate an integrated EAC financial system.

Lack of a local regional credit rating agency that would facilitate the rating of both government and corporate debt issuance so as to boost both financing for those institutions in need of finance and also investment for domestic and foreign investors who want to exploit the EAC regional growth potential.

Much as the EAC regional institutions have tried to outlaw and even fight any Non-Tariff barriers that could affect intra-regional trade, there are still some significant ones like the levies/ fees on weigh bridges for transporters/ traders who are engaged in cross-border trade. These are still existent and some are quite arbitrary, and they visibly act as disincentive to regional integration across the EAC.

Challenges to EAC Integration (Land Tenure System) Property Market

Land ownership/tenure system:

Land is a key factor of production, and in economics, it entails the fertile soils, water bodies, vegetation, but also the mineral resources therein. This renders land to be so pivotal in real production and contributes to the financial system significantly.

There are varying systems across East Africa that would complicate real integration ie Uganda and Kenya have a policy of private ownership of land and it is easier for foreigners to acquire land in these economies. On the other hand, in Rwanda land almost belongs to the government; yet in Tanzania, much as there is private ownership of land but it is practically hard to foreigners to acquire land.

NB: There is need to harmonize this discrepancy since land (its availability and ownership systems) is very instrumental in the production process.

How to Boost the EAC Financial System

There should be provision and development of new investment opportunities through diversification of risk in tailor-made structured investment vehicles that would both tap into funds from the large informal sector and also help to cover lots of eventualities. Most regulation is retail-centered yet retail investors don't make the market move in any significant way. Therefore, regulation ought to be revised and rendered pro-institutional investing since this is the global trend to boosting financial systems world over.

Improve availability of quality information on comparative returns and profitability on different investments especially on financial assets like stocks, bonds, etc vis-à-vis other alternative investments like property which many investors are used to (and trust).

Intermediaries should improve corporate finance business development, sales knowledge and skills so as to stimulate more issuance from the securities issuers (financing wing) and also the absorptive capacity of issuances (investment wing).

There is need to establish and/or integrate the central securities depositories into one financial system infrastructure for the whole of East African Community region to boost efficiency and convenience.

The tax systems should be comprehensively revised basically in regards to the framework for financial markets so that taxation on savings, investment vehicles, and corporate financial transactions be reconsidered.

There is further need to beef up legal framework for undeveloped potential financing pipeline avenues so as to incentivize their growth such as private equity and venture capitalism due to their likely impact on the financial system.

In the face of slumping commodities prices, EAC economies ought to explore avenues to boost growth; avoiding a prolonged slowdown is quite critical to reviving the region's growth momentum and key goals. These are function of: raising incomes of the poor, strengthening education and health care, but also ensuring widely shared economic benefits; and they can be achieved through advancement in production structures, diversifying EAC economies, and majorly lessening the dependence on commodities.

EAC Unified Currency

Many firms can't do business with some East African countries like Burundi and South Sudan now, even if they get deals because of their weak currencies (that are almost become papers with no value). The financial system risks and political risks have rendered their currencies almost value-less, unreliable in that it would be better if the East African Community establishes a unified currency so as to standardize value and economic transactions but also to safeguard and insure businessmen who trade in the region. Such a currency would be so incremental to the whole region since the "Central Bank of Eastern Africa" would be charged with maintaining its right exchange rate which in turn would enhance the region's economic position globally by boosting the levels of international trade undertaken and also the international competitiveness of the region as a bloc, and individual economies in particular. This is because a rise in the currency renders the exports less competitive worsening the trade deficit, and a fall in the currency value will render exports cheaper in the global market but making imports more expensive and less competitive in the domestic markets, thus affecting the region's global competitiveness.

Regional Integration (Creation of Regional Value-chains)

African exports are highly focused on commodities, accounting for over 50% of Sub-Saharan Africa exports (with the exception of Uganda whose share of primary commodity exports has dropped from 90% of total merchandise exports in 2002 to approximately 57% by 2015; and processed commodities rise from 8% to 35%). If we foster regional integration, we shall create regional value-chains and thus become more efficient; which will help East African Community to be a key player in global value-chains, which today increasingly characterizes world trade. Records have it that close to 30% of world trade is undertaken through cross-border value-chains. Regional integration will give access to markets for exports, allow traded goods industries to achieve more optimal economies of scale.

Collective regional strategies and actions in East African will help to reap economies of scale or other efficiencies in pursuit of common goals to increase local productive capacities and increased access to global markets. Besides, this will facilitate harmonized treatment of regional issues such as regulatory framework and policies; regional infrastructure like the Standard Gauge Railway and the Oil pipelines; but also better management of shared natural endowments (resources) eg Lake Victoria, Lake Albert, Lake Tanganyika, River Nile, and the resources therein.

Besides, most East African economies are land-locked, which would significantly hinder their progress without regional integration due to major infrastructure investment needs and other associated costs if the regional integration is not in place.

H.E Kenyatta Uhuru (Kenyan president), during the World Economic Forum in May 2016 in Kigali- Rwanda stressed that for regional integration and development to take off, there is need for boosting the Intra-EAC trade amongst regional economies but also to establish what can work for the region (commodities, oil, knowledge-economy, etc). This is because the intra-regional trade is the lever for both real integration and development but the bloc should identify a niche that can work for the region.

BASICS OF EAC INTEGRATION (SOCIOLOGICAL)

In integration, there is need to look at cultures, people, practices, and other things comprehensively but not only regulations as most priority has been placed now. Putting all these backgrounds together is much more complex than regulations, and these must be well thought-out. Of course, this may not be such a big problem if everything is driven by the business sense; since business can change any culture, practices, people, and other basics like how mobile money has significantly changed culture (financial behavior) and ushered in efficiency in financial transactions and business processes.

This is particularly so because EAC has a diversity of people ie Burundi, Kenya, Rwanda, South Sudan, Tanzania, and Uganda (approx. 170 million people). Some due to their background, ought to be instructed to do a certain task; others are self-driven; other do at their own pace; yet others don't want anything; and other despite being threatened, they can't do a thing. Therefore, bring these people together to work in the same way regardless of whether there are regulations to guide them but as long as their work cultures and practices are very different, it poses a challenge. On the contrary, the business sense (environment) will definitely force them all to a certain direction if it is the major driver but NOT regulation/policy.

NB: Markets should determine what to do but not rules! There is need to listen to people and see what is more beneficial for all the parties so as to harmonious develop an integrated financial system for EAC that works for everyone. If not, some sections of EAC populations will object to the whole initiative because they don't see the business sense driving the process; and this is evidenced by some communities in Tanzania & also the new entrant South Sudan.

Chapter 42
INTEGRATED EAC FINANCIAL SYSTEM ENVIRONMENT

Financial integration can be defined as a process in which country's financial system gets increasingly linked, interconnected and integrated with those of other trading Partner Countries or regional economic grouping. Full financial sector integration involves integration of financial markets, including removal/ elimination of all forms of barriers (policy, legal and regulatory, institutional, and infrastructure inter-connectedness) with a view to enabling domestic institutions to engage in domestic and foreign markets, and/or foreign financial institutions to participate in domestic markets. Under conditions of a nearly fully integrated financial markets environment, domestic banking markets, insurance markets, capital markets, pensions, and other categories of financial markets (such as mobile money) become increasingly linked to other regional and foreign entities.

A country's financial system could be integrated to the regional bloc, or to the rest of the world in several ways, including becoming member to a regional economic community, by ratifying all Protocols that have been established to link up the financial markets of the community. By ratifying such Protocols, the Partner State agrees to harmonize and eliminate restrictions that constrain free flow of trade and capital, including harmonization of all financial rules, regulations and taxes and non-tax barriers between member Partner States.

Financial system integration across the six members of the EAC will provide additional opportunities for increasing competition and innovation, while overcoming the challenge of low scale, ultimately contributing to economic growth and poverty alleviation. It is critical, however, that the regulatory framework keeps up to date with a more vibrant and thriving financial sector. Exclusively, increasing financial integration will pose new challenges for central banks across the EAC to adapt the cross border regulatory and resolution framework.

EAC MONETARY STATISTICS AS AT MARCH 2016

Figure 8.5 Interest Rates in Percentage (%)

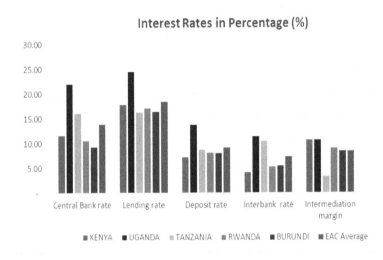

Source: EAC Secretariat (2016)

Figure 8.6 Monetary Aggregates in Million USD

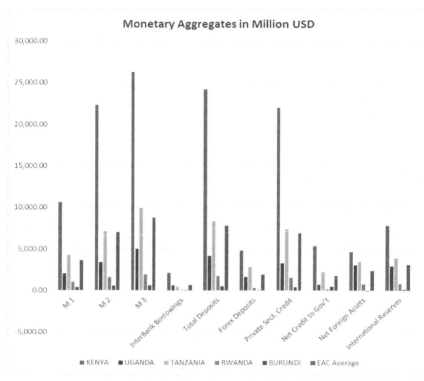

Source: EAC Secretariat (2016)

M1 (monetary base) refers to narrow money or high-powered money, which is simply notes and coins in circulation outside EAC Central banks.

M2 refers to Broad money, including time and sight deposits, retail and wholesale deposits, bank and savings institutions deposits, and other short-term deposits in the money markets. This measure of money gives the best indicator of effective money supply and represents an important source of liquidity for spending within a financial system.

M3 refers largely to money and all the quasi-money instruments (in the financial markets).

It is quite imperative to note that M2 and Private Sector credit are the major indicators of financial depth in a given financial system. By and large, the financial depth within the EAC regional Bloc is limited although drastically improving, thanks to branchless banking like mobile money, agency banking, among others.

Interbank lending is a short-term lending to other banks, it now constitutes one of the largest elements in banks' liquid assets. This may be used by a bank as a basis for expanding loans and thereby starting a chain of credit creation although those assets don't add to the liquidity of the banking system as a whole.

In most monetary fundamentals, it is quite evident that the stronger economies in the EAC regional Bloc are faring well and this proves that that larger economies practically enjoy the benefits of economies of scale. Nevertheless, despite that regional status quo, the Uganda financial system was way outcompeting her Tanzanian counterpart in interbank borrowing, which could imply that the Uganda banking system is more competitive, more liquid, more profit margins, and that she had better potential for credit creation than Tanzania (which is a larger economy than Uganda). Furthermore, on the metric of Net Foreign assets, Uganda is performing so well compared to all her peers, which could imply that the smaller economy has better financial system soundness (resilience); with more capacity of managing her external-economy vulnerabilities including shocks from the global financial system. These foreign assets can act as an implicit collateral against borrowing and they can lower the risk premium associated with financial vulnerabilities of frontier market economies.

Besides, the intermediation margin (defined as, the sum of net fee and commission income and income from financial service activities, net interest income and other financial items); in the Uganda financial system is way higher compared to her regional peers including Kenya (the regional giant economy), despite the fact that Uganda has the highest interest rate regime. This could imply that Uganda has improved her depth and breadth of her financial system and also her share of private sector credit as a percentage of GDP has been progressively growing, plus the deposits in the financial system as a share of GDP. Surprisingly, the Tanzania financial system is faring the poorest in the whole EAC region with just 3.260% in intermediation margin.

NB: Simple monetary theory assumes that the supply of money is independent of interest rates but in the real financial world, a rise in interest rates will often lead to an increase in money supply. But conversely, if monetary authorities rise interest rates, the supply of money may fall in response to a lower demand for money. The fall in interest rates will make borrowing cheaper leading to a rise in investment and exports, but also this boosts the level of economic activity in the economy. These will consequently see a rise in aggregate demand and a resulting rise in national income and output but possibly a rise in prices as well.

FINANCIAL MARKETS

There have been efforts by regulators to harmonize and later integrate the EAC financial markets through identical financial markets regulations, mutual recognition of financial products. Globally, this initiative has ever been undertaken in the Europe Union as a way of removing barriers and providing easier access to capital markets through the "Euronext". This is a pan-European stock exchange based in Paris with subsidiaries in Belgium, the Netherlands, Portugal, and the United Kingdom; in 2007, the Euronext merged with NYSE Group to form NYSE Euronext, which is debatably the first global stock exchange.

There has been a success story in West Africa, where Abidjan (Cote d'Ivoire) is domicile to all listings from economies of the West African Economic & Monetary Union, and the bourse is called "Bourse Regionale des Valeurs Mobilières".

RATIONALE FOR INTEGRATION OF EAC STOCK MARKETS

Financial markets are said to be integrated when the law and operations of one price hold; that is when securities with identical cash flows command the same price; firms, governments and households should be able to access finance on the same terms within and across national boundaries (EAC region).

As we draw from the successes and maybe the challenges of many regional stock markets (including the NYSE Euronext and the "Bourse Regionale des Valeurs Mobilières", discussed above), below are some of crucial reasons that underpin the development of an integrated EAC Stock market:

Increased scale and visibility of individual stocks since most of the listed stocks are quite insignificant while EAC stock market can enhance their visibility and scale as well.

Enhanced liquidity for more investment activities given the regional exposure but also the global visibility to large institutional investors.

Increased access of listed firms to a wider range of investors beginning with the more than 162 million people in East Africa, then the international investing community.

Boosting trading activities that is incremental to market capitalization & multiplier effect at macro level.

Lower transaction costs: management, compliance, and IT costs for market players since they will access to regional markets and investors without any regulatory or tax hindrances.

FUNDAMENTALS FOR OPERATION OF EAC FINANCIAL MARKET

In a bid to establish an efficient and integrated EAC financial market environment that works for the regional bloc and renders it globally competitive, the following need to be addressed:

- *There is need to harmonize regulation so as to instil confidence in investors across the board given an EAC country exposure.*

- *Financial markets ought to have pragmatic product design; products developed must respond to market needs.*

- *There must be a development of knowledge-based products eg securitization, IT products so as to diversify both offering & exposure. If EAC needs a certain information system, we should strive to produce it for our consumption; and the education system is crucial part of the knowledge-based economy.*

- *There is need to boost professionalism (skills set): the financial sector should be managed by professionals so as to sanitize the sector, and avoid gambling since technocrats (technical people) make informed decisions in this sector. Currently, the region is greatly deficient of professional and specialized financial sector human resources that can drive financial engineering and also boost the financial system.*

- *There is need to take advantage of existing opportunities to build national & EAC regional brands and products like mobile money, SACCOs systems, and commodities:*

- *Financial inclusion in mobile money revolution that has seen a drastic & significant development in all EAC financial systems. For instance, in Uganda, close to UGX 24 Trillion were transacted on mobile money in 2015; which accounts for a third (1/3) of Uganda's GDP at UGX 76 Trillion). Mobile money can deliberately be used as a financial product that mobilizes savings for infrastructural projects like the Standard Gauge Railway (SGR), and also for private equity investments in the whole EAC. This will help to finance our local needs (local solutions) but also take advantage of the high levels of liquidity in our financial systems partly caused by corruption, and mistrust in the banking system.*

- *SACCOs & microfinance revolution since people trust themselves more than the banking system. This would make our economies flourish and integrate as many investors in the informal sector into the formal financial system. These can also be used to mobilize local resources for development like SGR and other long-term capital needs for both government and business sectors. These will help to avoid some foreign capital flows which affect EAC sovereignty, some of which are relative expensive and with conditionality; EAC has tens of thousands of SACCOs and MFIs which can raise almost any funds required regionally*

- *Initiatives like the Rwanda National Unit Trust (RNUT) should be deliberately embraced by both individual economies in EAC but also establish a Unit Trust for East Africans (UTEA). This is because unit trusts reflect the social fabrics of the country; these ought to relate to each investor's tastes & interests. UTEA should have a variety of schemes to represent the major interest categories of East African so as to facilitate them to buy shares (invest in them) eg Matooke schemes (for lover of matooke across EAC); Football team schemes; Petroleum schemes; Coffee schemes, etc. These allow the pooling of resources of small holders in the whole EAC through buying units/shares and then such funds can be in invested in a blue-chip companies in EAC through either private or listed equities. This encourages diversification of risks due to a wide variety of products & schemes for every East African.*

- *Commodities & manufacturing: given the competitive advantage, EAC can resolve to purchase eg food items, I.T products, textiles, among other consumer and capital goods from within eg Uganda so as to strategically develop the manufacturing industry of that economy that will later boost the whole financial system (capital raising & investment opportunities for East Africans). This will foster both forward & backward linkages across the investment value-chain; but also EAC firms can position themselves as net suppliers/ producers of raw material to foreign firms in EAC eg agriculture, professionals in financial services & IT. This also entails provision of local cheap capital to both the services* and manufacturing foreign firms with an objective of creating dependence that will ultimately lead to acquisitions & mergers that help EAC to be competitive, creative, to develop local solutions & later indigenize its production systems.

CHALLENGES TO EAC CAPITAL MARKETS INTEGRATION

The integration of the EAC capital markets begun in 1997 when the East African Securities Regulatory Authority (EASRA) was established, and then re-energized in 2010 with a roadmap toward an integrated EAC capital markets put in place. EASRA is committed to having a unified/integrated financial markets environment by 2017, also called "EAC Stock market". But below are some of the challenges to its achievement:

Harmonization of key macroeconomic indicators such as: interest rates, inflation, currency differences; which are so key in facilitating financial transaction across the EAC region and building a rationale for business sense in an integrated stock market infrastructure.

A single efficient securities clearing and settlements system that smoothens stock market transactions and mitigates transaction cost and risks across the region.

Differing capital adequacies by various financial systems' regulators across the EAC region, which might bring in mistrust among the players in various EAC economies; and also predatory tendencies from firms of relatively developed financial systems of the EAC.

Improved liquidity requirement on the part of many stock markets especially the RSE and USE so as to favorably compete with NSE which has a relatively liquid market.

Political will on the part of each Member State's government, which necessitates the timely implementation of the resolutions towards the establishment of an operational EAC stock market.

Additional Financial Assets to be introduced in the EAC Capital Markets

- *REITs, these can be classified into: Investments REITs which hold mature assets & share out monthly income to owners; Development REITs are for new constructions.*
- *Single-stock futures*
- *Financial derivatives*
- *Forward exchange contracts ie currency hedging is in demand currently by investors with currency risk given the volatilities in the forex markets. This can be done with banks but later, it will traded on regulated platforms.*
- *Exchange-Traded Funds*
- *Securitization bonds*
- *Equity-linked debt instruments*
- *Structured debt instruments.*

THE EAC TAX SYSTEM

The EAC region has broad taxation systems covering income tax, value-added tax, customs & excise duty, and others. These are governed by independent legislations that make provisions for charges, assessment and collection of respective taxes. It is imperative to note that any goods imported from EAC and COMESA countries will be taxed at a lower preferential import duty rate; actually for the EAC imports the duty rate is zero.

Most East African economies offer tax incentives to both resident and non-resident corporate bodies, for instance, a newly listed firm on Nairobi Stock Exchange receive a reduced rate for the first 3 – 5 years following the year of listing.

Withholding tax: in Kenya, dividend paid to Kenyan resident and East African Community citizens' listed shares, the rate is 5% yet for non-residents it is 10%. In Uganda, the rate is 15%

across the board which needs revision so as to attract more local participation in the equities markets.

Single Customs Territory

Currently, there exists a single customs territory in the EAC region, which is good news for importers in the region since assessment and collection of taxes is done in the country of destination before the cargo is released from the first port of entry. This is aimed at establishing/attaining an EAC Customs Union which will give traders and manufacturers easier access to this huge EAC market but aso attract foreign, domestic and cross-border investments for investors who seek exposure to the EAC high-growth market. This single customs territory will respond to the need for intra-EAC regional trade that will enhance trade among the EAC member States but also leverage the EAC region as a unique foreign direct investments destination.

Double Taxation Agreements (DTAs): Kenya has signed DTAs with countries like Canada, Denmark, France, Germany, India, Norway, Sweden, UK and Zambia. It has further made treaties with Mauritius and United Arab Emirates (UAE); besides, East Africa community economies have ratified treaties with each other in regards to taxation so as to enjoy the benefits of an economic integration. There is need for EAC to establish DTAs with all economies that are significant potential investors but measures must be put in place to ensure that tax payers do not use the Double Taxation window to evade payment of tax.

Transfer pricing:

EAC economies continue to attract foreign investments, in particular multinational corporations (MNCs), which are keen to make an entry into the large EAC market. This presents challenges to regional tax bodies since they contend with sophisticated accounting systems used by MNCs which lead to tax evasion and/ or reduce tax liability of these corporations. Through the Income

Tax Acts and Transfer Pricing Rules of respective EAC tax bodies, there should be room to adjust profits of taxable persons in the country with a related non-resident person; where a business is such that it produces to the resident person either no profits or less than ordinary profits. The tax systems should require that transactions between persons in the EAC region and any related non-resident party be at arm's length ie the price charged for the transaction ought to be the same payable between independent enterprises. These Transfer Pricing rules apply as well to transactions between a branch and its head office and also other related branches.

These regulations require pricing arrangements in cross-border transactions such as sale of goods, provision of services, transfer of intangible assets and lending/borrowing money between related entities to be at an arm's length. This has seen many multinational corporations save a lot of funds in the way of tax liability due to such principle according to the East African tax systems. On the other hand, the region has lost lots of tax revenue to East African economies when foreign firms exploit this loophole and then deny the domestic economies of finance that would help to run domestic budgets and scale down on the debt to GDP ratio while also bettering the public sectors' capacity for local resource mobilization.

There is need for EAC tax systems to become more sophisticated so as to manage all craftiness and tax evasive initiatives majorly by foreign firms; this is because records have it that more than USD 60 Billion is lost by Africa in tax evasion each year.

EAC TAX REVENUE LOSSES

A 2016 report published by the Tax Justice Network-Africa indicates that the EAC loses close to USD 2 Billion as a result of unwarranted tax incentives such as tax holidays, capital gains tax allowances, royalty exemptions granted especially to foreign firms. That whopping figure of annual tax revenue loss that is almost equivalent to Rwanda's national budget of 2016/17 is broken down as follows: Kenya (USD 1.1 Billion); Uganda (USD 370 Million); Tanzania (USD 354 Million); and Rwanda (USD 176 Million). Analysts maintain that such tax incentives fuel competition at the EAC level, and derail any meaningful progress towards regional harmonization of tax policies and also the regional integration at large. EAC governments should review tax incentives structures with a view of obliterating all unproductive incentives and target such incentives that achieve special socio-economic objectives that benefit East Africans.

Chapter 43

REGULATORS OF THE FINANCIAL SYSTEM & RECOMMENDATIONS

"A well-regulated financial sector builds confidence among citizens to freely use financial services."

Figure 8.7

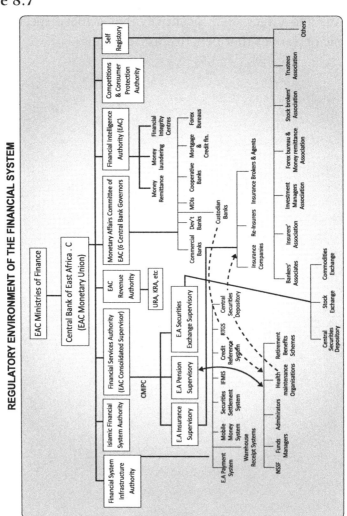

Source: Researcher's Data

EXISTING FRAMEWORK

Capital Markets Authority

This regulator is referred to as Capital Market Authority (CMA) in Kenya, Uganda and Rwanda yet in Tanzania it is Capital Markets and Securities Authority (CMSA) but their mandates are similar since they regulate capital markets and securities exchanges (including commodities exchanges). These are semi-autonomous bodies responsible for promoting, developing and regulating the capital markets industry in the East African Community, with the overall objectives of investor protection and market efficiency. The capital markets industry in EAC came into being in different years with the enactment of the Capital Markets Authority (CMA) Acts and relevant regulations; which later paved the way for the formation of the various stock exchanges in the EAC.

CMA has a number of functions, these include;

- *The development of all aspects of the capital markets with particular emphasis on the removal of impediments to, and the creation of incentives for longer term investments in productive enterprises.*

- *The creation, maintenance and regulation, through implementation of a system in which the market participants are self-regulatory to the maximum practicable extent of a market in which securities can be issued and traded in an orderly, fair and efficient manner.*

- *The protection of investors' interests and investments.*

- *The operation of an investor compensation fund that would hedge against foul play arising from unprofessional conduct of the market players.*

- *In their role as a regulator, the CMAs oversee the activities of the securities exchanges, licensed intermediaries such as broker/dealers and investment advisors. CMA also regulates the operation of Collective Investment Schemes.*

- *Regulating the business in stock exchanges and any other securities markets*
- *Registering and regulating the working of stock brokers, sub–brokers etc.*
- *Promoting and regulating self-regulatory organizations*
- *Prohibiting fraudulent and unfair trade practices*
- *Calling for information from, undertaking inspection, conducting inquiries and audits of the stock exchanges, intermediaries, self – regulatory organizations, unit trust funds and other persons associated with the securities market.*

RETIREMENT BENEFITS AUTHORITIES (PENSIONS)

This pension regulator is called Retirement Benefits Authority (RBA) in both Kenya and Tanzania yet in Uganda, it is the Uganda Retirement Benefits Regulatory Authority (URBRA). These regulate the pension industry in most EAC economies apart from some countries like Rwanda and Burundi that have consolidated regulation based in the central bank, and they were established:

- *To regulate the establishment, management and operations of the retirement benefits schemes in various EAC member States , in both the public and the private sector*
- *To supervise institutions which provide retirement benefits products and services*
- *To protect the interests of members and beneficiaries of retirement benefit schemes (pension schemes) by promoting governance principles, transparency and accountability*
- *To promote the development of the pension sector in Uganda*
- *To provide for the licensing of custodians, trustees, administrators and fund managers*

INSURANCE REGULATORY AUTHORITIES

These regulate the insurance industry and are aimed at stimulating its growth in most EAC financial systems apart from Rwanda that has a consolidated regulatory structure under the central bank.

REVENUE AUTHORITIES

These are semi-autonomous bodies that are charged with administering/implementing the tax laws on behalf of the Ministers of Finance of respective EAC countries after the tax bills have been passed by the Parliaments and later assented by the Presidents into laws/ Act. These tax regulators are established by an Act of Parliament in a bid to improve the tax administration in the respective countries; and they are under the Ministries of Finance whereby they assess and collect taxes from the public on the behalf of their respective Ministries. They performs the following functions as an agency:

- *They administer and give effect to the laws or the specified provisions of the laws specified in their statutes through assessing and collecting tax revenues according to the laws.*

- *They advise the minister on revenue implications, tax administration and aspects of policy changes relating to all taxes referred to in the tax statutes.*

- *They perform other functions in relation to revenue as the respective finance ministers may direct it.*

WAREHOUSING RECEIPT SYSTEM AUTHORITY (CASE OF UGANDA)

It begun its operations in July 2015, though it was enacted in 2006, and regulation enforced in 2007; it is mandated to operationalize the warehousing receipt system. It currently promotes and regulates warehousing through the following: inspecting warehouses; sensitizing stakeholders; providing quality & quantity assurance (controls); provision of market information system through the electronic WRS not only in Uganda but also internationally; capacity building of stakeholders; market linkages to the commodities exchange

Vision: "An excellent structured commodities trading system"

Mission: "To promote the development of infrastructure that supports structured commodities trading system & value addition

COMPONENTS OF WRS

- *Policy & legal framework (guiding in things to be done)*
- *Physical infrastructure (warehouses)*
- *ICT infrastructure (with electronic component that enables transactions)*

These facilitate the flow from commodities exchange to the general economy/ financial system. The electronic system receipt serves to save time and resources in establishing the validity of one client's commodities by another willing to trade.

UWRSA has a general mandate for all commodities though now it is basically specializing in those that are standardized, and has standards through UNBS eg agricultural products (maize, beans, sorghum, soya beans, coffee, cotton, etc) but others coming on board like oil, minerals, timber, etc. the authority helps farmers to trade their commodities in a structured way by linking rural farmers to formal/commercial markets in western world & other formal and standardized markets.

There are 2 types of WRS:

- *Regulated WRS which operate through the UWRSA.*
- *Non-regulated WRS that operate through contractual law whereby a collateral manager with experience in handling such commodities help two parties to sign a Tripartite Agreement clearly their roles & responsibilities ie trader – bank – collateral manager. This is done to manage risks basically on the part of the banks.*

However, there is need to establish a unified EAC level warehousing receipt systems authority so as harmonize policies and regulation in this crucial industry which is frankly the backbone (linked to agriculture and extractive industries/ real sectors) of the EAC regional bloc that has potential to procure a revealed comparative advantage for the EAC bloc.

PROPOSED REGULATORY FRAMEWORK FOR EAC FINANCIAL SYSTEM

With the establishment of an integrated financial system for the EAC region, there is a strong need for revising the regulatory framework so as to suit the new status. These regional bodies are not meant to replace or render the national bodies irrelevant or less important but they are aimed at spearheading the harmonization of policies and regulations. This synchronization should facilitate intra-regional trade and transactions, but also standardize procedures and ways of doing business within their respective industries/ sectors. A harmonized policy formulation for the EAC regional bloc is so key in boosting intra-regional competitiveness but also global excellence for the regional bloc. These should not work as barriers to innovation and business transactions but it should incentivize the whole process so as to create an environment of a relatively balanced and equitable development of the EAC financial system, and later significantly contribute to the long-desired monetary union. A two-tier legal and regulatory system is desirable in the financial subsystem of the EAC regional Bloc, and this consist of the EAC level regulatory agencies to set broad EAC legal frameworks such as: Monetary Affairs Committee; the Consolidated Financial services Authority; the Financial systems Infrastructure Authority; the Islamic Financial system Authority; the EAC Revenue Authority; the Financial Intelligence Authority; the Competitions & Consumer Protection Authority; and the Self-Regulatory Organizations.

On the other hand, all national level regulators ought to be in place in their jurisdictions for the efficient day-to-day supervision of activities and players in their respective industries/ sectors. This is because, supervision and empowerment at the domestic level is so imperative in the development and uptake of products in a given sector but also facilitation for healthy competition.

And the following is the proposed model which will all be premised and domiciled under the East African Central bank (some are here below and others are in the final chapter "Integrated Financial System Environment":

EAST AFRICA CENTRAL BANK (MONETARY AFFAIRS COMMITTEE)

This regulator will be charged with managing and harmonizing the monetary policy of the region and the whole central banking activities but also supervising the EAC banking system for macroeconomic stability and financial system soundness. The East Africa Central bank can borrow a leaf from the Bank of Central African States which caters for the following economies: Cameroon, Gabon, Republic of Congo, Equatorial Guinea, Chad, and Central African Republic. This will encompass activities of commercial banks, development banks, Microfinance Deposit-taking Institutions, foreign exchange bureaus, mortgage finance institutions, credit financial institutions, among other banking services.

FINANCIAL SERVICES AUTHORITY

This regulator will be ensure an integrated and consolidated supervision as well development of the financial services industry in the EAC region for the harmonious development of all the Member States and all the sectors within this industry. This will be headed by a director general of the financial services authority, whereby the Insurance, pensions, and securities exchanges sub-sectors will be departments also headed by directors

There should be an integrated/ consolidated regulator (supervisor) for financial services sector ie pensions, capital markets, and insurance under what is called the "Financial services Authority" (FSA). This is aimed to: lower supervision costs; have a common pool of resources; good coordination that can prevent a financial crisis since the global financial crisis of 2008/09 was partly caused by piece-meal (fragmented) supervision in the US financial services industry. If capital markets, insurance, pension, and others are under one regulator (FSA) headed by a Director General; whereby all the others are departments headed by Directors, this would lessen duplication of roles and activities by various regulators.

INTEGRATED EAC FINANCIAL SERVICES REGULATION

It has now become a practice among developed and developing financial systems to adopt a form of integrated regulation in the financial services industry thus eliminating the piece-meal regulation and supervision which is believed to have been a great catalyst of the 2008/09 Global Financial Crisis due to sub-prime mortgage scenarios. Once this is put in place, the integrated financial system for the EAC will attract foreign investors who are already used to this kind of regulation in their home economies, and it will incentivize them to have exposure to the EAC financial system. This regulatory approach is quite coherent and leads to relative efficiency and reduce transaction costs in dealing with regulated communities. As a matter of fact, many a financial centers world over have opted for this consolidated regulatory environment (securities, banking and insurance) as a means of attracting foreign investors, and these include among others: UK, Luxembourg, Gulf economies, Switzerland, Singapore. Nevertheless, I would advocate for a twin approach to financial services regulation in the EAC; whereby the Financial Services Authority works as a consolidated regulator for the securities, pensions, and insurance sectors, while on the other hand the Central banks (possibly under the Central Bank of East Africa Community or even individual Central banks) supervise and regulate the banking system

FINANCIAL SYSTEM INFRASTRUCTURE AUTHORITY

This body will be so crucial in regulating all the financial infrastructure in the EAC region so as to ensure efficiency in financial services delivery, manage financial system risks but also foster greater integration within the region and also financial deepening (development and inclusion) across the EAC region. This will entail payment systems, mobile money services, warehousing receipt systems, securities settlement systems, IFMIS, credit reference services, RTGS, and central securities depositories.

ISLAMIC FINANCIAL SYSTEM AUTHORITY

Just like for the case of the conventional financial system regulation, there is also need for an integrated financial services regulation for Islamic finance in the EAC so as to harmonize and streamline development in this complementary financial system. There is need to establish an Islamic finance standard setting body and also empower a single regional/national Shariah Advisory Board whose role is to provide guidance on product authenticity through qualification for the whole Islamic financial system. This body would set rules, guidelines and policies for all the sub-sectors of this upcoming financial system. The Shariah board would be responsible for reviewing the investment framework for Islamic finance like permissible products and other Shariah/corporate governance issues among the players in this industry. Besides, there ought to be a legally accepted Association of Islamic Financial Institutions across the whole system that provide Islamic financial products. Furthermore, the EAC financial system should recognize standards/regulation that pertain to Islamic-based accounting, investment, governance and auditing standards.

Given the deliberate establishment of the Islamic financial system in the EAC region, there is need to put in place an efficient regulatory framework that will ensure the success of this alternative financial system in the region. This regulator will supervise, development and guide the activities of these sub-sectors within the Islamic financial system: capital markets, insurance, pensions, asset management, and banking, among others across the EAC region for harmonious development of this newly established yet high-growth potential financial system.

FINANCIAL INTELLIGENCE AUTHORITY

With the growth of money laundering issues, terrorism financing and transferring of hot money for various reasons world over, there is need to regulate the flow of money within the EAC and also from outside the region so as to efficiently manage the financial system soundness and the macroeconomic stability across the EAC bloc. This will serve to ensure the harmonious develop of both the real economy and the financial sector within the EAC region through monitoring the activities of money remittance services, along with the activities (transactions) on the financial system infrastructure basically mobile money services, among others.

There is need to establish an EAC Financial Intelligence Authority to coordinate the implementation of the EAC regional Anti-Money Laundering (AML) regime; but it should also be responsible for the receipt and analysis of financial disclosures from any accountable persons within the region, and dissemination of financial intelligence to competent authorities. This would collect information on suspicious transactions, large cash and monetary transactions and within/ cross EAC border movement of cash and negotiable bearer instruments from reporting entities (banks, corporations and other financial institutions; and thereafter send financial intelligence reports to the appropriate law enforcement agencies. This EAC regional body should be mandated to coordinate and build strategic partnerships with key stakeholders in the EAC financial system all the country level Financial Intelligence Authorities so as to counter money laundering, terrorism financing but also undertake National Risk Assessments so as to contribute to the management of financial system and systemic risks within the EAC bloc.

REVENUE (TAX) AUTHORITY

This regional body will supervise, harmonize and promote the tax system of the EAC region so as to ensure that EAC governments raise the requisite finances for supporting their budgets but also to stimulate the harmonious development of all the sectors within the respective economies through prudent taxation policies and systems. This comes at a time when the EAC bloc is losing volumes of money through tax evasion and avoidance by both domestic firms but majorly foreign companies, which funds would have been invested in infrastructure development, public goods and services, and also stimulating private sector competitiveness. Actually, international organizations like OXFAM are advocating for this initiative, where by both regional blocs such as EAC but also the world should establish regional tax bodies and a global tax body respectively so as to harmonize tax policy, regulation and deal with tax avoidance.

A HARMONIZED TAX SYSTEM FOR EAC FINANCIAL SYSTEM

The EAC region has for long been striving to position herself as a friendly investment destination globally through the harmonization of tax systems (legislations) in a bid to boost investments, eliminate harmful tax competitions, and boost regional competitiveness in the global economy. Such initiatives date back in 1997 with the development of an Agreement on Avoidance of Double Taxation under the permanent Tripartite Commission. Through the line committees of the EAC, tax harmonization in the region could be viewed from two perspectives: harmonization of the tax rates, and the harmonization of the tax legislation. But from the time of inception, the various organs and committees of the EAC had, up to mid-2016, failed to agree on the harmonized domestic tax rates across the EAC because each country has its domestic issues to deal with, and the fact that smaller economies worry about significant revenue losses compared to larger economies. But by and large, at least the EAC has been able to harmonize Customs duties and the Common external tariff. By 2016, there was a Draft EAC Domestic Taxes Policy Framework, which among others highlight the harmonization of VAT, income tax and excise duty.

In a bid to achieve the benefits of the Common Market Protocol and also attain the EAC Monetary Union, the better option would be to harmonize legislation and the regulatory framework within the EAC since this will facilitate intra-regional trade and heavily attract foreign investors. This approach is easier and more practical for the varying levels of economic development amongst EAC economies, and also help them retain some levels of sovereignty basically in revenue collection.

But the bottom line is that a clearly understood, stable and effective tax system should be the priority of EAC governments and institutions.

EAC COMPETITION & CONSUMER PROTECTION AUTHORITY

Globally, some of the key drivers of efficiency and productivity within financial systems are innovation and healthy/regulated competition since these are crucial prerequisites that ensures that economies responds to the needs of their players and efficiency benefits easily passed on across the value-chain. Innovation should be driven by the business sense and environment, but also market players within the EAC region through a competitive identification of opportunities and financial products engineering that is geared at meeting both local and global investor needs.

Given the aggressive innovation and competition environment across the EAC financial sector, and an apparent absence of a recourse mechanism, coupled to an uneven coverage and enforcement systems of consumer protection framework; there is a lot that needs to be desired. There is currently scanty regulation on consumer protection across the EAC with varying levels and mandates to address these issues within the region's financial sub-sectors; hence the need for a full-bodied integrated EAC financial sector consumer protection authority.

Therefore, a necessary regulatory authority should be established for the EAC region so as to facilitate innovation, competition and consumer protection to enable new entrants to challenge the old-timers. This EAC regional level Competition and Consumer Protection Authority (CCPA) will also among others accomplish the following tasks:

- *To drive healthy market (financial system) growth through attracting business from within the EAC and also other regions;*
- *To stimulate financial engineering (creation of market-driven and sophisticated financial products) to match with both EAC regional and global financial system developments.*
- *To regulate monopoly and price control related issues;*
- *To champion consumer protection in the financial sector;*
- *To collaborate the EAC Court of Justice to deal with matters like individual complaints;*
- *To ensure sound business practices among financial institutions related to competition and market position abuse.*

SELF-REGULATORY ORGANISATIONS (SROS)

This regulatory environment is comprised of professional bodies that serve to guide the professional behaviour and operations of their members as they work within the financial system but it also entails empowering institutions to develop their own regulations that guide operations in a certain sector so as to stimulate its development. Among the SROs within the EAC region, there are: Bankers' Associations; Association of Investment managers; Insurers' Associations; stock brokers; Forex Bureaux and Money Remittance Associations; capital market registrars; trustees' associations; etc.

Besides, there is a strong need of adopting a self-regulatory business environment like in many developed and emerging economies; UK and India are moving to consumer-driven regulatory frameworks and self-regulatory institutions. This has a benefit of boosting creativity of the players and the rules are justified from the business perspective; hence, incentivizing more efficiency locally, competitiveness within EAC and in the global financial system, and fostering creativity that is greatly lacking in our domestic financial markets. On the contrary, there is need to establish EAC Standards Board to harmonize all standards in the services sector; this will serve to make EAC compete favorably on the global economy.

Deregulation is very key and most organizations must be self-regulatory, which is a way of delegation on the part of the government.

EAC Investment Promotion Agency

An East African Community Investment Board should be established (and/or empower the East African Business Council –EABC) to attract and encourage investments in the region. It should target both domestic and foreign investors through facilitating the licensing, immigration, but also negotiating tax incentives and exemptions for them from various East African Community regulatory authorities. However, for foreign investments, there ought to be quotas on minimum local ownership (at least 5% to 10%) so as to develop local capacity, and also for sustainability purposes; and this should indicate a regulation of listing part of the ownership of foreign firms on the stock exchange. This is aimed at promoting local ownership and participation in key sectors after a specified period of time in operation, but also to boost the activity of the domestic stock markets an further channel the benefits to the domestic real economy. This ought to be done in key sectors/ areas like: financial services industry (asset/fund management, insurance, and banking); telecommunication and construction; oil and gas; but also in the PPPs (public private partnerships). This East African Investment Promotions Authority should help individual economies to sign bilateral and multilateral investment treaties with a diversity of countries for the benefit of East African economies. But this body should help East Africa make better trade deals with partners especially companies in the extractive industry.

Besides, there is also need, by the EAC Governments, to review past investment agreements since these are responsible for the current revenue shortfalls in the region and Africa at large. These have led to financial distress across the EAC region in the context of corporate and public finance which has catalyzed a couple of corporations to close shop since many multinationals and foreign investors were given tax breaks and incentives in the 1980s and 1990s yet they earn their incomes within EAC region. Such trade pacts ought to urgently be revisited so as to reverse the tax shortages that are responsible for spiraling poverty levels

RECOMMENDATIONS (DEDUCTIONS FOR THE PART 8)

This section is a build-up from all earlier Chapters (the banking system and financial institutions, securities markets, and infrastructure), how they can better be developed to facilitate efficient, integrated and globally competitive institutions and markets that work for East Africans. This is also a general deduction for the whole Book that further proposes avenues of how the EAC financial system can attain and develop a vibrant regional integration in the financial subsystem.

By agreeing to integrate its financial markets (system), a Partner State agrees in principle to create an enabling environment through deliberate efforts aimed at the harmonization of policies, legal and regulatory frameworks governing domestic financial markets, and the creation of best-practice standards and benchmarks anchored to international frameworks such as Basel I, II, III, etc; IOSCO; ICPs; IOPS; and CGAP for banking, capital markets, insurance, pensions and microfinance markets respectively.

INTEGRATED BANKING SYSTEM

An efficient and stable banking system is a precondition for a country/regional integration to attain sustainable growth, especially in the EAC whereby financial intermediation largely takes place through the banking system in the way of taking deposits from the general public and availing it to all financial agents.

In the context of the EAC banking market, it would be prudent for regulation and supervision of all banking activities to be undertaken in line with International Standards both at the national and EAC levels, these standards are called Basel Committee's Core Principles for Effective Banking supervision (BCP).

Harmonizing policies and regulation within the EAC regional bloc is aimed at achieving a single market in banking services as a means of promoting sustainable growth and higher levels of financial inclusion amongst the populations of the six members States. In a bid to attain a fully functional and integrated EAC banking market, there is need to benchmark and/or be in harmony with the various BCP such as:

Supervisory agency's mandate and status – whereby the six Central banks should have clear mandates regarding supervision of banking activities but also enjoy the requisite operational independence.

Banking intermediaries ought to maintain adequate records in accordance with internationally acceptable accounting policies and practices, but also publish financial information on a regular basis.

The six Central banks should be equipped with a wide range of supervisory tools so as to take corrective and remedial action when need arises.

The regulation, licensing and minimum requirements of the six member States should be quite consistent in the following areas – list of permissible banking activities, licensing criteria, capital adequacy, major acquisitions, risk management systems for most risk exposures, and transfer of significant ownership.

INTEGRATED SECURITIES MARKETS

The role of securities markets in a financial system can't be overemphasized in the exchange of securities and financial resources amongst financial agents.

In the context of an integrated securities market, investment services should be provided freely and financial instruments traded within the EAC and possibly offshores. With guidance from international standards and best practices, this single securities market do the following:

It should promote the emergence of an efficient, transparent and integrated trading infrastructure and establish a high level of investor confidence. This should include all markets and exchanges but well categorized for simplicity; and cover all regulated activities of market players across the investment value-chain; plus all asset universe such: as transferable securities, money market instruments, units in pooled investment vehicles, derivative instruments, commodities futures, exchange-traded funds, depositary receipts, etc;

Besides the above, the EAC regulation should embrace even other sophisticated securities, currencies, interest rates, climatic variables, inflation rates, indices, commodities, among others to be settled in cash or physically;

The harmonized regulation should include initial capital based on the nature of investment services offered as guided by the EAC regional standards;

It should also include the institution of an investor compensation scheme by financial intermediaries within the EAC bloc to protect investor interests and value; and also maintenance of investor confidence in the financial system;

An integrated securities market should have systems developed to protect against insider dealing (illegal use of inside information to gain unfair advantage over other market participants) by using nonpublic information, but also market manipulation (a complex form of market abuse that is hard to prove and consequently punish. Securities markets need integrity, both insider trading and market manipulation harm the integrity of financial markets and public confidence in securities and derivatives. This further calls for the EAC institutions to try to stipulate certain benchmark behavior or patterns of transactions as examples to highlight lawful and unlawful trading practices. Thus, the main goal of regulation should be to enhance investor confidence and also boost the integrity of financial system in the regional investing community.

INTEGRATED INSURANCE SYSTEM

An efficient and vibrant insurance system is a pre-requisite for the EAC bloc to attain viable growth since insurance funds are significant players in financial markets through holding large quantities of corporate and government securities.

In the context of an integrated insurance market for the EAC bloc, it would be prudent for regulation and supervision of all insurance services to be undertaken following the core principles and methodology of the International Association of Insurance Supervisors (IAIS) as benchmarks for the regional operations. This will allow for greater access to insurance markets across the EAC bloc and deepening investment opportunities on the part of the insurance firms within the framework of the international standards.

An integrated insurance market for EAC would work if the key issues of supervision and regulation are rather harmonized across the various EAC insurance systems within the framework of the international best practices such as: clear mandate responsibility and empowerment of the insurance supervisor; harmonized legal framework on the general business of insurance with the region and also the players interactions with foreign insurance firms and systems.

There ought to be common standards in the areas of: solvency minimum requirements; licensing of firms; disclosure requirements; governance systems; competence of managers and other controllers; requisite protection of interests of policyholders; prudential requirements (risk management systems); hedges against fraud, money laundering and terrorism financing through the insurance system.

INTEGRATED PENSION SYSTEM

Globally, investment professional affirm that a sound and vibrant pension system is a huge requirement for economies and economic integrations to attain the desired economic development thanks to their significant participation in the overall financial system.

By early 2016, the various EAC governments had been successfully enacting laws that are particular to the pension sector and of course subsequent regulators such as Kenya (RBA Act) although not so comprehensive enough; Tanzania (RBA Act); Uganda (URBRA Act) though not yet harmonized with the NSSF Act but it strives to liberalize the pension sector. There are huge inconsistencies in the regional pension laws in line with licensing, consumer protection provisions, and the wide asset management of members' funds.

In the perspective of an integrated market for pension services, it would be rational for the EAC bloc regulation and supervision to be in harmony with the following core principles and methodology of the International Organization of Pension Supervisors (IOPS) as benchmarks regional operations: clear mandate, responsibility and empowerment of the supervisor; operational independence of supervisors from political and/or commercial interference. Besides, the employment of a risk-based supervisory approach; competence of directors and controllers; prudent man's rule in pension investments; separation of roles and employing fund managers and custodians; ensure well designed investment policy statements are equally crucial for a sound insurance market for the EAC bloc.

The EAC regional bloc's pension market common standards should further entail the broad areas of: licensing; disclosure requirements; governance systems; competence of management; investment policies and principles; relationships with foreign insurance firms and systems.

BIBLIOGRAPHY

PART 1 (FINANCE IN A FINANCIAL SYSTEM)

AfDB (2014) *Eastern Africa Quarterly Bulletin* – 3rd Quarter 2014. African Development Bank Group

Bank of Uganda Annual Report 2010/ 2011

EADB Monthly Economic Updates (October 2015; January 2016)

Jomana, A (Sept. 2012) *South Sudan Financial System*. International Network for Economics & Conflict

Marvin, Powell (July 2015) Bitcoin: Economics, Technology, and Governance. CFA Digest, Vol. 45, No. 7: CFA Institute

National Bank of Rwanda Annual Financial Stability Report June 2015

The Economist (19-25 March 2016) *Central Banks and Digital Currencies: Redistributed Ledger.* The Economist Newspaper Ltd

Villasenor, J., Darrell, W., & Lewis, R (2015) *The 2015 Brookings Financial & Digital Inclusion Project Report: Measuring Progress on Financial Access and Usage.* Center for Technology Innovation at Brookings

World Bank (2015) *The 2014 Global Financial Inclusion Database.* Global Index

World Bank (Sept. 2015) *Searching for the Grail: Can Uganda's Land Support its Prosperity Drive?* Uganda Economic Update. 6th Ed. World Bank Group.

PART 2 (ISLAMIC FINANCIAL SYSTEM)

Ananthakrishnan, Prasad (Sept. 2015) *Global Aspirations: Islamic Financing is Transcending its Geographical Boundaries.* Finance & Development – IMF Publication. USA

Ashraf, H. M., & Shabana, H. M ((2015) Prospects & Outlook of Islamic Wealth Management: Post Global Financial Crisis. International Sharia Research Academy (ISRA) Islamic Finance Journal

Shabana, H. M., & Mahbubi, A. M (2015) Africa and East Asia: The Emerging Market of Islamic Finance. ISRA Islamic Finance Journal. Malaysia

Ssonko, George (March 2016) *Islamic Finance: A Legislative Milestone towards an Inclusive Financial Sector.* Financial Services Magazine. Uganda Institute of Banking & Financial Services

PART 3 (FINANCIAL INSTITUTIONS)

Anyanzwa, James (5-11 December 2015) *High Exchange, Interest Rates Hit Banks' Profits.* The East African. Nairobi.

African Alliance Securities (2013), *Uganda Banking Sector Overview*. African Alliance Uganda Publications.

Bank of Uganda Annual Report 2012/ 2013

Bank of Tanzania Annual Report. 18th Ed. Directorate of Banking Supervision

Bank of Tanzania Financial Stability Report (Sept. 2015)

Banking in Africa (2013) Sector Report. KPMG

Beck, T. and Hesse, H., (2006), Bank Efficiency, Ownership and Market Structure: Why Interests Spread so High in Uganda? World Bank Working paper series WPS4027. The World Bank: Washington, D.C.

CBA Financial News (13 May 2016). Commercial Bank of Africa Publications

Demekas, Dimitris (Sept. 2015) *Wider Field of Vision: Stress Testing Must Be Adapted & Broadened to Assess the Stability of the Financial System as a Whole.* Finance & Development – IMF Publication. USA

Irungu, Geoffrey (25 November 2015) *Kenya Banks Rank Poorly among Peers in Region says IMF.* Business Daily. Nairobi

Jomana, A (Sept. 2012) *South Sudan Financial System.* International Network for Economics & Conflict

Mbugua, Pauline (2015) *A Tour of the East African Insurance Industry.* Paper presented at African Insurance Organization Conference 2015 at Lome-Togo.

Mugerwa, Paul (2016) "NSSF @ 30 Years – Financial Performance". In *"The NSSF Chronicle: Social Protection Driving Economic Growth".* Fountain Publishers Ltd

Mugerwa, Paul (2013) *Appraising the Investment Philosophy of Central Banks in Developing Economies for National Wealth Creation: A Case for Bank of Uganda.* Unpublished.

Mugerwa, Paul (2016) *The Insurance Industry Paradox in Uganda.* Paper presented during "Insurance, Pension & Investment Symposium" at Bugema University on 22nd March 2016 organized as a Collaboration between the Academia and the Financial Sector in Uganda.

Mugerwa, Paul (2016) *Sovereign Assets Preservation and Asset Allocation by the Six East African Central Banks.* (This paper was slated to be presented in Annual Malaysia Business Research Conference in Kuala Lumpur, Malaysia on 23rd August 2016)

Mugume, A. (2008), Market Structure and Performance in Uganda's Banking System. Makerere University Printery

Mugume, A. Apaa, J. & Ojwiya, C. (2009), Interest Spreads in Uganda: Bank

Specific Characteristics or Policy Changes? The Bank of Uganda Staff Papers Journal

National Bank of Rwanda Annual Report 2014/15

Nkamleu, G.B. & Mugisha, F. (2015) *South Sudan*. African Economic Outlook. African Development Bank Group

Oxford Business Group (2015) The Report Kenya 2014

Sanya, S. & Gaertner, Matthew (2012) *Assessing Bank Competition within the East African Community*. IMF Working Paper

The World Bank Annual Report 2015

PART 4 (COMMODITIES & FINANCIAL MARKETS)

African Securities Exchanges Association, (2009), African Securities Exchanges Association Yearbook 2009

Bank of Uganda; Annual Supervision Report; December 2010; Issue No. 1

Beck, T., Fuchs, M., & Marilou, U. (2010) *Finance in Africa: Achievements & Challenges*. World Bank Group

CMA-Kenya (2015) *Quarterly Statistical Bulletin* – Quarter Ended September 2015

CMA-Kenya (2014) Capital Markets Master Plan Kenya 2014 – 2023

CMA-Uganda (2016) Capital Markets 10 Year Master Development Plan

Dhanji, Shazmir (November 2015) *The Introduction of a Derivative Exchange on the Nairobi Bourse*. The Exchange. Dar es Salaam

Mugerwa, Paul (2014) *Capital Markets Monitoring Systems and Financial Performance of Listed Firms in Uganda*. Proceedings of 25th International Business Research Conference in Cape Town, South Africa 14th January, 2014; ISBN 978-1-922069-42-9

Mugerwa, Paul (2015) *Developing Efficient Commodities Spot & Multi-asset Derivatives Exchange in Uganda*. (To be published in Financial Services Magazine – June 2016 Issue by The Uganda Institute of Banking & Financial Services

Mwanyasi, Rufus (July 2015) *The Rebirth of Africa's Capital Markets*. Forbes Africa

Nairobi Securities Exchange Annual Report 2014

Nsamba, Charles (July 2015) *The Evolution of Stock Exchanges: a Closer Look at Uganda*. CMA-Uganda Journal.

Olingo, Allan (14-20 May 2016) *Kenya, Uganda Shillings rise against the Dollar as Tanzania and Rwanda currencies Slump.* The East African. Nairobi

Rwanda Stock Exchange Annual Report 2014

Shirima, Charles (November 2015) *President Kikwete Launches Tanzania's Commodities Exchange.* The Exchange. Dar es Salaam

PART 5 (FINANCIAL ASSETS)

Arnold, Glen (1998) *Corporate Financial Management.* Financial Times- Prentice Hall

Barker, Richard (2001) *Determining Value: Valuation Models and Financial Statements*

Bodie, Z. Kane, A. and Marcus, A. J (2009), Investments. 8th Ed: McGraw-Hill

Magali, Azema-Barac (2010) *Be Dynamic in Your Asset Allocation.* PineBridge Investments Research- New York

Strong, A. Robert (2009), *Portfolio Construction, Management and Protection.* 5th Ed: South Western University

PART 6 (AGENTS/ PLAYERS IN THE FINANCIAL SYSTEM)

MoFPED (2015) *Report on Public Debt, Guarantees, Other Financial Liabilities and Grants for Financial Year 2014/15.* Presented by Hon. Minister of Finance, Matia Kasaija, to Parliament on 1st April 2015.

MoFPED (2015) *Annual Economic Performance Report 2013/14.* Directorate of Economic Affairs – MoFPED January 2015.

Mugerwa, Paul (2015) *The Ugandan Financial System: Scrutiny of the Institutions, Markets, Assets, Agents & Intermediation.* Local Edition. EPS Publishers Ltd (September 2015). Finance/Investment Textbook for Higher Education & Technicians

World Bank (April 2016) *From Smart Budgets to Smart Returns: Unleashing the Power of Public Investment Management.* Uganda Economic Update. 7th Ed. World Bank Group.

PART 7 (FINANCIAL INFRASTRUCTURE, RISKS & INTERMEDIATIONS)

A.M Best Country Risk Report 2015

East Africa Analyst (Oct.- Dec. 2015) *Cross-border Mobile Money Services: Key Growth Area for Regional Telecoms.*

Mugerwa, Paul (2015) *The Ugandan Financial System: Scrutiny of the Institutions,*

Markets, Assets, Agents & Intermediation. International Edition. EPS Publishers Ltd (December 2015). Finance/Investment Textbook for Higher Education & Technicians

Stephen, Odoki (2014) The Uganda's Financial Outflow Conundrum. In Bank of Uganda Official Internal Newletter. Vol.1 Issue No.8 November 2014

PART 8 (INTEGRATED EAC FINANCIAL SYSTEM)

African Development Bank -AfDB, (2010), *Financial Sector Integration in Three Regions of Africa* (Tunis: African Development Bank Group).

Anyanzwa, James (14-20 May 2016) *East Africa Member States Fail to Reach Consensus on Common Tax Rates.* The East African. Nairobi

Christensen, Benedicte (2013) *Financial Integration in Africa: Implications for Monetary Policy & Financial Stability*

EAC Secretary (2011) *EAC Financial Sector Development and Regionalization Project 1: Project Appraisal Document.* World Bank Group

Eastern Africa Regional Integration Strategy Paper 2011-2015. African Development Bank

EY (2014) *Eastern Africa Banking Sector.* Ernest & Young Africa

Njoka, David (5-11 December 2015) *Rationale for Regional Integration.* The East African (Nairobi)

Okidi, Michael (5-11 December 2015) *The Journey to the EAC Integration is Steadily on Course.* The East African (Nairobi)

Tax Justice Network- Africa Report (2016) *Still Racing Towards the Bottom? Corporate Tax Incentives in East Africa.*

INTERVIEWS & INTERACTIONS DURING THE RESEARCH PROJECT

The scholar did thorough and comprehensive interactions with finance gurus within the EAC regional bloc and globally (those he deemed so incremental to the study). Among the key interviewees within and outside the EAC region that I interacted with in the course of my research undertakings between June 2015 and June 2016, were:

EAC & SUPRANATIONAL INSTITUTIONS

World Bank Group: Officials
International Center for Education in Islamic Finance: Professor
Shariah Advisory Council, Central Bank of Malaysia: Technical Member

Islamic Development Bank Group: Expert

East African Development Bank: Director General's office

East African Insurance Supervisors' Association: Chairman

International Shariah Research Academy for Islamic Finance (ISRA): CEO; and Senior Researcher

Economic Policy Research Center: 2 Senior Research Fellow

Inter-University Council for East Africa: Executive Secretary; 2 Other Officials

EAC Capital Markets, Insurance & Pensions Committee (CMIPC): Officials.

Macroeconomic & Financial Management Institute of Eastern & Southern Africa: Director

Examready Financial Markets Consulting (South Africa)

Cadogan Financial Ltd (UK): Consultants

EAC Secretariat: Deputy Secretary General P&I; and EAC-FSDRP Regional Financial Policy Advisor

EAC Financial Sector Development & Regionalization Project (FSDRP): Technical Project Manager

East African Securities Exchanges Association: Chairman

Shrikaam Fincom Consulting Pvt. Ltd: Consultant (Financial & Commodities Markets)

Thompson Reuters: Official

EAC Capital Markets, Insurance & Pensions Committee (CMIPC): Officials

UGANDA

Ministry of Finance: Macroeconomic Advisor to government; and 3 Commissioners.

Capital Markets Authority: CEO; and Director, Research & Markets.

Insurance Regulatory Authority: CEO; and Director, Research.

Uganda Retirement Benefits Regulatory Authority: CEO.

Uganda Warehouse Receipt System Authority: CEO; and Quality Manager.

Uganda Securities Exchange: CEO; and Director, Business Development.

National Social Security Funds: Managing Director; Head, Investments.

Uganda Bankers' Association: Chairman; and CEO.

Investment Managers' Association of Uganda: Chairman.

Financial Sector Deepening- Uganda: Consultants

Private Sector Foundation: 2 Directors

Financial services firms: fund managers; stock brokers; insurance firms; pension schemes; endowment firms.

Banking Institute; Insurance institute; Universities' Business schools: CEOs and Deans.

Association of Islamic Finance Professionals in Uganda: Chairman; and 1 Researcher

Islamic Chamber of Commerce & Industry Uganda: President

RWANDA

National Bank of Rwanda: Financial Markets Dep't; & (Director; 2 Managers) Non-Bank Financial Supervision (Director)

Capital Markets Authority (Rwanda): CEO; and Financial Analyst.

Rwanda Stock Exchange: CEO; and Financial Analyst.

Financial services firms: stock brokers; insurance firms; commodities exchange.

University of Kigali: 2 Professors (Finance) & DVC-Academics.

TANZANIA

Central Bank of Tanzania: Financial Markets Dep't (Director; and Portfolio Manager)

Capital Markets & Securities Authority: CEO; and Director - Research, Policy & Planning.

Tanzania Insurance Regulatory Authority: Commissioner

Dar es Salaam Stock Exchange: CEO; and Principal Accountant.

Financial services firms: stock brokers; forex bureaus; commodities exchange

KENYA

Central Bank of Kenya: Financial Markets Dep't (Director)

Capital Markets Authority: CEO; and 2 Directors.

Insurance Regulatory Authority: CEO

Nairobi Securities Exchange: CEO; and 3 Specialists.

Financial services firms: fund managers; stock brokers; insurance firms.

BURUNDI & SOUTH SUDAN

Central Banks: Financial Markets Dep't.

Insurance Regulatory & Control Agency (Burundi): Secretary General.

University of Juba: Dean, School of Business & Head of Department.

APPENDICES
RWANDA STOCK EXCHANGE

	2009	2010	2011	2012	2013	2014	up to Sept
1. EAC Stock Markets							
RWANDA STOCK EXCH.							
Equities trading statistics							
RSE Shares Volume traded (mn)	0.07	0.08	118.1	103	105.4	92.6	136.2
Turnover in billion (Frw)	0.01	0.01	20.8	18.1	53.5	45.2	37.6
Turnover in USD million	0.02	0.02	34.6	28.7	79.9	64.5	51.8
No. of deals	49	50	1,794	1,636	2,095	1,552	970
Market capitalisation in Frw Billion	381.4	701.8	960.8	1,070.60	1,326.20	1,354.00	2,820.38
Market capitalization(USD Billion)	0.6	1.2	1.6	1.7	2	2	3.8

NAIROBI STOCK EXCHANGE

Year	2006	2007	2008	2009	2010	2011	2012	2013	2014	2015 (Sept.)
Equity Turnover (KshsBn)	94.9	88.6	97.5	38.2	103.5	78.1	86.8	155.8	215.7	209.38
NSE Share Volume Traded (Mn)	1,454.70	1,938.20	5,856.50	3,169.10	6,479.80	5,684.70	5,464.20	7,576.20	8,233.40	6,812.14
Market Capitaliz ation (Kshs Bn)	791.6	851.1	853.7	834.2	1,089.20	1,035.80	1,072.90	1,691.50	2,141.40	2,112.43

DAR es SALAAM STOCK EXCHANGE

Year	2008	2009	2010	2011	2012	2013	2014	2015
Equity Turnover (TZS Bn)	24	33.81	53.16	48.77	44.45	73.53	272.38	785
DSE Share Volume Traded (Mn)	26.39	44	170	211	67	147	257.9	
Market Capitalization (TZS Trillion)				10	18	18.2	22	20.1

UGANDA SECURITIES EXCHANGE

Year	2005	2006	2007	2008	2009	2010	2011	2012	2013	2014	2015
Equity Turnover (UGX Bn)	7.7	48.4	85.2	89.7	19.7	42	40.7	26.4	245.1	466.3	187.42
Share Volume Traded (Mn)	11.1	273.9	484.1	216.9	123.2	226.5	168.2	345.1	2,353.90	2,116.90	769.2
Market Capitalization (UGX Trillion)	3.9	4.4							202.1	255.3	24.9
Deals	1,042	8.065	14,338	15,659	5,698	4,960	4,748	3,668	5,205	6,147	7,084

NB: For trend analysis purposes and simplicity of interpretation by readers on Volume traded, Kenya was reduced by a factor of 100; and Uganda by a factor of 10 so as to develop the visual representation on graphs. This is why the researcher presents the absolute figures in the Appendix Section

EAC MONETARY Aggregates as at March 2016

	KENYA	UGANDA	TANZANIA	RWANDA	BURUNDI
M 1	10,610.050	2,001.874	4,261.868	976.975	378.159
M 2	22,295.689	3,404.074	7,105.686	1,592.338	551.954
M 3	26,236.535	5,016.632	9,932.325	1,925.978	625.064
InterBank Borrowings	2,097.484	597.700	451.160	71.121	3.053
Total Deposits	24,213.022	4,177.042	8,342.092	1,752.943	506.764
Forex Deposits	4,796.251	1,612.557	2,826.639	333.640	73.110
Private Sect. Credit	21,979.857	3,314.583	7,379.033	1,524.505	415.828
Net Credit to Gov't	5,356.680	689.349	2,241.658	157.718	443.656
Net Foreign Assets	4,645.422	3,037.389	3,454.700	727.816	-98.333
International Reserves	7,766.239	2,888.461	3,948.838	816.810	93.305

Interest Rates in Percentage (%)					
	KENYA	UGANDA	TANZANIA	RWANDA	BURUNDI
Central Bank rate	11.50%	22.00%	16.00%	10.50%	9.21%
Lending rate	17.788	24.370	16.261	17.090	16.340
Deposit rate	7.169	13.735	8.640	8.128	7.980
Interbank rate	4.098	11.330	10.394	5.182	5.400
	10.619	10.635	3.260	8.962	8.360
Nominal Exchange rate (local currency per 1 USD)	101.485	3,365.497	2,179.600	786.406	1,637.540

ADDENDUM ON INSURANCE INDUSTRY IN EAC REGION

OTHER NEW DEVELOPMENT IN EAC INSURANCE SECTOR

Insurance sector in Uganda will be operating in the Oil & Gas sector through an Oil & Gas co-insurance syndicate of 17 insurance companies, this initiative is currently under construction and preparations for its smooth rolling out. Worth noting is that the Uganda insurance industry attained Gross Written Premiums (GWP) for 2015 worth UGX 611 Billion.

In terms of the pensions; retirement benefits sector: - Ministry of Finance is developing an EAC policy to harmonize the pensions; retirement benefits sector to allow for portability of the benefits from one EAC country tom another, which will truly be good news to EAC citizens across the board.

In terms of regional integration developments; the East African Insurance Association (EAIA) is an umbrella body for regional insurers that also contributes to harmonizing business in the industry; and also the East African Insurance Institute Association (EAIIA) that is in charge of harmonizing and synchronizing training and research provisions in the insurance industry in the EAC regional bloc.

CHALLENGES TO THE INSURANCE INDUSTRY

Background

The industry enjoys huge opportunities which include positive demographics: a very young population (median age approx. 16 years); a growing middle class (nearing 40% in some countries) - most with smartphones; and an increasingly large diaspora getting more interested in investing back home. There's a whole new generation of savvy consumers with disposable incomes, and also the large infrastructure projects being built, besides massive opportunities in commercial agriculture. It is worth noting that the insurance market is closely linked to economic growth: when incomes rise there are more insurable assets. On the other hand, it is equally imperative to appreciate that the East African insurance market represent a diverse picture (different levels of economic development amongst the six economies).

Despite such great optimism in the drastic growth of the insurance industry in East Africa largely hinged on political stability and economic growth, with millions of U.S dollars in foreign direct investments in the oil-gas & extractive, agriculture, infrastructure, financial services, tourism and manufacturing industries in various EAC economies (Kenya, Tanzania, Uganda, Rwanda, Burundi and South Sudan), there are lots of challenges that face the industry:

Challenges -

There is a huge trust deficit gap whereby people don't buy insurance because they don't trust the providers; this is because claims are not paid quickly, fairly or correctly. Across the EAC region, would-be clients don't think that the promise of paying a claim is reliable, consistent and achievable given the prevalent negative publicity of huge unsettled claims.

Consumer educations is really wanting, with very high levels of generally financial illiteracy (and specifically low and distorted knowledge of the insurance services. East African governments have a role of better supporting the industry through efforts that raise awareness of insurance and educate consumers about the need to purchase adequate risk protection.

Traditional marketing strategy by many insurers and brokers that has failed to have a blend traditional strategies and modern technology distribution infrastructure such as internet, mobile money and mobile phone platforms to ensure relevance and convenience to consumers.

There is a strong need to establish the credit ratings of corporations within the EAC regional bloc but also to further beef up the bankruptcy laws so as to further facilitate and incentivize the insurance industry's capacity in underwriting companies' risk exposures.

Besides, there is also need to reduce the claim settlement times, and better client focus; all of which would equip the insurance sales agent's job in pitching clients in the industry.

Generic product provision that don't suit the market and that don't facilitate consumers' rational decision-making. Product expansion is necessary to meet the dynamic and changing needs of the region. The industry hardly understands the diverse needs of the clientele in the market which has consequently seen insurance brokers continue to push a one shoe fits all perspective.

There is a predominant and systemic weakness across the regional insurance industry of the lack of management skills and product knowledge in the local talent; this would require developing generic and elite training courses for new staff, but also hiring outside consultants so as to facilitate the transfer of technical knowhow and technology as well.

Information management inefficiency. Insurance thrives on data; the more it is at their disposal, the greater their competitive advantage. Unfortunately, there is a significant lack of volumes and velocity of data for analysis purposes; besides, many insurers are not positioned to leverage fully on available data and new sources of information and real time analysis that are publically available partly due to absence of data management infrastructure and governance architecture.

Regulatory challenges. Progressive changes in the regulatory and compliance atmosphere such as the implementation of risk-based supervision by financial services regulators, and other emerging trends in the whole industry such as the Islamic financial system are ushering in an increasingly complex regulatory environment. This leads to multiple supervisors/overseers which all come with their complex standards and guidelines that would significantly affect the way how players in the insurance industry operate. This also affects their profitability due to increased costs in the short run and institutional capacity-building requirements.

GLOBAL HISTORICAL INSURANCE FACT FILES

1) *Insurance dates way back to early human society (B.C) but also got sophisticated in the "Enlightenment Era of Europe" where the specialized varieties of insurance were developed.*

2) *The first written insurance policy appeared in prehistoric times on a Babylonian monument with the codes of King Hammurabi carved into it "The Hammurabi Code".*

3) *The first method of transferring or distributing risk in a monetary economy were practiced by Chinese and Babylonian traders in 2nd Millennia B.C.*

4) *In the 1st Millennium B.C, the inhabitants of Rhodes created "the General Average". This refers to a loss that must be borne partly by someone other than the owner of the goods that were lost/ destroyed (in Marine Insurance).*

5) *In 1884, Chancellor Otto Von Bismarck passed the Workers' Compensation Insurance Act which became the basis for what is now called, "Workers' Compensation".*

6) *Plate glass insurance particularly intended for shopkeepers to protect them from the high expenses of repairing large shop windows, originated in France in 1829 with the establishment of 'La Parisienne'.*

7) *Fidelity Insurance was one of the earliest forms of accident insurance successfully offered by corporate bodies in the U.K. It was instituted in1840 by the Guarantee Society, which was established to protect employers from fraud/ embezzlement by staff.*

8) *Accident Insurance became available in the 19th Century and the first company to offer it was the Railway Passengers Assurance Company in 1884 in England.*

9) *Universal Insurance was first initiated by Governments in the late 19th Century against sickness and old age. It was very common in Germany and Prussia through the welfare programs.*

10) *Property Insurance as it is commonly known today can be traced back to the Great Fire of London in 1666.*

11) *The first person to purchase a liability insurance cover was Gilbert J. Loomis in 1897.*

12) *The first Fire Insurance Company was formed in the U.S in Charleston, South Carolina in 1735.*